$39.50

INTRODUCTION TO
GROUP
COUNSELING

EDITED BY

DAVE CAPUZZI
Portland State University

DOUGLAS R. GROSS
Arizona State University

LOVE PUBLISHING COMPANY ®
Denver, Colorado 80222

Library of Congress Catalog Card Number 91-077047

Copyright © 1992 Love Publishing Company
Printed in the U.S.A.
ISBN 0-89108-220-4

Contents

Prologue

As we approach the close of the twentieth century and look forward to the twenty-first century, the world in which we live and work continues to change and become more complex. Vast and far-reaching changes are occurring in the nature and structure of the social, family, and economic systems in which we live and the industrial and occupational structures where we work. We live in a global society and economy. Cultural diversity and change are the rule, not the exception.

At the same time, however, we need to recognize that there is an opposite force at work in these systems and structures that has an impact on people, and that force is constancy. Although changes will occur, and with increasing rapidity, the familiar configurations of our economic, occupational, industrial, social, and family environments and structures as we know them today, in all probability, will still be visible in the future.

The impact of living and working in a rapidly changing world in which the forces of change and constancy are at work is substantial. Stress, physical and psychological abuse, alcoholism and drug abuse, suicide, and marital discord are not abstractions for some individuals. They are very real and often result when individuals try to respond to the changing situations and circumstances of their lives—situations and circumstances that seemingly are beyond their control.

As individuals search for meaning in their lives and try to deal with their changing situations and circumstances in positive, constructive ways, they often seek the assistance of professional counselors. To respond effectively, counselors today and tomorrow must have substantial professional expertise. Knowledge of and skills in using theoretical constructs, a wide range of counseling methods and techniques, and multiple people and paper resources are essential. Group counseling in particular, holds a great deal of promise in helping individuals deal with change.

Introduction to Group Counseling is important because it brings relevant group counseling literature, research, and applications together in one place, to provide you, as a beginning or a practicing counselor, with the necessary foundational knowledge you require. It also brings together, in one place, the latest information about client goals and problems that are particularly responsive to group counseling methodology. Finally, this introductory book is important because it brings to you the latest in techniques and the underlying research that supports these techniques.

This introductory book to group counseling is more than isolated chapters of information about client goals and problems and the group counseling theory and techniques to respond to them. *Introduction to Group Counseling* also provides you with an overall configuration of group counseling knowledge and applications that cannot be derived from its separate chapters alone. You will obtain an overall picture, a gestalt, of group counseling. This allows you to view and come to understand the theory, the process, and the results of the process more completely.

Because the goals and problems clients bring to the counseling relationship cannot be resolved by simply applying the techniques of group counseling in a vacuum, it is critical for you to have an overall picture of group counseling as well as an understanding of the specifics involved. What is required is an overall understanding of group counseling theory and research that provides guiding principles to help select and direct the use of appropriate techniques.

Introduction to Group Counseling provides you with the guiding principles as well as the corresponding techniques to be an effective group counseling provider. This is important because group counseling is an especially powerful approach to assist clients in achieving their goals and resolving their problems, particularly in the complex worlds of today and tomorrow. Group counseling takes clients out of the isolation in which they sometimes exist, and the alienation they often feel as a result, and puts them into guided contact with people, the context where many problems clients face need to be resolved in the first place.

In *Introduction to Group Counseling,* foundational knowledge for group work is presented first, followed by presentations by group work experts who share their knowledge and skills about working with clients with eating disorders, suicidal ideation, gay, lesbian, or bisexual orientation, disabilities, and issues related to abuse. Finally, attention is given to professional, ethical, and cross-cultural perspectives in group counseling. It is an introductory book but at the same time it is a book that goes beyond the content and procedure usually found in introductory books. It will serve you well in your quest for knowledge and skill in understanding and applying group counseling methods and techniques to assist clients of all ages and circumstances.

Norman C. Gysbers, Ph.D.
University of Missouri at Columbia
January 31, 1992

Preface

The therapeutic elements of a positive group experience have been documented through empirically based research, client self-reports, descriptions by group leaders, and the emergence of paradigms derived from a variety of theoretical perspectives. These curative factors have been described by terms such as acceptance, altruism, universalization, belonging, security, instillation of hope, increased awareness of emotional dynamics, interpersonal learning, and many other descriptors. The role of professional counselors in educational, corporate, mental health, private practice, and rehabilitation settings calls for knowledge, experience, and competence in facilitating groups. Therefore, the aspiring group leader has to start developing the knowledge and competencies necessary to provide a powerful, growth enhancing opportunity for clients involved in group counseling.

Group work is demanding and requires the professional counselor to add knowledge and skills to the foundation in individual counseling provided by coursework and supervised practice. Individuals who are trying to decide if group work is the specialization they want will find the information in this text helpful as a point of departure in the decision-making process.

The book is unique in format and content. The contributed-authors format enables state-of-the-art information by experts in their respective group work specializations. The content goes beyond that usually addressed in introductory group work texts. Chapters on group work with clients who have eating disorders, suicidal clients, gay, lesbian, and bisexual clients, clients with disabilities, and adult victims of abuse are cases in point. The first four chapters provide prerequisite information on the foundational aspects of group work that makes subsequent chapters on group work with special populations easier to assimilate. This format and content are intended to increase the book's readability, interest level, and knowledge needed in today's world.

Students enrolled in a beginning course in group work will find the book useful for the future as well as the present. The book provides a comprehensive overview of major issues connected with group work, as well as insight and practical guidelines for group work in general and group work with specialized populations. Although the specialized populations addressed are primarily adult, the overall developmental focus encompasses younger populations as appropriate. The concept of cultural diversity, certainly a major issue in group work, is incorporated throughout the book and also is accorded a chapter of its own (Chapter 15), "Cross-Cultural Considerations." We know that one book cannot cover all the factors involved in preparing a person to be a group leader. Rather, we are attempting to give readers a broad perspective on group work.

With few exceptions, each chapter contains information specific to a topic and includes discussion of age-specific variations, where appropriate, for special populations (for example, clients with eating disorders). The many case studies are intended to help the reader identify with and make applications to current or future clients. The text is divided into three parts: Foundations for Group Counseling; Group Counseling: Special Populations; and Professional and Ethical Issues in Group Counseling.

Part One, Foundations for Group Counseling (Chapters 1 through 4), leads off with information dealing with the historical, definitive, theoretical, research, and practical perspectives that provide the foundation for all types of group work. These chapters are entitled "Group Counseling: An Introduction," "Group Counseling: Stages and Issues," "Group Counseling: Elements of Effective Leadership," and "Group Counseling: Theory and Application."

Part Two, Special Populations (Chapters 5–14), covers a wide spectrum: self-enhancement, addictions, eating disorders, physical disabilities, abuse/incest, and suicide. Also included are strategies and approaches for group work surrounding gay and lesbian orientation, career and lifestyle concerns, couples and family issues, and handling loss. Each chapter presents a conceptual frame of reference for dealing with the special needs of these populations, and also specialized approaches and techniques that have been effective.

Topics of Part Three, Professional and Ethical Issues in Group Counseling (Chapters 15 and 16), are "Group Counseling: Cross-Cultural Considerations" and "Group Counseling: Ethics and Professional Issues." Applications to the group leader, group members, and the group counseling process are discussed.

The editors and contributors have attempted to present current information in each of the 16 areas of focus. We hope that *Introduction to Group Counseling* will provide the reader with a solid foundation and a sound basis for decision making in regard to group counseling as a profession.

Meet the Editors

Dave Capuzzi, Ph.D., N.C.C., is past president of the American Association for Counseling and Development (AACD) and is Assistant Dean for Academic Development for the School of Education and professor of counselor education at Portland State University, Portland, Oregon.

From 1980 to 1984, he was editor of *The School Counselor.* Dr. Capuzzi has authored a number of textbook chapters and monographs on the topic of preventing adolescent suicide and is co-editor and author, with Dr. Larry Golden, of *Helping Families Help Children: Family Interventions with School Related Problems* (1986) and *Preventing Adolescent Suicide* (1988). In 1989 he co-authored and edited *Youth at Risk: A Resource for Counselors, Teachers and Parents* and in 1991, *Introduction to Counseling: Perspectives for the 1990's* with Douglas R. Gross.

A frequent speaker and keynoter at professional conferences and institutes, Dr. Capuzzi also has consulted with a variety of school districts and community agencies interested in initiating counseling and intervention strategies for adolescents at risk for suicide. He has facilitated the development of suicide prevention, crisis management, and postvention programs in communities in 23 states.

Douglas R. Gross, Ph.D., has been a faculty member in the Counseling Program at Arizona State University, Tempe, for 23 years. His professional work history includes public school teaching, counseling, and administration. Dr. Gross has been president of the Arizona Counselors Association, president of the Western Association for Counselor Education and Supervision, chairperson of the Western Regional Branch Assembly of the American Association for Counseling and Development (AACD), President of the Association for Humanistic Education and Development, and Treasurer and Parliamentarian of AACD.

Dr. Gross has contributed chapters to four texts: *Youth at Risk: A Resource for Counselors, Teachers and Parents* (1989), *Foundations of Mental Health Counseling* (1986), *Counseling: Theory, Process and Practice* (1977), and *The Counselor's Handbook* (1974). His research has appeared in the *Journal of Counseling Psychology*, the *Journal of Counseling and Development*, the *Association for Counselor Education and Supervision Journal*, the *Journal of Educational Research*, *Counseling and Human Development*, the *Arizona Counselors Journal*, the *Texas Counseling Journal*, and the *AMHCA Journal.*

Dr. Gross also serves as a consultant to several alcohol and drug programs in the state of Arizona.

Meet the Authors

Richard Pearson, Ph.D., is associate professor of counselor education, Syracuse University. He received his doctorate from the University of Illinois. As teacher and writer, his scholarship has focused on small-group leadership skills, adult life transitions, support groups, and informal support networks. His current program development and research activities center on primary prevention and counselors in rural schools.

Jack Clark, A.C.S.W., is clinical director for the New Arizona Family, Residential, and Outpatient Programs in Phoenix, Arizona. He received his masters in social work degree from the Jane Adams College of Social Work, University of Illinois at Chicago. He consults throughout Arizona and nationally with social service and chemical dependency programs, and maintains a private practice. He holds affiliate memberships in the Academy of Certified Social Workers, the National Association of Social Workers Register of Clinical Social Workers, and the Phoenix Society of Clinical Hypnosis.

The late ***Charles Hawes,*** M.C., received his bachelor of arts degree from Kalamazoo College and master of counseling degree from Arizona State University. He was project coordinator for the New Arizona Family Dual Diagnosis Program and worked as a social worker and counselor of the chemically dependent, both individually and in groups. He actively participated in workshops and conferences, and taught college-level courses in chemical dependency. Mr. Hawes died prior to publication of this text.

Melissa Blanchard, M.Ed., obtained a master of educational psychology degree from the University of Utah, Salt Lake City, with a concentration in rehabilitation counseling. As project coordinator at the New Arizona Family's long-term residential treatment facility, substance abuse counseling is her focus. She also teaches college-level courses in chemical dependency counseling and is a member of the Phoenix Society of Clinical Hypnosis. Her doctoral work is in human development. Additional areas of interest include therapeutic group dynamics, research, and human development.

Mary Lou Frank, Ph.D., is a psychotherapist at Arizona State University where she coordinates the campus eating disorders program, heads the eating disorders team, and is a faculty affiliate with the counseling psychology department. She received both her B.A. degree and M.Ed. in counseling from Colorado State University, Fort Collins, and M.S. and Ph.D. in counseling psychology also from Colorado State University. Dr. Frank's multifaceted professional career includes training, supervision, outreach, and consultation.

Hanoch Livneh, Ph.D., is associate professor for counselor education and coordinator of Rehabilitation Counseling Specialization, Counselor Education Program, Portland State University, Portland, Oregon. He received his B.A. degree in psychology from the Hebrew University, Jerusalem, Israel (1971) and his M.A. (1973) and Ph.D. (1976) degrees in rehabilitation counseling psychology from the University of Wisconsin, Madison. Prior to joining Portland State University in 1988, Dr. Livneh served as the director of the rehabilitation counseling program and as professor of counseling and educational psychology at Rhode Island College.

Robert E. Pullo, Ph.D., C.R.C., is an associate professor and coordinator of the Rehabilitation Services Program, Department of Human, Health, and Family Studies, University of Maine at Farmington. He received his M.Ed. degree in rehabilitation counseling from Northeastern University, Evanston, Illinois, and his Ph.D. in rehabilitation counseling psychology from the University of Wisconsin. Dr. Pullo's interests focus primarily on the psychosocial impact of disability in the areas of vocational rehabilitation and substance abuse rehabilitation.

Anita Vinson, M.Ed., is a counselor in private practice in Portland, Oregon. A gestalt therapist, she also incorporates object relations theory and self-psychology into her work. In addition to individual and couples work, she facilitates groups for incest survivors, women with a history of early childhood trauma, and families, and she works with children in play therapy. For the past three years she has conducted graduate training seminars for therapists who work with adults who were molested as children. She has served as a public school counselor for grades K–6 and as a mental health consultant for a Head Start program and a group home for developmentally disabled adults. She received her M.Ed. in counseling from North Texas State University, Denton.

Reese M. House, Ed.D., N.C.C., is a professor of education in the Oregon State University College of Education, Corvallis, and chair of the Department of Counselor Education. He has worked as a counselor educator since 1969. In addition to working with gay and lesbian clients, his areas of interest and expertise include death, dying, and loss issues; AIDS education and counseling; and group work in counseling and gerontology. Dr. House has a doctorate in counseling from Oregon State University and a master of arts degree from Ball State University, Muncie, Indiana.

Virginia Tyler, M.S., N.C.C., works with individuals, families, and groups on issues of loss and grieving. As counselor and Bereavement Care Coordinator for Evergreen Hospice in Albany, Oregon, she works with individuals and families living with life-threatening illness and coordinates ongoing counseling support after a death. In addition to facilitating grief and loss groups in the community, particular areas of interest and expertise include grieving children, people with AIDS and their families, and ethical issues, including euthanasia, raised by life-threatening illness. She received her M.S. in counseling degree from Western Oregon State College/Oregon State University.

Ardis Sherwood-Hawes, M.S., is a counselor at the Women's Center at Clark College in Vancouver, Washington. She specializes in issues related to women who are disadvantaged. She plans to obtain her doctoral degree in counseling psychology and establish a private practice focusing on marriage counseling and family therapy.

Art Terry, Ph.D., is an assistant professor and supervisor in the practicum/internship component of the graduate program in counseling education at Portland State University, Portland, Oregon. Dr. Terry is one of the charter members of the Oregon Career Development Association (OCDA) and was president for the 1989–1990 term. He is completing his third term as member of the Governor's Commission on Occupational Information for the State of Oregon (OOICC).

Max Hines, Ph.D., is a licensed consulting psychologist and marriage and family therapist in Minneapolis, Minnesota. His interest and expertise in group therapy and in marital and family therapy is reflected in his chapter and in his guest editorship of a special issue of the *Journal for Specialists in Group Work*: The Interface of Group and Family Therapy." Dr. Hines is a core faculty member at the Minnesota School of Professional Psychology and maintains a private practice involving direct service and consultation to other therapists and agencies.

Ann Vernon, Ph.D., N.C.C., is professor and coordinator of counseling at the University of Northern Iowa, Cedar Falls. Dr. Vernon is a former elementary school counselor and currently has a private practice, where she works primarily with children and adolescents. An approved supervisor of rational-emotive therapy, Dr. Vernon is director of the Midwest Center for Rational-Emotive Therapy. Dr. Vernon is a consultant and workshop leader in the areas of communication, stress, parenting, counseling techniques, and rational-emotive therapy. She is past president of the Iowa Association for Counseling and Development and currently serves as public relations coordinator. Dr. Vernon received her M.A.E. and Ph.D. degrees from the University of Iowa.

Betty Newlon, Ed.D., is an associate professor and head of the Division of Educational and Professional Studies at the University of Arizona, Tucson, where she is involved in the training and supervising of graduate students in the mental health and community counseling program.

Miquel Arciniega, Ph.D., is an associate professor in the division of psychology in education, Arizona State University, Tempe. Dr. Arciniega has been director of minority counseling projects and institutes, teacher corps, and centers for bilingual/bicultural education. He has consulted extensively for federal, state, and local agencies in counseling minorities and has also consulted with AID (Aid for International Development) in Central and South America.

Holly Forester-Miller, Ph.D., L.P.C., is an associate professor of counseling at the University of West Virginia College of Graduate Studies, Institute, West Virginia. She served on the ethics committee for the Association for Specialists in Group Work (ASGW) that revised the *Ethical Guidelines for Group Counselors* (1989). Dr. Forester-Miller has served on the editorial board for JSGW, on the professional development committee for ASGW, has chaired the research committee for ASGW, and was founder and president of the West Virginia Association for Specialists in Group Work.

Robert L. Rubenstein, Ed.D., L.P.C., is an assistant professor of counseling in the College of Graduate Studies, University of West Virginia Institute. As an elementary school counselor, he conceived, organized, and implemented groups for children covering a variety of topics. As a counselor educator, Dr. Rubenstein focused on courses related to organization of school programs as well as professional and ethical issues related to school counselors. Dr. Rubenstein has served as president of the West Virginia School Counselors Association and is a former chairperson for the Ethics Committee of the West Virginia Association of Counseling and Development.

PART ONE

Foundations for Group Counseling

Group counseling encompasses many knowledge and skill modalities in which the group leader must be proficient. The first part of this text provides an overview of the historical context of group work as well as basic knowledge and skill areas pertinent to group facilitation.

Chapter 1, "Group Counseling: An Introduction," leads off with basic information and terminology. This is followed by a brief overview of the history of group work, examples of goals for groups, a discussion of different types of groups, assumptions underlying approaches to group composition, therapeutic factors in groups, personal characteristics of group leaders, and myths connected with group work.

The stages and transitions inherent in the group experience, as well as the issues these stages and transitions present for the leader and the members of a group alike are analyzed in chapter 2, "Group Counseling: Stages and Issues." After beginning with a case study, revisited at the end of the chapter, the early and current conceptualizations of stage theory and member behavior are discussed. A composite conceptualization of the developmental stages of groups incorporates definitive personal involvement, group involvement, and enhancement and closure stages. In conjunction with each of the four stages, member and leader behaviors are identified.

Chapter 3, "Group Counseling: Elements of Effective Leadership," explores leadership style: authoritarian, democratic, laissez-faire, leader-centered, group-centered, interpersonal, intrapersonal, and charismatic. It also covers skills related to pre-group screening and organizing for groups. Various member roles are outlined. The authors set forth the skills the group leader must master to facilitate the definitive, personal involvement, group involvement, and enhancement and closure stages discussed in chapter 2. Chapter 3 concludes with consideration of techniques for dealing with difficult members.

Chapter 4, "Group Counseling: Theory and Application," takes five selected theoretical/therapeutic approaches and applies them to groups: Adlerian, Gestalt, person-centered, rational-emotive, and transactional analysis. Rather than reiterating theory available in texts on individual counseling and psychotherapy, these theoretical concepts are translated into group leader behaviors and techniques. The chapter concludes with an integrative theme considering relationship, leader role, member role, process, and outcome variables in light of the five theoretical approaches.

1

Group Counseling: An Introduction

Dave Capuzzi and Douglas R. Gross

*L*ike other institutions and training activities, group counseling reflects both the culture and the history of the moment as influenced by national, regional and local concerns (Klein, 1985). The transition from the 20th to the 21st century in the United States poses challenges and possibilities for those who are considering work in group counseling. If the 1950s symbolized the "individual in society," the 1960s "the individual against society," the 1970s "the individual's conflict with self," and the 1980s "the individual's integration into the family," the society of the 1990s and beyond may be characterized as "the individual's integration with the machine" (Shapiro & Bernadett-Shapiro, 1985).

In the 21st century, much of the work in educational, career, and day-to-day living situations will be done by computers; connections among colleagues, friends, and family members will be maintained by telephone lines, word processors, and modems (Capuzzi & Gross, 1991). The replacement of consistent social contact with friends and co-workers by the video display terminal and telecommunication networks will create a much greater need for interpersonal communication on a person-to-person basis. Groups will provide an antidote to isolation, and more and more counselors, therapists, and other human development specialists will be called upon to serve as group facilitators. The counseling and human development professional faces crescendoing opportunities and escalating responsibilities in group work.

THE HISTORY OF GROUP WORK

Beginnings

Group counseling can be traced back to the very first decade of the 20th century (Gazda, 1985). Joseph Hersey Pratt, a physician, applied the "class" method in providing assistance to patients with tuberculosis in Boston, Massachusetts. At about the same time, J. L. Moreno, also a physician, began to develop psychodramatic methods with children and adults in Vienna, Austria. By the 1920s, Alfred Adler, also in Vienna, had introduced families to group guidance methods. In the city of New York, S. R. Slavson analyzed aspects of the small therapy group during the 1930s. At about the same time, the forerunner of group counseling models in educational settings was developed by R. D. Allen, whose approach built on the early group guidance work of Boyden.

In 1947, a multidisciplinary group of researchers and practitioners from university and community settings throughout North America attended a history-making conference in Bethel, Maine. The National Training Laboratory (NTL) in Group Development of the National Education Assocation (NEA) held its first "laboratory session" and T-groups (the "T" stands for training) and the laboratory method were born (Bradford, Gibb & Benne, 1964). Using themselves as experimental subjects, participants at the Bethel conference created a "laboratory" situation in which participants' behavior was more important than any group facilitator intervention or technique. It provided a safe place for group members to explore their own behaviors and feelings and others' responses to them as people separate from social, work, and family roles. Under NTL direction, conferences like this one continued each summer, and the T-group movement grew and attained national visibility.

As time passed, T-groups appeared on university campuses and in other settings. The T-group provided a fresh concept with tremendous appeal as opportunities were extended for group members to become more "sensitive," to "grow emotionally," and to "realize your human potential." People began hearing about the "human potential movement" and about exciting developments in California, particularly at the Esalen Institute at Big Sur and at the Center for the Studies of the Person, founded by Carl Rogers and his colleagues. A variety of marathon and encounter groups proliferated. It was an era of openness, self-awareness, and getting in touch with feelings.

The 1960s and 1970s

The 1960s were a time of social upheaval and questioning. There were riots on university campuses and in cities as civil rights groups struggled to raise the consciousness of the nation after years of unfair discrimination and prejudice. Charismatic leaders such as John F. Kennedy and Martin Luther King, Jr. became the idolized champions and international symbols of a people's determination to change a society and to promote social responsibility. The nation united in grief-stricken disbelief as its heroes were martyred, and determination to counter the human rights violations of the decades escalated. As the 1960s ended, the encounter group movement, emphasizing personal consciousness and closer connection with others, reached its zenith, and then gradually waned as events such as the Watergate scandal, the first presidential resignation in the history of the United States, the Charles Manson killings, the group killings at the Munich Olympics, the rise of fanatic cults, and others made people in all parts of the country question the extent to which permissiveness and "human potential" should be allowed to develop (Janis, 1972; Rowe & Winborn, 1973).

For professionals in education and mental health, however, the 1960s and 1970s were decades of high interest in group work despite the highs and lows of societal fervor and dismay. Mental health centers conducted more and more group sessions for clients, while counselor education, counseling psychology, psychology, and social work departments on university campuses instituted more and more course work and supervised experiences in aspects of group work. In 1973 the Association for Specialists in Group

Work (ASGW) was chartered, and by 1974 it had become a division of the American Association for Counseling and Development (at that time known as the American Personnel and Guidance Association). Similar developments took place in the context of other large professional groups such as the American Psychological Association (APA) and the National Association of Social Workers (NASW).

The 1980s

Interest in group work and in working with specialized populations grew during the 1980s. Groups sprang up for alcoholics, adult children of alcoholics, incest victims, adults molested as children, overweight people, underassertive individuals, and victims of violent crimes. There were groups for the elderly, people dealing with death and other losses, individuals with eating disorders, smokers, and victims of the holocaust (Shapiro & Bernadett-Shapiro, 1985). This increasing specialization brought with it a need for higher standards for preparation of group leaders, as evidenced by the development of ethical standards for group work specialists (Association for Specialists in Group Work, 1983) and the inclusion in the standards of the Council for the Accreditation of Counseling and Related Educational Programs (1988) of specific group work specialist preparation guidelines for the graduate-level university educator. The specialization also precipitated what has become known as the self-help group, composed of individuals who share a specific concern. Usually, self-help groups are not facilitated by a professional, which can be in conflict with the values and standards of professional group counseling (Capuzzi & Gross, 1991).

The 1990s

The practice of group counseling will continue to require greater expertise and ability to participate in and apply the results of needed research. The history-making national conference for group work specialists, conceptualized and sponsored by the ASGW in early 1990 in Florida, symbolized the importance of group work and marked the beginning of the trend to provide professional counselors with continuing education experiences aimed entirely on aspects of group work.

GOALS FOR GROUPS

Although many group work leaders believe that the goals for each counseling group should be established by the members and leaders of those groups, general goals for groups have some consensus (George & Dustin, 1988). As early as 1957, Frank proposed a general statement of group goals as helping members to:

— release their feelings constructively.
— strengthen self-esteem.
— face and resolve their problems.
— improve their skills in recognizing and resolving interpersonal and intrapersonal conflicts.
— fortify their ability to consolidate and maintain therapeutic gains.

In 1963, Kelman proposed a similar set of general goals, which added the dimensions of overcoming feelings of isolation, developing hope for increased adjustment, learning to accept responsibility, developing new relationship skills, and enhancing commitment to change. Corey, Corey, Callahan, and Russell (1982) suggested that group facilitators have two kinds of goals: general and process. General goals have to do with establishing a psychological environment within the context of a group that is conducive to supporting members as they work toward their personal goals. Process goals relate to teaching members appropriate methods of sharing their own concerns and providing feedback to others in the group. This differentiation provides a helpful guideline. Carroll and Wiggins (1990) have identified general goals for helping members of a group:

1. Become a better listener.
2. Develop sensitivity and acceptance of others.
3. Increase self-awareness and develop a sense of identity.
4. Feel a sense of belongingness and overcome feelings of isolation.
5. Learn to trust others as well as self.
6. Recognize and state areas of belief and values without fear of repression.
7. Transfer what is learned in the group to the outside by accepting responsibility for solving one's own problems. (p. 25)

In addition, Carroll and Wiggins (1990) proposed certain process goals helpful to group members:

1. Help members stay in the here and now.
2. Prevent story telling related to the there and then.
3. Help members to confront others with care and respect.
4. Learn to give nonevaluative feedback.
5. Learn to risk by speaking from the first person. (p. 26)

Both of the above lists are only partial and could be modified depending on the group leader's style and philosophy, and on the type of group. For example, a group of adults molested as children would modify the process goals so each member could disclose some there-and-then information relative to their own experiences as victims of sexual abuse, because they may not have been able to verbalize their thoughts and feelings in the past. In any case, these goals provide general guidelines only, and the different experience and process of each group call for flexibility in goals.

TYPES OF GROUPS

Group therapy, group counseling, and group guidance have different connotations. In general, *group therapy* is considered to be longer term, more remedially and therapeutically focused, and more likely to have a leader with doctoral-level preparation and a more "clinical" orientation. *Group counseling* may be differentiated from group therapy by its focus on conscious problems, by the fact that it is not aimed at major personality changes, by an orientation toward short-term issues, and by its lesser emphasis on treatment of the more severe psychological and behavioral disorders (Corey & Corey, 1987). *Group guidance* usually refers to intervention in a classroom group in a kindergarten through grade

12 setting in which the leader presents information or conducts mental health education. In contrast to group therapy or group counseling involving no more than 8 to 10 participants, a group guidance experience could involve 20 to 40 participants, lessening opportunities for individual participation and group leader observation and intervention.

Other distinctions are made between types of groups. The *T-groups* originated at the National Training Laboratory in Bethel, Maine. The *encounter group*, initiated by Carl Rogers, became known as the "personal growth group" because of its emphasis upon the individual personal development of each of its members (Gladding, 1991). Both T-groups and encounter groups are sometimes called *sensitivity groups*.

J. L. Moreno's *psychodrama* is a type of group in which participants stage a production in which they play themselves at times and sometimes play the alter-egos of others. Through acting out their issues and concerns and "processing" the experience afterward, members progress to higher levels of self-awareness and begin to exert better control over their own emotions and behaviors.

Marathon groups were first introduced in the 1960s by George Bach and Fred Stoller. Marathon groups are intense experiences extending 24 hours, 48 hours, or even longer, and they require that group members stay together. Because fatigue and intensity are aspects of the marathon, participants' defenses break down, truthfulness and openness increase, and personal growth can take place differently than in groups conducted once a week for an hour and a half. (Provisions should be made for participants to receive individual or small group follow-up after participating in a marathon group.)

The *task group* is still another modality. Saltmarsh, Jenkins, and Fisher (1986) classified task groups as volunteer groups, mission groups, goal groups, and working groups. Emphasis in a task group is on control, efficiency, and completing some kind of project through collaborative efforts. Unlike the other groups, the task group does not have a goal of personal growth, self-awareness, behavior change, or understanding group dynamics.

A Paradigm for Classifying Groups

For purposes of this chapter, the four-part paradigm suggested below (Scheidlinger, 1985) is presented as a starting point for classifying groups. Sources, including Corey (1990), Dinkmeyer and Muro (1979), Gazda (1984), and Ohlsen (1977), elaborate on group types.

Category 1: Group Psychotherapy   Group psychotherapy refers to a psychosocial process in which a mental health professional, trained in psychology or counseling psychology as well as psychopathology, elicits emotional interactions in small, carefully constructed groups to assist individuals in overcoming personality and interpersonal dysfunctions. This type of group generally has a clinical orientation, which includes assessment of each potential group member's strengths and weaknesses as well as suitability for group membership. Group psychotherapy professionals require extensive educational and supervisory experience prior to independent practice because of the long-term nature of the group psychotherapy process and the chronic nature of group members' problems.

Category 2: Therapeutic Groups   Therapeutic groups encompass all the group approaches (other than group psychotherapy) that counseling and human development pro-

fessionals use in inpatient, outpatient, or private practice settings. These groups are usually offered as an auxiliary group or in conjunction with the primary mode of treatment
(which could have an individual, group, or a family focus). Often, therapeutic groups are
directed at remediation or toward optimal functioning. Art therapy, movement therapy,
socialization, and behavior therapy groups are a few examples that might be contained in
this category.

Category 3: Human Development and Training Groups   Human development and training groups perhaps might be more closely allied to affective and cognitive mental health
education than to therapeutic groups. This does not mean that participation in this type of
group precludes personal growth and an enhanced sense of well-being. The personal
expressive, consciousness-raising, and sensitivity groups in this category may have purposes such as decreasing social isolation, making relationships more genuine, coping
with divorce, death or other losses, dealing with life transitions, understanding sexuality,
and the like.

Category 4: Self-Help Groups   Self-help groups are usually voluntary groups for participants who share a common problem or need. Many self-help groups are conducted without a professional group leader. Alcoholics Anonymous, Al-Anon, Parents Without Partners, and Overeaters Anonymous are examples of self-help groups that are relatively well
known and established in most communities.

Some group leaders prefer the term *mutual-help groups* to the term "self-help"
because self-help is only a first step (Silverman, 1986). The individual becomes aware of
a problem and then attempts to do something about it. As soon as the individual seeks
another person to share experiences and discuss options, self-help becomes mutual help.
Eligibility for participation in these groups usually is based on the individual's acknowledging a shared problem and expressing an interest in joining.

Closed and Open Groups

Closed and open groups are subcategories for group psychotherapy, therapeutic groups,
human development and training groups, and self- or mutual-help groups. A *closed group*
is characterized by members who remain together until the group terminates. In an *open
group*, new members are added during the life cycle of the group (Gruner, 1984).

Each of these models has advantages and disadvantages. Open-ended groups permit
members to resolve problems and issues in their own time frame and then leave the
group. New members may enter the groups as openings occur. Although new members
coming in at various times may be viewed as adding stimulation to the group, the group
as a whole may go through a process of regression, with accompanying fluctuations in
cohesion and trust. In contrast, closed groups offer stability of membership and facilitate
cohesion and trust. Because all members of a group do not progress at the same rate,
however, some group members might lose the advantage of being able to work hard and
terminate in a manner consistent with their own ability to learn, resolve intrapersonal or
interpersonal issues, and obtain closure based on an appropriate resolution (Gruner,
1984).

COMPOSITION OF GROUPS

The composition of a group influences many aspects of how a group functions (Waltman & Zimpfer, 1988; Yalom, 1985). Two general approaches to combining members of groups are heterogeneous and homogeneous.

Heterogeneous or Mixed-Sex Group Composition

Beasley and Childers (1985) discussed five fundamental assumptions underlying groups composed of both men and women:

1. This kind of group is a microcosm of society.
2. Self-defeating behavior can be identified and confronted more easily in a group approximating the composition of society.
3. The group focus is on the present rather than on the past.
4. Reality testing can and does occur.
5. The heterosexual group situation generates anxiety that produces change.

Social Microcosm   Creating a group environment representative of the world in which an individual interacts on a daily basis is said to maximize opportunities for learning and realization of potential (Hansen, Warner, & Smith, 1980). Not all group research supports the assumption that creating a microcosm through heterogeneous grouping promotes personal growth for both women and men.

In some studies, women in a mixed-sex group, compared with those in all-female groups, talk less, talk primarily to the men, share less personal information, and are less involved in topics (Carlock & Martin, 1977). Although some studies have indicated that men in heterogeneous groups are more personal and self-disclosing and initiate and receive more interaction than they do in all-male groups (Aries, 1976; Carlock & Martin, 1977; Reed, 1981), it will be interesting to see if these findings continue to be reported with the same frequency as researchers begin to study the group phenomenon created by Robert Bly and other proponents of the men's movement.

Confrontation of Self-Defeating Behavior   Based on the premise that a person's true self will emerge in a group reflecting society in general, this assumption presupposes that group members' dysfunctional behavior will become more clearly evident in a heterogeneous group. Then, other group members, as well as the group leader, can confront the behavior and provide constructive feedback (Beasley & Childers, 1985). Some evidence supports this assumption. A person's self-perception evolves from feedback through the years from interactions with both men and women, so a mixed-sex group would seem to be the best avenue for clarifying self-perception. But the evidence is not clear. For example, women could risk negative feedback by revealing characteristics such as assertiveness, competitiveness, and independence (Broverman, Broverman, Clarkson, Rosenkrantz, & Vogel, 1970). Because of the concern that heterogeneous groups may tend to reinforce stereotypical behavior for men and for women (Reed, 1981), the group leader should be alert to that possibility when facilitating a mixed-sex group.

Focus on the Present   Yalom (1985) maintained that groups focusing on the present augment their potency and effectiveness. It augments the development of each group member's social microcosm and promotes feedback, self-disclosure, and the acquisition of social skills. Focusing on the present may be easier in heterogeneous groups (Aries, 1973) and should be considered when making decisions about group composition.

Reality Testing   In groups, participants can discuss new alternatives and test the reality of these alternatives by having other group members provide feedback. Reactions from both genders, in the context of a safe and well facilitated group, may help a group member gain confidence and accept responsibility for behavior in a way that will transfer to heterosexual relationships outside the group (Beasley & Childers, 1985). On the other hand, if women's behaviors are circumscribed in a mixed-sex group, heterogeneous group composition may limit women's communication and exploration of new options.

Generation of Sex-Based Anxiety   Much research shows that heterogeneous groups produce more anxiety than do homogeneous groups (Aries, 1973; Carlock & Martin, 1977; Hansen et al., 1980; Melnick & Woods, 1976). Yalom (1985) contended that this anxiety is positive because change usually follows a period of anxiety and a state of ambiguity. This anxiety ideally propels members to participate in problem solving, consideration of new behaviors, and so on. Active participation and interest in self-enhancement are generally valued in the context of the group experience.

Homogeneous or Same-Sex Group Composition

A homogeneous group consists entirely of members of a given population or members who share a specific need, concern, or situation (Beasley & Childers, 1985). The cohesiveness theory underlies this approach to group composition and supports the idea that similarity of members can lead to a great deal of cohesion, openness and exploration of issues.

All-Female Groups   Some feminist groups have excluded men from membership because of the perception that men tend to dominate the conversation and the decision-making process (Bardwick, 1971; Meador, Solomon, & Bowen, 1972). When women are in the presence of men in a group, they tend to withdraw, become passive, defer to more dominant men, and assume other patterns of communication (Aries, 1973; Carlock & Martin, 1977).

According to some group leaders (Halas, 1973; Meador et al., 1972), groups composed solely of women are more conducive to change for women than are mixed-sex groups. In summarizing the research on women's consciousness groups, Kravetz (1980) reported the following consistent outcomes:

- ❑ Increased self-awareness, self-respect, and self-esteem.
- ❑ Greater awareness of the effects of traditional sex roles and sexism.
- ❑ More awareness of a commonality with other women.
- ❑ Improved relationships and a sense of solidarity with other women.
- ❑ Positive changes in interpersonal relationships and roles.
- ❑ Participation in work and community activities to change the options and opportunities of women.

All-Male Groups   Washington (1982) suggested that men's groups provide opportunities for members to share the stress and anger they experience, to discuss concerns and insecurities and to develop the confidence they need to change behaviors. Research such as that done by Twentyman and McFall (1975) and MacDonald, Lindquist, Kramer, McGrath, and Rhyne (1975) indicated that all-male groups helped members improve and rehearse behaviors and confront personal issues, which resulted in improving their relationships with women.

Some research (Aries, 1973; Reed, 1981) suggested that men's self-disclosures in all-male groups frequently take the form of storytelling and metaphors with frequent references to competition, self-aggrandizement, and aggression.

THERAPEUTIC FACTORS IN GROUPS

A therapeutic factor in a group is "an element occurring in group therapy that contributes to improvement in a patient's condition and is a function of the actions of a group therapist, the patient, or fellow group members" (Bloch, 1986, p. 679). This definition is important because it helps distinguish between therapeutic factors and necesssary conditions for change in a group as well as group interventions or techniques. An example of a condition for change is the presence of a group leader and group members to listen and provide feedback. "Making the rounds" is an example of a Gestalt intervention or technique that a group leader might employ. Conditions and interventions or techniques increase the impact of therapeutic factors in groups.

As George and Dustin (1988) noted, Corsini and Rosenberg (1955) published the first major work that presented a unifying paradigm of therapeutic factors shared by group leaders from a variety of theoretical perspectives. After considerable clustering of statements reflecting therapeutic factors, they formed the following nine-category classification system:

1. Acceptance: a sense of belonging.
2. Altruism: a sense of being helpful to others.
3. Universalization: the realization that one is not unique in one's problems.
4. Intellectualization: the process of acquiring knowledge about oneself.
5. Reality testing: recognition of the reality of issues such as defenses and family conflicts.
6. Transference: a strong attachment either to therapist or to co-members.
7. Interaction: relating within the group that brings benefits.
8. Spectator therapy: gaining from the observation and imitation of fellow members.
9. Ventilation: the release of feelings and expression of previously repressed ideas.

In 1957, Hill interviewed 19 group leaders in an attempt to further refine the classification of therapeutic elements in groups. He proposed the six elements of catharsis, feelings of belongingness, spectator therapy, insights, peer agency (universality), and socialization. Berzon, Pious and Farson (1963) used group members rather than group leaders as a basis for information about therapeutic factors. Their classification included:

1. Becoming more aware of emotional dynamics.
2. Recognizing similarity with others.
3. Feeling positive regard, acceptance, sympathy for others.
4. Seeing self as seen by others.
5. Expressing self congruently, articulately, or assertively in the group.
6. Witnessing honesty, courage, openess, or expressions of emotionality in others.
7. Feeling warmth and closeness in the group.
8. Feeling responded to by others.
9. Feeling warmth and closeness generally in the group.
10. Ventilating emotions.

A very different set of therapeutic factors connected with group experiences was proposed by Ohlsen (1977). His list differs from earlier proposals in that it emphasizes group members' attitudes about the group experience (Capuzzi & Gross, 1991). Ohlsen's paradigm includes 14 elements, which he labeled "therapeutic forces":

1. Attractiveness of the group.
2. Acceptance by the group.
3. Expectations.
4. Belonging.
5. Security within the group.
6. Client readiness.
7. Client commitment.
8. Client participation.
9. Client acceptance of responsibility.
10. Congruence.
11. Feedback.
12. Openness.
13. Therapeutic tension.
14. Therapeutic norms.

In what is now considered a landmark classification of "curative factors," Yalom (1970, 1975, 1985) proposed a list of therapeutic elements based on research he and his colleagues conducted:

1. Instillation of hope.
2. Universality.
3. Imparting of information.
4. Altruism.
5. The corrective recapitulation of the primary family group.
6. Development of socializing techniques.
7. Imitative behavior.
8. Interpersonal learning.
9. Group cohesiveness.
10. Catharsis.
11. Existential factors.

These listings are representative of the many possibilities for viewing the therapeutic elements of a positive group experience.

PERSONAL CHARACTERISTICS OF GROUP LEADERS

Many professionals in the field have described the personal traits and characteristics of effective group leaders (Corey & Corey, 1987; Dinkmeyer & Muro, 1979; Kottler, 1983). As expressed by Gerald Corey (1985):

> It is my belief that group leaders can acquire extensive theoretical and practical knowledge of group dynamics and be skilled in diagnostic and technical procedures yet be ineffective in stimulating growth and change in the members of their groups. Leaders bring to every group their personal qualities, values, and life experiences. In order to promote growth in the members' lives, leaders need to live growth-oriented lives themselves. In order to foster honest self-investigation in others, leaders need to have the courage to engage in self-appraisal themselves. In order to inspire others to break away from deadening ways of being, leaders need to be willing to seek new experiences themselves. In short, the most effective group direction is found in the kind of life the group members see the leader demonstrating and not in the words they hear the leader saying. (p. 39)

We believe that the group leader must possess certain characteristics to be effective. Arbuckle (1975), Carkhuff and Berenson (1977), Jourard (1971), Truax and Carkhuff (1967), and Yalom (1975) have presented their views on this topic. Corey's (1990) orientation is summarized here as a starting point for the beginning counselor.

Presence

The group leader's capacity to be emotionally present as group members share their experience is important. Leaders who are in touch with their own life experiences and associated emotions are usually better able to communicate empathy and understanding because they can relate to similar circumstances or emotions.

Personal Power

Personal power is derived from a sense of self-confidence and a realization of the group leader's influence on a group. Personal power channeled in a way that enhances the ability of each group member to identify and build upon strengths, overcome problems and cope more effectively with stressors is both essential and curative.

Courage

Group leaders have to be courageous. They must take risks by expressing their reactions to aspects of group process, confronting, sharing a few life experiences, acting on a combination of intuition and observation, and directing the appropriate amount of group movement and discussion.

Willingness to Confront Oneself

Dealing with group members takes courage. It is not easy to role model, confront, convey empathy, and achieve a good balance between catalyzing interaction and allowing the group to "unfold." It also takes courage on the part of the group leader to confront self. As Corey (1985) so aptly stated:

Self-confrontation can take the form of posing and answering questions such as the following:

❏ Why am I leading groups? What am I getting from this activity?
❏ Why do I behave as I do in a group? What impact do my attitudes, values, biases, feelings, and behavior have on the people in the group?
❏ What needs of mine are served by being a group leader? And to what degree?
❏ Do I ever use the groups I lead to satisfy my personal needs at the expense of the members' needs? (p. 40)

Self-confrontation has to be an ongoing process for the group leader, because the leader enhances the capacity of members in a group to ask related questions about themselves.

Self-Awareness

Serving in any kind of a counseling role would be difficult without a highly developed sense of self-awareness. Needs, defenses, apprehensions, relationship conflicts and unresolved personal issues of any kind all come into play in the process of facilitating a group. These can enhance or detract from one's ability to lead the group, depending upon the group leader's level of awareness and the extent to which these factors make the leader's role more difficult. Many counselor education departments require graduate students to obtain personal counseling outside the department, to resolve "unfinished business," so personal issues do not impede their ability to serve constructively in a counseling role.

Sincerity

Sincerity, on the part of a group leader, relates to the leader's genuine interest in the welfare of the group and individual group members. Sincerity also reflects the leader's ability to be direct and to encourage each member to explore aspects of self that could easily be distorted or denied completely.

Authenticity

Effective group leaders are able to be real, congruent, honest and open as they respond to the interactions in a group. Authenticity means that the leader knows who he or she really is and has a sense of comfort and acceptance about self, which results in an ability to be honest about feelings and reactions to the group in a way that is constructive to individuals as well as the group as a whole.

Sense of Identity

Group leaders often assist members of a group in the process of clarifying values and becoming inner- rather than outer-directed. A group leader who has not clarified personal values, meanings, goals, and expectations may have trouble helping others with the same process.

Belief in Group Process

Group leaders must be positive about the healing capacity of groups and their belief in the benefits of a group experience. If they are unsure, tentative, or unenthusiastic, the same tenor will develop among group members. Although the outcome of a group experience does not totally depend on its leader, the leader does convey messages, both verbally and nonverbally, that impact the overall benefit of the experience.

Creativity

Group leaders who can be spontaneous about their approach to a group can often catalyze better communication, insight, and personal growth than those who rely on structured interventions and techniques. Creative leaders usually accept those who are different from themselves and are flexible about approaching members and groups in ways that seem congruent with the particular group. In addition, a certain amount of creativity and spontaneity are necessary to cope with the unexpected. In a group situation the leader is continuously presented with comments, problems, and reactions that cannot be anticipated before a given session.

Stamina and Energy

Unlike an individual counseling session, during which the counselor listens to and interacts with one client, group leadership requires "tracking," remembering, and diagnosing several clients simultaneously. This set of circumstances requires more alertness, observation, responsiveness and proactivity and energy. Therefore, a group leader should not overschedule groups. Many leaders prefer the co-facilitation model so the co-facilitator or co-leader can assume part of the responsibility for group process and observation.

MYTHS CONNECTED WITH GROUP WORK

Counselors who are group leaders are usually quite enthusiastic about the benefits to clients who participate in a small-group experience. The outcomes of a competently facilitated group experience can engender personal growth (Capuzzi & Gross, 1991) that affects clients well into the future. Group work, as with other forms of therapeutic assistance (e.g., individual or family), can be for better or for worse (Carkhuff, 1969). Many group leaders follow a belief system that can be challenged by empirical facts. The following myths connected with group work are given quite a bit of attention here, with the hope that group leaders will not base their practices on a belief system not supported by research (Anderson, 1985; Capuzzi & Gross, 1991).

Myth #1: Everyone Benefits from Group Experience

Groups do provide benefits. Research on the psychosocial outcomes of groups demonstrates that groups are a powerful modality for learning, the results of which can be used outside of the group experience itself (Bednar & Lawlis, 1971; Gazda & Peters, 1975; Parloff & Dies, 1978). At times, however, membership in a group can be detrimental. Some research shows that one of every 10 group members can be hurt (Lieberman, Yalom, & Miles, 1973).

The research findings that seem to relate most to individuals who are harmed by group experience suggest some important principles: (a) those who join groups and who have the potential to be hurt by the experience have unrealistic expectations, and (b) these expectations seem to be reinforced by the leader who coerces the member to meet them (DeJulio, Bentley, & Cockayne, 1979; Lieberman et al., 1973; Stava & Bednar, 1979). To prevent harm, members' expectations for the group have to be realistic, and the leader must maintain a reasonable perspective.

Myth #2: Groups Can Be Composed to Assure Effective Outcomes

The fact is that we do not know enough about how to compose groups via the pre-group screening interview. In general, objective criteria (age, gender, socioeconomic status, presenting problem, and so forth) can be applied to keep groups homogeneous in some respects, but behavioral characteristics should be selected on a heterogeneous basis (Bertcher & Maple, 1979). The most consistent finding is that groups should be composed so that each member is compatible with at least one other member (Stava & Bednar, 1979). This seems to prevent the evolution of neglected isolates or scapegoats in a group. The essence of group process in terms of benefit to members and effective outcomes is *perceived mutual aid* (helping others, a feeling of belonging, interpersonal learning, instillation of hope, and so on) (Butler & Fuhriman, 1980; Long & Cope, 1980; Yalom, 1975).

Myth #3: The Group Revolves Around the Leader's Charisma

Although leaders do influence groups tremendously, two general findings in the research on groups should be noted. First, the group, independent of the leader, has an impact on outcomes. Second, the most effective group leaders are those who help the group develop so that members are primary sources of help to one another (Ashkenas & Tandon, 1979).

As noted by Anderson (1985), research on leadership styles has identified four leader functions that facilitate the group's functioning:

> (1) *Providing:* This is the provider role of relationships and climate-setting through such skills as support, affection, praise, protection, warmth, acceptance, genuineness, and concern.
> (2) *Processing:* This is the processor role of illuminating the meaning of the process through such skills as explaining, clarifying, interpreting, and providing a cognitive framework for change, or translating feelings and experiences into ideas.
> (3) *Catalyzing:* This is the catalyst role of stimulating interaction and emotional expression through such skills as reaching for feelings, challenging, confronting, and suggesting; using program activities such as structured experiences; and modeling.
> (4) *Directing:* This is the director role through such skills as setting limits, roles, norms, and goals; managing time; pacing; stopping; interceding; and suggesting procedures. (p. 272)

Providing and processing seem to have a linear relationship to outcomes: The higher the providing (or caring) and the higher the processing (or clarifying), the higher the positive outcomes. Catalyzing and directing have a curvilinear relationship to outcomes. Too much or too little catalyzing or directing results in lower positive outcomes (Lieberman et al., 1973).

Myth #4: Leaders Can Direct Through Structured Exercises or Experiences

Structured exercises create early cohesion (Levin & Kurtz, 1974; Lieberman et al., 1973); they help create early expression of positive and negative feelings. At the same time, they restrict members from dealing with group themes such as affection, closeness, distance, trust, mistrust, genuineness, and lack of genuineness. All of these areas form the basis for group process and should not be hampered by too much structure. The best principle around which to plan and use structured exercises to get groups started and to keep them going can best be stated as: Overplan and underuse.

Myth #5: Therapeutic Change in Groups Comes About Through Here-and-Now Experiences

Much of the research on groups indicates that corrective emotional experiences in the here-and-now of the group increase the intensity of members' experience (Levine, 1971; Lieberman et al., 1973; Snortum & Myers, 1971; Zimpfer, 1967). The intensity of emotional experiences, however, does not seem to be related to outcomes. Higher level outcomes are achieved by group members who develop insight or cognitive understanding of emotional experiences in the group and can transfer that understanding into their lives outside the group. The Gestaltists' influence on groups in the 1960s and 1970s (Perls, 1969) suggested that members should "lose your mind and come to your senses" and "stay with the here-and-now." Research suggests that members "use your mind *and* your senses" and "focus on the there-and-then as well as the here-and-now."

Myth #6: Major Member Learning in Groups Is Derived From Self-Disclosure and Feedback

Most of the learning of members in a group is assumed to come from self-disclosure in exchange for feedback (Jacobs, 1974). To a large extent, this statement is a myth. Self-disclosure and feedback per se make little difference in outcome (Anchor, 1979; Bean & Houston, 1978). Rather, the *use* of self-disclosure and feedback seem to make the difference (Martin & Jacobs, 1980). Self-disclosure and feedback seem useful only when deeply personal sharing is understood and appreciated and the feedback is accurate (Berzon, Pious, & Farson, 1963; Goldstein, Bednar, & Yanell, 1979; Frank & Ascher, 1951). The actual benefit of self-disclosure and feedback relates to how these processes generate empathy among members. Empathy, or the actual experience of being understood by other members, is what catalyzes personal growth and understanding in the context of a group.

Myth #7: A Leader Does Not Have to Understand Group Process and Group Dynamics

Groups have a natural evolution and unfolding of processes and dynamics. Anderson (1979) labeled these as trust, autonomy, closeness, interdependence, and termination (TACIT). Tuckman (1965) suggested the more dramatic terminology of forming, storming, norming, performing, and adjourning. Two reviews covering more than 200 studies of group dynamics and group process (Cohen & Smith, 1976; La Coursiere, 1980) revealed remarkably similar patterns (despite differences in the terms chosen as descriptors) in the evolution of group processes. Group leaders must understand group processes and dynamics to do a competent job of enhancing benefits from group participation.

Myth #8: Changes in Group Participants Are Not Maintained

Groups can be powerful! Members can maintain changes as long as six months to a year later even when groups meet for only three or four months (Lieberman et al, 1973). The positive effects of having participated in a group can be subtle but pervasive. For example, graduate students at Portland State University who took part in a 10-week off-campus personal growth group focusing on art therapy reported that skills they learned in the group, such as the need for creativity in their lives, relaxation techniques, insight into personal family dynamics, and ways of working with daily stress, continued to be relevant and useful a year later.

Myth #9: A Group Is a Place to Get Emotionally High

As noted by Corey (1985), feeling good after a group session is a positive outcome but is not the main reason for being in a group in the first place. Some group members have periods of depression after group participation because they don't find, on a daily basis, the kind of support they received from other members of the group. Group members should be prepared for this possibility and assisted in their ability to obtain support, when appropriate, from those around them.

Myth #10: A Group's Purpose Is to Make Members Close to Every Other Member

Although genuine feelings of intimacy and cohesiveness develop in effective groups, intimacy is the byproduct and not the central purpose of the group. Intimacy develops as individual members risk self-disclosure and problem solving and other group members reach out in constructive ways (Corey, 1985).

Myth #11: Group Participation Results in Brainwashing

Professional groups do not indoctrinate members with a particular philosophy of life or a set of rules about how each member "should be." If this does occur in a group, it is truly a breach of professional ethics and an abuse of the group. Group participation encourages members to look within themselves for answers and to become as self-directed as possible (Corey, 1985).

Myth #12: To Benefit from a Group, a Member Has to Be Dysfunctional

Group counseling is as appropriate with individuals who are functioning relatively well and who want to enhance their capabilities as it is for those who are having difficulty with certain aspects of their lives. Groups are not only for dysfunctional people (Corey, 1985).

SUMMARY

Group counseling has its roots in the early 1900s, when it was applied in medical settings and with children, adults, and families. The first "laboratory," or T-group, emerged in 1947, later branching out to university and other settings. Interest in group work has increased dramatically over time, illustrated by the recent flood of self-help groups, led by either professionals or lay people.

Among the goals for groups are to facilitate the release of feelings, to strengthen members' self-esteem, to help members face and resolve their problems, to help them learn how to recognize and solve interpersonal and intrapersonal conflicts, and to facilitate their maintaining therapeutic gains. Goals are of two basic types: general (relating to a conducive environment) and process (having to do with methods of sharing and feedback).

Distinctions can be made between group therapy (more likely to be longer term and have a therapeutic emphasis), group counseling (having a focus on conscious problems and an orientation toward short-term issues), and group guidance (in which the leader presents information or conducts mental health education to a larger group). Specialized types of group experiences include sensitivity groups, psychodrama, marathon groups, and task groups, among others. Groups can be classified into four primary categories: group psychotherapy, therapeutic groups, human development and training groups, and self-help groups. These can be either heterogeneous (mixed sex) or homogeneous (same sex) and can be closed (in which members stay together until the group is terminated) or open (in which new members are added as other leave.

Therapeutic factors in a group include acceptance, altruism, universalization, intellectualization, reality testing, transference, interaction, spectator therapy, and ventilation. Translated into leader qualities, these entail presence, personal power, courage, willingness to confront oneself, self-awareness, sincerity, authenticity, a sense of identify, belief in the group process, creativity, and stamina and energy. Myths that can detract from group effectiveness are that everyone benefits from group experience, groups always have advantageous outcomes, the group revolves around the leader's charisma, groups should be limited to the here and now, and dysfunctional people are the only ones who can benefit from groups, among other misconceptions. Groups can be either powerful and growth-enhancing or stifling and hindering. The more a leader is aware of the goals, purposes, and dynamics of groups, the better equipped he or she will be to provide an optimal experience for group members.

REFERENCES

Anchor, K. N. (1979). High and low-risk self-disclosure in group psychotherapy. *Small Group Behavior, 10,* 279–283.

Anderson, J. D. (1979). Social work with groups in the generic base of social work practice. *Social Work With Groups, 2,* 281–293.

Anderson, J. D. (1985). Working with groups: Little known facts that challenge well-known myths. *Small Group Behavior, 16*(3), 267–283.

Arbuckle, D. (1975). *Counseling and psychotherapy: An existential-humanistic view.* Boston: Allyn & Bacon.

Aries, E. J. (1973). Interaction patterns and themes of male, female and mixed groups. *Dissertation Abstracts International, 35,* 3084. (University Microfilms No. 74-27, 772).

Aries, E. J. (1976). Interactional patterns and themes of male, female and mixed groups. *Small Group Behavior, 7,* 7–18.

Ashkenas, R., & Tandon, R. (1979). Eclectic approach to small group facilitation. *Small Group Behavior, 10,* 224–241.

Association for Specialists in Group Work. (1983). *Professional standards for training of group counselors.* Alexandria, VA: Author.

Bardwick, J. M. (1971). *Psychology of women.* New York: Harper & Row.

Bean, B. W., & Houston, B. K. (1978). Self-concept and self-disclosure in encounter groups. *Small Group Behavior, 9,* 549–554.

Beasley, L., & Childers, J.H., Jr. (1985). Group counseling for heterosexual, interpersonal skills: Mixed or same-sex group composition. *Journal for Specialists in Group Work, 10*(4), 192–197.

Bednar, R., & Lawlis, G. (1971). Empirical research in group psychotherapy. In S. L. Garfield & A. E. Bergin (Eds.), *Handbook of psychotherapy and behavior change* (2nd ed., pp. 420–439). New York: John Wiley.

Bertcher, H. J., & Maple, F. F. (1979). *Creating groups.* Beverly Hills, CA: Sage.

Berzon, B., Pious, C., & Farson, R. (1963). The therapeutic event in group psychotherapy: A study of subjective reports by group members. *Journal of Individual Psychology, 19,* 204–212.

Bloch, S. (1986). Therapeutic factors in group psychotherapy. In A. J. Frances & R. E. Hales (Eds.), *Annual review* (Vol. 5, pp. 678–698). Washington, DC: American Psychiatric Press.

Bradford, L. P., Gibb, J. R., & Benne, K.D. (Eds.). (1964). *T-group theory and laboratory method: Innovation in re-education.* New York: Wiley.

Broverman, I. K., Broverman, D. M., Clarkson, F. E., Rosenkrantz, P., & Vogel, S. R. (1970). Sex role stereotypes and clinical judgments of mental health. *Journal of Consulting Psychology, 34,* 1–7.

Butler, T., & Fuhriman, A. (1980). Patient perspective on the curative process: A comparison of day treatment and outpatient psychotherapy groups. *Small Group Behavior, 11,* 371–388.

Capuzzi, D., & Gross, D. R. (1991). *Introduction to counseling: Perspectives for the 1990s.* Boston: Allyn & Bacon.

Carkhuff, R. R. (1969). *Helping and human relations: A primer for lay and professional helpers: Vol. 2. Practice and research.* New York: Holt, Rinehart & Winston.

Carkhuff, R. R., & Berenson, B. G. (1977). *Beyond counseling and therapy* (2nd ed.). New York: Holt, Rinehart & Winston.

Carlock, C. J., & Martin, P. Y. (1977). Sex composition and the intensive group experience. *Journal of the National Association of Social Workers, 22,* 27–32.

Carroll, M. R., & Wiggins, J. (1990). *Elements of group counseling: Back to the basics.* Denver: Love Publishing.

Cohen, A. M., & Smith, D. R. (1976). *The critical incident in growth groups: Theory and techniques.* La Jolla, CA: University Associates.

Corey, G. (1985). *Theory and practice of group counseling* (2nd ed.). Pacific Grove, CA: Brooks/Cole Publishing Company.

Corey, G. (1990). *Theory and practice of group counseling* (3rd ed.). Pacific Grove, CA: Brooks/Cole Publishing Company.

Corey, G., & Corey, M. S. (1987). *Groups: Process and practice* (3rd ed.). Pacific Grove, CA: Brooks/Cole Publishing Company.

Corey, G., Corey, M. S., Callahan, P. J., & Russell, J. M. (1982). *Group techniques.* Pacific Grove, CA: Brooks/Cole.

Corsini, R., & Rosenberg, B. (1955). Mechanisms of group psychotherapy: Processes and dynamics. *Journal of Abnormal & Social Psychology, 51,* 406–411.

Council for Accreditation of Counseling and Related Educational Programs. (1988). *Accreditation procedures manual and application.* Alexandria, VA: Author.

DeJulio, S. J., Bentley, J., & Cockayne, T. (1979). Pregroup norm setting: Effects on encounter group interaction. *Small Group Behavior, 10,* 368–388.

Dinkmeyer, D. C., & Muro, J. J. (1979). *Group counseling: Theory and practice* (2nd ed.). Ithaca, IL: Peacock Publishers.

Frank, J. (1957). Some determinants, manifestations, and efforts of cohesiveness in therapy groups. *International Journal of Group Psychotherapy, 7,* 53–63.

Frank, J., & Ascher, E. (1951). The corrective emotional experience in group therapy. *American Journal of Psychiatry, 108,* 126–131.

Gazda, G. (1984). *Group counseling* (3rd ed.). Dubuque, IA: Wm. C. Brown.

Gazda, G. M. (1985). Group counseling and therapy: A perspective on the future. *Journal for Specialists in Group Work, 10*(2), 74–76.

Gazda, G. M., & Peters, R. W. (1975). An analysis of research in group psychotherapy, group counseling and human relations training. In G. M. Gazda (Ed.), *Basic approaches to group psychotherapy and group counseling* (pp. 38–54). Springfield, IL: Charles C Thomas.

George, R. L., & Dustin, D. (1988). *Group counseling: Theory and practice.* Englewood Cliffs, NJ: Prentice Hall.

Gladding, S. T. (1991). *Group work: A counseling specialty.* New York: Merrill.

Goldstein, M. J., Bednar, R. L., & Yanell, B. (1979). Personal risk associated with self-disclosure, interpersonal feedback, and group confrontation in group psychotherapy. *Small Group Behavior, 9,* 579–587.

Gruner, L. (1984). Membership composition of open and closed groups. *Small Group Behavior, 15*(2), 222–232.

Halas, C. (1973). All-women's groups: A view from inside. *Personnel & Guidance Journal, 52,* 91–95.

Hansen, J. C., Warner, R. W., & Smith, E. J. (1980). *Group counseling: Theory and process* (2nd ed.). Chicago: Rand McNally.

Hill, W. F. (1957). Analysis of interviews of group therapists' papers. *Provo Papers, 1,* 1.

Jacobs, A. (1974). The use of feedback in groups. In A. Jacobs and W. W. Spradline (Eds.), *The group as an agent of change* (pp. 31–49). New York: Behavioral Publications.

Janis, I. L. (1972). *Victims of groupthink: A psychological study of foreign-policy decisions and fiascos.* Boston: Houghton Mifflin.

Jourard, S. (1971). *The transparent self* (rev.). New York: Van Nostrand Reinhold.

Kelman, H. C. (1963). The role of the group in the induction of therapeutic change. *Journal of Group Psychotherapy, 13,* 399–432.

Klein, E. B. (1985). Group work: 1985 and 2001 [Special issue]. *Journal for Specialists in Group Work, 10*(2), 108–111.

Kottler, J. A. (1983). *Pragmatic group leadership.* Pacific Grove, CA: Brooks/Cole Publishing Company.

Kravetz, D. (1980). Consciousness-raising and self-help. In A. M. Brodsky & R. Hare-Mustin (Eds.), *Women and psychotherapy* (pp. 267–281). New York: Guilford.

La Coursiere, R. (1980). *The life-cycle of groups: Group development stage theory.* New York: Human Sciences.

Levin, E. M., & Kurtz, R. P. (1974). Participant perceptions following structured and nonstructured human relations training. *Journal of Counseling Psychology, 21,* 514–532.

Levine, N. (1971). Emotional factors in group development. *Human Relations, 24,* 65–89.

Lieberman, M. A., Yalom, I. D., & Miles, M. B. (1973). *Encounter groups: First facts.* New York: Basic Books.

Long, L. D., & Cope, C. S. (1980). Curative factors in a male felony offender group. *Small Group Behavior, 11,* 389–398.

MacDonald, M. L., Lindquist, C. V., Kramer, J. A., McGrath, R. A., & Rhyne, L. D. (1975). Social skills training: Behavior rehearsal in groups and dating skills. *Journal of Counseling Psychology, 22,* 224–230.

Martin, L., & Jacobs, M. (1980). Structured feedback delivered in small groups. *Small Group Behavior, 1,* 88–107.

Meador, B., Solomon, E., & Bowen, M. (1972). Encounter groups for women only. In L. Solomon & B. Berzon (Eds.), *Perspectives on encounter groups.* San Francisco: Jossey-Bass.

Melnick. J., & Woods, M. (1976). Analysis of group composition research and theory for psychotherapeutic and group oriented groups. *Journal of Applied Behavioral Science, 12,* 493–512.

Ohlsen, M. M. (1977). *Group counseling* (2nd ed.). New York: Holt, Rinehart & Winston.

Parloff, M. B., & Dies, R. R. (1978). Group therapy outcome instrument: Guidelines for conducting research. *Small Group Behavior, 9,* 243–286.

Perls, F. (1969). *Gestalt therapy verbatim.* New York: Bantam.

Reed, B. G. (1981). Gender issues in training group leaders. *Journal for Specialists in Group Work, 6,* 161–170.

Rowe, W., & Winborn, B. B. (1973). What people fear about group work: An analysis of 36 selected critical articles. *Educational Technology, 13*(1), 53–57.

Saltmarsh, R. E., Jenkins, S. J., & Fisher, G.L. (1986). The TRAC model: A practical map for group process and management. *Journal for Specialists in Group Work, 11,* 30–36.

Scheidlinger, S. (1985). Group treatment of adolescents: An overview. *American Journal of Orthopsychiatry, 55*(1), 102–111.

Shapiro, J. L., & Bernadett-Shapiro, S. (1985). Group work to 2001: Hal or haven (from isolation)? [Special issue]. *Journal for Specialists in Group Work, 10*(2), 83–87.

Silverman, P. R. (1986). The perils of borrowing: Role of the professional in mutual help groups. *Journal for Specialists in Group Work, 11,* 68–73.

Snortum, J. R., & Myers, H. F. (1971). Intensity of T-group relations as function of interaction. *International Journal of Group Psychotherapy, 21,* 190–201.

Stava, L. J., & Bednar, R. L. (1979). Process and outcome in encounter groups: the effect of group composition. *Small Group Behavior, 10,* 200–213.

Truax, C. B., & Carkhuff, R. R. (1967). *Toward effective counseling and psychotherapy: Training and practice.* Chicago: Aldine.

Tuckman, B. W. (1965). Developmental sequences in small groups. *Psychological Bulletin, 63,* 384–389.

Twentyman, C. J., & McFall, R. M. (1975). Behavioral training of social skills in shy males. *Journal of Counseling & Clinical Psychology, 43,* 384–395.

Waltman, D. E., & Zimpfer, D. G. (1988). Composition, structure and duration of treatment: Interacting variables in counseling groups. *Small Group Behavior, 19*(2), 171–184.

Washington, D. S. (1982). Challenging men in groups. *Journal for Specialists in Group Work, 7,* 132–136.

Yalom, I. D. (1970). *The theory and practice of group psychotherapy.* New York: Basic Books.

Yalom, I. D. (1975). *The theory and practice of group psychotherapy* (2nd ed.). New York: Basic Books.

Yalom, I. D. (1985). *The theory and practice of group psychotherapy* (3rd ed.). New York: Basic Books.

Zimpfer, D. G. (1967). Expression of feelings in group counseling. *Personnel & Guidance Journal, 45,* 703–708.

2

Group Counseling: Stages and Issues

Douglas R. Gross and Dave Capuzzi

As George left the group counseling classroom that evening, he could not help but think of all of the issues the class had been discussing during the past few weeks. He would finish his program within the next year, and he knew that the expectations in any position would require both group and individual counseling. He felt comfortable with his individual skills, and his practicum experience had substantiated his ability in this domain. His current concern centered on his ability to work with groups. This was his second class in groups, and there seemed to be so many things to remember, so many factors to consider, and so many issues to be addressed. As he drove home that evening, George felt overwhelmed. In talking with others in the class, he felt that many shared his concern. He wondered if he would ever feel comfortable in this area and what would happen in his internship when asked to lead or co-lead groups. "Will I be able to function effectively as a group leader?" is a question that continued to plague him.

Many concerns and questions arise in the group counseling area. According to Gill and Barry, 1982, "Every trainer of group counselors and most group counseling trainees have been either the sender or receiver of these statements" (p. 302). They address the anxiety surrounding group counseling for the experienced and novice group leader alike. The individuals selected to lead groups are immediately struck by the complexity and the challenge groups present. In addressing this issue, Ward (1985) stated:

> Group work is challenging and complex because groups are complex. Groups are complex because each group member has complex thoughts, feelings, and behaviors. The complexity is magnified many times because most group members who have psychological exploration, growth, and change as their goals interact with one another and with the group leaders in intricate patterns. In addition, if members have an opportunity to interact over a period of time, the group develops a set of overt and covert guidelines or group norms that help regulate individual behavior and interactions between and among members. (p. 59)

The challenge and complexity of group work are further substantiated in the literature by Maples (1988), Shulman (1986), and Waldo (1985). Each of these authors, although dealing with differing aspects of group work, arrives at similar conclusions related to issues of challenge and complexity. They highlight areas such as group membership, leadership styles, group methods, issues surrounding confidentiality, resistance, silence, conflict, termination and follow-up, and stages and transitions inherent in the group experience. Add to these the complexity of each individual involved, and it is easy to see why group work generates anxiety for the leader and for the members and sets the stage for a real challenge.

In this chapter we explore the stages and transitions inherent in the group experience and discuss issues including resistance, conflict, and termination as they relate to group stages and transitions. We present a conceptualization of stages of group development based on a literature review and on our own experiences in working with groups, integrating member and leader behaviors at each stage and concluding with recommendations on how group leaders can apply these stages, transitions, functions, and tasks.

STAGES AND TRANSITIONS

The distinct stages that groups move through as they pass from opening to closure are difficult to describe in definitive terms. The nature of the group, the membership, and the leadership style all influence this developmental process. A second set of factors arises from the open or closed nature of the group. A closed group, which maintains the same membership through its lifetime, is more easily described in terms of stages of development than is an open group, in which members come and go. Groups that add new members as old members leave complicate the developmental process. Any developmental scheme, therefore, is based more upon experience than upon hard and fast rules governing groups' development.

Another caution regarding the presentation of stages of group development centers upon the concept that, based upon a myriad of factors, group stage development is not a discrete and neatly separated process. In discussing this point, George and Dustin (1988) stated:

> The stages described do not occur in discrete and neatly separated points in the life of a real group. There is considerable overlap between the stages, as groups move from one stage to the other in a somewhat jerky, hesitant manner. As a result, there may be some movement toward the next stage and then regression to the previous stage. (p. 102)

In spite of these caveats, authors apparently agree on a generalized pattern of stages and transitions in groups (Berg & Landreth, 1990; Corey, 1985; Kormanski & Mozenter, 1987; Tuckman, 1965; Tuckman & Jensen, 1977; Yalom, 1975, 1985; Zimpfer, 1986). The stages or phases identified within this pattern are outlined in Table 2.1. Before discussing these stages, however, the following background information is presented as significant foundational material to later stage development.

Early Conceptualizations

A great deal has been written about the phases through which groups progress from inception to closure. Much of the early work in this area stems from authors such as

Thelen and Dickerman (1949), Bales (1950), and Miles (1953). They conceptualized stages of groups based on the problem-solving behaviors exhibited in task groups. In these early developmental schemas, the emphasis was on tasks the group was expected to accomplish, such as getting organized, sharing ideas and opinions, and reaching solutions through suggestions. From this task orientation, specific member roles in groups were examined. What started as group *maintenance behaviors* (member behaviors utilized to either promote or impede the progress of the group), were translated into *interactional behaviors*, which added a dimension to the early emphasis on task behaviors. Subsequent approaches to stage development in small groups combined task and member behaviors into descriptions of group process over time.

An example of how task and member behaviors are combined is found in the work of Bennis and Shepard (1956). Integrating the work of Bales (1953) with their own concepts, they developed a conceptualization of group movement based upon their observations while teaching group dynamics to graduate students. As a result of those observations, they proposed that groups generally move through six developmental phases from beginning to termination:

1. Dependence-flight.
2. Counterdependence-fight.
3. Resolution-catharsis.
4. Enchantment-flight.
5. Disenchantment-fight.
6. Consensual validation.

This conceptualization indicates that groups begin in a somewhat dependent stage and growth takes place as they strive to move toward interdependent functioning.

Expanding on the work of Bennis and Shepard, Reid (1965) discussed the developmental stages of groups in terms of an "authority cycle." He viewed the growth and development of the group in direct relationship to the leader's authority. Groups move from dependence upon an established leader through counterindependence and counter-

Table 2.1   STAGES/PHASES OF GROUP DEVELOPMENT

STAGES/PHASES AUTHOR	1	2	3	4	5
Tuckman (1965) Tuckman & Jensen (1977)	Forming	Storming	Norming	Performing	Adjourning
Yalom (1975, 1985)	Orientation	———Conflict———		Intimacy	Termination
Corey (1985)	Orientation	Transition	Working	Consolidation/Termination	
Kormanski & Mozenter (1987)	Awareness	Conflict	Cooperation	Productivity	Separation
Berg & Landreth (1990)	———Precommitment———			———Commitment———	

dependence until interdependence with the original authority leader has been established. According to Reid, a crisis within the group may cause it to fall back to dependence on the established leader and begin the circular developmental pattern again. Like Bennis and Shepard, he stressed that growth occurs in groups as they move from degrees of dependence to degrees of interdependence.

Other writers (Bion, 1961; Gazda, 1971; Gibb, 1964; Kaplan & Roman, 1963; Mills, 1964; Ohlsen, 1970; Schutz, 1958) aided in the early development of stage theories applied to the group process. Each described the various stages through which groups progress. Their descriptions discuss not only the content of each of the stages but also the behaviors individual group members display at each of these stages.

Current Conceptualizations

Based upon the work noted in the preceding discussion, the authors listed in Table 2.1 expanded upon these early theories. All of the authors identified in Table 2.1 view the movement of groups from origination to termination from a stage/phase perspective. A perusal of the table indicates that they differ in terminology to describe each stage and also in the number of stages. They do show, however, a great deal of consistency in their descriptions of group members' behaviors in these stages.

Stage 1   Some of the descriptors applying to Stage 1 are:

❏ Orienting
❏ Testing the environment
❏ Identifying boundaries
❏ Coming together
❏ Seeking acceptance
❏ Seeking approval
❏ Developing commitment
❏ Searching for structure and meaning
❏ Getting acquainted
❏ Defining goals
❏ Building a culture
❏ Exploring expectations
❏ Learning group functioning
❏ Seeking one's place in the group
❏ Reviewing and defining power

Whether these behaviors are viewed from an individual's perspective or from the group's perspective, Stage 1 in group development seems to be one of definition for the individual member and the group alike. Individuals seem to be defining for themselves where and perhaps if they fit in the group, what role they will take in the group, degrees of acceptance and approval within the group, and expectations both for self and for others as these relate to the group process.

If the "group" can be viewed as an entity unto itself separate from its individual parts, aspects of further definition appear. This entity, called "group," is seeking to define its structure and meaning, its functions, its goals, and its boundaries. Through such definition, the "group" attempts to build *a networking system connecting its individual parts*, its members. The degree of success in this endeavor often rests in the strength of the constructed network and the skills of the group leader in building this network.

A second factor identifed by research centers on the *affective aspects* of this stage. The term "anxiety" appears in many of the descriptions as a common response to the beginning stage of group involvement. The amount of anxiety seems to be related to perceptions of risk, threat, power, member behaviors, leader behaviors, and expectations, either perceived or real. The degree of anxiety varies from member to member and from group to group, but it does seem to be present, to some extent, in the beginning stages of all groups.

A third factor involves *dependence versus independence*. Aspects of dependence seem much more pronounced during this initial stage than in the other stages identified. Perhaps the unknown elements of the new group are responsible for this response. Perhaps the testing, seeking, and exploring to find one's place in the group are the catalysts for this type of behavior. Perhaps a more dependent stance is necessary in attempting to reach a definition of self in relationship to the group.

Stage 2 Labeled by terms such as storming, conflict, transition, and precommitment, Stage 2 is characterized by active personal involvement in which the individual begins to test his or her position and power in the group and also the behavioral parameters of the group and its members. The following terms are descriptive of Stage 2:

❑ Conflict
❑ Polarization
❑ Resistance
❑ Dominance
❑ Control
❑ Power
❑ Anxiety
❑ Defensiveness
❑ Struggle
❑ Confrontation

These terms depict not only action and reaction but also interaction on the part of the individual members as they attempt to establish self within the group structure. Words such as struggle, conflict, and confrontation attest to the individual's need to move from the safety of passive involvement to the more risk-oriented position of active involvement. Most of the descriptors for Stage 2 signify a movement from observation to participation, and this participation is generally viewed as action oriented.

Stage 3 In describing Stage 3, terms such as norming, conflict, working, cooperation, precommitment, and commitment are applied. Yalom (1975, 1985) believes that conflict is part of both Stages 2 and 3 but that the conflict associated with Stage 3 is a more productive interaction out of which group cohesion develops. Berg and Landreth (1990) view this period of group development as one of transition in which greater degrees of commitment develop, leading to more productive interactions within the group. The following terms describe the types of behaviors identified in Stage 3:

- ❑ Cohesiveness
- ❑ Standardization
- ❑ Role clarification and adoption
- ❑ Intimacy
- ❑ Problem exploration
- ❑ Action exploration
- ❑ Development of belonging
- ❑ Development of inclusion
- ❑ Development of solidarity
- ❑ Conflict resolution
- ❑ Development of helping skills
- ❑ Enhanced risk taking
- ❑ Decreased aggression
- ❑ Increased compromise

Activities in Stage 3 involve blending, merging, and moving from independence to more interdependence, in which individuality is not lost but instead becomes enmeshed in the group. Stage 3 encompasses behaviors and activities that are more group-specific than member-specific. Whereas in Stage 2, the individual, through testing, checking, and confrontation, was striving for greater self-involvement, members in Stage 3 are most accurately viewed in terms of group involvement. The group, its purposes, processes, and membership, comes ahead of the individual to maximize its development.

Stages 4 and 5 For the purposes of discussion, Stages 4 and 5 will be presented as overlapping, because the authors cited vary in the number of stages they present and also in the words they use to describe these stages. Descriptive words such as performing/adjourning, intimacy, termination, consolidation/termination, productivity, separation, and commitment are applied. In his earlier conceptualization, Tuckman (1965) discussed only four stages. He added a fifth stage, adjournment, in his later work (Tuckman & Jensen, 1977). Corey (1985) delineated four stages, and described Stage 4 in terms of consolidation/termination. Yalom (1975, 1985) and Kormanski and Mozenter (1987) see five distinct stages and label the last two intimacy and termination and productivity and separating, respectively. In the view of Berg and Landreth (1990), the last stage is commitment, with several phases within this stage. Whether viewed as being one or two stages, the following terms describe the final portion of group development:

- ❑ Developing roles
- ❑ Channeling energy
- ❑ Resolving issues
- ❑ Increasing self-disclosure
- ❑ Increasing honesty
- ❑ Increasing spontaneity
- ❑ Increasing responsibility
- ❑ Increasing integration
- ❑ Increasing interpretation
- ❑ Increasing behavioral reaffirmations

❑ Increasing intensification of feelings
❑ Increasing sadness and anxiety and dependence
❑ Preparing for separation
❑ Evaluating
❑ Ending

Drawing upon the growth and development that have taken place during the previous stages, the final segment is best viewed in terms of self- and group-enhancement and closure. Enhancement is seen in more group involvement and personal development as these apply to the group and to the individual. Group development is furthered by greater depth of problem exploration, action orientation, solidarity, integration, and problem resolution. Personal dynamics are seen when areas such as honesty, spontaneity, intimacy, feelings of belonging, inclusion, and integration come to fruition.

The cyclical nature of group development (Reid, 1965) becomes obvious as the group approaches culmination. As individuals begin to see closure as a reality, loss anxiety, and dependence evolve in questions such as: Will I be able to take what I have learned and apply it outside the group? Will I be able to function without the group? The loss anxiety and dependence inherent in these questions apply to Stage 1 behaviors, and the leader will have to be skilled to turn this anxiety and dependence into positive attributes as members leave the group. In discussing the closure process, Berg and Landreth (1990) had the following observations:

> A certain ambiguity of feelings can be anticipated that approximates the grieving process. Leave taking will produce denial and withdrawal in some and elation in others. Overriding these natural feelings of loss and anticipation should be a general optimism and a sense of completion. The group leader needs to take special care in dealing fully with feelings of anxiety associated with leaving the group. (p. 109)

COMPOSITE CONCEPTUALIZATIONS

Based upon the preceding information, we add our view of the developmental stages of groups, calling upon our own collective experience. In our view, this developmental process consists of four stages: (a) definitive stage, (b) personal involvement stage, (c) group involvement stage, and (d) enhancement and closure stage.

Definitive Stage

The length of time accorded this stage in group development varies with the group and is best explained in terms of the individual group members' defining for themselves the purpose of the group, their commitment to it, their potential involvement in it, and the degree of self they are willing to share. Characterizing this stage of development are questions such as: Whom can I trust? Where will I find support? Will I be hurt by others' knowing about me? How much of myself am I willing to share? These questions and the lack of immediate answers typify members in the definitive stage as showing increased anxiety, excitement, nervousness, and self-protective dialogue. The dialogue during this stage tends to be of a social nature (small talk) as the members test the waters of group involvement. To help group members deal effectively with the definitive stage, the group leader needs skills in dealing with issues such as trust, support, safety, self-disclosure, and confidentiality.

In the definitive stage in group development, individuals define, demonstrate, and experiment with their own role definitions; they test out the temperament, personality, and behaviors of other group members; and they arrive at conclusions about how personally involved they are willing to become. The individual's movement through this stage can be enhanced or impeded by the group's makeup (age, gender, number, values, attitudes, socioeconomic status, and so on), the leadership style (active, passive, autocratic, democratic), the group's setting (formal, informal, comfortable, relaxed), the personal dynamics the individual brings to the group (shy, aggressive, verbal, nonverbal), and the individual's perceptions of trust and acceptance from other group members and from the group leader.

The definitive stage is crucial in group development and can determine for the individual, and, therefore, for the group, future involvement, commitment, and individual and group success or failure in the long run.

Member Behaviors

❑ Members evaluate the leader in terms of skill, ability, and capacity to trust.
❑ Members evaluate other members in terms of commitment, safety, and confidentiality.
❑ Members evaluate self in terms of risk taking, sharing self with others, and their willingness to fully participate.
❑ Members search for meaning and structure within the group.
❑ Members search for approval from members and from the leader.
❑ Members search for their place within the group.
❑ Members define self in relationship to other members and the leader.
❑ Members define the group experience in terms of other life experiences.

Leader Behaviors

❑ The leader attempts to foster inclusion of all group members.
❑ The leader explains the rules and regulations that will operate within the group.
❑ The leader explains the structure, timelines, and leader behaviors that members can expect within the group.
❑ The leader attempts to model the behaviors expected of the group members.
❑ The leader is aware of the various emotions within the group and attempts to deal effectively with these.
❑ The leader discusses issues of confidentiality, behavior, and goals and expectations for the group.
❑ The leader attempts to draw from the members their goals and expectations for the group.
❑ The leader attempts to provide an environment that facilitates growth.

Personal Involvement Stage

Once individuals have drawn conclusions about their commitment and role in the group, they move into the personal involvement stage of group development. This stage is best described in terms of member-to-member interactions—the sharing of personal information, confrontation with other group members, power struggles, and the individual's growing identity as a group member. Statements such as "I am," "I fear," "I need," and "I care" are characteristic of this stage of group involvement. Through speech and behaviors, the individual member demonstrates the degree of personal sharing he or she is willing to invest and confirms the commitment made during the definitive stage.

The personal involvement stage is one of action, reaction, and interaction. Both fight and flight are represented in this stage as individuals strive to carve their place within the group. This carving or creating process often involves heated member-to-member interactions followed by retreat to regroup and battle again. The battles that ensue not only enhance the member's place within the group but also aid in firmly establishing the group as an entity in its own right.

The personal involvement stage offers the individual the opportunity to try out various behaviors, affirm or deny perceptions of self and others, receive feedback in the form of words or behaviors, and begin the difficult process of self-evaluation. Individual involvement in this stage of group development is critical to the eventual outcome of the group.

Member Behaviors

❑ Members openly challenge members and the leader as they strive to find their place in the group.
❑ Members test their personal power within the group in attempts at manipulation and control.
❑ Members struggle as they try to find safety and comfort in sharing themselves with others.
❑ Members resist integrating the feedback they receive, as the suggested changes may be too painful to implement.
❑ Members join with other selected members in attempts to build safety and security.
❑ Members increase their commitment to self and also to the group and its goals and purposes.
❑ Members become more willing to share self with others and take a more active role in the group process.
❑ Members expand their ability to share feelings, ideas, and needs as these relate to the group process.

Leader Behaviors

❑ The leader demonstrates awareness of the emotional makeup of the group and encourages affective expression.
❑ The leader participates in the struggle, confontation, and conflict that is part of this stage.
❑ The leader communicates to the members the appropriateness of this type of member-to-member reaction and interaction.
❑ The leader allows members to move through this stage at their own pace, knowing the dangers of rushing the process.
❑ The leader provides an environment conducive to more and more comfort and safety.
❑ The leader encourages members to explore new ways of behaving within the group.
❑ The leader acknowledges his or her own struggles as the group moves to deeper levels of interaction.

❑ The leader stresses the importance of all members of the group aiding in the transition from definition to involvement.

Group Involvement Stage

With the information about self gained in the personal involvement stage, group members move into the group involvement stage, characterized by self-evaluation and self-assessment of behavior, attitudes, values, and methods used in relating to others and also by members' channeling their energies to better meet group goals and purposes. During this stage the term *member* and the term *group* become somewhat more synonymous.

Degrees of cooperation and cohesiveness replace conflict and confrontation as members, more confident in their role in the group, direct more of their attention to what is best for the group and all of its members. This stage reveals increasing role clarification, intimacy, problem exploration, group solidarity, compromise, conflict resolution, and risk taking.

The group, with its purposes and goals, is merging with the individual purposes and goals of its members. Individual agendas are being replaced by group agendas, and the members are identifying more with the group. Bonding is taking place between members as they join forces to enhance the group and, in turn, enhance self in relation to the group. References to "insider" and "outsider" differentiate the group and the members' life outside the group. Members grow protective of other group members and also of the group itself. The group and its membership take on special significance unique to those who are part of the process. This melding of member and group purposes and goals is necessary to the group's ongoing success.

Member Behaviors

❑ Members develop confidence in self and their ability to relate effectively in the group environment.
❑ Members develop better helping skills and apply these to working with other group members and to self.
❑ Members devote increasing energy to aiding the group to meet its purposes and goals.
❑ Members direct more attention to cooperation and cohesiveness and less to conflict and confrontation.
❑ Members take more of a perspective of belonging and inclusion and less of non-belonging and exclusion.
❑ Members operate more in a problem exploration/solution mode than in a problem developmental mode.
❑ Members provide support for other members and the group as a whole.
❑ Members demonstrate more solidarity as in their view of members and the group.

Leader Behaviors

❑ The leader encourages and facilitates development of individual strengths within the group.
❑ The leader encourages members in their development of group identity and solidarity.
❑ The leader provides more opportunity for members to serve in the leadership role within the group.
❑ The leader gives positive direction as the members move from individual to group-directed purposes and goals.

❑ The leader demonstrates, in verbalization and behaviors, the benefits to be derived from individuals' working cooperatively together.

❑ The leader demonstrates, in words and through his or her behaviors, the benefits to be derived, for individual members and for the group, from reinforcement of positive change.

❑ The leader involves himself or herself to a greater extent as a participant, sharing in the changing dynamics of the group.

❑ The leader involves himself or herself more in a helping capacity than in a leader capacity to enhance the development of individual members and the group.

Enhancement and Closure Stage

The final stage in a group's life is often described as the most exhilarating but also the saddest aspect of group work. The exhilaration stems from the evaluation and reevaluation that are so much a part of the final stage. The evaluative aspect consists of reevaluation of the group process and individual and group assessment of change, in conjunction with individual and group reinforcement of individual member change, and a commitment to continue self-analysis and growth. Members have an opportunity to share what they feel have been significant growth experiences during the group tenure, and they receive feedback, generally positive, from other group members and the leader. Members are encouraged to review the process of the group and to measure changes that have taken place since their first entering the group to this period just before closure. Member statements at this stage of group development tend to be along the line of: "I was . . . now I am," I felt . . . now I feel," "I didn't . . . now I do," and "I couldn't . . . now I can."

The sadness in this final stage centers on leaving an environment that provided safety, security, and support and individuals who offered encouragement, friendship, and positive feedback. A major concern seems to be whether the individual will ever be able to replace what he or she found in the group and whether he or she will be able to take what was learned in the group and apply it elsewhere. The answer to both questions is generally yes, but the individual is too close to the experience to have this self-assurance. Our experience indicates that this stage often ends with members' unwritten agreement to continue group involvement and, more specifically, to continue contact with members of the present group. Most group members find, after distancing themselves from the group, that neither of these activities is essential. The gains they made from the group experience will serve them well as they move into other facets of their life.

Member Behaviors

❑ Members evaluate the amount of self-progress they have made during the life of the group.

❑ Members evaluate the extent to which the group accomplished its purposes and goals.

❑ Members share their perceptions of the strengths and weaknesses of other members and the leader.

❑ Members share their concerns about what will happen after the group ends.

❑ Members attempt to evaluate the group experience in terms of their other life experiences.

❑ Members try to build contacts with group members and the leader that will continue after closure.

❑ Members start to deal with the loss that group closure will bring.
❑ Members consider alternative actions to take the place of what the group provided.

Leader Behaviors

❑ The leader assists group members in evaluating their growth and development during the tenure of the group.
❑ The leader aids group members in resolving any issues that remain.
❑ The leader facilitates closure by initiating certain activities early in this last stage.
❑ The leader makes sure each member in the group receives appropriate feedback.
❑ The leader reviews the dynamics of the group and its members based upon his or her perception.
❑ The leader reviews, for each member, both strengths and weaknesses from his or her perspective.
❑ The leader encourages the emotional venting that is necessary in the closure process.
❑ The leader encourages each member to discuss what he or she plans to do after the group ends.

The movement from group initiation to group termination varies. Groups differ in this movement process for a myriad of reasons. And no one conceptualization has all the answers or addresses all the issues inherent in the group process. This framework does provide, however, guidelines and directives, for working with groups.

SUMMARY

To address the concerns expressed by our hypothetical student, George, and to summarize the content of this chapter, the following outline is presented.

1. Knowledge of group stages provides information on typical member behaviors and the developmental process of groups as they move from initiation to termination.
2. Knowledge of group stages offers directives to those in a leadership role.
   a. During the early stages of group development, the leader has to address the anxiety and dependence of group members.
   b. During the early stages of group development, the leader should establish operating procedures and structure that will help alleviate some of this anxiety and dependence.
   c. During the middle stages of group development, the leader should facilitate empowerment of group members to work on personal and group issues. These are the working stages, the producing stages of the group, and the stages that foster both individual and group development.
   d. During the final stages, the leader must be aware of the dichotomy of exhilaration and sadness that characterizes these stages. Allowing members to discuss and deal with both ends of this emotional continuum will provide for positive closure.
3. Knowledge of group stages allows the leader to plan and structure the group to better meet the needs of its members.
4. Knowledge of group stages enables the leader to instruct and orient the members in regard to possible experiences in moving from initiation to termination of the group.

5. Knowledge of group stages helps the leader to better judge the types of individuals who would benefit most from the group experience and enhance the group outcome accordingly.

6. Knowledge of group stages enables the leader to better understand the cyclical nature of groups and be better prepared to deal with forward and backward movement within the group and with the behaviors and emotional reactions that can be expected throughout the group's life.

7. Knowledge of group stages allows the leader to integrate his or her experiences in groups with information from past and current research. In so doing, he or she is able to restructure or reconceptualize the process to best advantage for all.

8. Knowledge of group stages permits the leader to measure or evaluate the developmental process within his or her groups by comparing it with what others in the field are saying.

9. Knowledge of group stages allows the leader to become comfortable with the overall process of group work through an understanding of certain dynamics that are generally predictable.

10. Knowledge of group stages offers the leader the freedom to work within the known parameters of the group process and also to create and develop his or her own conceptualizations within this process.

REFERENCES

Bales, R. F. (1950). *Interaction process analysis: A method for the study of small groups.* Cambridge, MA: Addison-Wesley.

Bales, R. F. (1953). The equilibrium problem in small groups. In T. Parson, R. F. Bales, & E. A. Shils (Eds.), *Working papers in the Theory of Action* (pp. 111–161). Glencoe, IL: Free Press.

Bennis, W. G., & Shepard, H. A. (1956). A theory of group development. *Human Relations, 9,* 415–437.

Berg, R., & Landreth, G. (1990). *Group counseling: Concepts and procedures* (2nd ed.). Muncie, IN: Accelerated Development Inc.

Bion, R. W. (1961). *Experiences in groups.* New York: Basic Books.

Corey, G. (1985). *Theory and practice of group counseling* (2nd ed.). Pacific Grove, CA: Brooks/Cole.

Gazda, G. M. (1971). *Group counseling: A developmental approach.* Boston: Allyn & Bacon.

George, R. L., & Dustin, D. (1988). *Group counseling: Theory and practice.* Englewood Cliffs, NJ: Prentice Hall.

Gibb, J. E. (1964). Climate for trust formation. In L. P. Bradford, J. R. Gibb, & K. D. Benne (Eds.), *T-group theory and laboratory method: Innovation in re-education* (pp. 279–309). New York: Wiley.

Gill, S. J., & Barry, R. A. (1982). Group-focused counseling: Classifying the essential skills. *Personnel & Guidance Journal, 60,* 302–305.

Kaplan, S. R., & Roman, M. (1963). Phases of development in an adult therapy group. *International Journal of Group Psychotherapy, 13,* 10–26.

Kormanski, C. L., & Mozenter, A. (1987). A new model of team building: A technology for today and tomorrow. In J. W. Pfeiffer (Ed.), *The 1987 annual: Developing human resources* (pp. 255–268). San Diego: University Associates.

Maples, M. F. (1988). Group development: Extending Tuckman's theory. *Journal for Specialists in Group Work, 13,* 17–23.

Miles, M. B. (1953). Human relations training: How a group grows. *Teachers College Record, 55,* 90–96.

Mills, T. M. (1964). *Group transformation.* Englewood Cliffs, NJ: Prentice Hall.

Ohlsen, M. M. (1970). *Group counseling.* New York: Holt, Rinehart and Winston.

Reid, C. (1965). The authority cycle in small group development. *Adult Leadership, 13*(10), 308–331.

Shulman, L. (1986). Group work method. In A. Glitterman & L. Shulman (Eds.), *Mutual aid groups and the life cycle* (pp. 23–50). Itasca, IL: F. E. Peacock.

Schutz, W. D. (1958). *FIRO: Three dimensional theory of interpersonal behavior.* New York: Rinehart.

Thelen, H., & Dickerman, W. (1949). Stereotypes and the growth of groups. *Educational Leadership, 6,* 309–316.

Tuckman, B. W. (1965). Developmental sequence in small groups. *Psychological Bulletin, 63*, 384–399.

Tuckman, B. W., & Jensen, M. A. (1977). Stages of small group development revisited. *Group & Organizational Studies, 2*, 419–427.

Waldo, M. (1985). A curative factor framework for conceptualizing group counseling. *Journal of Counseling & Development, 64*(1), 52–58.

Ward, D. E. (1985). Levels of group activity: A model for improving the effectiveness of group work. *Journal of Counseling and Development, 64*(1), 59–64.

Yalom, I. D. (1975). *The theory and practice of group psychotherapy* (2nd ed.). New York: Basic Books.

Yalom, I. D. (1985). *The theory and practice of group psychotherapy* (3rd ed.). New York: Basic Books.

Zimpfer, D. G. (1986). Planning for groups based on their developmental phases. *Journal for Specialists in Group Work, 11*, 180–187.

3

Group Counseling: Elements of Effective Leadership

Dave Capuzzi and Douglas R. Gross

Many factors contribute to the outcomes of group counseling (Conyne, Harvill, Morganett, Morran, & Hulse-Killacky, 1990; Zimpfer & Waltman, 1982). Studies have focused on the relationship between group counseling outcomes and counselor personality (Cooper, 1977; Kellerman, 1979), counselor experience (Heikkinen, 1975; Wittmer & Webster, 1969), group membership (Heslin, 1964; Shaw, 1981), leader directiveness (Brown, 1969; Chatwin, 1972), counselor self-disclosure (Dies, 1973, 1977) and counselor-group interaction (MacLennan, 1975). Although the results conflict, effective leadership of groups clearly is a complex, demanding, and important consideration for the group leader.

LEADERSHIP STYLES

Lewin's Three "Classics"

Lewin's (1944) identification of authoritarian, democratic, and laissez-faire leadership styles provided the group leader with a point of departure for understanding this element of group leadership. *Authoritarian* group leaders assume a position as the "expert" and direct the movement of a group. They may interpret, give advice, explain individual and group behavior, and generally control most aspects of group process. This style of leadership may be preferred by professionals with strong psychoanalytic, medical, or teaching backgrounds and may be one in which the leader does little self-disclosing.

Democratic group leaders are more group- and person-centered in the way they interact with group members. They place more stress upon the responsibility of each participant to create a meaningful individual and group experience. Trust in the ability of members and the phenomenon of the group experience is implicit. Professionals who subscribe to a Rogerian frame of reference or who align themselves with humanistic or phenomenological viewpoints are more likely to adopt a democratic leadership style.

In contrast to the first two of Lewin's identified styles, *laissez-faire* group leaders do not provide structure or direction to a group. Group members are expected to take responsibility for making the group experience beneficial. As Gladding (1991) noted, some group leaders (usually inexperienced) select this style in an attempt to be "nondirective" (a misnomer in and of itself), as a way to avoid decision making and enhance their likeability, or because they believe a completely unstructured group works best. Some evidence shows that many laissez-faire groups accomplish little during the life of the group. Several studies, as identified by Zimpfer and Waltman (1982), have investigated the relationship between the extent to which the group leader takes an active, directive role and success with certain group members. Low-anxiety members, for example, may do well in a group with little structure, whereas low-trust members may prefer a distinctly leader-centered group.

Leader-Centered and Group-Centered Styles

Another way to conceptualize leadership styles is based on the degree to which the group is leader-centered or is group-centered (Gladding, 1991). In a leader-centered group, the focus is on the leader and what the leader thinks will benefit group members. In this kind of a group, a predetermined theme, sequence of structured exercises, or format for each group session might be emphasized, with the leader directing interaction quite assertively at times. Group members are expected to cooperate with the leader and to deal with personal issues as they fit into the leader's agenda. In contrast, a more group-centered style would encourage members to establish the agenda for the group and to more freely discuss personal concerns, issues, and plans. Each of these styles can facilitate growth of group members, depending upon the group's purpose, the expectations and personalities of group members, and the leader's ability to apply techniques and interventions in a comfortable, congruent, and sensitive manner.

Interpersonal and Intrapersonal Styles

In 1978, Shapiro described two leadership styles: interpersonal and intrapersonal. Leaders with an *interpersonal* style (Corey, 1990) emphasize the importance of understanding and processing interactions among group members and relationships that develop within a group as group sessions progress. Interest centers on the nature, quality, and dynamics of the interaction among members and *what* is occurring in the here and now of the group. Leaders with an *intrapersonal* orientation are likely to explore *why* group members make certain responses by focusing upon individual members and the conflicts, concerns, and dynamics within individual members of a group. This style is directed more toward the past, and it facilitates insight and resolution of internal conflicts. At times, individual counseling or therapy may take place in the context of group experience.

Charismatic Leadership Style

Group members have a tendency to admire and respect the group leader, particularly in the early stages of a group (Rutan & Rice, 1981). Group leaders may derive some of their power as group leaders from a combination of traits (such as personableness, appearance, verbal ability) that are particularly appealing to group members.

Group leaders whom others perceive as charismatic may have an advantage during the early stages of a group, in terms of their ability to facilitate the beginning stage of a group. On the other hand, group members may become dependent upon the leadership and initiatives of a leader with charisma if they view the leader as an ego ideal. And some charismatic leaders may begin to enjoy the admiration of group members to such an extent that they fail to encourage autonomy of the participants (Rutan & Rice, 1981). In any case, group leaders should try to develop the skills needed to promote the personal growth of group members and to guide the group from the beginning to middle and later stages of the life of a group.

DEVELOPING YOUR OWN LEADERSHIP STYLE

When professionals are in the position of providing leadership to a group, they should first understand their own inherent qualities, characteristics and inclinations. But the leader has to go far beyond the assessment of personal qualities discussed in chapter 1. In addition to self-awareness and understanding of how personality traits and personal qualities can enhance or detract from what the leader contributes to a group experience, he or she must master a set of core knowledge and skills in the process of developing a personalized leadership style.

In 1990, the Association for Specialists in Group Work, a division of the American Association for Counseling and Development, published a revised version of its training standards, entitled *Professional Standards for Training of Group Work Generalists and of Group Work Specialists*. These standards specify knowledge and skill competencies as well as education and supervision requirements. Some examples of the specified *knowledge* competencies are an understanding of the basic principles of group dynamics, awareness of the specific ethical issues unique to group work, understanding the specific process components in typical stages of a group's development, and comprehension of the therapeutic factors inherent in a group experience. Examples of specified *skill* competencies are the ability to explain and clarify the purpose of a particular group, ability to encourage participation of group members, ability to open and close sessions effectively, and ability to help group members integrate and apply what they have learned in the group. Depending upon whether the group leader wishes to be prepared at a beginning (generalist) or advanced (specialist) level, *education* requirements range from a minimum of two group work courses to a wide range of related coursework in areas such as organizational development, sociology, community psychology, consultation, and others. *Supervision* requirements involve group observation, co-leading, and leading expectations, ranging from 30 to 55 clock hours (minimum) depending on the type of group work under study. (Appendix A gives a complete set of training standards.)

The point is that professionals interested in becoming competent group leaders must develop a leadership style that integrates personal qualities with a myriad of knowledge and skill competencies engendered through master's or doctoral coursework, as well as requirements for group observation and supervised practice. In many ways, developing a leadership style is an integrative, sequential, and creative endeavor resulting in the group leader's ability to transmit knowledge and skill competencies in a unique, individualized way, linked and integrated with a variety of personal characteristics, to encourage emotional, cognitive, and behavioral changes on behalf of each member of a group.

LEADERSHIP SKILLS

Conducting Pre-Group Screening.

Group leaders have to develop expertise in screening potential group members. As noted in the *Ethical Guidelines for Group Counselors* (Association for Specialists in Group Work, 1989), leaders must screen prospective members of a group to select individuals whose needs and goals are congruent with the group goals, who will not be detrimental to the group, and whose well-being will not be jeopardized by the group experience.

Screening may be accomplished through individual interviews, group interviews of potential group members, an interview as part of a team staffing, or completion of a written questionnaire. The pre-group screening process must provide prospective members with information about participation expectations, goals, payment methods and fee schedules, termination and referral procedures, client rights, and so on. Group leaders also must inquire about prospective members' current and past experience with counseling and provide clients with a written disclosure statement of the group leader's qualifications and the nature of the services to be provided. (See Appendix B at the end of this book for a complete statement of the *Ethical Guidelines for Group Counselors*, which addresses screening procedures.)

As Gladding (1991) noted, selection of group members through pre-group screening also grants potential members the opportunity to assess their readiness and interest in being a group member. Group leaders who have not conducted a group before should conduct pre-group screening under the supervision of an experienced group work specialist.

Organizing for Groups

The Physical Setting   Group sessions may be conducted in a variety of settings, as long as the room allows privacy and relative freedom from distraction for participants (Yalom, 1985). Some leaders seat participants around a circular table; others prefer placing chairs in a circle so members' nonverbal or body language responses are more readily observed. When group sessions are observed or videotaped, group members must give permission ahead of time and must have the opportunity to ask questions about and discuss the purposes of observation and taping procedures.

Length and Frequency of Meetings   As noted by George and Dustin (1988), the agency or the setting may dictate the duration and frequency of group sessions. The group leader has to simultaneously consider the purpose of the group and the scheduling. Some groups require longer time periods and more frequent scheduling than do others. Typical groups require 1½-hour sessions to provide for a "warm-up" period and for the participation of each person in the group. Sessions scheduled for more than 2 hours, unless they are specifically designed as part of a marathon group, generally become nonproductive and fatiguing for all concerned. Groups conducted in educational settings, such as high schools or middle schools, may of necessity be limited to a 40- or 50-minute time period based upon the school's standard class schedule. Ideally, groups should meet once or twice a week to promote the continuity of the group experience.

Size of the Group   Yalom (1985) suggests that the ideal size of a counseling/therapy group is seven or eight; five to ten members constitute an acceptable range. He believes that a minimum number is required to function and interact as a group; a group of fewer than five often results in a sequence of individual therapy or counseling sessions within the context of a very small group. Many of the advantages of a group, particularly the opportunity to receive validation and feedback from a microcosm of society, are lost as the size of the group diminishes.

Other Aspects of Organization   Several additional possibilities for group leaders to consider in conjunction with groups they lead or co-lead are as follows (Yalom, 1985):

1. Weekly, written summaries, describing some aspects of the group experience during a given week could be mailed to group members, providing a means to maintain reinforcement and continuity.
2. In addition to the disclosure statement mentioned earlier, written material could be distributed describing the "group rules," purposes, expectations, and so on. Material of this nature also reinforces group participants. It may be particularly helpful after the first session, because members may not have been able to totally integrate information about what a group experience would be like, because of anxiety.
3. Group members might be afforded an opportunity to see a movie or a videotape presenting information about group participation, similar to the information that could be shared in item #2.
4. Group members could be given the option of watching videos of their own group after each session. This would give members a chance to evaluate their participation and to obtain feedback from other group members. As noted earlier, group members must have provided written permission before filming.
5. Group members could be offered pre-group training sessions during which they would be taught skills for self-disclosure, expressing feelings, staying in the here-and-now, and so forth. Obviously, this suggestion depends upon the time and resources available to the group leader and group participants and may work better in the context of "inpatient" rather than "outpatient" situations.

RECOGNIZING MEMBERSHIP ROLES

As emphasized by Vander Kolk (1985), when a group is formed and begins to meet, all of the members begin with just one role, that of group member. As time passes, however, role differentiation occurs as members interact and become more comfortable about being themselves in the group. In most groups, a combination of roles exists. This combination results in a dynamic interaction among members, which energizes or de-energizes the group, as a whole, in some way. For example, a group composed of a number of task-oriented members might focus on identifying objectives for the group experience and monitoring interactions to ensure movement and progress during each session.

Another group might consist of several task-oriented members and several process-oriented members who value spontaneous interaction and disclosure. This group might find itself in conflict from time to time if task-oriented members feel time is being spent nonproductively and process-oriented members feel they are not always able to complete interactions or express deep feelings without others pressuring them to refocus on the original objectives established for the session.

The group leader has to recognize the types of roles group members are taking and make appropriate interventions to maintain balanced interaction and movement through the definitive, personal involvement, group involvement, and enhancement and closure stages of a group (described in chapter 2). One way of conceptualizing membership roles in groups is to view roles as facilitative, maintenance, or blocking in nature.

Facilitative Roles   Facilitative roles serve to keep the group on task and to clarify aspects of communication. Members who behave in facilitative ways contribute to the group constructively and increase the likelihood of participation and cooperation. Table 3.1 presents some examples of facilitative roles in groups.

Maintenance Roles   Maintenance roles help develop social-emotional bonds among members of a group and usually contribute to cohesiveness and feelings of connectedness. Group members who fill maintenance roles usually are quite sensitive to the affective components of a group experience and respond in ways that either escalate or reduce tensions related to affective aspects of intra- and interpersonal communication. Table 3.2 summarizes selected maintenance roles.

Blocking Roles   Individual needs of group members (Vander Kolk, 1985) often inhibit a group's progress. Group leaders must recognize these blocking roles and learn to recognize and diffuse problematic behaviors in individuals so the entire group does not become unproductive. Table 3.3 outlines some of the possible blocking roles that members of a group might bring to a group experience.

FACILITATING THE GROUP STAGES

Facilitating the Definitive Stage

As discussed in chapter 2, the definitive stage of the developmental process of a group is critical for group members to define for themselves and each other the purpose, quality, and involvement level. Members have questions about trust, support, safety, self-disclosure, confidentiality and many other aspects of group participation. The group leader has to be sensitive to members' questions and uncertainties during initial sessions and be able to model behavior that encourages constructive communication and gradual movement toward achieving individual and group goals. Several group specialists (Corey, 1990; Gladding, 1991; Nolan, 1978) have discussed the importance of mastering special skills which are unique to group work. Among the skills vital to the definitive stage of a group are:

1. *Active listening*. Paying attention to and paraphrasing the verbal and nonverbal aspects of communication in a way that lets members know they have been listened to and have not been evaluated.
2. *Supporting*. Providing reinforcement and encouragement to members to create trust, acceptance, and an atmosphere in which self-disclosure can occur when appropriate.
3. *Empathizing*. Communicating understanding to members by being able to assume their frames of reference.
4. *Goal setting*. Assisting with the planning process by helping members define concrete and meaningful goals.

5. *Facilitating.* Opening up communication between and among group members so that each person contributes in some way to the group experience and begins to feel some involvement with others and with the group experience.
6. *Protecting.* Preventing members from taking unnecessary psychological risks in the group.
7. *Modeling.* Teaching members the elements of constructive communication by demonstrating desired behavior in conjunction with each interaction with group members.

Table 3.1   FACILITATIVE ROLES IN GROUPS

Role	Description
Initiator	Energizes the group; presents new ideas, new ways of looking at things, stimulates the group to move toward some sort of action. Responses to the initiator may be positive, if the group is ready to move ahead, or negative, if it prefers inaction.
Information Seeker Opinion Seeker	Both request data of a factual or judgmental nature from the group. Information seeker simply requires cognitive information for clarification; opinion seeker focuses on values and the group's affective aspect. Each can be facilitative when data would be helpful to the group. An information seeker can dwell on data to the exclusion of affective concerns; on the other hand, the opinion seeker can put people on the defensive by pressing for value judgments and self-disclosure before a member is ready.
Information Giver Information Seeker	An information giver may spontaneously provide cognitive data, or respond to the information seeker. An opinion giver may also offer values or judgments on his/her own or in response to the opinion seeker.
Elaborator	Explains and gives examples of the topic, thus developing a meaning for what the group discusses; a rationale for group ideas evolves and the elaborator suggests how the ideas might work out.
Coordinator	Acts as a reality base for the group; ties ideas to practicality, prevents meandering into unrealistic discussions; pulls together group ideas; tries to have group organize its activities.
Orienter	Tells the group where it is in regard to goals and direction; summarizes what group has done and whether it is "on course."
Evaluator	Describes group's accomplishments and how well it is functioning; may evaluate usefulness or logic of a procedure, suggestion, or group discussion.
Procedural Technician	Carries out technical tasks (arranging chairs, brewing coffee).
Recorder	Writes down or remembers the group's decisions, plans, and suggestions.

Source: From *Introduction to Group Counseling and Psychotherapy* (p. 139) by C. J. Vander Kolk, 1985, Columbus, OH: Charles E. Merrill. Copyright ©1985 by Charles E. Merrill. Reprinted by permission of Merrill, an imprint of Macmillan Publishing Company.

Certain practical tasks also must be accomplished. Establishing ground rules, for example, is something the group leader usually does during the first and, if necessary, subsequent sessions. Attendance at all meetings, no physical violence, no smoking during meetings, no sexual relationships with other members of the group, and no coming late (Vander Kolk, 1985) are examples of group rules that may be established. The leader should explain all of the ground rules, and the rationale behind each. Group members may add ground rules as the group continues to meet, as long as none of these rules endangers the well-being of group members.

Table 3.2 VITALIZING AND MAINTENANCE ROLES

Role	Description
Encourager	Accepts others' ideas by praising, agreeing with, or stimulating ideas from participants; wants good feelings and a sense of security for the group. Excessive use of this role may direct attention from this person to the others.
Harmonizer	Attempts to mediate conflict and tension to keep group in harmony rather than polarized. May deal with subgroups in conflict. May brush real conflicts aside without a thorough working through.
Compromiser	Contracts with the harmonizer in cognitive orientation toward resolving group issues; may seek alternatives acceptable to the participants. When compromiser is part of the conflict, is often willing to give up status, see other points of view, or compromise in a way that resolves the problem.
Expediter	Oversees establishing group norms and guiding adherence to those norms. May try to get everyone to participate or suggest length of individual contributions. Role is similar to a leader's assistant or referee. Group members can become annoyed with someone who takes this role too seriously.
Standard Setter	Wants group process and goals to meet a criterion for acceptance by others. Sets high standards for norms and objectives. May evaluate quality of interactions. Often unsure of himself/herself; wants high standards as a means of reassurance.
Group Observer and Commentator	Notes group process, relates observations or conclusions. Contributions may be descriptive, interpretive, or evaluative. In the extreme, this member may be distancing himself/herself from the group, becoming a less involved participant.
Follower	Goes along with whatever group wants; quiet; offers little of self, preferring to be friendly observer. Usually too insecure and fearful to initiate ideas or discussion; not really a vitalizer.

Source: From *Introduction to Group Counseling and Psychotherapy* (p. 140) by C. J. Vander Kolk, 1985, Columbus, OH: Charles E. Merrill. Copyright ©1985 by Charles E. Merrill. Reprinted by permission of Merrill, an imprint of Macmillan Publishing Company.

Confidentiality is another aspect of the definitive stage that should be discussed. The group leader must stress the importance of confidentiality and possible violations (for example, talking about the disclosures of group members outside the group, telling individuals outside the group the identity of those participating in the group). This topic will receive more attention in chapter 16.

In addition to establishing ground rules and discussing confidentiality, the leader should give some thought to how much structure he or she wishes to provide at the beginning of a group session. Leader and member introductions, exercises in dyads or triads followed by sharing in the total group, guided fantasies followed by discussion of the experience, sentence completion exercises, and responding to a written questionnaire and subsequent discussion are a few examples of how structural elements promote involve-

Table 3.3 ANTI-GROUP ROLES

Role	Description
Aggressor	Disagrees with ideas and discussion. May disapprove of behavior, feelings, and values. May impose beliefs or ways of doing things on others. May be jealous, insecure, need attention. Some groups fight back; others react passively.
Blocker	Stubborn about what should and should not be discussed; resists wishes of total group. Negativism can impede group progress.
Recognition Seeker	Boasts; engages in other behavior to attract group attention.
Self-Confessor	Reveals feelings and insights unrelated to group's immediate dealings. Personal expressions distract group from concentrating on its task.
Playboy	Nonchalant or cynical toward group; engages in horseplay or other behaviors that communicate lack of involvement, thus disrupting group cohesiveness.
Dominator	Tries to manipulate others to recognize his/her authority; less aggressive than manipulative. Behaviors include interrupting, flattery, asserting status, giving directions. Interferes with sense of equality among participants.
Help Seeker Rescuer	Elicits sympathy from group by excessively dwelling on personal problems, confusions, and inadequacies. Giving attention may reinforce dependent behavior. Rescuers may meet own needs by accommodating help seekers, but both roles are unproductive.
Self-Righteous Moralist	Has need to be always right and others always wrong. Authority on moral issues. Does not care to be liked; wants to be respected for moral integrity. Imposes moral standards on others. Will at first be quiet, then assert position persistently without conceding or admitting error. Projects image of moral superiority that soon alienates participants. Yalom (1970) suggests these people are disturbed by feelings of shame and anger, but usually believe they have no problems.

ment and productivity. The amount of structure needed to catalyze group interaction will always depend on pre-group screening, the purpose of the group, the age and functionality of group members and the leader's style. As a rule of thumb, we recommend that the leader provide and use structure when needed but does not depend on group exercises to the extent that members are unable to express their concerns, desires, and issues.

Finally, the leader should think about how to close a group session in a way that provides time for reflection, summarization, and integration. Corey and Corey (1987) recommended setting aside at least 10 minutes at the end of a group for these purposes so group members do not feel frustrated at a lack of closure or what might be perceived as an abrupt ending. This might be an ideal time to suggest introspection, behavioral rehearsal, or other homework to group members, if applicable.

Table 3.3 ANTI-GROUP ROLES (continued)

Role	Description
Do-Gooder	May be a modified form of self-righteous moralist who wants to do what is "right." Is helpful, kind, understanding toward others. Does not usually impose "good" behavior on others, but wants acceptance from others.
Informer	Possible variation on the do-gooder. Occurs when group members interact and know each other outside group sessions; informer shares information about someone's behavior outside the group. Purpose of "squealing" is to enhance one's status with and acceptance by others, or as act of revenge.
Seducer	Uses manipulation, usually in the form of active or subtle attempts to control others by getting others to reach out to him/her or pretending to be fragile. Seductive behavior also avoids genuine closeness.
Hostile or Angry Member	Manipulates others by intimidation or avoids needs such as affection. Joking, sarcasm, and ridicule are signs of hostility. Result is greater self-protection on part of other participants to avoid attacks.
Monopolist	Talks incessantly about experiences, ideas, and information that is usually only tangentially related to group goals. Self-centered talk may be set off by similarity of another member's problem with an experience of the monopolist. May tell stories, relate what h/she has read, or relate personal upheavals in great detail. At first, group is relieved to have someone carry the ball; after several sessions, there is often fighting, absenteeism, and dropouts. Leader and group must deal with underlying anxiety of the monopolist.
Withdrawn, Nonparticipating, Silent Member	Opposite end of continuum from monopolist. Nonfacilitative group members may resent these members' seeming noninvolvement, or resent attention they get when other members try to draw them out.

Source: From *Introduction to Group Counseling and Psychotherapy* (pp. 142–143) by C. J. Vander Kolk, 1985, Columbus, OH: Charles E. Merrill. Copyright ©1985 by Charles E. Merrill. Reprinted by permission of Merrill, an imprint of Macmillan Publishing Company.

Facilitating the Personal Involvement Stage

The personal involvement stage of a group is best depicted as one of member-to-member interactions, the sharing of personal information, confrontation with other members of the group, power struggles, and the individual's growing identity as a member of the group. It is a stage of action, reaction, and interaction and requires the group leader to demonstrate awareness of the emotional makeup of the group and the intra- and interpersonal struggles that are part of this stage of a group. Besides the skills the leader must apply during the definitive stage, the following skills are required during this challenging stage of group life:

1. *Clarifying*. Helping members sort out conflicting feelings and thoughts to arrive at a better understanding of what is being expressed.
2. *Questioning*. Asking questions to gain additional information or promote self-exploration and description of feelings and thoughts.
3. *Interpreting*. Providing tentative explanations for feelings, thoughts and behaviors that challenge members to explore in more depth their motivations and reactions.
4. *Reflecting feelings*. Letting members know they are being understood in a way that goes beyond the content of their communication.
5. *Confronting*. Challenging members to become aware of discrepancies between words and actions or current and previous self-disclosures.
6. *Initiating*. Being proactive to bring about new directions in individual sharing or interpersonal communication.
7. *Giving feedback*. Offering an external view of how a member appears to another by describing concrete and honest reactions in a constructive way.
8. *Self-disclosing*. Describing here-and-now reactions to events in the group.
9. *Blocking*. Preventing counterproductive behavior by one or more group members.

Some practical considerations also must be dealt with during the personal involvement stage of any group. As self-disclosure becomes more open and interactions among members become more straightforward and more focused on the here and now, some group members may become threatened and remain silent to avoid taking risks. When this happens, the group leader should use his or her skills to acknowledge the way those members may be feeling and encourage them to participate without demanding more participation than they are able to contribute at the time. The longer members remain silent, the more difficulty they may have entering into dialogue and spontaneous interaction. Also, the silent member often engenders suspicions and criticisms by other group members who begin to wonder why the silent members are not involved in the group.

Silence is not the only way members who become threatened by the dynamics of the personal involvement stage react. Benjamin (1981), Corey (1990), Sack (1985) and Yalom (1985) offer these additional possibilities the group leader should recognize:

1. *Intellectualization*. Members who are feeling threatened by the openness of communication may focus completely on their thoughts to avoid making connections with either their own or others' emotions. Use of a cognitive pattern of communication should signal the leader that these members may not be comfortable with their feelings.

2. *Questioning*. Questions by members can direct the discussion to why something was said or has happened rather than on how members are feeling and what they are experiencing now. Questions often disguise a statement about true feelings.
3. *Advice giving*. Advice rarely helps another group member resolve personal issues or solve problems independently, but it does provide a means for the advice giver to avoid struggling with internal issues and empathizing and adopting the internal frame of reference of other group members.
4. *Band-aiding*. Band-aiding is the misuse of support for the purpose of alleviating painful feelings. Group members who band-aid prevent themselves and others from fully expressing their emotions.
5. *Dependency*. Dependent group members invite advice giving and band-aiding by presenting themselves as helpless and "stuck." This, too, prevents complete and accurate self-disclosure by those who feel threatened by aspects of group interaction.

The group leader may be verbally attacked by one or more members, either because the leader has modeled some inappropriate behavior or because members feel threatened by the energy or the interactions in the group. The leader has to work through the criticism, during the session, by encouraging those who have negative feelings toward the leader to describe those feelings. Perhaps a give-and-take discussion can lead to acceptable resolution of the difficulty. If a leader does not provide an opportunity for the members to do this, their feelings may escalate to the point that group sessions become counterproductive.

Facilitating the Group Involvement Stage

As explained in chapter 2, the group involvement stage is characterized by much self-evaluation and self-assessment of behavior, attitudes, values, and methods in relating to others, and also by members channeling their energies toward meeting the group's goals and purposes. During this stage the terms "members" and "group" become somewhat more synonymous. The group, with its purposes and goals, is merging with members' individual purposes and goals. Individual agendas are replaced by group agendas, and the members identify more with the group.

Facilitating this stage of the group's life requires the leader to use all of the skills needed during the definitive stage and, from time to time, some of the skills important to positive resolution of the personal involvement stage. Additional skills that may be needed include:

1. *Linking*. Stressing the importance of interpersonal communication within the group by connecting what one member is feeling or doing to what another member is feeling or doing.
2. *Providing group identity*. Encouraging members in their development of a group identity.
3. *Suggesting direction*. Providing suggestions as the members progress from individual to group-directed purposes and goals.
4. *Sharing leadership*. Encouraging members to assume leadership responsibility within the group when appropriate.

5. *Participating in the group.* The leader's involving himself or herself as a member of the group and by sharing leadership as opportunities arise.
6. *Reinforcing cooperation.* Demonstrating, on verbal and nonverbal levels, the benefits of cooperative participation.

Practical considerations for constructive leadership during this stage relate to the higher level of self-disclosure and intimacy that members have developed. One situation that often arises comes from sudden insights that a member gains as another member self-discloses and problem-solves. Because members are now readily able to put aside personal agendas and listen and empathize as others in the group share during this stage, one or more participants may become aware of incidents (e.g., interactions designed to prevent intimacy from occurring) that are emotionally laden. At times, these memories may be extremely difficult to share and then integrate into a new perspective or set of behaviors. During these circumstances, the leader must provide the safety and support needed to guide resulting disclosure and group response and interaction. Insights about previously denied experience can be powerful and quite difficult for an individual to handle.

Risk-taking in the group may be high during the group involvement stage, and self-disclosure may progress more rapidly than is necessary or appropriate for the participant or the group as a whole. The leader may have to slow down the rate and intensity of self-disclosure to safeguard members from unnecessary psychological risks. Because of the cohesive atmosphere that has developed during this stage, other members may reinforce self-disclosure or offer suggestions that the leader might have to ward off so the risk is not escalated.

Group efforts to help another member with a problem sometimes become detrimental during this stage. Unlike the advice giving and band-aiding in the personal involvement stage, these efforts are not meant to redirect the group away from discussing emotional or painful issues. Instead, they derive from the strong feelings of closeness that have developed, and they occur following intense discussions and thorough exploration. The problem arises when a participant receives so many suggestions for resolving a problem that the member begins to feel confused and at a loss to deal with the many options presented. The group leader needs to intervene so an option or two can be carefully considered and then either adopted or discarded. Or the leader might more appropriately encourage participants to discuss a specific problem or area in future sessions after they have identified their own solutions.

During the group involvement stage, group members begin discussing their desire to establish on the "outside" the same kind of cooperation, cohesiveness, and communication patterns they enjoy during group sessions. This is an important topic to discuss so members do not come to expect the same level of cooperation and the same degree of self-disclosure in all groups or, conversely, assume that nothing can improve in established outside circles. Members may also express how much they look forward to group sessions and how much they dislike the idea of their group terminating at some future point. This latter sentiment may begin to be expressed as the group moves toward the enhancement and closure stage.

Facilitating the Enhancement and Closure Stage

This is the final stage in group development and is often described as simultaneously the most exhilarating and the saddest aspect of group work. The exhilaration stems from evaluation and reevaluation as members are encouraged to review the group process and to measure changes from entering into the group to this period just before closure and termination. The sadness centers on leaving an environment that has provided safety, security, and support and individuals who have offered encouragement, friendship, and positive feedback related to one's growth potential.

Facilitation of this stage requires the leader to draw upon many of the skills used during previous stages in addition to the following:

1. *Evaluating.* Assessing both individual and group process during the group's tenure.
2. *Resolving issues.* Assisting the member and the group to achieve closure on remaining issues.
3. *Reviewing progress.* Helping group members obtain an overview of the progress and change that have taken place since the group was initiated.
4. *Identifying strengths and weaknesses.* Encouraging members to pinpoint the strengths they have developed in the group, as well as the weaknesses they have acknowledged and begun to overcome, so they can apply this learning outside the group after it terminates.
5. *Terminating.* Preparing a group to finalize its history, assimilate the experience, and separate from the group as sessions come to an end.
6. *Referring.* Recommending possibilities for individual or group counseling after this group ends.

Practical considerations for the group leader are numerous. Corey (1990), George and Dustin (1988), Jacobs, Harvill, and Masson (1988), Ohlsen, Horne, and Lawe (1988), Vander Kolk (1985), and others discuss aspects of closure and termination connected with this stage. The group leader can draw upon the following suggestions during the last few sessions of the enhancement and closure stage, although these by no means represent an exhaustive listing of possibilities:

1. *Reminders.* Make sure members are aware of the approaching termination date, to enable them to achieve the essential review and closure. This suggestion applies to groups that have a predetermined closure date established by the members themselves or by a set of external circumstances.
2. *Capping.* During the last few sessions of a group, do not encourage members to initiate discussions of intensely emotional material or to facilitate powerful emotional interchange in the group as a whole. Capping means easing members and the group out of affective expression and into intellectual consideration of progress, change, and strengths, because time is running out for processing of new emotional material.
3. *Logs.* If members have been keeping written logs chronicling the group experience, suggest that they share particularly meaningful segments as the group reaches its conclusion. This can be an excellent vehicle for evaluation, review, and providing feedback.

4. *Unfinished business*. Ask group members to share and work on the resolution of any unfinished business. Allow enough time to adequately achieve resolution (whether individually or group-focused).

5. *Homework*. Suggest that each group member identify, discuss, and commit to some homework to be completed after the group ends. This may help group members integrate learning and develop perspectives for the future.

6. *Making the rounds*. Offer members the opportunity to look at each person and provide some final feedback (or to hand each person some written feedback). This can provide the basis for one or more sessions aimed at easing the emotion sometimes associated with the end of a positive group experience. To allow feedback to be adequately discussed and processed, the leader should allow more than one group session to make the rounds.

7. *Saying good-bye*. Allow each member to express his or her unique personality and perspective in saying good-bye when a group is ending. Suggest that members frame this good-bye as it relates to the group as a whole, each participant, or both.

8. *Future planning*. Discuss how group members can approach the future in a proactive way. This helps participants integrate new learning and plan to meet future needs. Members need plenty of time to think about how they will function in the absence of the group support.

9. *Referrals*. Make arrangements for members who need further counseling, whether group or individual. Discuss the possibilities during a specifically scheduled group session. Members may decide to share with the total group their decision for follow-up counseling.

10. *Questionnaires*. Use questionnaires to assess the strengths and weaknesses of a particular group experience if desired. If these are filled out before the group ends, share excerpts with the group, with advance permission of the members.

11. *Follow-up interviews*. Ease the apprehension often associated with the end of a group by offering the opportunity for individual follow-up sessions. Members can utilize the follow-up meeting to discuss post-group progress, difficulties, or issues, and obtain the support needed to continue in productive ways.

12. *Group reunions*. Organize group reunions. The reunion might be in the form of a group session, a potluck dinner or picnic, or group attendance at a lecture, as examples. The purpose of the follow-up is to give members a chance to reconnect, share, and provide support and encouragement.

DEALING WITH DIFFICULT MEMBERS

Counselors at times face some difficult group members. Typical patterns, originally presented by Dyer and Vriend (1973), are listed here with suggestions as to how the group leader might respond (Capuzzi & Gross, 1991). The 10 examples concretize the use of skills discussed in facilitating the four stages of a group.

1. A group member speaks for everyone.

   A group member commonly says something like, "We think we should . . .," "This is how we all feel," or "We were wondering why. . . ." Often this happens when a member does not feel comfortable making statements such as, "I think we should . . ." or "I'm wondering why . . ." or when a group member is attempting to garner support for a point of view. The difficulty with allowing the "we" syndrome to operate in a group is that it inhibits members from expressing their individual feelings and thoughts. The group leader might give *feedback* ("You mentioned 'we' a number of times. Are you speaking for yourself or for everyone?") or *linking* ("What do each of you think about the statement that was just made?").

2. A member speaks for another member in the group.

"I think I know what he means" and "She's not really saying how she feels; I can explain it for her" are examples of one group member speaking for another. When one member speaks for another, it often connotes a judgment about the ability of the other member to communicate or that the other member is about to share uncomfortable information. Regardless of the motivation behind the statement, the group member who permits another group member to do the talking for him or her needs to assess the reason for this and whether the same communication patterns happen outside the group. The "talker" needs to evaluate his or her inclination to make decisions for or rescue others.

Appropriate leader skills here include *questioning* ("Did Jim state your feelings more clearly than you can?" or "How does it feel to have someone rescue you?") and *interpretive statements* ("Did you feel June needed your assistance?" or "Do you find it difficult to hold back when you think you know what someone else is going to say?").

3. A group member focuses on persons, conditions, or events outside the group.

Many times group counseling sessions can turn into gripe sessions. Group members tend to enjoy complaining about a colleague, a friend, or a partner if they are allowed to reinforce one another. The difficulty with this is that the interaction might erroneously substantiate that others are at fault and that group members do not have to take responsibility for these aspects of their behavior.

The group leader might use skills in *initiating* ("You keep talking about your wife as the cause of your unhappiness. Isn't it more important to ask yourself what contributions you can make to improve your relationship?") or *clarifying* ("Does complaining about others really mean you think you would be happier if they could change?").

4. A member seeks the approval of the leader or a group member before or after speaking.

Some group members nonverbally seek acceptance by nodding, glancing, or smiling at the leader or another group member. These members may be intimidated by authority figures or by personal strength or have low self-esteem and seek sources of support and acceptance outside themselves. One tactic is for the leader to look at another member, forcing the speaker to change the direction of his or her delivery. Another is to give *feedback* ("You always look at me as you speak, almost as if you're asking permission").

5. A member says, "I don't want to hurt her feelings, so I won't say what I'd like to say."

Especially in the early stages of a group, this sentiment is common. Sometimes it happens when a member believes another member of the group is too fragile for feedback. Other times the member is revealing apprehension about being liked by other group members. The group leader should explore reasons for the reticence to offer feedback, which can include reinforcing cooperation by asking the member to check with the person to whom feedback may be directed to validate these fears.

6. A group member suggests that his or her problems are someone else's fault.

This example may seem to overlap with the third one, but it presents a different problem than a group gripe session. When a group member periodically attributes difficulties and unhappiness to another person, the leader might use *blocking* statements ("Who is really the only person who can be in charge of you?" or "How can other people determine your mood so much of the time?"). We are not suggesting a stance that would be perceived as lacking empathy and acceptance, but the leader should facilitate members' taking responsibility for self.

7. A member might suggest that "I've always been that way."

This suggestion indicates irrational thinking and lack of motivation to change. Believing that the past determines all of one's future can limit one's future growth. The group leader must help these members identify irrational thoughts that cause them to be ineffective in specific areas and learn that they are not doomed to repeat the mistakes of the past. *Interpreting* ("You're suggesting that your past has such a hold over you that you will never be any different") and *questioning* ("Do you feel that everyone has certain parts of his life over which he has no control?") are possible statements to stimulate examination of faulty thinking and assumptions.

8. A member in the group suggests, "I'll wait, and it will change."

Frequently, group members are willing to discuss their self-defeating behavior during a group session but are not willing to make an effort to change outside the group. At times they take the position that they can postpone action and things will correct themselves. A competent group leader will use *initiating* to help members develop strategies for doing something about their problems outside the group and will assign *homework* as a means of tracking or checking in with members to evaluate progress.

9. A member shows discrepant behavior.

When discrepancies appear in a member's behavior, the group leader must intervene. Discrepancies may occur in what a member is currently saying and what he or she said earlier, lack of congruence between what a member is saying and what he or she is doing in the group, a difference between how a member sees himself or herself and how others in the group see him or her, or a difference between how a member reports feelings and how nonverbal cues communicate what is going on inside. Statements used to identify discrepancies may be *confrontational* in nature because the leader usually has to describe the discrepancies so the group member can begin to identify, evaluate, and change aspects of the behavior.

10. A member bores the group by rambling.

Sometimes members use talking as a way of seeking approval, and it may become "overtalk." In response, the leader might ask other members to give *feedback* to the "intellectualizer" and let him or her know how the rambling affects others. If this behavior is not addressed, other members may become angry and hostile toward the offender.

SUMMARY

The group leader's style, personality, experience, and skills have many ramifications for group experiences and outcomes. The three classic styles identified by Lewin are authoritarian, democratic, and laissez-faire, which may relate somewhat to the purpose of the group and its composition. In another conceptualization, groups can be seen as leader-centered or as group-centered. A third way of looking at leader style is to characterize it as interpersonal or intrapersonal. Group members tend to admire leaders who have charisma, though this carries the danger of the leader's relying too much on this characteristic and less on facilitating autonomy of group members. Leaders are encouraged to develop their own unique style, through self-awareness and understanding of their own personal traits and qualities. In any case, leaders should acquire some specific skills common to all group needs.

In planning for a group experience, leaders should conduct pre-group screening, which may be done through interviews or completion of questionnaires, to select members whose needs and goals are compatible with those of the intended group and who will not be detrimental to other group members or themselves. In screening, potential members should receive full information about all aspects of the group and what to expect.

When organizing for a group, the leader has to consider the physical setting, length and frequency of meetings, and size of the group (within a recommended range of 5–10). Other organizational aspects may include weekly summaries, written material, movies or videotapes, and pre-group training sessions.

Members assume various roles within a group, including maintenance, anti-group, and facilitative, and sub-roles of each, which the leader should be aware of in facilitating the group experience. The leader also has to apply a repertoire of skills in leading each of the stages in a group's development. In a group's life, the leader is likely to encounter difficult members and behaviors, which he or she must counteract to ensure that the group progresses as intended from beginning to termination.

REFERENCES

Association for Specialists in Group Work. (1989). *Ethical guidelines for group leaders.* Alexandria, VA: Author.

Association for Specialists in Group Work. (1990). *Professional standards for training of group work generalists and of group work specialists.* Alexandria, VA: Author.

Benjamin, A. (1981). *The helping interview* (3rd ed.). Boston: Houghton Mifflin.

Brown, R. (1969). Effects of structured and unstructured group counseling with high- and low-anxious college underachievers. *Journal of Counseling Psychology, 16,* 209–214.

Capuzzi, D., & Gross, D. R. (1991). *Introduction to counseling: Perspectives for the 1990s.* Boston: Allyn & Bacon.

Chatwin, M. (1972). Interpersonal trust and leadership style in group counseling. *Dissertation Abstracts International, 32:*6120A.

Conyne, R. K., Harvill, R. L., Morganett, R. S., Morran, D. K., & Hulse-Killacky, D. (1990). Effective group leadership: Continuing the search for greater clarity and understanding. *Journal for Specialists in Group Work*, *15*(1), 30–36.

Cooper, G. L. (1977). Adverse and growthful effects of experimental learning groups: The role of the trainer, participant, and group characteristics. *Human Relations*, *30*, 1103–1109.

Corey, G. (1990). *Theory and practice of group counseling* (3rd ed.). Pacific Grove, CA: Brooks/Cole.

Corey, M. S., & Corey, G. (1987). *Groups: Process and Practice* (3rd ed.). Pacific Grove, CA: Brooks/Cole.

Dies, R. R. (1973). Group therapist self-disclosure: An evaluation by clients. *Journal of Counseling Psychology*, *20*, 344–348.

Dies, R. R. (1977). Group therapist transparency: A critique of theory and research. *International Journal of Group Psychotherapy*, *27*, 177–200.

Dyer, W. W. & Vriend, J. (1973). Effective group counseling process interventions. *Educational Technology*, *13*(1), 61–67.

George, R. L., & Dustin, D. (1988). *Group counseling: Theory and practice*. Englewood Cliffs, NJ: Prentice Hall.

Gladding, S. T. (1991). *Group work: A counseling specialty*. New York: Merrill.

Heikkinen, C. A. (1975). Another look at teaching experience and closed-mindedness. *Journal of Counseling Psychology*, *22*, 79–83.

Heslin, R. (1964). Predicting group task effectiveness from members' characteristics. *Psychological Bulletin*, *62*, 248–256.

Jacobs, E. E., Harvill, R. L., & Masson, R. L. (1988). *Group counseling: Strategies and skills*. Pacific Grove, CA: Brooks/Cole.

Kellerman, H. (1979). *Group psychotherapy and personality: Intersecting structures*. New York: Grune & Stratton.

Lewin, K. (1944). The dynamics of group action. *Educational Leadership*, *1*, 195–200.

MacLennan, B. W. (1975). The personalities of group leaders: Implications for selection and training. *International Journal of Group Psychotherapy*, *25*, 177–184.

Nolan, E. J. (1978). Leadership interventions for promoting personal mastery. *Journal for Specialists in Group Work*, *3*, 132–138.

Ohlsen, M. M., Horne, A. M., & Lawe, C. F. (1988). *Group counseling* (3rd ed.). New York: Holt, Rinehart & Winston.

Rutan, J. S. & Rice, C. A. (1981). The charismatic leader: Asset or liability? *Psychotherapy: Theory, research and practice*, *18*, 487–492.

Sack, R. T. (1985). On giving advice. *AMHCA Journal*, *7*, 127–132.

Shapiro, J. L. (1978). *Methods of group psychotherapy and encounter: A tradition of innovation*. Itasca, IL: F. E. Peacock.

Shaw, M. E. (1981). *Group dynamics: The psychology of small group behavior*. New York: McGraw-Hill.

Vander Kolk, C. J. (1985). *Introduction to group counseling and psychotherapy*. Columbus, OH: Merrill.

Wittmer, J., & Webster, G. B. (1969). The relationship between teaching experience and counselor trainee dogmatism. *Journal of Counseling Psychology*, *16*, 499–504.

Yalom, I. D. (1985). *The theory and practice of group psychotherapy* (3rd ed.). New York: Basic Books.

Zimpfer, D., & Waltman, D. (1982). Correlates of effectiveness in group counseling. *Small Group Behavior*, *13*(3), 275–290.

4

Group Counseling: Theory and Application

Douglas R. Gross and Dave Capuzzi

The group procedures class was just beginning, and Dr. Burns asked if anyone had questions about the material that was to be read prior to class. Greg, a first year student, raised his hand and said he was confused about the information dealing with theory applied to groups. When Dr. Burns asked Greg to be more specific in his question, Greg said that when he had taken the counseling theory class last semester, he had understood that the various counseling theories had been developed to work with the individual, that the research done in developing these theories was all completed on individual cases. His confusion stemmed from the fact that the author of the assigned material seemed to be simply transferring these theoretical concepts from the individual to the group. His question was, "How do I transfer these individual concepts into a group of eight or ten members?"

Dr. Burns's response of "carefully" brought laughter from the class. He continued, however, by stating that Greg had a good question, one that continues to concern even the most experienced group leaders. The class spent most of the period discussing the issue. As with many such questions, the class arrived at no definitive answers, and every student left that evening with several questions regarding the relationship of counseling theory to group interaction and how to use individual-based approaches with groups.

This scenario has probably taken place, in one form or another, in every group class. The student's question and surrounding confusion continue for all professionals who operate in the broad arena of group counseling.

Writing in 1978, Shapiro made the following statement:

> There is an apparent paradox in the notion of group psychotherapy. The locus of therapy is the group, and yet the group is not in need of treatment. Unless the group in question is a natural group (family, management, etc.), group therapists are using a group format to treat individuals. The goal of the leader is not to alter the group per se but to provide treatment and growth for the members of the group. This problem is reflected in the development of thera-

peutic approaches to groups. Most of the extant group therapies are in fact individual therapies which subsequently were applied in group settings for reasons of economy. (pp. 44–45)

This statement encapsulates one of the major dilemmas emanating from discussions
of theoretical/therapeutic concepts applied to groups. The dilemma revolves around the
transferability of concepts, techniques, and approaches, which originally were developed
for and directed toward the individual, into a group modality. Authors such as Thompson
and Kahn (1970), Hansen, Warner, and Smith (1976), Corey and Corey (1977), Lieberman
(1983), Olsen, Horne, and Lawe (1988), and George and Dustin (1988) have all addressed
difficulties and cautions that the counselor making the transition from individual to group
counseling has to face. These should not be interpreted to mean that transferability is
impossible. On the contrary, current practice indicates that all theoretical/therapeutic
approaches have been applied across both individual and group counseling. Based upon
statements by Lakin (1985), Shaffer and Galinsky (1989), and Wright (1989), many of the
factors that dictate the selection of one or more theoretical/therapeutic approaches in the
individual realm have applicability in the group domain. The selection of a theoretical
system is often based upon the individual's philosophical position and what he or she
believes regarding the nature of the individual as this relates to development and change.
It also may stem from an experiential position based upon the individual's education and
working background in selected theoretical systems. Regardless of the reasons, those who
choose to work with groups should do so with a basis in theory. To do otherwise places
the individual and the group in the following situation described by Corey and Corey
(1987):

> Attempting to lead groups without having an explicit theoretical rationale is like flying a
> plane without a flight plan. Though you may eventually get there (and even find detours excit-
> ing), you're equally likely to run out of patience and gas and do nothing but fly aimlessly in
> circles. Group leaders without any theory behind their interventions will probably find that
> their groups never reach a productive stage. (p. 7)

Responding to this issue, we are exploring in this chapter selected theoretical/thera-
peutic approaches and applying them to groups. The initial discussion focuses on selected
theoretical systems and examples of their application in the group setting. This is followed by an integration of the five theoretical systems with identified variables of relationship, leader role, member role, process, and outcome.

THEORETICAL SYSTEMS

We have selected five theoretical systems that we believe are representative of theories
with wide acceptance in the group setting: Adlerian, Gestalt, person-centered, rational-
emotive, and transactional analysis. The Bibliography at the end of this chapter provides
sources of more in-depth discussion on each of these theories.

Adlerian Theory

Adlerian psychology is both an individual and a social psychology. The individual
aspects define humans as unified organisms whose behaviors are purposeful and goal-

directed and not necessarily determined by genetic endowment, environmental press, or early sexual impressions. Individuals give meaning to their lives. They have the creative power and the self-determination to influence not only their personal/social development but also certain events. Through their unique powers, individuals strive to achieve an identity and to belong.

The social aspects hinge on the premise that individuals are motivated primarily by social interest. This is translated into a "need to belong." According to Manaster and Corsini (1982), social interest is possibly the single most distinctive and valuable concept in Adlerian psychology. It involves individuals' attitudes in dealing with the social world and includes a concern and striving for a better world for all humans. This social connectedness and individuals' needs to be useful to others are what give people measures of happiness and success. Based upon this social interaction, individuals strive to master three main relationships as they move through life: friends, work, and family.

The basic motivational forces, according to Adlerians, are best described in terms of striving from a perceived negative to a hoped for positive position in life, striving in the direction of a unique goal or ideal self, striving to belong in the social world of the individual, striving to understand one's spiritual nature, and striving to better comprehend the "I" and "me" aspects of self. None of these driving forces stands alone. They are interrelated, and movement in one area impacts movement in another.

These strivings are influenced by a number of factors, any one of which may encumber the individual in his or her development and movement toward goals:

1. Fictional goals (unconscious assumptions regarding what must be done to develop worth as an individual, such as striving for superiority).
2. Birth order (the individual's chronological and psychological position within the family).
3. The family constellation/atmosphere (variables related to personality, relationships, developmental issues, structural factors, attitudes and values within the family).

This planned and orchestrated movement is termed one's "style of life" and, based upon these identified factors, may lead individuals to a lifestyle characterized by positive growth and development or to one characterized by maladjustment. The key rests with individuals and their perception and interpretation, which translate into assumptions and goals that direct the formation of their style of life.

In summarizing the major concepts underlying Adlerian psychology, Gilliland, James, Roberts, and Bowman (1984) identified seven:

1. Humanistic (individual and society valued over the organization).
2. Holistic (individual is indivisible).
3. Phenomenological (importance of the individual's perspective).
4. Teleological (future orientation and striving for goal attainment).
5. Field theoretical (interactional nature of the individual with the social and physical environment).
6. Socially oriented (individual responds to and contributes to society).
7. Operational (methodology in place).

Concepts/Leader Dynamics The Adlerian group leader has to be able to:

— establish a working relationship in which the leader and members are equal.
— communicate to the members feelings of mutual trust and respect.
— aid the members in exploring the personal goals, beliefs, feelings, and motives that are determining factors in development of the members' style of life.
— assist the members in gaining insight into their fictitious goals and self-defeating behaviors that impede them from formulating effective life goals.
— help members to accept responsibility for their freedom and personal effectiveness in order to develop feelings of self-worth.
— aid members in considering alternative lifestyles and assist them in strengthening their commitment to change.
— help members to enhance their involvement with others and to extend their social interest as this applies to self and others.
— aid members in accepting self with the assets and the liabilities that comprise the self.
— assist members in developing a sense of belonging and the sense of community, because their self-meaning is tied closely to their social purpose.
— aid members in exploring alternative behaviors and gaining new insights, and be able to empower them to put these behaviors and insights into action.

Techniques According to Dreikurs (1957), the Adlerian approach to working with groups has four phases:

1. Developing and maintaining the proper therapeutic relationship.
2. Analyzing of the dynamics that operate within the individual.
3. Fostering the individual's insight into understanding self.
4. Helping the individual to discover new alternatives and make new choices.

In each of these phases, certain techniques have been found to enhance group members' growth and development. These techniques, however, are not limited to only one phase; their use throughout the group process is highly effective in bringing forth positive group interaction. The leader should:

— model appropriate social skills and show social interest to demonstrate acceptance.
— contract to demonstrate the equality of the leader-member relationship.
— make use of active listening skills (restatement, reflection, summarization, and so on).
— employ visual imagery to help members clarify and put into concrete terms some of the absurdities of their thinking and behavior.
— call upon early recollections to aid members in identifying emotional patterns and feelings and discovering the basis for negatives carried from childhood into adulthood.
— make use of paradoxical intention by having members attempt to increase debilitating thoughts and behaviors.
— use confrontation, in a constructive fashion, to point out discrepancies between what group members say and their actions.

— assess members' current functioning in work and social relationships.

— assess members' goals and how these translate into individual lifestyles.

— observe members' interactions, as this may be descriptive of their feelings regarding self and their social skills development.

— observe members' nonverbal behaviors and do not be afraid to interpret from these observations.

These are just samples of the leader techniques that have application in an Adlerian group. Special techniques, as reported by Gilliland et al. (1984), with names such as "The Question," "Catching Oneself," "Spitting in the Soup," "Push Button," "Encouragement," "Midas Technique," "Pleasing Someone," and "Avoiding the Tar Baby" are specific to Adlerians and are used in both individual and group modalities. Each technique is designed to deal with the identified group phases discussed in chapters 2 and 3 and is explained more fully in the sources listed in the Bibliography.

Gestalt Theory

Gestalt counseling is rooted in Gestalt psychology, a school of perception that originated in Europe before World War I. Gestalt psychology began with studies of the perceptual field as a whole and then broke down this field into parts (figure and background), identifying the characteristics of each of these parts and their relationships. Using the body of knowledge collected in this academic field, Fritz Perles translated the perceptual approach to psychology into Gestalt therapy, which moved it from the primarily academic realm into the arena of counseling and therapy.

As applied to counseling and therapy, Gestalt theory views the individual (organism) as being fully responsible for determining the essence of his or her being and his or her reality. In this sense, Gestalt theory may be viewed as both phenomenological and existential. This view credits individuals with the ability to find their own way in life and to accept the responsibilities that come from the decisions made in this journey. Individuals must accept responsibility for the problems created by their decisions and at the same time accept the responsibility of dealing effectively with these problems. The major goal of counseling is to aid individuals in attaining greater awareness of their potential, which will, in turn, allow the individuals to exercise this potential in positive growth.

Gestalt theory explains motivation as striving toward some degree of balance or equilibrium. This striving is natural and is represented by movement between the polarities of equilibrium and disequilibrium. According to Polster and Polster (1973), this striving for balance provides the organism with perceptual order, which is best viewed in terms of a figure set against a background. When the individual perceives a need (figure), a state of disequilibrium exists. When that need is met, the figure melds into the background and a new need (figure) takes its place. Therefore, the individual tends to remain in a constant state of flux.

To further understand the individual, the principle of holism—the individual's interdependent combination of body and spirit and his or her relationship to the environment—must be taken into consideration. The individual is viewed as a physical and psychological totality, and this totality is also unified with the environment. Through the individual's aggressive capacity, he or she is able to interact with the environment and assimilate from that environment what is needed for growth and change. Gilliland et al. (1984) commented about the individual's integration of body, spirit, and aggressive capacity:

> Connecting these three aspects of personality theory together presupposes that a person exists in a field that includes the self and environment. Although the individual and the environment are separate, the process of interaction between them cannot be split (holism). Moreover, human aggressive capacity comes into play at the contact boundary between the organism and the environment by means of contact or withdrawal (the opposite of contact). More specifically, when an object has been contacted or withdrawn from in a way satisfying to the individual, both the object and the need associated with it disappear into the background. The situation is finished; another Gestalt is completed. (p. 96)

The same three aspects play a role in the development of dysfunctional behavior. Instead of using these factors for growth, the individual uses them to protect the organism, and in so doing develops defense structures that prevent positive growth and change. Words including introjection, projection, retroflection, and confluence describe these nonproductive defensive behaviors, which render the individual's perceptions unclear so that he or she is in danger of erecting rigid, artifical boundaries that do not permit the successful completion of need satisfaction.

Gestaltists believe that counseling/therapy must approach the individual from an experiencing perspective through which the individual can deal with the barriers that detract from effective functioning. This is done through a here and now orientation that deals with present functioning, because current behavior is most representative of the barriers. By dealing with behaviors in the here and now, through sensing, feeling, and experiencing the barriers, the individual is able to move through the impasse and reformulate his or her life for more productive results.

Naranjo's (1970) listing of nine "moral injunctions," which he states are not only implicit in Gestalt counseling but also give implied direction to the counselor's work, synthesizes the information as:

1. Live now. Be concerned with the present rather than the past or future.
2. Live here. Deal with what is present rather than with what is absent.
3. Stop imagining. Experience the real.
4. Stop unnecessary thinking. Rather, taste and see.
5. Express rather than manipulate, explain, justify, or judge.
6. Give in to unpleasantness and pain just as to pleasure. Do not restrict your awareness.
7. Accept no *should* or *ought* other than your own. Adore no graven image.
8. Take full responsiblity for your actions, feelings, and thoughts.
9. Surrender to being as you are. (pp. 49–50)

Concepts/Leader Dynamics The following theoretical concepts are presented in terms of leader behaviors. The leader needs to be able to:

— establish an environment in which leader and members share equally in the process of change.
— allow members to find their own way in life and accept the responsibility that goes with this.

— focus members on their experiences in the present moment (here and now).
— recognize the blocks/barriers that impede members' growth, and be willing to bring these to the members' attention.
— aid members in accepting all aspects of themselves, and encourage their sharing of hidden and self-disguised aspects of self.
— assist members in understanding, accepting, and dealing with the concept that they are responsible for their existence.
— confront members with their defensive structures and their unwillingness to take responsibility for self.
— aid members, through experiments, in addressing the unfinished business in their lives.
— help members try out new forms of behaviors, to open them up to the full spectrum of their being.
— help members recognize the splintered parts of self and work toward integrating these parts.

Techniques   Gestalt therapy does not lend itself well to the concept of phases and stages. The listed techniques have special significance in Gestalt therapy, but their use is not limited to one stage. Rather, their application throughout the group experience is seen as highly effective in bringing about positive member interaction and change. The leader should:

— become actively involved with members of the group.
— demonstrate, through exaggeration, the meanings of gestures, posture, and movement in communication.
— experiment with exercises that will help group members gain greater awareness.
— demonstrate, through dialogue and exercises, willingness and ability to stay in the here and now.
— apply active listening skills (e.g., restating, paraphrasing, summarizing).
— enlist other members of the group in providing feedback.
— demonstrate intensive interaction with one member as a learning model for all members.
— use confrontational skills to startle or shock members into greater awareness of their self-defeating behaviors.
— be a creative agent of change to enhance members' self-awareness.
— observe and give direct feedback on group members' nonverbal behaviors.

These are just a few examples of leader techniques that have application in a Gestalt-oriented group. Special techniques identified by Corey (1985), Polster and Polster (1973), and Zinker (1977), termed "language exercises," "nonverbal language," "dialoguing," "empty chair," "making the rounds," "rehearsal," "reversal," "dream work," "unfinished business," and "exaggeration," are specific to Gestalt counseling and are used in both individual and group settings. The sources in the Bibliography offer these suggested techniques.

Person-Centered Theory

Person-centered counseling arose from the work of Carl Rogers. Based upon its major tenets and belief structures, it may be viewed as both phenomenological (human behavior is based on the individual's perception of reality and the values and attitudes attached to that perception) and holistic (human existence is best understood by viewing individuals as a whole and in relationship to the contexts in which they live their lives). The theory sets forth an optimistic view of human potential. The "organismic valuing process" Rogers described is inborn and provides the individual the capacity to make wise choices that will maintain and enhance the organism. People make bad choices, choices that are self-destructive, not because of a failure of the organismic valuing process but, rather, because this process has been subverted by the individual's accepting (introjecting) the values, beliefs, and experiences of others.

The uniqueness of the individual, which is stressed in Person-centered theory, is explained developmentally through the potential that exists within the organism. The organism enters the world with both an organismic valuing process and the tendency toward self-actualization. The infant is able to evaluate what feels good (what actualizes self) and through this process forms a self-concept from experiences, values, meanings, and beliefs that enhance the "I" or "Me" of self. With self-concept come perceptions of relationshps with others and the values attached to these.

As the organism matures, the self becomes identified as an entity separate from others and from the environment. With this awareness, a new need appears: the need for positive regard. This need initially can be fulfilled only through interaction with others and is, fortunately, reciprocal. The need is fulfilled by receiving positive regard from others or by perceiving that a person's own behavior has met another's need.

With the emergence of self-awareness and the need for positive regard, the individual becomes concerned with self-regard and seeks experiences that result in positive valuing of the self by others. When a person receives unconditional positive regard from others, the need for positive self-regard is almost automatically fulfilled and no problems are likely to arise. The individual remains congruent and bases his or her behavior on his or her organismic valuing process.

In the course of human development, trouble arises when significant others negatively value some of the individual's positive self-experiences. When this happens, the need for positive regard and the organismic valuing process are thrown into conflict and "conditions of worth" develop. To maximize the positive regard received from others and to feel personally worthwhile, the individual is forced to deny or distort the value of some of these experiences. In doing so, the individual becomes incongruent and no longer simply assimilates and symbolizes experiences. The person now denies or distorts experiences that are threatening to the distorted self-concept, and hence to the need for positive self-regard, in order to be accepted into the unrealistic self-structure. This defensive pattern becomes circular. More and more behavior is based on the need for positive regard than on the organismic valuing process, and the person becomes increasingly incongruent, defensive, and rigid, compulsively acting to protect his or her erroneous self-image (Noble, 1977).

Rogers (1959) made some statements regarding what changes he expected successful counseling to produce:

1. People come to see themselves differently.
2. People accept themselves and their feelings more fully.
3. People become more self-confident and more self-directing.
4. People become more the person they would like to be.
5. People become more flexible, less rigid, in their perceptions.
6. People adopt more realistic goals for themselves.
7. People behave in a more mature fashion.
8. People change maladjustive behaviors.
9. People become more accepting of others.
10. People become more open to the evidence of what is going on within them and outside of themselves.
11. People change basic personality characteristics in constructive ways. (p. 232)

Concepts/Leader Dynamics   The following theoretical concepts are presented in terms of leader behaviors. The leader needs to be able to:

— establish a facilitative climate within the group characterized by congruence, unconditional positive regard, and empathic understanding.
— provide an environment in which all group members perceive the constructs of safety and mutual trust.
— establish an environment in which leader and members share equally in the process of change.
— be congruent (genuine) in relationships with members and able to communicate this to the members.
— have unconditional positive regard for all members and be able to communicate this to the members.
— have empathic understanding and be able to communicate this to all members.
— support members' finding their own way in life and accepting the responsibility that goes with this.
— refrain from giving advice and direction and allow members to positively activate their organismic valuing process.
— use one's being as an agent of change that will serve as a catalyst for change within the group.

Techniques   Person-centered counseling is not presented in terms of stages or listings of techniques. According to Gilliland et al. (1984):

> Since person-centered counseling is essentially a "being" and a relationship-oriented approach, it is important to note that Rogerian-based strategies for helping people are devoid of techniques that involve doing something to or for the client. There are no steps, techniques, or tools for inducing the client to make measured progress toward some goal; instead the strategies are geared to the experiential relationships. (p. 78)

With this caveat in mind, the leader should make use of:

— silence as a way of communicating acceptance and understanding.
— the active listening skills (e.g., restatement, paraphrasing, summarizing).
— confrontation to demonstrate congruence and positive regard for group members.
— attending behaviors to focus fully on group members.
— communication skills to verbally and nonverbally communicate the depth of empathic understanding for group members.
— self-disclosures, when appropriate, to communicate willingness to be real and to model safety and trust within the group.
— members' resources to enable and promote self-empowerment.

In operationalizing the person-centered approach, the emphasis is on the facilitative relationship rather than on a set of techniques. The Bibliography includes resources for further information on how to apply person-centered concepts.

Rational-Emotive Theory

Rational-emotive therapy (RET), a cognitive approach to human development and counseling, stems from the work of Albert Ellis. Ellis assumes that many types of emotional problems result from irrational patterns of thinking. People with emotional problems develop belief systems that lead to implicit verbalizations or self-talk resting on faulty logic and assumptions. What individuals tell themselves is intimately related to the way they feel and act.

As reported in Blackham (1977), the basic foundation of Ellis's theorizing is contained in his A-B-C-D-E paradigm:

A = an external event to which a person is subjected.
B = a sequence of thoughts or self-verbalizations in which the person engages in response to the external event.
C = the feelings and behaviors that result from B.
D = the therapist's attempt to modify the sequence of thoughts or self-verbalizations.
E = the presumed affective and behavioral consequences resulting from intervention by the therapist.

Undergirding this paradigm is the belief that human problems are not based in the actual situation or event that triggers the discomfort but, instead, the thinking (views, beliefs, attitudes) that individuals attach to the situation or event. For example, someone who is rejected in attempting to develop a relationship (situation) cognitively processes the rejection (interprets) according to views, beliefs, and attitudes and, based upon that interpretation, reacts in an irrational manner. The person blows the situation out of proportion (catastrophizes), moves beyond the situation, and feels both rejected and rejectable, and, therefore, will not be able to establish a meaningful relationship in the future.

Ellis contends that people are born with the ability to think and respond both rationally and irrationally. As a result of individuals' interactions with the environment and the significant persons who frequent that environment, too often the propensity for irrational thinking surfaces as a more consistent mode of operating. This should not be interpreted to mean that external forces exert total control. According to Ellis, individuals, based upon instinctual influences, tend to desire that all things happen for the best, and that they get whatever they desire. Therefore, both internal and external factors operate in influencing individuals whose behaviors are determined more from irrational than rational approaches to problem solving. In Ellis's view, this is the basis for human maladjustment.

Rational-emotive therapy also posits a hopeful view in that it holds that individuals have a strong growth/actualizing potential, and this potential facilitates their ability to replace irrational approaches to problem solving with more rational ones. This same potential facilitates their seeking counseling and provides the counselor with what he or she may need to facilitate change.

The following statement from Ellis (1982) incorporates the basic tenets of RET and also provides direction for the group leader who is operating from this theoretical viewpoint:

> In RET group therapy, the therapist not only actively and directively shows members bringing up their emotional problems that they are largely creating these problems themselves by devoutly and rigidly inventing and holding on to irrational beliefs, not only vigorously questions and challenges these beliefs and helps rip them up, but he or she also encourages and pushes all the group members to look for and dispute the shoulds, oughts, and musts of the other members and to help them give up their perfectionism and dictatorialness. All group participants are steadily taught to use the scientific method with themselves and others: to phrase logically, to vigorously undermine, and to empirically contradict the disordered disturbance-creating cognitions of the other members. (pp. 384–385)

Concepts/Leader Dynamics   The leader needs to be able to:

— develop a group climate characterized as instructional, didactic, confrontative, and challenging.
— instruct group members as to the nature of their faulty thinking and the reasons behind such thinking, and provide them with directions for changing.
— separate the behavior of group members from their personhood and focus on the behaviors reported.
— set aside his or her need for a warm personal relationship with members of the group, as this may be counterproductive to change and growth.
— confront members with their thinking and resulting behaviors and encourage other members of the group to do the same, to aid in the reeducative process of RET.
— detect the irrational belief structures of group members and cause them to reach this same type of understanding.
— dispute the "crooked" thinking of members and teach them ways of disputing or challenging this same thinking.
— teach group members the fundamental principles of RET (A-B-C-D-E formulation) that will empower them to strive for greater self-direction.
— provide relevant experiences, through homework, outside of the group, to reinforce and enhance learning and change.
— use principles of contingency management and skill training as viable options for growth and change.

Techniques   Rational-emotive therapy is not presented in terms of stages of group development but, instead, in terms of levels or perspectives. According to Gilliland et al. (1984), the techniques that have application in RET may be viewed from three perspectives: (a) cognitive-explicatory, (b) evocative-emotive, and (c) behavioristic-active-directive. Techniques that derive from all three of these perspectives include:

— presentation, instruction, and demonstration to help members gain an understanding of their behaviors.
— role playing as a form of behavioral rehearsal within the group for members' effective operation outside the group.
— distracting methods to get the members involved in activities that will stop them from dealing solely with their self-defeating thinking and behaving.
— humor directed at members' behaviors so they can begin to see how ridiculous their current ways of thinking and behaving are.
— emotionally charged language, which will have impact on the members and which they, in turn, can use on self.
— shame-attacking exercises that will force group members to place themselves in embarrassing situations. These are intended to show that others' reactions are not what the members expected.
— exaggeration to get points across to group members. This underlines the ideas and behaviors under discussion and alerts members to their tendencies to exaggerate the end results of their behaviors.

The Bibliography at the end of this chapter lists sources of further information on RET techniques.

Transactional Analysis

Transactional analysis (TA) is based on the ideas and concepts originally developed by Eric Berne (1964), popularized in his book, *Games People Play*. Building on the early work of Berne, TA proponents have added structure and concepts that continue to expand this evolving view of human development and change (Dusay & Dusay, 1979; Goulding & Goulding, 1979; James & Jongeward, 1971; Karpman, 1981; Schiff & Day, 1970; Wollams & Brown, 1979).

Addressing TA from a global perspective brings into clear focus the significance of early decision making that sets the parameters for future behavior. The three ego states (parent, adult, child) form early in life, and each carries with it a script on how one is to behave, think, and feel. The developing individual takes in messages, verbal and nonverbal, delivered by the environment and by significant persons within that environment, processes these, and develops from them a set of scripts that form the framework for behavior. Individuals are not passive in this process; they make decisions and develop their own life script. Because the individual is able to decide and, therefore, determine the original life script, he or she also can redecide and change the script. This redecision and rescripting become central issues in the process of counseling.

From a TA perspective, personality development is viewed in terms of:

1. Ego states.
2. Strokes.
3. Injunctions.
4. Decisions.
5. Script formation.
6. Life positions.

The ego states (parent, adult, child) are the foundation for the personality, from which individuals build the cognitive, affective, and behavioral dynamics that direct their lives.

The first ego state to develop is that of the child. This development begins shortly after birth. During the first few years of life, the child incorporates within this ego state rudimentary configurations of the adult ego state and the parent ego state. This "early adult," called the "little professor," processes information and makes decisions based on this processing. The "early parent" incorporates the infant's perception of parental behaviors and the messages this behavior transmits. As development proceeds, the fully developed adult ego state and parent ego state emerge from these early configurations. Each is separate and distinct, but the interplay of the three, based upon the scripts written for each, forms the basis of behavior.

Strokes, the second key concept, are units of attention that stimulate the individual and serve as a motivational force for human interaction. This attention may be positive or negative. The rule seems to be that even negative strokes are better than no strokes at all. Strokes may stem from both internal and external sources, and, if not readily available, the individual may devise "games" and "rackets" (transactions that allow the individual to gain needed strokes) to provide this motivational force.

Injunctions, decisions, and script formation, the next three concepts, are most easily understood in combination. Injunctions are parental messages that children receive at an early age. These messages are generally prescriptive in terms of ways of being: "Don't be, don't feel, don't love, don't trust." Upon hearing and processing these messages, the child makes decisions regarding these directives. Based upon those decisions, he or she forms a script for living his or her life. If the messages are reinforced and repeated, the foundation for this early scripting becomes strong.

Life positions, the last of the major concepts, represent the resolution of the three-part process of injunctions, decisions, and script formation. These form the framework within which individuals structure and operate the behavioral, cognitive, and affective domains of their life. According to Harris (1967), individuals adopt one of the following four life positions:

1. I'm OK — You're OK.
2. I'm OK — You're not OK.
3. I'm not OK — You're OK.
4. I'm not OK — You're not OK.

Each position is descriptive of the individual's developmental process and also how he or she interacts with the environment and the people who frequent that environment. The boundaries between the positions are not hard and fast. Even though individuals usually operate more in one position than the others, movement across all four positions is possible. The life position "I'm OK — You're OK" is considered a "winner's script." The other life positions are viewed as "losers' scripts" and set the stage for maladjustment in later life.

In sum, transactional analysis is based on the philosophy that individuals are OK and have potential and desire to move toward a positive growth-oriented position. This potential is often stifled because of early decisions, and a redecision process is necessary for individuals to realize their growth potential. Awareness seems to be a key to this change process. Individuals need to become aware first of their current scripting and how this impacts on their way of being, and then of their power and ability to change the scripts and create for themselves a more positive and productive way of living.

Concepts/Leader Dynamics   The group leader with a TA orientation needs to be able to:

— develop a therapeutic contract with the group members that stresses equality and identifies the goals that leader and members mutually agree to.
— instruct group members in the specific tenets and specialized terminology of transactional analysis.
— analyze at least four elements for group members: (a) structures, (b) transactions, (c) games, and (d) scripts.
— establish a working relationship with group members that is best described as a partnership in which equality is a key ingredient.
— enhance group members' awareness of their scripts, resulting from early decisions, and their power and ability to change these scripts.
— provide positive strokes to group members, and instruct them in the significance these strokes play in motivating behavior.
— reinforce the redecisions group members make during the group process, and encourage them to act upon these redecisions.
— function in the cognitive/rational domain of human behaviors, as these are major forces for change in the redecision process.
— challenge group members to change current patterns of thinking/feeling/behaving and to move to more growth-producing patterns.
— enhance group members' autonomy to reduce dependence on the leader or on other group members.

Techniques   Although stages or phases for groups are not specified in transactional analysis, a TA group probably would follow a pattern of: (a) establishing a facilitative climate, (b) developing contracts that identify goals, (c) working though various analyses of structures, transactions, games, and scripts, and (d) terminating with specific directives for action oriented change. In each of these stages/phases, the leader would:

— use active listening skills to encourage member participation.
— confront members to challenge them in the redecision process.
— role play to encourage members to try out their new scripts.

— consult the myriad of books and publications that instruct in principles of transactional analysis.

— develop contracts to keep members on target as this relates to goals.

— enhancing the redecision process, draw upon members' committment to change.

— make use of self-scripting to model more positve ways of being.

— give strokes to motivate members to change.

The Bibliography provides sources for further exploration of transactional analysis.

AN INTEGRATION OF THEORETICAL APPROACHES

The five theories presented in this chapter offer the group leader options in working with groups. At first glance, each of these approaches seems to represent a unique underpinning for group process. But the five approaches actually have many aspects in common, which enhances the possibility for integrating these theories and applying them to the ongoing group process. Five factors address this integrative theme and allow group leaders to use a blended theoretical approach in their work with groups: (a) relationship variables, (b) leader role variables, (c) member role variables, (d) process variables, and (e) outcome variables.

Relationship Variables

A working relationship is basic to all five theoretical approaches. Although the terms describing this working relationship vary, each presents a need for trust, safety, mutual respect, and leader competence, and in four of the five, "equality" as this relates to leader-member interaction. In all five, the working relationship is the foundational building block on which all other aspects of group dynamics rest. Each stresses the importance of taking time to build this foundational structure and to assure that group members understand the nature of this relationship. From the integrative perspective, a working relationship must be established first, regardless of which of the theoretical positions is followed. All other aspects of the group process stem from this relationship.

Leader Role Variables

In all five theoretical positions, the leader's role is an active one. Descriptors such as develop, instruct, analyze, establish, enhance, provide, reinforce, demonstrate, aid, confront, communicate, and observe are action-oriented and give the leader specific directions to take an active role in his or her interaction with the group. It could be argued that the person-centered approach does not call for leader action, but the person-centered leader must be able to communicate unconditional positive regard and empathy and be congruent in his or her interactions with group members.

Therapeutic conditions are, in themselves, action-oriented as they require the leader to possess these "conditions" and also to demonstrate and communicate these to group members. From the integrative perspective, active leader participation is necessary in all five theoretical approaches. The type of action may vary, but action-oriented leadership seems to be a key element in all five.

Member Role Variables

Themes relating to the role members are to play in the groups permeate all five theoretical approaches. These themes focus on being responsible, committed to change, willing to risk, willing to try out new behaviors, willing to share self with others, able to deal with affect, cognitions, and behaviors, willing to do the "hard work" that change demands, and openness to new information, insights, and awareness. These themes stress the active role that members must take and also the concept that, if change is to occur, members must assume major responsibility for this change. From the integrative perspective, the role of members has the same underlying message, regardless of the theoretical approach: If you desire change, you must be willing to take major responsibility for that change and be willing to take the necessary action to make that change possible.

Process Variables

The area that seems to have the most variability across the five theoretical approaches is the process dimension. It encompasses the various experiential activities that take place within groups to attain the desired goals. Even here, however, the five approaches have some similarity. Self-disclosure, role playing, giving and receiving feedback, observing others, using active listening skills, modeling, demonstrating, encountering, and dialoguing are common to all five approaches. The differences are not as much in terms of process as in the unique way these processes are employed in each of the five approaches. For example, in the person-centered approach, giving and receiving feedback is seen as an ongoing means to facilitate group interaction and member growth. From the Gestalt orientation, giving and receiving feedback might be structured to give group members exaggerated exposure to the various affective responses associated with giving and receiving feedback. The group may do this at a specific time to emphasize a specific point.

From the integrative perspective, regardless of the theoretical approach selected, the process variable dimension is not nearly as diverse as one might expect. The diversity is not so much in the "what" of process as in the "how" and perhaps the "why" of process. All five approaches provide a process to expand the affective, cognitive, and behavioral realms of group members.

Outcome Variable

The greatest similarity across all five theoretical approaches is in intended group outcome. In discussing outcomes, concepts including increasing awareness, changing dysfunctional behaviors, enhancing self-concept, fostering insight, accepting responsibility, and increasing degrees of trust in self and with others find application across all five approaches. Regardless of theoretical approach, the desired outcomes all center on change. The words used to describe this change vary from theory to theory, but the end result is to have group members function more effectively in affective, cognitive, and behavioral domains. From the integrative perspective, outcome variables are directed in the rather specific area of positive change—change in the way group members feel about themselves and their world, change in the way group members think about themselves and their world, and change in the way group members behave as a result of changes in the way they feel and think. Notwithstanding the differences in some of the fundamental principles of the five theoretical approaches presented, such differences do not exist in terms of outcome variables.

Implementation

In sum, the following are recommended to effectively integrate individual counseling approaches in working with groups.

- ❑ Be familiar with all theoretical approaches even though they were originally developed for work with the individual. Each will provide insight into human development and change and how to apply this insight in the group setting.
- ❑ Attempt to integrate aspects of various theoretical approaches in working with groups. An eclectic approach will prove beneficial to the group leader and consequently to group members.
- ❑ Apply theoretical approaches as they were intended to be used—as facilitative guides to better understand individual dynamics and to assist individuals in the change process. They were not conceived as the true and only way of explaining the human condition.
- ❑ Do not rely solely on one approach to the exclusion of the others. Base your approach in working with groups on a broad knowledge base, and take from this base what will make your group work most effective.
- ❑ Experiment with many approaches to group work until you find the combination of principles and techniques that best fits your personal philosophy regarding people and your personal style of being with people. The approach you finally develop should be much more a reflection of you than of any single theoretical position.

SUMMARY

Group approaches are derived largely from theories and therapies developed for individuals. Because theory has to form the foundation for group counseling, group leaders should become knowledgeable about the major theories and learn how to integrate these and apply them within the group modality. The five individual theories highlighted in this chapter are: Adlerian, Gestalt, person-centered, rational-emotive, and transactional analysis.

The five variables that enable leaders to blend these theories in their work with groups are: relationship, leader role, member role, process, and outcome. In all five theories, the working relationship is the basis for the group dynamic, and most advocate equality in leader-member interactions. All five theories propel the leader into an active role, particularly in providing optimum therapeutic conditions. Member role permeates all the theoretical precepts, and all agree that individuals ultimately have to take responsibility to change whatever they want to change. Process presents the most diversity of the five factors, but more in the "why" and "how" than in the "what" of the process. The theories are similar in the outcome variable; all center on evoking positive change in people.

Most important, group leaders should take their knowledge of various theories, experiment with different approaches, and strive to find the way that works best for them and for the group, reflecting the leader's personal philosophy and personal style.

REFERENCES

Berne, E. (1964). *Games people play*. New York: Grove Press.

Blackham, G. (1977). Procedures for promoting behavior change: Behavioral and cognitive approaches. In G. Blackham (Ed.), *Counseling theory, process and practice* (pp. 133–163). Belmont, CA: Wadsworth Publishing.

Corey, G. (1985). *Theory and practice of group counseling* (2nd ed.). Pacific Grove, CA: Brooks/Cole.

Corey, G., & Corey, M. S. (1977). An overview of eight models of group process. In G. Corey & M. S. Corey (Ed.), *Group process and practice* (pp. 24–30). Pacific Grove, CA: Brooks/Cole.

Corey, G., & Corey, M.S. (1987). *Group process and practice* (3rd ed.). Pacific Grove, CA: Brooks/Cole.

Dreikurs, R. (1957). Group psychotherapy from the point of view of Adlerian psychology. *International Journal of Group Psychotherapy, 7*, 363–375.

Dusay, J., & Dusay, K. M. (1979). Transactional analysis. In R. Corsini (Ed.), *Current psychotherapies* (2nd ed., pp. 374–427). Itasca, IL: F. E. Peacock.

Ellis, A. (1982). *Rational emotive therapy and cognitive behavior therapy*. New York: Springer.

George, R. L., & Dustin, D. (1988). *Group counseling theory and practice*. Englewood Cliffs, NJ: Prentice Hall.

Gilliland, B., James, R., Roberts, G., & Bowman, J. (1984). *Theory and strategies in counseling and psychotherapy*. Englewood Cliffs, NJ: Prentice Hall, Inc.

Goulding, M., & Goulding, R. (1979). *Changing lives through redecision therapy*. New York: Brunner/Mazel.

Hansen, J. C., Warner, R. W., & Smith, E. M. (1976). Group counseling theories: Synthesis and analysis. In J. C. Hansen, R. W. Warner, & E. M. Smith (Eds.), *Group counseling: Theory and process* (pp. 250–278). Chicago: Rand McNally.

Harris, T. (1967). *I'm OK — you're OK*. New York: Harper & Row.

James, M., & Jongeward, D. (1971). *Born to win: Transactional analysis with gestalt experiments*. Reading, MA: Addison-Wesley.

Karpman, S. (1981). The politics of theory. *Transactional Analysis Journal, 11*(1), 68–75.

Lakin, M. (1985). Helping groups in our times. In M. Lakin (Ed.), *The helping group: Therapeutic principles and issues* (pp. 21–28). Reading, MA: Addison-Wesley.

Lieberman,, M. A. (1983). Comparative analysis of change mechanisms in group. In R. R. Dies & K. R. MacKenzie (Eds.), *Advances in group psychotherapy: Integrating research and practice* (pp. 191–208). New York: International Universities Press.

Manaster, G. J., & Corsini, R. S. (1982). *Individual psychology: Theory and practice*. Itasca, IL: F. E. Peacock.

Naranjo, C. (1970). Present centeredness techniques, prescriptions and ideals. In J. Fogan & I. Shepherd (Eds.), *Gestalt therapy now* (pp. 45–55). Palo Alto, CA: Science and Behavior Books.

Noble, F. (1977). Procedure for promoting behavior change: Humanistic approach. In G. Blackham (Ed.), *Counseling theory, process and practice* (pp. 165–183). Belmont, CA: Wadsworth Publishing.

Ohlsen, M. M., Horne, A. M., & Lawe, C. F. (1988). *Group counseling* (3rd ed.). New York: Holt, Rinehart and Winston.

Polster, E., & Polster, M. (1973). *Gestalt therapy integrated*. New York: Brunner/Mazel.

Rogers, C. R. (1959). Significant learning in therapy and in education. *Educational Leadership, 16*(4), 232–242.

Schiff, J. L., & Day, B. (1970). *All my children*. New York: Evans.

Shaffer, J. B. P., & Galinsky, M. D. (1989). The gestalt therapy workshop. In J. B. P. Shaffer & M. D. Galinsky (Eds.), *Methods of group therapy* (pp. 118–140). Englewood Cliffs, NJ: Prentice Hall.

Shapiro, J. L. (1978). Major theoretical orientations. In J. L. Shapiro (Ed.), *Methods of group psychotherapy and encounter: A tradition of innovation* (pp. 40–63). Itasca, IL: F. E. Peacock.

Thompson, S., & Kahn, J. H. (1970). Group psychotherapy. In S. Thompson & J. H. Kahn (Eds.), *The group process as a helping* technique (pp. 55–74). New York: Pergamon Press.

Wollams, S., & Brown, M. (1979). *TA: The total handbook of transactional analysis*. Englewood Cliffs, NJ: Prentice Hall.

Wright, H. (1989). Therapeutic properties of group. In H. Wright (Ed.), *Group work: Perspectives and practice* (pp. 89–99). London: Scutan Press.

Zinker, J. (1977). *Creative process in gestalt therapy*. New York: Brunner/Mazel.

BIBLIOGRAPHY

Adler, A. (1958). *What life should mean to you*. New York: Capricorn.

Adler, A. (1964). The individual psychology of Alfred Adler. In H. L. Ansbacher & R. R. Ansbacher (Eds.), *The individual psychology of Alfred Adler*. New York: Harper & Row.

Berne, E. (1961). *Transactional analysis in psychotherapy*. New York: Grove Press.

Combes, A. W. (1989). *A theory of therapy: Guidelines for counseling practice*. Newbury Park, CA: Sage Publications.

Ellis, A. (1962). *Reason and emotion in psychotherapy*. New York: Lyle Stuart.

Ellis, A. (1973). *Humanistic psychotherapy: The rational-emotive approach*. New York: Julian Press.

Perls, F. (1969). *Gestalt therapy verbatim*. Moab, UT: Real People Press.

Perls, F. (1973). *The Gestalt approach and eye witness to therapy*. New York: Bantam Books.

Rogers, C. (1961). *On becoming a person*. Boston: Houghton Mifflin.

Rogers, C. (1980). *A way of being*. Boston: Houghton Mifflin.

PART TWO

Special Populations

With the foundational information in Part One, Part Two: Special Populations, provides information and approaches to group work in ten specific areas. Each of these demands a specific informational base and also effective techniques and approaches to deal with them. The chapters in Part Two provide knowledge combined with an applicational base for working in these specific areas.

The growing prominence of self-help groups in the field of mental health is an affirmation that contact with others who are facing similar difficulties can empower individuals to act on their individual and collective needs. Chapter 5, "Group Counseling: Self-Enhancement," applies the information in the first four chapters to self-help groups with a focus on self-enhancement.

The chapter attempts to answer the questions: Why have self-help groups become so widely used? What does self-enhancement mean in relation to self-help groups? Why is self-enhancement a major focus in counseling intervention? What aspects of group structure, process, and content are most effective in self-enhancement? In answering these questions, the author discusses the emphasis on individualism, individuals' responsibility to others, individual and contextual determinants of self-enhancement, and the physical and social contexts of self-enhancement as these relate to the role each plays in either supporting or complicating self-enhancement as an approach to aiding individuals in the growth process. This discussion turns to consciousness raising, instilling hope and commitment, and empowerment.

Chapter 6, "Group Counseling for People with Addictions," imparts information on the topics of physiological, psychological/cognitive, and sociological factors affecting groups, and counterproductive group processes with chemically dependent populations. The chapter blends the idealized empirical view with the pragmatic, practice-based perspective.

Chapter 7, "Group Counseling for Individuals with Eating Disorders," deals with the specific disorders of anorexia nervosa, bulimia nervosa, and compulsive overeating. Current research regarding these disorders is presented together with the issues, implications, and applications related to group work with this population.

Chapter 8, "Group Counseling for People with Physical Disabilities," provides information on (a) the merits of group counseling with individuals who have physical disabilities, (b) a delineation of the needs of those with disabilities, (c) the therapeutic factors deemed effective in working with this population, and (d) the goals of groups whose members have disabilities.

Chapter 9, "Group Counseling with Victims of Abuse/Incest," discusses the factors that should be considered in selecting group members, the stages of group work with these people, the concepts of transference and concomitant factors, and age-specific variations in group approaches with children and adolescents.

Chapter 10, "Group Counseling with Gays and Lesbians," provides gay and lesbian culture-specific information dealing with issues such as values, attitudes, and language. Based upon this foundation, the authors address (a) gay-affirmative counseling, (b) gay and lesbian professional counselors, (c) types of groups in the gay/lesbian community, and (d) specific gay and lesbian groups. Each of these areas includes techniques and approaches that have proven effective. Special attention is also directed to AIDS groups.

Chapter 11, "Group Counseling with Couples and Families," introduces the reader to the subject, then presents an overview of multiple family group counseling (MFGC) and an overview of couples group counseling. Each of these sections explores indicators and contraindicators, group counseling procedures, group dynamics, stages of group development, co-facilitation models, and case examples demonstrating the information presented.

Chapter 12, "Group Counseling: Career and Lifestyle Issues," defines career group counseling and presents a rationale for its use. This chapter contains a review of available career research and provides information on the application of techniques to career and lifestyle issues. Group models and components of group programs with relevance to career and lifestyle issues are presented. The chapter concludes with current and future trends in dealing with career and lifestyle issues.

Chapter 13, "Group Counseling for Issues Related to Suicide," begins with a discussion of the statistics on the prevalence of suicide and the significant factors that research has found to be indicative of suicidal risk. Using this information as a foundation, the author devotes the major portion of the chapter to suicide intervention groups. These groups are discussed in terms of guidelines for leaders, short-term versus long-term therapy models, group membership, group limitations, and goals and functions. Techniques and interventions are presented and broken down by age-specific categories. Prevention, intervention, and postvention group models for working in the area of suicide are included together with examples.

Chapter 14, "Group Counseling: Loss," provides strategies for group work dealing with loss—defined in its broadest context to include death, separations, departures, loss of dreams, expectations, power, and freedom. The strategies are tied to stages of the grieving process and common feelings associated with loss. Special attention is directed at the death of a mate and at loss resulting from the transition to later adult years.

As these chapters indicate, the effective use of group approaches is based upon a combination of knowledge and the ability to apply that knowledge in the group setting. These chapters also offer evidence that group knowledge and skill have wide application in the helping professions.

5

Group Counseling: Self-Enhancement

Richard E. Pearson

*T*o make self-enhancement a focal point of group counseling, though not controversial, may at first seem a bit arcane. Why not just talk about autonomy, self-direction, or self-efficacy? Why self-enhancement? The growing prominence of self-help groups as mental health resources for individuals with personal and interpersonal difficulties has highlighted the importance and utility of self-enhancement. Implicitly and explicitly, these groups point out the significance of self- and peer-based help. They affirm the view that contact with others facing similar difficulties can empower ordinary individuals to act on their individual and collective needs and interests. Self-enhancement and empowerment are major themes running through self-help and other nonprofessionally oriented helping approaches. Perhaps something is going on here to which group leaders should pay attention.

To state that groups will contribute to the personal and interpersonal competence of members is to state the obvious. But when self-enhancement becomes a central focus of group work, the meaning of "growth in clients' effectiveness" becomes narrower. It brings up the possible contradiction that counseling groups might not contribute significantly to helping members act in self-enhancing ways.

The assertion that the ability to "self-enhance" is a possible but not necessary subset of personal effectiveness suggests that we question what self-enhancement is and what place it has in the counseling process.

❑ What is self-enhancement?
❑ Why should self-enhancement be a focus in counseling intervention?
❑ What variations of group structure, process, and content are most effective in contributing to self-enhancement?

A VIEW OF SELF-ENHANCEMENT

Consider the following assertions:

❑ Self-enhancement consists of actions, by individuals, that represent their intention to promote their interests (e.g., well-being, rights, opportunities).
❑ Self-enhancement action varies as a function of individual-based (e.g., motivation, skill) and context-based (e.g., peer support, social norms) variables.
❑ Self-enhancement can be considered a multilevel construct, reflecting the intention to promote one's interests in social settings ranging from informal, face-to-face relationships (e.g., family, peer group) to relationships that are an aspect of one's membership in formal, distant associations (e.g., the community, the nation).
❑ Self-enhancement can be pursued through a wide range of actions ranging from high-profile, apparent behaviors such as defiance to quieter, less noticeable actions such as biding one's time or letting small slights "roll off your back."

Self-enhancement is, then, a construct well within the boundaries of counseling concern. Its aim of encouraging individuals toward self-direction raises a familiar counseling theme. Because it is rooted in a person's attitudes and behavioral repertoires, self-enhancement is reasonably addressed by the standard array of individual and group interventions. Fostering clients' self-enhancement ability clearly is something that counselors might address. But we should also ask why.

THE SIGNIFICANCE OF SELF-ENHANCEMENT AS A FOCUS IN COUNSELING

For a variety of reasons, contributing to members' self-enhancing ability might be perceived as an important outcome of a counseling group. These reasons can be viewed as clustering around two considerations: pragmatics and ideology.

Self-Enhancement as Pragmatics

From a practical position, because virtually all forms of assistance offered in counseling groups are time-limited, it makes sense to prepare people for life after the group by equipping them with the attitudes, knowledge, and skills (cognitive and behavioral) that will allow them to maintain and extend the gains the group experience has helped them achieve. From this perspective, groups that operate under a "learning to learn" strategy are most effective. At the same time individuals' presenting concerns are addressed, they are enlisted as active partners in resolving those concerns. Because of this dual focus (responding to the present/preparing for the future), the nature of the process becomes just as important to the group leader as the effectiveness in resolving those concerns.

Keeping group members actively involved in resolving their concerns presumably increases the likelihood that they will acquire problem-solving strategies, knowledge, and skills and be able to bring them to bear in solving future concerns. This can be seen in the following passage from Carl Rogers's early book, *Counseling and Psychotherapy* (1942). Rogers asserts that counselors should focus on current and future issues alike:

The aim is not to solve one particular problem but to assist the individual to *grow*, so that he can cope with the present problem and with later problems in a better integrated fashion. If he can gain enough integration to handle one problem in more independent, more responsible, less confused, better organized ways, then he will also handle new problems in that manner. (pp. 28–29)

Self-Enhancement and the Pragmatics of Prevention   In a similar vein, strengthening self-management and self-enhancement resources, and preparing individuals to handle future life demands more effectively, can be viewed as a preventive strategy that wards off a variety of difficulties (Conyne, 1987). When viewed as prevention, counseling can help thwart acquiring dysfunctionality and ameliorate suffering. For example, acquiring effective parenting skills as a result of participating in a group for first-time parents can help a couple approach the responsibilities and pressures of child rearing in a more relaxed, effective way than they would otherwise. This could be expected to translate into a nurturing, supportive, family environment. If so, the family will foster children who are more robust in terms of their personal and interpersonal effectiveness than might have been the case without the parents' involvement in the parenting group.

Self-Enhancement and the Conservation of Professional Help   Another possible benefit from helping people pursue their own self-enhancement is that it could ease the demand for always-scarce professional helping resources. Self-enhancement would reduce the need for counseling. Professional helpers tend to view families and peer groups as hothouses for the growth of dysfunctionality (Heller, 1979), but natural networks can be reservoirs of positive assistance as well. Enhancing individuals' access to the resources of family, peer, neighborhood, and work support systems can lead to the resolution of personal and interpersonal difficulties without resorting to formal, professional assistance (Pearson, 1990).

A case can be made (and many group-centered cultures and subcultures would make that case) that knowing one's place within the group, looking to it for assistance, and being willing to accept its helping efforts represent a superior general strategy for dealing with life's demands. Perhaps, after all, the preference for individual autonomy or integration into the group is as much a matter of personal and group ideology as it is a determination of which general strategy is most efficient.

Self-Enhancement as Ideology

The importance attached to self-enhancement usually derives from individual, subjective judgments about what is good and right. These value judgments are involved in one's definition of the effective, admirable person. Fostering self-enhancement abilities can be held as a proper concern in group counseling because it moves individuals closer to widely-held formulations of personal effectiveness.

Self-Enhancement as Personal Ideology   Observers of the American scene (for example, Alexis de Tocqueville, Ralph Waldo Emerson, Max Weber) have noted that independence and self-reliance are prized in the national ethos. Standing on one's own, making one's own way, underlie the notion of the effective, successful person (Bellah, Madsen, Sullivan, Swidler, & Tipton, 1985). To be dependent, not able to care for oneself, or to need reassurance and confirmation from others, is to be considered weak in body or character, incompetent, unsuccessful, yea, pitiable.

Given this perspective, promoting movement toward autonomy and self-direction seems to represent a reasonable outcome for counseling groups. Pragmatic considerations aside, many helping professionals in America assume that autonomy is "better" than dependence. In a careful analysis of the roots and consequences of this emphasis on individual achievement and self-direction, Bellah et al. (1985) specifically call attention to how psychotherapy "reinforces the traditional individualism of American culture, including the concept of utilitarian individuals maximizing their own interests" (p. 104).

Goble (1970) noted that the "third force" perspectives articulated by Abraham Maslow, Carl Rogers, Rollo May, and others can be understood (at least in part) as a reaction to the dominant role that psychoanalytic and behavioral perspectives had, until then, exerted in American psychology. Both psychoanalysis and behaviorism have a strong deterministic tone, viewing the individual as essentially reactive in nature, and functioning in response to instinctive or environment-based forces (Allport, 1962). When extended to human service activities, these perspectives have tended to generate strategies that emphasize helper control and helpee compliance. With their assumption of individuals' potential for independence and self-direction, person-centered and other third force theorists and practitioners conceptualize the helping process as being based on respect for people's growth potential, and highlighting the importance of counselor-counselee collaboration.

The emergence of self-enhancement, empowerment, and self-help constructs in professional and popular literatures might be viewed as the current face of the longstanding American propensity to prize the self-defining, competent, achieving individual as the model of personal effectiveness. Although this pragmatism draws helping professionals toward the means/ends utility of behavioral approaches, and our fascination with mysteries (what's behind the closed door?) entices us to find psychoanalytic and other "depth" perspectives intriguing, our bedrock values are most compatible with views of the helping process that speak the language of autonomy, self-direction, and personal responsibility.

Self-Enhancement as Social Ideology   At another level, self-enhancement can be viewed as central to the proper relationship between society and the individual. The American *Declaration of Independence* is based on the view that governments exist to preserve the rights of individuals. One of those basic rights, specifically cited, is the freedom to pursue one's happiness (to act to further one's interests and needs). Governments that unwarrantedly restrain self-enhancement subvert their *raison d'etre* and deserve to be overthrown. Because the government is created by and for us, we as citizens have the responsibility of active involvement in the ongoing process of monitoring and shaping it to be responsive to our needs. Participation in the processes of government is, thus, not only a basic right but also a duty.

In her analysis of mutual help organizations, Marie Killilea (1976) pointed out that this widespread social phenomenon not only has deep, longstanding cultural and historical roots but it also reflects important dimensions of contemporary American life. She saw mutual help groups as expressions of the American ideal of participation and self-determination. Just as the consumer movement represents individuals' attempt to influence the production and distribution of material goods, so the mutual help movement can be considered an expression of individuals' desire to influence decisions that shape the character and delivery of mental health services.

Viewed from this perspective, the line between the personal and the political dissolves. When individuals seek out the assistance of a medical or a mental health professional they enter a system that is as clearly defined in terms of its assumptions about power, responsibility, and rights and privileges as any explicitly "political" system. Vattano (1972) suggested that the self-help phenomenon can be understood as a reaction to a mental health establishment that has, in some respects, become unresponsive to the needs and influence of its recipients. Through self-help groups, individuals seize ownership of the helping process. Rather than being channeled into a passive "patient" role, they are able to enter into decision-making and help-delivery processes.

At a societal level, the consumerism and demand for participation that self-help groups represent can be seen as resulting in what Killilea (1976) labeled an "alternative care giving system." At an individual and immediate social network level (in this instance, the helping group), it often enables individuals to pursue their own interests and needs. In the process, they not only become empowered to "self-enhance" but also experience the boost in self-worth and personal efficacy that commonly result from having the opportunity or responsibility to assist their peers (Reissman, 1965).

Increased self-worth, heightened personal efficacy, growing self-enhancement—certainly these are outcomes of interest to the counselor who works with groups. Group leaders can learn some lessons from the structure, process, and outcome of self-help groups.

Self-Enhancement and Responsibility to Others   Determining who or what to use as the standard for identifying where an individual's personal or collective interests really lie brings one into the domains of personal and social ideology with which group leaders must (or ought to) wrestle as they take on the audacious task of presuming to act as agents for others' growth and development. Given that one person's self-enhancement may be seen by another as self-indulgence or exploitive self-aggrandizement, interventions to facilitate others' ability to act in their own interests must be carried out within some framework of understanding about the proper balance between an individual's rights and responsibility to others.

Though individualism and self-enhancement can be viewed as foundational American values, these values have mixed consequences. Untrammeled individualism has been blamed for diverse contemporary social phenomena including (to mention just a few): the decline of volunteerism, dangerously high levels of personal debt, weakening of the extended and nuclear families, escalating incidence of addiction, neglect of elders, and underfunding of the public schools. Tension between individual striving and responsibility to others is not new to American life. As Bellah et al. (1985) pointed out, however, the weakening of civic and religious traditions, which historically have acted to counterbalance individual striving, has disrupted traditional strategies for accommodating self-enhancement and responsibility toward the collective. The resulting imbalance precipitated a range of crises that threaten the coherence and unity of American society.

The question is whether an individualism in which the self has become the main form of reality can really be sustained. What is at issue is not simply whether self-contained individuals might withdraw from the public sphere to pursue purely private ends, but whether such individuals are capable of sustaining either a public *or* a private life. (p. 148)

How can counseling intervention strike a balance between fostering individuality and maintaining the integrity of the collective? Person-centered theory has proposed the existence of an essentially positive human nature. If genuinely given a chance for expression, a person's most basic tendency is to ". . . value those objects, experiences, and goals which make for his own survival, growth, and development, and for the survival and development of others" (Rogers, 1989, p. 183). From the person-centered perspective, counseling that is genuinely effective will lead to the emergence (or further emergence) of people who will (because that is their "nature") be inclined to make choices that fairly balance their own needs and interests and those of others. Thus, the challenge is not how to *make* others be responsible but, rather, how to *allow* them to be.

Others (for example, psychoanalytic theorists) who hold a less sanguine view of the basic stuff of humanity tend to stress the importance of strengthening responsible behavior by maintaining a functional level of internalized social control. Optimum personal effectiveness occurs when the superego sets down limits of what is acceptable that are sufficiently broad to allow a reasonable array of real-world alternatives in satisfying physical and social needs while still maintaining effective control over self-gratification impulses.

Similarly, behaviorally oriented theorists and practitioners cite the necessity of ensuring that individuals are quickly confronted with, and held responsible for, the consequences of their actions. Skinner (1971), for example, asserted that much contemporary antisocial behavior (e.g., industrial pollution) is the result of too great a lag between actions and their consequences. As society becomes ever more complex, and as communities become more and more impersonal, connections between many classes of action and their consequence can become blurred. With this distortion comes a decline in the effectiveness of the process through which individuals are "taught" to behave responsibly.

Turning more specifically to groups, this matter of avoiding possible discontinuity between the consequences of individuals' self-enhancement and the needs of the collective is important, especially when focusing upon groups as vehicles to foster self-enhancement. Those who witnessed the heyday of the human potential movement of the 1970s recall that one criticism leveled at small-group activities was that they concentrated too heavily on encouraging self-direction, self-expression, and self-preoccupation, to the detriment of responsibility toward, and concern for, others. How may counseling groups in general, and groups supporting growth in members' self-enhancement ability, in particular, work toward balancing individual and collective interests?

DETERMINANTS OF SELF-ENHANCEMENT

The extent to which self-enhancement in individuals varies as a function of individual- or setting-based variables is an essential consideration. Narrow identification with sociological or psychological perspectives might cause group leaders to emphasize either the importance of contextual or of individual factors in developing and maintaining attitudes and behaviors that support self-enhancement. Group leaders might see the willingness and ability to pursue one's interests as being rooted primarily in a supportive, confirming social context (family, neighborhood, school, community, nation) that presents self-assertion as normative, appropriate behavior. Conversely, they might view self-enhancement as being dependent primarily upon personal characteristics such as ego-strength, self-assertion skills, or internal locus of control.

Espousing one or the other view—that self-enhancement is primarily the consequence of contextual- or of individual-based variables—quickly translates into a preference for counseling strategies that center either on individual clients or on their social/physical contexts. An individual focus translates into traditional individual and group interventions that consider individuals to be separate, autonomous entities. In contrast, as Pattison (1973) noted, group leaders might consider self-enhancement (and most other behavior clusters) to be the manifestation of social forces acting upon individuals. This channels counselors and other human service workers toward interventions that, like family counseling or network therapy (Attneave, 1976; Rueveni, 1979), directly involve the social systems within which individuals lead their lives.

In the arena of counseling practice, hard and fast dichotomies have a way of crumbling. Group leaders have ample opportunity to see individuals being shaped by situations, as well as situations being transformed by the actions of individuals. Certainly, some families and neighborhoods foster hopelessness and powerlessness in their members, just as other families and neighborhoods are transformed by the growth in personal awareness and skill of their members.

In attempting to understand the presence or absence of self-enhancing behavior in group members, perhaps the most useful stance is to remain sensitive to the operation of both individual- and context-based factors, and to expect to find both domains functioning in an interdependent way. This willingness to consider both individual- and context-based factors in self-enhancement will, in turn, open up a wider range of counseling interventions and strategies to foster the self-enhancing ability of group members.

Individual Determinants of Self-Enhancement

Where does self-enhancement come from? What individual attitudes, beliefs, perceptions, or skills support or allow its expression? Having identified the individual-based characteristics upon which self-enhancement rests, group leaders can search for interventions that increase individuals' self-enhancement ability and activity. In helping group members develop or increase whatever prerequisite attributes or skills they lack, they become empowered to act in their own interests.

One way of organizing the individual-based variables that can affect individuals' willingness or ability to carry out self-enhancing actions is to consider these variables as falling into one of three categories:

1. Variables that relate to individuals' *awareness.*
2. Variables that relate to hope or *intention.*
3. Variables that relate to *knowledge or behavioral skill.*

Table 5.1 presents and elaborates on these categories and traces general strategies and specific interventions that can foster self-enhancement ability and activity.

Table 5.1 SELF-ENHANCEMENT: DETERMINANTS AND INTERVENTIONS

Individual-Based Determinant	Awareness of need for self-enhancement	Intention to take self-enhancing action	Skills required for self-enhancing
Strategy	Consciousness raising	Instilling hope, commitment	Empowerment
Focus of Specific Interventions	• Problem recognition (consciousness) • Possession of information relevant to the problem • Understanding of relevant information	• Hope • Commitment to act	• Skill acquisition • Ability to transfer and elaborate skills

Using the group counseling context to affect individuals' awareness, intentions, and skills is, of course, a broader matter than merely promoting self-enhancement. In this book, however, a major concern is to identify how generic group counseling processes and activities can be put to work to further group members' ability to take actions that will improve their status *vis-a-vis* their needs, interests, and rights.

Contextual Determinants of Self-Enhancement

Kurt Lewin's (1951) concept of *life space* has three major facets: the "me" (the individual's awareness of his or her physical and nonphysical self), the "not me" (the environment) and the "foreign hull" (those aspects of the current context of which the individual is not aware). Lewinian perspectives also hold that, in all but the most intellectually limited or emotionally regressed individuals, the "not me" (the context) is experienced as a differentiated phenomenon; parts of the environment are differentiated from each other (e.g., this chair is different from that suitcase), and the perceptual process imposes patterns and relationships upon these otherwise separate parts of the context (e.g., this chair and that sofa in the other room are both furniture).

One of the most general ways to organize the context is to posit two broad categories: the physical environment and the social environment. The *physical environment* consists of the nonhuman (animate and inanimate) objects and derivative processes (e.g., weather, distance) that constitute the life space. The *social environment* is made up of human beings and their actions (e.g., my mate, social support, condemnation) that the individual perceives as part of the present setting.

The Physical Context and Self-Enhancement As technology advances, people increasingly acquire the ability to transcend, or at least lessen, many of the limits formerly posed by the physical environment. For example, distances that in past eras reduced or eliminated options for action, assistance, and understanding can now be bridged through physical travel and electronic information exchange. In spite of technological advancement, however, one cannot completely escape the influence of his or her physical setting. A malfunctioning automobile, furnace, or elevator is a quick reminder of the fragility of the technological buffer that insulates people from the demands of physical reality.

Individuals and groups with restricted access to relevant technology are most apt to be affected by limitations imposed by the physical context. For example, living in a rural area does not necessarily eliminate alternatives for action. An automobile, a fax machine, a telephone, a computer, and a modem can put a rural dweller in touch with extensive information networks and well placed helpers. But if rural residence is accompanied by lack of access to supportive technological resources, tasks such as gaining necessary information, communicating needs and views, and locating and mobilizing the assistance of others can be problematic.

One of the unique benefits of the group setting is the opportunity it allows individuals to exchange, and pool, needed information. Isolated individuals (whether their isolation comes from the lack of transportation and communication resources accompanying rurality or from the anomie and sense of personal danger found in deteriorated urban settings) often are not even aware of the existence of others who share their concerns. Physical isolation, too, can cut off information about the alternatives available for constructive, self-enhancing action. The group setting, involving as it does the gathering of people, can reduce members' physical isolation, allowing them to gain access to information about the nature, scope, and remediation of their concerns.

Social Contexts and Self-Enhancement   Although the physical environment sometimes complicates self-enhancement action, the social context usually is a more important consideration, because a person's most important primary and secondary needs typically are mediated by the characteristics and processes of the social context. For instance, in modern life, access to food is apt to depend more on a person's relationship to others (family members, employers) than on the vagaries of climate and soil conditions in the area.

Social contexts can affect self-enhancement activity in a variety of ways. Two mechanisms found in social contexts are of particular interest to group leaders: social norms and social support.

Social Norms   Defining culture as a set of meanings that group members hold in common, Olmsted (1959) suggested that group norms can be considered an aspect of culture. Norms embody the group's position regarding the correct understanding of, and response to, situations. With regard to self-enhancement, group norms of special note are those that relate to defining:

— what an individual's proper rights and interests are.
— what actions are appropriate in the pursuit of self-enhancement.

Norms relating to the nature and scope of individual rights can have a notable impact on determining when self-enhancement is appropriate. If, for example, a group's norms hold that members of a particular gender or religious or ethnic group should not work in a certain discipline, even the objects of this discrimination may not be able to perceive that rights and interests are being usurped. Much of what has been called consciousness raising can be understood as the process of sensitizing unaware individuals to how existing norms work against their interests. Self-help approaches to combating racism, sexism, ageism, and other forms of exploitation often begin with those affected people developing an understanding of how existing norms work against their interests. Without this awareness, they are likely to view self-enhancement as irrelevant or inappropriate. Similarly, without a change in group norms concerning the appropriate limits of rights, individuals acting upon their own view of what is proper are likely to earn labels such as "uppity," "unappreciative," "selfish," or "dangerous."

One of the most valuable functions of self-help groups is to provide individuals a context with norms that (unlike those of the broader social context) are more supportive of what they believe their needs and interest are. For example, self-help groups of stigmatized or exploited individuals confirm that their difficulties are not all of their own making. Also, the self-help group can reinforce the view that members need to be accepted, be treated with equity, and receive assistance are reasonable. The shifting of one's normative referents is a central part of consciousness-raising efforts.

Even given general acceptance of the appropriateness of self-enhancement, norms can limit and shape the actions individuals might take in furthering their rights and interests. For instance, the deliberate, circumspect process of working through channels might be considered commendable whereas confrontive strategies such as picketing or presenting a list of nonnegotiable demands may be condemned as inappropriate. Again, the company of others who are in the same boat can reinforce individuals who are pursuing a confrontive, high-profile strategy to promote their interests. Collective will and support can offer members alternatives with the potential to budge the status quo and move it in the direction of needed change.

Social Support Shumaker and Brownell's (1984) view that social support is a resource whose function is to help individuals cope with life demands overlaps many other positions found in the literature. Supporters "support" by providing resources individuals need in attempting to deal with a wide range of ordinary and extraordinary problematic life events.

Social norms can exert a powerful influence on one's willingness to offer supportive assistance. If a person's self-enhancement efforts are viewed as inappropriate, relatives and peers are apt to be indifferent to (or perhaps even oppose) entreaties for support. Thus, young adults who assert what they believe are their valid interests in the employment setting may be viewed by co-workers as trouble makers or overstepping their "place." Rather than supporting their self-assertion, co-workers may react with ridicule or ostracism.

Further, support may not be forthcoming from the informal social network because of supporter-based deficiencies (Pearson, 1990). These people may lack the inclination to be supportive or may not have the skills, information, or resources needed to help individuals undertake self-enhancing activity. For example, the parents of an adolescent, Bob, might approve of his efforts to assert his interests in the face of stereotyping and discrimination in an educational setting because of his epilepsy, but lack information, skills, and material resources needed to take self-enhancement action. Thus, despite their supportive intentions, the parents have limited ability to offer support.

Elsewhere (Pearson, 1983) I have termed support groups "surrogate support systems" that provide individuals with emotional and material support not available from the informal support network because of *network-based barriers* (e.g., supporter's lack of willingness or skills) rather than because of the operation of *barriers in those individuals* (e.g., the individual's lack of skill or information, or dysfunctional attitudes). In the latter case (support deficiency stemming from person-based barriers), I suggest traditional individual and small-group counseling or psychotherapy interventions.

GROUP COUNSELING AND SELF-ENHANCEMENT

The process and (to a lesser extent) content of counseling groups can be directed specifically to the goal of promoting members' movement toward effective self-enhancement. Referring back to Table 5.1, the *process* can contribute to: (a) members' awareness of the need for self-enhancement (consciousness raising); (b) strengthening members' intention to take self-enhancing action (instilling hope/commitment); and (c) helping members acquire or improve the knowledge and skills required for self-enhancement (empowerment). The *content* of group interaction, too, can contribute to members' self-enhancement skills. As examples, groups can provide information that is useful in pursuing one's interests, and "packages" blending materials and activities that further members' skills in domains such as self-assertion, decision making, or self-esteem can strengthen self-enhancement efforts. In any case, the process dimension of group life is generic, found across groups, whatever their content and desired outcomes.

Group process requires a focus on *how* group goals are pursued. It relates to the characteristics of the instrument (group activities and events) through which the group seeks to achieve its purposes. For example, the process of one counseling group might be described as tightly tied to the decisions of a central leader who pursues the group's goals by closely adhering to a predetermined agenda. The process of another counseling group might be described as featuring someone who fills a position called "leader" but who really seems to exert no more influence than any other group member as the group moves from activity to activity in an apparently spontaneous, unplanned fashion.

As McLuhan (1964) and others have pointed out, characteristics of the medium through which communication takes place often have a strong impact upon the communication itself. Similarly, the characteristics of the process through which a group pursues its ends can have a powerful influence upon group outcomes. Thus, process is not unrelated to outcome; rather, it can influence what, and to what degree, outcomes will be achieved.

Dorothy Nolte's (1989) insightful poem "Children Learn What They Live" explores the connection between the process and outcome of child rearing. Three stanzas of that poem seem particularly relevant to counseling as a means of fostering individuals' self-enhancement ability:

> *If children live with encouragement,*
> *They learn confidence.*
>
> *If children live with security,*
> *They learn to have faith.*
>
> *If children live with approval,*
> *They learn to like themselves.*
>
> (pp. 95–96)

More directly focused upon counseling, Rogers and other relationship-oriented theorists and practitioners have taken a similar position—that the process of the helping relationship should reflect the goals of those in counseling. If counseling seeks to move individuals toward greater self-acceptance, the group leader's behavior, then, should reflect a high level of acceptance of the person. Similarly, if group leaders hope for greater self-direction and autonomy in group members as an outcome of group work, the process should offer opportunities for the members to enter into decision making that determines group activity and outcome.

If group leaders accept the "process shapes outcome" thesis, the examination of group counseling as a vehicle for fostering self-enhancement logically turns to a consideration of how major elements of group process—leadership and therapeutic mechanisms have been chosen for discussion here—can contribute to self-enhancement in the group counseling situation.

Leadership

In their review of the theory and research related to group leadership, Cartwright and Zander (1968) noted a movement away from considering leadership to be a specific person, or a position in a group's role structure, toward thinking of leadership as a function. Accordingly, leadership consists of any contribution (e.g., exerting influence, providing information, offering comfort, making suggestions) to the group's ability to achieve its goals.

The Functional Perspective   One of the most important consequences of viewing group leadership from a *functional perspective* is that it leads to the recognition that group leadership may be a *shared* function. Although only one person might conceivably provide all the many and varied resources a group needs to achieve its goals, a careful, unbiased examination of group life more likely will reveal that a number of members (at any given point, or across longer time frames) are actually contributing to the group's success. Even in groups that do not explicitly espouse a shared leadership pattern, members other than the designated leader quietly carry out actions that can be considered leadership from the functional perspective.

A functional view of leadership also veers away from the traditional view that all leaders are a certain type of person (e.g., charismatic, powerful) doing similar things (e.g., directing, coordinating, evaluating) in all groups. Rather, the functional perspective holds that as group goals and resources vary, so will the content and structure of leadership. Thus, leadership in a task-oriented group with only one person who possesses the information and skills upon which group success rests is apt to be very different from a person-oriented group with many members who have the resources needed to foster and support personal growth.

Group-centered leadership is one of the most conspicuous features of self-help groups. Even in groups that adhere to a "leader of the meeting" format, the "leader" clearly is an equal among equals, having no special prerogatives or influence (Levy, 1979). Designating one member as the leader does not interfere with the group's usual manner of pursuing its goal (peer-based help).

These groups, then, stand as good examples of the implementation (by design, chance, or intuition) of a function-centered, shared model of leadership. They have as their basis a self-help model of assistance that ". . . emphasizes empowerment, self-determination, mutuality, [the] noncommodity character of help, prosumerism, antibig, antibureaucratic, and experiential wisdom, among other values" (Borkman, 1990, p. 328). That they are also powerful contributors to the development of self-enhancement-relevant resources such as social support, hope, self-esteem, and skill acquisition should make the leadership processes of self-help groups of interest to group leaders. Can any principles and practices, gleaned from an examination of the leadership function in these groups, be extrapolated to the group counseling situation in which a concern for supporting members' movement toward self-enhancement is central?

The Group Leader as Facilitator   Like it or not, group members *will* try to be helpful to each other. Though professional eyes may see these helping efforts as ineffective (at best) or noxious (at worst), it is virtually impossible to keep members from comforting, giving advice, confronting, or otherwise taking a host of actions that their inclinations and experience cause them to believe will be helpful. Flying in the face of the assumptions of many professional help models, self-help groups place untutored peer help center stage as the method through which growth is to be achieved (Hurvitz, 1970). Most of these groups have no continuing, formal leadership structure.

Though counseling groups are characterized to varying extents by self-help, and peer-based helping processes, a counseling group is not a self-help group (Borkman, 1990, Pearson, 1983). However much professionally trained leaders take a group-centered stance and stress the commonality with group members, professional ethics and (perhaps) institutional role stamp us as special people, with special responsibilities, in the group. Inescapably, counseling groups have a formal, designated leader.

Even though the reality of this formal role means leaders will never be (or ought to be) simply group members, they can take a range of positions regarding their extent of control in groups. If leaders focus upon growth in clients' self-enhancement ability as a goal for group work, leaders should move toward a functionally oriented, shared view of group leadership. This allows leaders to bring to counseling groups some of the benefits of self-help groups by strengthening members' self-enhancement ability. In doing so, the leader should function primarily as a facilitator, to allow members to express their self-directing and self-help resources within the group. This can be achieved by:

— communicating (implicitly and explicitly) to group members a functional, shared perspective on group leadership.
— pursuing a general strategy of power sharing by encouraging members to enter into decisions about the group's life.
— identifying existing member resources (e.g., information, feedback, acceptance, caring, material assistance) that can help the group move toward its goals, and encouraging members to provide those resources to the group.
— helping members fill gaps in their own resources by supporting development of skills needed for group progress (e.g., listening skills, understanding, and skills needed for effective group management) and, again, encouraging them to contribute these newly developed resources to the group.

As a facilitator, the group leader seeks to support and empower group members (as individuals and as a group) in pursuing their growth. The leader acts as a stimulus and a resource rather than as an expert who takes responsibility for members' conduct and learning. As in self-help groups, members' ability to manage themselves and contribute to each other's growth is supported. Concomitantly, leaders would expect group members to reap the benefit of the increased self-esteem typically associated with taking increased responsibility for, and initiative in, pursuit of their own growth (Reissman, 1990).

Therapeutic Mechanisms

Yalom (1985), building on an earlier schema of Corsini and Rosenberg (1955), identified 11 basic mechanisms that can be considered the source of growth in therapeutic groups. Ranging from the relatively concrete categories of "information sharing" and "development of socializing techniques" to the much more abstract "universality" (recognition that one's difficulties and concerns are shared by others), these mechanisms are basic processes in group life that promote and support members' movement toward greater effectiveness. All of the basic therapeutic mechanisms Yalom described would be expected to be observed (in some form and to some degree) in any effective personal growth-oriented group. The concern here, however, is with processes that have the most potential in developing, or furthering, members' self-enhancement ability.

Referring to the view (presented in Table 5.1) that self-enhancement rests upon awareness, intention, and skill, I believe that of the therapeutic mechanisms identified by Yalom, those most central to the quest for self-enhancement are: universality, instilling hope, altruism, identification/modeling, and group cohesiveness.

Universality   Perhaps even before a person can hope for change, he or she has to be aware that change is necessary. Whether one's problem comes from individual adjustment difficulties (e.g., substance abuse) or stems from external sources (e.g., racial, ethnic, sexual, or age discrimination), constructive action to resolve the problem is not apt to start until the individual acknowledges that a problem exists.

Consciousness raising groups seek to help members recognize and affirm that the status quo is not responding to their interests and needs. The status quo may reflect the way a city government operates or how male-female relationships are structured in a marriage. Raising awareness often demands more than simply presenting data confirming a situation of exploitation, neglect, or personal dysfunction. Denial and avoidance processes operating in individuals can make it difficult for them to recognize a problem. Also, habituation can make it hard for people to step far enough out of their situations to see that a string of chronic, but minor, hassles of scattered individuals are part of a broader pattern of societal discrimination.

The group setting can contribute to consciousness raising through a format that explicitly centers upon relating personal experience and presenting objective information about exploitive or discriminatory situations and patterns. Data about inequity in applying and enforcing of laws can help people realize that individual or collective action is needed to protect their interests. Personal accounts of individuals who have recognized their disadvantage and acted to oppose it can spur group members to examine their own life situations for possible inequity and disrespect.

Even in groups that do not focus explicitly upon consciousness raising, a considerable amount of this basic process can be expected. Voicing and exchanging life experiences are at the heart of the group process. This exchange provides a rich opportunity for individuals to observe patterns and issues that run across the experience of the separate members. As other group members tell their stories, a woman may realize that her personal experience of sexual harassment at work is not an isolated occurrence but, rather, part of a widespread pattern many women face in many different work situations. Similarly, a child in a support group for elementary students in divorcing families can, as member after member talks about feeling powerless and ignored, come to realize that as personal the pain of family disruption is, others share it; it is a problem out there and not of his or her making.

The process of universalization counteracts the sense of isolation and uniqueness that people in conflict and suffering often feel (Levy, 1979). Being with others who are in the same boat often causes people to feel that, at last, they are understood and accepted. Groups can give individuals access to new norms and points of comparison that make their concerns and difficulties seem less abnormal. In addition, the recognition of commonality can help group members become aware that their own difficulties are only a part of a broader problem. Understanding that one's problem is an instance of a more general pattern serves to demystify and deintensify the problem. It also can form the basis for individual and collective action to deal with that problem. The group setting can be a vehicle for instrumental activity, as well as a channel for expressing one's understandings, feelings, and aspirations.

Instilling Hope   Heightening the expectation that improvement will come is common to curing interventions across a wide range of cultural contexts (Frank, 1961). The often noted potency of placebo treatment can be traced to the patient's expectation of improvement. Frank observed that one of the most common ways of increasing hope is to have a high-prestige person sanction, or be involved in, the helping intervention. Generalizing this phenomenon to the group setting leads to the desirability of gaining the support and approval of influential people in our group efforts. Another tack would be to enhance the leader's prestige to group members to strengthen the intervention.

Self-help groups are different in the sense that hope comes from observing fellow sufferers who have been able to benefit from participation in the group (Hurvitz, 1970; Levy, 1979). Self-help groups have implicit and explicit processes for building hope in group members. In groups following the 12-step model, the emphasis upon recovery as a continuing process rather than an outcome results in members' being at various stages of recovery, from the "first timer" to the veteran with many years of abstinence, at any given meeting. The opportunity for members to see and interact with peers who have gone through the same struggles implicitly teaches that people do get better, that there is hope. As Hurvitz (1970) noted: "The continued participation by those peers who have been helped by the fellowship supports the expectations of new members that they will receive the help they need and serves as a self-fulfilling prophesy" (p. 46).

More explicitly, self-help groups present direct messages of hope to members. When new members hear a veteran say, "The program does work; the fact that I have been able to turn my life around is testimony to its power—work it!" they gain hope for a way out of their seemingly insurmountable difficulties. When members of a TOPS group see the before-and-after pictures of their group leader, they are supported in their hope that the program can also help them shed their unwanted weight.

Awareness of a problem leads to despair unless that awareness is coupled with hope for a solution to the problem. Any group that seeks to bolster members' self-enhancement resources and activities would do well to pay attention to the processes and procedures through which self-help groups instill hope in their members. Counseling groups that operate with an open-ended, continuing framework (members move into and out of the group as individuals rather than having all members start and end the group at the same time) have a built-in possibility for new members to associate with others who are farther along in the growth process. A format that provides opportunities for "veterans" to talk about their trials and successes can make explicit the implicit message, "People can change; things can get better." Groups that have a closed format might provide for a hope-instilling mechanism by having successful "graduates" of the group return to share their stories.

Altruism   The power of altruism (contributing to the well-being of others) to promote growth in the helper has been widely noted. Frank (1961) cited the curative value of altruism as a principle common to healing procedures in a wide range of cultural settings. Reissman (1965) and Levy (1979) have highlighted the positive value of altruism to the helper, and what might be called a "growth through helping" principle underlying the potency of self-help groups. More recently, Reissman (1990), noting that the role of "help receiver" tends to corrode individuals' feelings of competence and adequacy, has suggested mutual help as an appropriate paradigm for human services in the 1990s. He chided that in most professionally led helping interventions (e. g., counseling, psychotherapy), the help receiver is cast in a role of passivity and inadequacy:

> Besides these iatrogenic difficulties inherent in the helpee's role, the recipient of help is automatically deprived of the benefits accruing to the helper: increased status and self-esteem, the so-called "helpers high" (Luks, 1988), and all the specific helping mechanisms involved in learning through teaching and the helper therapy principle. . . . (p. 222)

Reissman asserted that making peer help and cooperation a central part of the ethos of the helping group strengthens the "growth through helping mechanism" of an intervention. In a counseling group, the benefits of helping can be furthered in a number of ways, some of which relate to the leader's attitudes and values, others more with procedural issues.

Perhaps the most important influence in determining the level of peer-to-peer assistance is the extent to which the group leader is willing to sanction and encourage peer-to-peer help rather than considering it to be an annoying, negative influence. Many group leaders neglect the possible benefits of peer help, either because they do not recognize its therapeutic potential or because they see it as a mechanism that is detrimental to their own impact upon the group.

A functionally oriented, shared model of group leadership encourages peer help. Recognizing that many of the resources needed for group progress may be distributed among members can counterbalance unexamined assumptions about the uniqueness and unmatched efficacy of professional help that preparation programs of helping professionals spawn or do little to temper (Reissman, 1990). The group leader should realistically assess the helping resources that group members have, rather than assuming that because they "need help," they are devoid of helping resources.

Furthermore, the group leader will encourage members to be involved with each others' growth and make sure that the flow of members' helping resources is not obstructed by an assumption that the group belongs to the leader—an assumption that causes members to think their proper role is to be passive recipients of the expert's efforts. As the leader moves toward considering leadership as a group function, a process is set in motion that results in group members becoming "prosumers" (producers) in the helping process. Reissman (1990) described the prosumer model of help as promoting reciprocity, destigmatizing the negative attitude toward receiving help, empowering help-receivers, and forming communities.

When observing genuine gaps in members' helping resources, the leader should consider ways of helping members develop and gain access to those resources. This may be as indirect as modeling good listening skills, with the assumption that it will stimulate members to gradually acquire that valuable group resource. Or it may be explicit. For example, the leader might stop group interaction to give a mini-lecture on how to impart and receive feedback, or make a process observation on the characteristic decision-making strategy the group is using, then encourage members to examine the consequences of, and alternatives to, that strategy.

The ideologically based reasons for adopting self-help groups' reliance on peer help are many. As we have seen, there are also many therapeutically-based reasons. As important as ideological and therapeutic considerations are, however, the group leader must recognize that supporting and encouraging altruism will increase the likelihood that the group experience will be empowering and competence-building for group members. One broad benefit of this empowerment may well be improved attitudes, intentions, and skills members need to pursue self-enhancement.

Identification and Modeling   If leaders direct their attention to the inadequacies and dysfunctionalities of group members, the observation that those members identify with one another and use each other as models will be cause for alarm. The concern that group members will "just sit around and reinforce each others' pathology" accompanies a view of group process in which the leader is the primary therapeutic resource, bearing the responsibility of countering the pathogenic possibilities of member-to-member contact.

Clearly, self-help groups take a different stance regarding peer influence. Instead of being concerned that member-to-member influence will be negative, the self-help-group is founded on the assumption that peers can help each other toward resolving their difficulties. Powell (1987) has pinpointed peer-based modeling as a central growth-enhancing mechanism of self-help groups. People at different levels of "recovery" (a term used here to refer to movement away from a wide range of dysfunctional conditions) demonstrate the wide range of relevant models.

> The prospective imitator usually will be encouraged by the differences among models. Variety increases the chance that he or she can match an effective pattern. The success experienced by models also encourages imitation. For even before imitation occurs, the prospective imitator-member shares vicariously in the success of the model. To the extent prospective imitators perceive important similarities to the model, they will be encouraged. (Reissman & Gartner, 1987, p. 110)

Identification and modeling in self-help groups clearly can influence a myriad of attitudes and behavior. Members can "catch" functional attitudes such as hope, perseverance, concern for others, patience, and existential equanimity. Also, members can glean from other members specific coping strategies such as asking for help, publicly admitting failures, and substituting constructive for destructive behaviors. How can identification and modeling be extrapolated to a group that seeks to promote members' self-enhancement?

If group members are to acquire the awareness, intentions, and skills that support self-enhancement, the group has to include individuals who can successfully model those attitudes and behaviors. A continuing, open-ended group format extends the range of models available to group members. A "self-help ethos" (Reissman & Gartner, 1987) emphasizing members' responsibility to both offer and receive help may help them view their "work" in the group as continuing well after they have attained some success in resolving the difficulties that brought them to the group. Simply the presence of these successful veterans, who are now getting on with their lives, looking after their interests, can provide new members with models for growth. Moreover, explicitly casting these members in the role of mentors and guides can highlight the cluster of behaviors and attitudes called self-enhancement.

The group leader who works in a closed format will have to be creative in broadening the range of models available to group members. Inviting back successful graduates of earlier groups to interact with members may be helpful. And the possibility of involving veterans (and other good models) in a "sponsor program," based on the practice (in 12-step groups) of linking new members with individuals who are farther along in the recovery process might be explored. However it is done, recognizing the power of identification and modeling in self-help groups alerts group leaders to ways of getting a piece of the action in professionally led groups.

Group Cohesiveness   According to Cartwright and Zander (1968), group cohesiveness varies as a function of the extent to which group members perceive the group as an effective vehicle for satisfying their needs. As members increasingly believe they need the group, they are more attracted to it. Cartwright and Zander also asserted that one of the consequences of group cohesiveness is enhanced member receptivity to group influence. Evidence of the influence of a cohesive group can be seen in group members' attitudinal and behavioral homogeneity with regard to issues and situations relevant to the group's operation. Because the group is important to its members (i.e., the satisfaction of important needs is, at least to some extent, dependent upon the group), they tend to want to meet group expectations.

By accepting and continuing membership in a group, individuals accept a body of norms that often differs markedly from those of the broader social context. For example, the counseling or psychotherapy group's stance that taking the risk of talking about one's inadequacies and vulnerabilities is good, even necessary, departs widely from the everyday wisdom embodied in caution-endorsing sayings such as "better to be quiet and thought a fool than to speak and be known as one" or "don't air your dirty linen in public." As people enter more and more deeply into what Hurvitz (1970) called the "fellowship" of a self-help group, their membership in that group becomes a stronger influence in defining who they are, what they do, and what they will do. The group becomes a new reference group for them.

Besides this exposure to growth-enhancing influence, a cohesive group provides a strong sense of belonging. Though self-help groups can be confrontive in identifying and criticizing dysfunctional behavior, the fact that criticism comes from peers—others who are, or have been, in the same circumstances—can, paradoxically, heighten the sense of being with others who really understand and care.

This is apt to be true especially if the self-help group is one that Killilea (1976) has characterized as an organization of "the deviant and stigmatized" (p. 61). In groups such as these, the sense of fellowship is more than just a general feeling of being with others who have problems, too. Self-help groups whose members share the experience of rejection, stigmatization, and (often) discrimination bond tightly to form a powerful new reference group, one in which individuals can compare themselves with others and gain "consensual validation leading to a reduction or elimination of members' uncertainty and sense of isolation or uniqueness regarding their problems and experiences" (Levy, 1979, p. 254).

In addition to the cohesiveness fostered by meeting members' *expressive* needs (e.g., to be accepted, or to express their feelings and beliefs openly), many self-help groups are attractive to members because they serve the *instrumental* need to change an unresponsive or noxious social context. Support groups for parents of children with handicapping conditions, for example, not only offer understanding and acceptance, but also they often become instruments for self-advocacy and social/political action as well. Collective action to make the community, school, or corporation more responsive to members' interests can produce a powerful sense of community that increases members' sense of belonging, self-esteem, and personal efficacy. Thus, group cohesiveness is both contributor to, and consequence of, acquiring the awareness, hope, and skill upon which self-enhancement rests.

Some groups may be composed of individuals (e.g., obese adolescents, women in traditionally male-dominated occupations, adults with handicapping conditions, students from recently immigrated families) who are collectively affected by negative attitudes and actions in the social setting. These homogeneous groups may serve a dual purpose: to meet members' expressive needs and to support instrumental action. The group is a place where emotional needs are met, and it also can be an impetus for members to consider, and act upon, the need to influence their nonsupportive social context.

The group solidarity that fosters sharing of a specific difficulty can heighten members' awareness that their interests are being violated, instill hope for positive change, and facilitate acquisition of knowledge and skills needed for self-enhancing activity. In groups that explore the relationship between individuals' suffering and societal influences, the line between the personal and the political tends to disappear. When members realize that much of their individual difficulty results from a system that disregards (or deliberately works against) their interests, subsequent political action, supported by collective strength, becomes an act of personal growth.

In heterogeneous groups, attraction to the group can be based on the actuality that the group helps its members meet expressive needs. These groups, though lacking the strong sense of common identity that pervades a homogeneous group, can still generate considerable cohesiveness simply by members' recognizing that amidst their diversity runs a commonality—trying to learn how to deal more effectively with life concerns.

Garden variety, heterogeneous groups can also serve an instrumental function for their members. Even though group members have different specific goals and target their actions on different people or settings, a sense of mutuality can develop. Group members can become directly involved in the progress of one another. They can be enlisted in helping each other gain the beliefs, knowledge, and skills needed for self-enhancement. The "opening go-round" ritual of some groups, in which members report on their progress or lack thereof (such as the "weighing in" procedure of weight control self-help groups) is an example of how groups can formalize member-to-member involvement in each others' progress. Progress can be reinforced, and failures can be confronted, then examined to determine what went wrong, and what information, skill, or resource might be needed.

CONCLUSION

Fostering self-enhancement has an honorable place in the history of counseling. It is still alive, well, and growing, not only because of longstanding societal prizing of independence and self-direction but also because of the vigor contributed by a more recent phenomenon, self-help groups.

The cross-fertilization of professionally led groups and peer self-help groups should be a mark of respect for the power and versatility of the self-help group movement rather than the opening moves of a strategy of cooptation. Self-help groups do very well on their own. People make their way to them not only because these groups are often more available (physically and psychologically) than professionally led groups but also because they have virtues beyond the reach of counseling, psychotherapy, or case work groups. Self-help groups are not substitutes for, or pale reflections of, the "real thing." Among their many values is that they happen to be good vehicles for people to grow in self-enhancement ability.

Even though the process, content, and outcome of self-help groups and counseling groups may overlap considerably, the two are quite different. Group leaders who pursue the goal of promoting self-enhancement ability in members can borrow from self-help groups, make referrals to them, perhaps even act as resources for them. But no one benefits from attempting to blur the distinctions between these two group forms.

SUMMARY

Self-enhancement is a valid focus in counseling. It can be linked to some of the most fundamental theoretical, philosophical, and pragmatic underpinnings of counseling practice, especially counseling in the context of dominant American culture. Individuals' willingness and ability to engage in self-enhancement varies as a function of their own characteristics, and of properties in the physical and social contexts within which they live. The processes of formal groups (support, counseling) and informal groups (families, peers, co-workers) can inhibit or foster individuals' self-enhancement.

The growing influence of self-help groups attests to their appeal in fostering self-enhancement ability in group members. This can be perceived as a worthy outcome of any counseling group experience as well, so group leaders should note relevant aspects that might be incorporated into professionally led groups.

Increasing self-enhancement in group members is influenced by the style of leadership from a functional standpoint (in which a role of facilitator and shared leadership are suggested), and the therapeutic mechanisms of universality, instilling hope, altruism, identification and modeling, and group cohesiveness. These elements, common to self-help groups, are infused in professionally led groups by the leader's sensitivity and action relating to the overlapping dynamics of the two types of groups.

REFERENCES

Allport, G. W. (1962). Psychological models for guidance. *Harvard Educational Review, 4*, 373–381.

Attneave, C. N. (1976). Social networks as the unit of intervention. In P. J. Guerrin (Ed.), *Family therapy: Theory and practice* (pp. 220–232). New York: Gardner Press.

Bellah, R. N., Madsen, R., Sullivan, W. M., Swidler, A., & Tipton, S. M. (1985). *Habits of the heart: Individualism and commitment in American life.* Berkeley: University of California Press.

Borkman, T. (1990). Self-help groups at the turning point: Emerging egalitarian alliances with the formal health care system? *American Journal of Community Psychology, 18*(2), 321–332.

Cartwright, D., & Zander, A. (1968). *Group dynamics: Research and theory* (3rd ed.). New York: Harper and Row.

Conyne, R. K. (1987). *Primary prevention counseling: Empowering people and systems.* Muncie, IN: Accelerated Development.

Corsini, R., & Rosenberg, B. (1955). Mechanisms in group psychotherapy: Processes and dynamics. *Journal of Abnormal Social Psychology, 51*, 406–411.

Frank, J. (1961). *Persuasion and healing.* Baltimore: Johns Hopkins Press.

Goble, F. G. (1970). *The third force: The psychology of Abraham Maslow.* New York: Grossman Publishers.

Heller, K. (1979). The effects of social support: Prevention and treatment implications. In A. P. Goldstein & F. H. Kanfer (Eds.), *Maximizing treatment gains: Transfer enhancement in psychotherapy* (pp. 335–382). New York: Academic Press.

Hurvitz, N. (1970). Peer self-help psychotherapy groups and their implications for psychotherapy. *Psychotherapy: Theory, Research, and Practice, 7*(1), 41–49.

Killilea, M. (1976). Mutual help organizations: Interpretations in the literature. In G. Caplan & M. Killilea (Eds.), *Support systems and mutual help: Multidisciplinary explorations* (pp. 37–93). New York: Grune & Stratton.

Levy, L. H. (1979). Process and activities in groups. In M. A. Lieberman & L. D. Borman (Eds.), *Self-help groups for coping with crisis* (pp. 234–271). San Francisco: Jossey-Bass.

Lewin, K. (1951). *Field theory in social science.* New York: Harper.

Luks, A. (1988). Helper's high. *Psychology Today*, pp. 39–42.

McLuhan, M. (1964). *Understanding media: The extensions of man.* New York: McGraw-Hill.

Nolte, D. L. (1989). Children learn what they live. In Z. Zigler, *Raising Positive Kids in a Negative World* (pp. 95–96). New York: Ballantine Books.

Olmsted, M. S. (1959). *The small group.* New York: Random House.

Pattison, E. M. (1973). Social system of psychotherapy. *American Journal of Psychotherapy, 18*, 396–409.

Pearson, R. E. (1983). Social groups: A conceptualization. *Personnel & Guidance Journal, 61*(6), 361–364.

Pearson, R. E. (1990). *Counseling and social support: Perspectives and practice.* Newbury Park, CA: Sage Publications.

Powell, T. J. (1987). *Self-help organizations and professional practice.* Silver Spring, MD: National Association of Social Workers.

Reissman, F. (1965). The "helper" therapy principle. *Social Work, 10*, 27–32.

Reissman, F. (1990). Restructuring help: A human services paradigm for the 1990s. *American Journal of Community Psychology, 18*(3), 221–230.

Reissman, F., & Gartner, A. (1987). The surgeon general and the self-help ethos. *Social Policy, 18*, 23–25.

Rogers, C. R. (1942). *Counseling and psychotherapy: New concepts in practice.* Boston: Houghton Mifflin.

Rogers, C. R. (1989). Toward a modern approach to values: The valuing process in the mature person. In H. Kirschenbaum & V. L. Henderson (Eds.), *The Carl Rogers reader.* Boston: Houghton Mifflin.

Rueveni, U. (1979). *Networking families in crisis: Intervention strategies with families and social networks.* New York: Human Services Press.

Shumaker, S. A., & Brownell, A. (1984). Toward a theory of social support: Closing conceptual gaps. *Journal of Social Issues, 40*(4), 11–35.

Skinner, B. F. (1971). *Beyond freedom and dignity.* New York: Alfred A. Knopf.

Vattano, A. (1972). Power to the people: Self-help groups. *Social Work, 17*(4), 7–15.

Yalom, I. (1985). *The theory and practice of group psychotherapy* (3rd ed.). New York: Basic Books.

6

Group Counseling for People with Addictions

Jack Clark, Melissa Blanchard, and Charles W. Hawes

Groups are the primary treatment (modality) utilized in the chemical dependency (CD) treatment centers in America today. Over time, groups have prevailed over individual counseling because of their clinical efficacy and cost effectiveness. The literature is replete with examples of the clinical effectiveness of group work. Agazarian and Peters (1981) clearly illustrate the advantages over individual counseling, especially because chemically dependent individuals often express their symptoms in interpersonal terms.

Flores (1988) points out that a limitation operating within groups of chemically dependent individuals is the typical defensive style group members use to reinforce an individual's denial (a central operating element in the addiction process). This pervasive defensive style among group members requires the leader to be directive, at least in early stages of group development, utilizing this dynamic to the group's advantage. Despite the limitations imposed by the typical defensive style, multiple benefits accrue for group work, ranging from the curative process that can be tapped within a group to the power of the group to influence the behavior of its members.

Cost effectiveness of groups over individual sessions is explained by simple mathematics. A single counselor can see six to eight clients in a 1½- to 2-hour period versus treating corresponding numbers of clients individually, the latter taking 6 to 8 hours of counselor time. Zimberg, Wallace, and Blume (1985) argue that this is only partially true because of associated time-consuming activities including, but not limited to, screening, family conferences, arranging for other services participants may require, record keeping, and allowing time before and after the group session for individual needs. In spite of these very real expenditures of counselor time, group work remains a cost effective method of treating the chemically dependent individual's specific counseling needs.

In this chapter, we attempt to blend the idealized empirical view with the pragmatic, practice-based perspective. As this is only an overview, additional education, training, and experience are necessary to fully appreciate the complexities associated with group work with chemically dependent individuals.

GROUP CONSTRUCTION

Group construction with groups of chemically dependent individuals is multifaceted and requires the group leader to have a clear picture of the generalized purpose the group will have. Feeders (third parties) provide a significant amount of the funding for groups today, and subsequently influence length of treatment session, duration and type of group service purchased, and, to some degree, outcome goals. As a result, an open information exchange between parties concerned relative to purpose and intent is critical in preventing misunderstanding and confusion. Clarification of feeder source intent, time constraints, and population characteristics will begin to allow a picture of the generalized purpose of the group to surface.

Time constraints are imposed by counselor and client availability, as well as by group design. For example, a third party may wish to purchase didactic groups with an awareness of chemical dependency, versus insight into intra/interpersonal issues, as the outcome. As a result, the frequency, duration, format, content, and process would be designed to meet that goal and, subsequently, make different demands on clients and on counselors than another design would. Population characteristics such as age, background, level of functioning, motivation, and individual goals for treatment require comprehensive assessment, both at the onset of the treatment experience and on an ongoing basis.

Selection and Assessment

The selection process begins with assessment and leads to matching the client to available service. Once the service has been implemented, ongoing assessment allows for adjustment of service to specific client need, and it ensures appropriate placement of clients. The critical role that the initial and the ongoing assessments play is pointed out clearly in the work of Daley, Moss, and Campbell (1987), who state that in order to develop appropriate treatment goals, adequate assessment of the client's total functioning should be undertaken and viewed as ongoing.

Various assessment instruments are available to assist the group leader in the assessment process. Of particular value is the reliability and validity the assessment measures offer to an otherwise subjective process. A good example is the Addiction Severity Index (ASI), a comprehensive clinical and research instrument useful in assessing the severity of the problem in areas commonly affected in substance abuse populations (McLellan et al., 1985). This is a particularly useful measure when readministered at regular intervals as a means to determine clinical improvement. Another instrument that assesses a variety of problem areas is the Substance Abuse Problem Checklist (SAPC). It utilizes a self-administered 377-item checklist featuring problem statements from various functional areas of life (Carroll, 1983). In addition, the group leader may want to become acquainted with other assessment aids such as the Michigan Alcoholism Screening Test (MAST), the Drug Abuse Screening Test (DAST), and the McAndrews subscale of the Minnesota Multiphasic Personality Index (MMPI), as well as the many other useful assessment instruments available.

The assessment process is most effective when the group leader incorporates clinical interviews and assessment aids. The information gathered assists the group leader in determining the appropriateness of placement in specific groups and in directing the focus of treatment to problem areas.

Placement of individuals in groups, a process referred to as *grouping*, should be done with great care. Levine (1979) states that no single activity on the part of the group leader can influence the nature and destiny of a counseling group as much as the selection and matching of individuals for membership. Levine elaborates that the potentials, limitations, and balance of a counseling group are inherent in its composition. *Homogeneity* (the ways members are similar) and *heterogeneity* (the ways members are different) are the two major considerations for mixing and matching members of a treatment group (Levine & Gallogly, 1985). Commonality of purpose, the capacity for insight, the level to which the chemical dependency has progressed, motivation to seek treatment, and degree of criminal justice system involvement all should be considered during the grouping process.

Other factors that may influence the group process within treatment groups are age, gender, racial, ethnic/cultural, and socioeconomic differences, and the capacity for relationships (Levine & Gallogly, 1985). The clinical interview and application of the assessment instrument yield valuable information that can enable a sound clinical decision on initial placement of an individual in a group. Ongoing assessment throughout the treatment process allows for adjustments if and when indicated. Adjustment may be necessary to fulfill the purpose of the group, through modification of structure or content, or to better match individuals to groups as new information surfaces.

Additional aspects to consider in this ongoing assessment process are how verbal or nonverbal an individual might be and how that relates to the group's general composition and purpose. A highly verbal, aggressive individual placed in a group of withdrawn individuals will dominate the group—a counterproductive dynamic. The level to which an individual can demonstrate self-control is worthy of consideration as well. A basic understanding and some degree of tolerance for impulsivity and acting out behaviors should be collectively present in the group if it has a member with a strong propensity to behave in this way. Mixing individuals who are significantly different in level of functioning can hamper group development and is generally not recommended. Occasionally the group leader has to operate under less than ideal conditions, of course, and with carefully applied skill can accomplish tasks consistent with available conditions.

Each member's expectations for the group, as well as the expected outcome, should be congruent, at least in a general sense, with group construction. Naturally, some disparity of expectations and hidden agendas will always be present, especially with group members who are coerced into treatment. With skill, understanding, empathy, and patience, however, the group leader and members can often break through deception and denial, when present, and evoke effective group process.

Treatment Conditions

Treatment conditions for a group vary and can be seen along a continuum from the most restrictive level to the least restrictive level of care. Included on this continuum are inpatient hospital, residential treatment centers, partial hospitalization/day care, intensive outpatient, outpatient/traditional, relapse prevention, aftercare, and a host of self-help support groups. The different types of treatment needs of individuals, their resources, and the specific treatment community resources are integral considerations in the selection process.

Historically, populations have tended to be categorized by the substance of abuse (alcohol or drug), with even further subdivision by specific type of drug. Within each of these exist even more subgroups, such as adult, adolescent, elderly. Carroll's (1986) work pointed out that, when demographics of age, race, and gender were controlled, research findings showed more similarities than differences among alcoholics, addicts, and poly-substance abusers with respect to personality needs, self-concept, psychopathology, and self-reported problems. Even so, recognizing the differences between individuals seeking treatment is useful, in order to be sensitive to the specific needs they represent. Of particular importance are issues relating to cultural and ethnic diversity, especially as they relate to group process.

The purpose and subsequent goals of group work with chemically dependent individuals vary, from personal goals of sobriety or other means of increasing level of functioning, to group work as a form of social control. Many paths lead people to seek treatment, and coercion—directly through the courts or indirectly through suggestion or implication—is playing an ever increasing role in the individual's motivation to seek treatment. This third-party influence on group work should be recognized, especially as it relates to group selection, process, and outcome. Groups that consist mostly of resistant, distrustful and angry court-referred individuals represent a much different dynamic and outcome than a more heterogeneously selected group.

Feeder sources supply individuals for groups. After screening and selection, groups are constructed to have outcomes consistent with the group composition. This process is most effective when all parties—the feeder source, the individuals making up the group, and the group leader—seek similar goals.

Balance between the ideal view and the pragmatic, practice-reality is the intent. Especially in agency or hospital practice, where the group leader operates within a program model under specific policies and procedures, the opportunity to freely construct groups may be limited. In these settings the group leader may be assigned previously established groups or be instructed to take on a group of clients currently registered in the program. This situation is not unusual in chemically dependent treatment programs.

Lack of control over group construction may give rise to problems in group development as well as accomplishment of the group's goals and objectives. Group work can and does take place under these conditions, but it may require more skill on the leader's part and also modification of group goals. Clinical supervision and staffing of difficult situations, usually available in hospital and in agency settings, assist in dealing with less than ideal circumstances.

Group Norms

Generally, group norms are established early in the group's development. These norms operate as a set of behavioral and ethical rules for the group.

The culture-building process within groups has critical significance to the ultimate functioning level of the group. The group leader's role is to shape this culture into one that will be conducive to a therapeutic process. Yalom (1975), who has written extensively on the critical nature of culture building within groups and the group leader's role in the process, points out the importance of this process by stating that, to a large extent, the group, rather than its leader alone, is the agent of change.

The idealized norms for chemical dependency groups are virtually identical to those for other types of groups: participation, nonjudgmental acceptance of others, self-disclosure, dissatisfaction with present behaviors, and the desire to change. Members should feel free to honestly express themselves, as well as to confront or question other members and the group leader. Yalom (1975) suggests that the group leader go about the important task of establishing norms "in an informed, deliberate manner" (p.110) to prevent counterproductive norms from developing. During the early stages of group development, and often throughout the group's tenure, the leader must take a directive stance to establish and reinforce norms.

In Yalom's (1985) work, he identifies two basic roles the group leader must assume in the group: (a) technical expert, and (b) model-setting participant. Both of these roles allow the leader to influence the shaping of the group's norms. Specific applications of these roles depend on the leader's particular clinical biases and personality, balanced by the group's composition and needs. In groups of chemically dependent individuals, the leader must shift back and forth, first providing information and guiding insight, then modeling open, empathic acceptance of others. The often discussed issue of confrontation, a critical function of chemical dependency treatment, occurs in the early stages of recovery, when the individual is in denial, and throughout the life of the group. This gives the leader an excellent opportunity to model appropriate methods of establishing personal boundaries and limit setting.

A norm specific to treatment/recovery groups is that of chemical/alcohol use. Norms must be established early in the group process to deal with members coming to group under the influence of chemicals. Specifically, will slips or relapse be tolerated and, if so, under what conditions? Acting out frustration, anger, authority issues, and so on, often result in reverting to chemical/alcohol use. The leader will have to assess the role the specific incident of chemical use might be playing in the total picture of the individual on both an intrapersonal and an interpersonal level, and differentiate use related to a relapse and use as a form of acting out behavior. The concrete, black-and-white thinking of group members may make this task less than simple. Group members may become uncomfortable or angry when other members fail to remain sober, regardless of the reason for it.

Relapse is a reality that usually is not expected but nonetheless happens with some frequency in groups of recovering individuals. Group leaders may see a lack of total abstinence as failure and blame either the individual or themselves. This kind of thinking results in anything from an increased dropout rate by members to discouraged, overly strict group leaders. The leader and the group members have to understand the reality of relapse and to incorporate this understanding into their established norms for behavior within the group. A plan of support should be established to deal with relapse. Group members and other supportive people (friends, family, employer, Alcoholics Anonymous sponsor) are some often-used sources of support during relapse crises. Having a group to bring the relapse experience back to, in order to share and understand and ultimately extinguish or prevent future relapses, is critical to the effectiveness of the group and the recovery process.

From time of inception to closure, the evolutionary process of the group will be dictated by the members and all they bring to the experience. The leader's personal self and professional self enter into this evolution. Whether an ideal self-monitoring, freely self-disclosing, and self-valuing group evolves depends not on any one part of the whole but on the whole itself.

PHYSIOLOGICAL, PSYCHOLOGICAL/COGNITIVE, AND SOCIOLOGICAL FACTORS

When working with addicted populations in groups, the leader must be prepared to handle a full range of presentations, defenses, and behaviors. Although similarities are inherent, stemming from the process of addiction, factors of a physiological, psychological/cognitive, and sociological nature produce many and varied presentations in recovering individuals. To successfully deal with this range of behaviors in the group is a challenge to the leader's expertise, experience, and knowledge of addiction. Group leaders need to have thorough knowledge of addiction, background factors, and physiological variables. In addition, they need clinical skills to handle disruptive or antitherapeutic defenses. Flexibility and insight are useful assets for the leader, to keep from being overwhelmed by the differences and also to help organize these presentations into a meaningful assessment and viable treatment plan for each group member.

Physiological Factors

Certain variables affecting recovery are physiological in origin and likely affect a large proportion of chemically dependent individuals. These neurophysiological similarities in chemically addicted people may be present regardless of whether the drug of choice is alcohol or any other variety of drugs.

Platelet MAO   Platelet MAO (monoamineoxidase), recognized as a stable biological marker in humans, has been linked to both chemical dependency and mental illness. MAO contributes to the breakdown of certain neurotransmitters including norepinephrine and dopamine. Studies have consistently shown lower platelet MAO levels in recovering alcoholics. The net result of lower levels of MAO is to increase the available amount of norepinephrine and dopamine. People with clinical depression have abnormal amounts of these neurotransmitters. Although monoamineoxidase inhibitors may be given as antidepressants, tricyclic antidepressants are most often prescribed because of the side effects associated with monoamineoxidase inhibitors in combination with certain foods. Altered MAO level is considered a factor in bipolar disorders, and increased dopamine activity has been thought to have a significant role in schizophrenia.

Behaviors associated with lowered levels of MAO are increased sensation seeking, extraversion, and avoidance of monotony (von Knorring, von Knorring, Smegan, Lingberg, & Edholm, 1987). Lowered MAO levels also might contribute to states such as agitation, anxiety, mood disturbance, and emotionality, which clinicians often observe in newly recovering individuals (Krippenstapel, 1987). These behaviors have direct relevance to those seen in groups and also are likely to be factors in relapse.

Teaching newly recovering individuals to understand their mood changes, their tendency to boredom, and their need for stimulation, and then learning to facilitate constructive alternatives is important. The group leader should be aware of these tendencies in individuals and be able to recognize them when they appear. Helping the recovering individual understand that biochemical reasons may underlie these discomforts helps the person accept them and reduces negative self-talk about being "different" or "weird." Means to manage these feelings might include attendanding more AA meetings, contacting others by telephone when bored, managing anger, and planning leisure time.

TIQs in the Brain   Higher levels of tetrahydroisoquinolines (TIQs) have been observed in the brain of chronic alcoholics and heroin addicts. These morphine-like substances ultimately replace the natural endorphins and enkelphalins in the brain. Natural endorphine production becomes damaged and results in diminished ability of recovering individuals to experience enjoyment and pleasure (Krippenstapel, 1987). If the group leader notices that members do not seem to experience pleasure, he or she might introduce into the group discussion ways to improve the quality of life, such as exercise, humor appreciation, leisure and recreational activities. We have found that when we explain underlying physical considerations to newly recovering individuals, they respond with interest and are more likely to experiment with suggested alternatives.

Post Acute Withdrawal   A leader in the area of relapse prevention, Terrance Gorski, has written about the phenomenon of *post acute withdrawal* as a period when certain physiological processes produce episodes of decreased functioning in newly recovering individuals (Gorski & Miller, 1986). Members of support groups have known about this for some time, with reference to "dry drunks" and the "30- (60-, 90-) day syndrome."

Symptoms of post acute withdrawal include lowered ability to handle stress, poorer motor coordination, sleep and appetite disturbances, emotional overreaction or emotional "numbness," and difficulty with certain mental processes such as attention, memory, abstract reasoning, and decision-making skills. Gorski and Miller place the cause on damage to the brain from the use of chemicals, in combination with less ability to handle stress (Gorski & Miller, 1986). Group leaders involved with recovering individuals must understand this phenomenon and have a good working knowledge of the ways to manage post acute withdrawal, to counter the chances of relapse.

Because stress figures so heavily in post acute withdrawal, compounded by the individual's diminished capacity to handle stress, the best way to alleviate post acute withdrawal is to lower stress. Rest, proper diet, expressing feelings, discussing fears about what is occurring, education, relaxation methods, and eliminating caffeine can all temper post acute withdrawal. Often, just knowing that this is a temporary physical condition can offset much of recovering persons' anxieties and negative self-talk about their ability to function.

Psychological/Cognitive Factors

The factors mentioned above, plus other biological factors, both preexisting and generated as a direct result of active addiction, lead to certain observable cognitive deficits in recovering individuals. Krippenstapel (1987) reported that alcoholics generally have a higher activity level than nonalcoholics, and the incidence of hyperactivity during childhood is higher in alcoholics. Also, a direct relationship seems to exist between MAO levels and mania, increased sensation seeking, and avoidance of monotony. Von Knorring et al. (1987) likewise reported lowered MAO levels, increased sensation seeking, and higher monotony avoidance among alcoholics. The implications for group work arising from these tendencies are significant.

Clinical observations support the assertion that newly recovering individuals are often bored and restless in groups that are lengthy or not interesting to them. Individuals who are not actively participating in the group are most likely to be bored and nonattentive. Although this might be blamed on resistance or denial, certain biological reasons might be contributing. Skilled group leaders will need to be aware of this problem if they find they are losing the attention of group members.

Eliciting responses from nonattentive members, and even using appropriate dramatic or controversial elements can help restore a nonattentive group. The group leader's charisma can be brought to bear as well. In a residential facility, for example, the residents often compare the various group leaders' approach to groups. Leaders who are charismatic and use drama skillfully often receive fewer complaints about their "boring groups." When residents anticipate a group by a "boring leader," this often leads to negative self-fulfilling prophesies among group members and heightens discomfort within the group. This is especially true with educational groups in a treatment program.

Another cognitive impairment often seen in recovering people is a problem with attention persistence. Krippenstapel (1987) points out that behaviors such as failing to do assignments, being at the wrong place for appointments, and in general not following instructions may in some cases be mislabeled as passive/aggressive resistance when actually it stems from attention problems. Even minor problems in this area have implications for treatment. Group leaders may have to be particularly clear in their directives. And, in our experience, repetition of significant information and ideas has usually yielded noticeably better results with alcoholics and addicts. AA members, who have known about this for some time, repeat many sayings to newcomers, such as, "Don't drink and go to meetings," "Keep it simple," and "One day at a time."

A higher level of emotionality, or the reactivity of individuals to stimulation, also characterizes recovering alcoholics and addicts. This is combined with lower levels of soothability after excitement. Somatic indications of this are found in galvanic skin response, blood pressure, and heartbeat, among other responses, in diagnosed alcoholics. Recovering individuals are going to look for ways to reduce or avoid situations that contribute to negative responses.

In observing the emotionality of individuals in the early stages of recovery, they initially seem to have an absence of emotions, or an absence of a range of emotions. Clinical observations and impressions seem to confirm that the emotions associated with fight/ flight (such as fear, anxiety, anger, hostility, and rage) are likely to be present and are usually associated with a wider variety of situations. In addition, limitations in coping skills restrict the variety of responses to situations. Individuals in groups are likely to have higher levels of psychic anxiety, somatic anxiety, and muscular tension—differences that have been measured by researchers (von Knorring et al., 1987).

Gorski and Miller (1986) discussed the relationship of post acute withdrawal to stress and related this to factors such as damage to the brain resulting from chemical use (including chronic toxicity and falls/injury to the head while intoxicated or high). During periods of post acute withdrawal, individuals show an inability to handle stress and difficulty in controlling emotions. Continued research and increasing medical knowledge of the effects of addiction will likely add much to our understanding of reasons for behaviors noted in newly recovering individuals. Although observers for some time have had difficulty in agreeing upon what constitutes a pre-addictive personality with associated stable traits, more evidence exists for similarities in people after they have been actively addicted.

The emerging theories surrounding addiction and recovery maintain that the process of recovery entails much more than simply a mirror image of the decline in active stages of using addictive chemicals. The process of growth in recovery may be linked to the Piagetian process of assimilation and accommodation. Recovering alcoholics are likely to have cognitive impairments. Neuropsychological impairment is likely in areas of problem solving, new task learning, retaining unfamiliar material, and engaging in deductive, logical thinking relative to unfamiliar conceptual material. This is reminiscent of the stages of cognitive development in the Piagetian model, with individuals progressing from concrete operations to formal operations.

Newly recovering individuals may have difficulty understanding certain concepts involved in the process of growth and change and ordering the world around them. Cognitive distortions common among newly recovering individuals are tunnel vision, euphoric recall, and cognitive distortion of current circumstances. For example, in euphoric recall the person magnifies past, pleasant events involved with chemical use, while minimizing or forgetting unpleasant consequences. In cognitive distortions of the present, the person may magnify problems of the here and now and minimize the benefits of sobriety. Tunnel vision makes the individual's entire existence seem either dismal or in the "pink cloud" that AA members often refer to in a newly recovering person. These cognitive distortions of reality unfortunately can have devastating results if they end in a relapse.

Intervention may be necessary when the group leader observes these thought patterns, and the client's reality of recovery may have to be explained and reframed with more use of the concrete and less of the abstract. The group leader may literally have to use explanations, concepts, and words that the recovering individual can comprehend and relate to. Among the reasons for the success of the book *Alcoholics Anonymous* was that it was written in language newly recovering people could understand.

Sociological Factors

Many sociological factors contribute to human functioning in social settings. In regard to chemically dependent individuals in groups, at least two are relevant to group functioning: *educational background* and *economic conditions* under which individuals live. Wide disparity between group members in either of these two areas will impede the development and actual functioning level of the group. During the assessment and group building processes, these two issues should be closely considered. If the leader cannot control who comes into the group, he or she must apply skill and effort toward minimizing these differences and, at the same time, try to identify areas of common experience and purpose, and increase members' insight into these areas.

COUNTERPRODUCTIVE GROUP PROCESS

Working in a group of chemically dependent members requires acute awareness of characterological behavior that is often defensive. Individual members can successfully defend these behaviors through a number of intellectual exercises. A group leader who is knowledgeable of and experienced with these intellectualizations can effectively intervene, using them to advantage. The goal is to disrupt and lessen members' need and habit for these counterproductive behaviors.

Denial and Resistance

Phenomenologically, denial and resistance seem to interact; the strength of one enhances the other. As a client emphatically denies or rejects the label of addict or chemically dependent or problem drinker, the stronger is the resistance or opposition to intervention by an outside force.

Denial can be unconscious, leading to self-deception by disguising motives to avoid recognition of personal qualities or behaviors that would decrease self-esteem, which is a threat to ego structure. A paradox exists because abuse of chemicals often derives from the addict's lack of self-esteem by virtue of the addiction and, concurrently, the person perpetrates behaviors so that self-loathing is obvious to everyone, especially the abuser.

Resistance is classically thought to be a psychological barrier keeping the unconscious impulses from conscious perception (Monte, 1980). It manifests from fears of change, rejection, dependence on the group or the group leader (Corey & Corey, 1987). Ellis (1985) also notes fears of disclosure and hopelessness.

Denial can run the gamut from (a) lack of recognition of the need for treatment, to (b) disbelief in the need to cooperate with the group, or (c) unwillingness or inability to accept the magnitude of the problem, or (d) not admitting any problems beyond the drug abuse. Often-heard statements in a group are: "I don't know what I'm doing here—I don't need treatment or anyone." Naturally, the less denial or resistance, the greater is the openness to intervention, information gathering, and willingness to ask for assistance.

Within the context of denial and resistance reside psychological defenses and behaviors well rehearsed by those who are chemically dependent. Minimizing, rationalizing, justifying, and projecting are some of the more common, entrenched, and less healthy coping mechanisms that allow for continued abuse.

Minimizing allows the addict to admit chemical use, while enabling the addict to lessen or reduce its impact on his or her life. Minimizing takes many forms. For example: "I've been using heroin only a year, so I don't have as much of a problem as others in this group."

Rationalizing means creating plausible excuses for one's behavior that are superficial and without recognition of the true motives and beliefs underlying the behavior. Example: "I'm able to control my cocaine use by buying only the purest grade, so I use it less often and less of it each time."

Justifying entails excuses that allow support of or vindication for a behavior. It grants freedom from guilt or responsibility. Examples: "Cocaine gives me the edge I need to beat the competition." "I don't need to speak up in the group because I learn better by listening."

Projecting places one's own behavior or ideas or impulses onto another, particularly behaviors or ideas that are objectionable or deemed negative. Example: "All the kids in high school drank beer and smoked grass, so I had to, too."

Defensive postures are well practiced and are manifested in a variety of ways. The group leader must use confrontation by self and by the group to get past these positions. The goal is for the individual to discover ways to see self and his or her behavior realistically.

The denial/resistance phenomenon has passive manifestations. A group member may combine any of the defensive postures in any way to maintain unhealthy beliefs and behaviors. A member may be nonparticipatory—silent and withdrawn, remarking that he or she learns best by listening and watching. The leader may effectively intervene by encouraging involvement and by appropriately expressing how the group member's behavior affects the leader, perhaps feeling as though kept at a distance. A member may maintain a superior "better than you other addicts" demeanor. This can stop group process, because others may be unwilling to expose themselves as less perfect. A nondefensive challenge by the group leader with a question as to what such a superior person is doing in the group, since he or she doesn't require help, will refocus the group. A group member acting dependent and helpless, hoping for advice and solutions from others, also exemplifies a passive stance. This member can remain feeble and effectively resist therapy and any change by not taking action. In these examples, the leader continues to admonish the group not to give answers or advice, and instead encourages the passive member to access his or her own power from the information already gleaned in group.

Opposite of passive denial/resistance are the more active demonstrations such as open hostility to the group, the leader, or the world in general. This often takes the form of caustic remarks or sarcasm. Sometimes a person uses a passive/aggressive style. For example, a male member may catch a female group member by surprise, commenting on her being a "real manhater" and then quickly apologizing or saying, "just kidding." This leaves the woman angry, hurt, intimidated. The group leader needs to explore the interaction, ask the woman about her feelings and thoughts, and then move to the man's motivation for his action (Corey & Corey, 1982).

Other forms resistance can take are members' defocusing from individual self or the group process and focusing instead on others; speaking only of superficial or inconsequential matters; and challenging the leader's competence, knowledge, or lack of personal experience with addiction (Corey & Corey, 1982). The leader must allow the resistance and challenge the denial, and not defend his or her own position or self, even though feeling threatened or angry or inadequate in the face of the opposition. Most important, the leader must teach through example.

Transference

Transference is demonstrated in the reproduction of past and often repressed experiences through one's present emotions and thoughts. The original object of the repressed material is replaced by another person in the client's mind. The concept of transference can be simplified by understanding that it involves a repeat of the past, which is unsuited to the present situation (Flores, 1988).

An example within the group setting is when a group member sees the leader as harsh, cold, and unreceptive when the group reality perceives the leader as vulnerable, warm, and open. This individual group member unrealistically places a memory of an important authority figure (mother, father, grandmother, or whomever) onto another important authority figure (group leader) in the present. Often, behavioral mannerisms trigger the transference. The group leader might use verbal phrases or have a physical body type or haircut or hair color or head movement similar to the original subject. If this goes unrecognized by the leader and the member, the original conflict/impairment/dysfunction is not addressed and the group member may remain stuck in an unresolved cycle of behavior patterns of the past, which reinforces the drug/alcohol use as a substitute or cover-up for the member's own defects as viewed from the past.

The group leader may wonder, after the initial stage of learning about each other and what the group means, if a group member remains hostile or withdrawn or inappropriately angry at the leader, whether transference may be operating. In questioning and probing the member's memories or in asking how the member experiences the leader, the leader can learn to whom the anger is really being directed. The group member might admit to existing awareness or be surprised and enlightened by the new awareness. Often the group member is surprised at the material and the feelings repressed from conscious functioning and how this impacts on relating to the leader, and how it had generalized to other authority figures. The unresolved past continues to distort the present. After becoming aware of transference, the leader and other group members can use this knowledge to help the individual member reexperience the past in the present, view the distorted thinking and behavior patterns and modify them, and thus impact the cycle of repetitive dysfunction with the hope of stopping it.

After six sessions in a therapy group, one female member continued eyeing the female co-leader with sidelong looks, unwilling to face her directly and unwilling to participate beyond monosyllables when encouraged to join in. Two previous interactions between this member and the female leader in the group had culminated in aggressive and abusive denunciation of the leader's cold and analytical personality and lifestyle in general. This member was often observed outside of the group being animated and chatty with the male co-leader and other group members.

At the seventh session the female co-leader gently challenged the woman's avoidance of and aggression toward her. In agitation, the woman left the group, returning moments later with a picture of her mother, a picture showing a striking resemblance in facial features and hairdo to the female co-leader. This information precipitated a major breakthrough, and both could begin to clarify and distinguish past experiences from present interactions. The client was able to divulge her perceptions of her mother as untrustworthy and controlling and unfeeling. She had learned it was in her best interest to avoid any direct interaction with her mother and give out as little information as possible about her activities. With this clarification, leader and member could define their relationship, place the past where it belonged, and experience a warm and close relationship in the present.

Other group members, too, can be objects of transference, representing a sibling rivalry, jealousy, an overdeveloped sense of responsibility, continual need for nurturance or approval, and so on. As a part of this, it is helpful to view the group as a family itself, a symbol of the individual's own family of origin (Brown & Beletsis, 1986), with the individual's behaviors being reenacted therein, as well as an experience of the group (substance abusers with differing histories and personalities) as its own uniquely defined family. The group also can serve as a microcosm of the larger community within which each member lives, works, and operates outside the group. An experienced group leader remains aware of these dynamics and open to informing the group of its here-and-now behavior that might be a replay from the past. And the group itself can apply the dynamics with each other.

As a word of caution, the leader and the group should be careful not to use knowledge of transference as a distancing mechanism to keep worries or feelings such as inadequacy or anger at bay or to keep other group members away. Labeling problems or confrontations as transference and then dismissing them could conceivably be avoiding here-and-now events that may accurately represent the present instead of the past. A perception of the group leader as wishy-washy, unreliable, and nonsupportive may be an astute observation of the present and not a comment of disappointment surrounding a father's lack of defense of his son against a punitive mother. For change to occur, repressed and present-moment feelings must be differentiated and expressed and then worked with therapeutically (Corey & Corey, 1987).

Countertransference

Countertransference refers to feelings a group member stimulates in the leader. These feelings may come out of the past and represent unresolved issues or struggles in the leader. As with client transference, countertransference in the leader is at odds with the present situation. Being aware of and addressing countertransference, if it occurs, is necessary for continued healthy expression by group members. To reveal these issues, however, may not always be wise or in the best interests of the group. For example, a leader may be particularly attracted to or dislike a specific member. Divulging this to the group might be hurtful and embarrassing to the member, accomplishing nothing beyond exposing the leader's dubious belief that he or she had to be totally honest with the group.

A common problem confronting the leader is one of power. As substance abusers often think and react in extremes, they may hail the leader as savior, wise one, expert. Quickly, clients bestow their own power on the leader as they did to the parent or mate or boss or drug. Just as quickly, the leader can be demoted and denounced when he or she fails to provide the answers or nurturance group members unrealistically expect. A leader may unconsciously keep members in a powerless position in the group and also not be able to sort out his or her own disappointment, anger, or hurt when members attack the leader as inadequate or uncaring. An unaware leader may then fall into the trap of reproducing the more verbally disagreeable members' failure patterns by punishing them.

Another common countertransference issue is the leader's belief that as a helper, he or she will be admired and loved by group members, in contrast to others in life. The leader thus comes to depend on members as the source of nourishment and feeling good. A characteristic of substance abusers is a continual need to be nourished, approved of, cared for, or filled up, because they do not believe they can do this for themselves. If transference/countertransference issues are unrecognized or dismissed without examination as unimportant, the leader can get caught up in meeting these member needs and at the same time be appreciated (loved) for doing so. The leader is rewarded and the member is rewarded, but the result may be that no change occurs and, ultimately, the client relapses.

Finally, the group member holding onto intense anger, hostility, distrust, and resentment (Flores, 1988) often manifests them in aggressive attacks on the leader. These barrages may bring forth similar reactive behaviors in group leaders who are insecure or unaware of their own personal issues related to authority or interpersonal relationships.

Continued self-evaluation, ongoing education, and close processing with a clinical supervisor can bring these issues to light and diminish possible deleterious affects of countertransference with clients.

Group Reinforcement

Peer pressure encourages change. As group members allow each other to change, they reinforce change. Sharing experiences and understanding the universality of behaviors create intimacy and acceptance, resulting in healing and forgiveness of self and others.

Although the group's capacity for healing is powerful, the group leader must be cognizant of group members' power to reinforce each other to resist change, sometimes not even consciously. For example, allowing members to dwell on how awful they are because of their days of abuse, known as "war stories," keeps them in the "there and then." This merely reinforces hopelessness to ever change or improve or get past their past. The leader must remember that however uncomfortable past and current addictive behavior is, it is a known quantity and gives more comfort than the fear created by facing the unknown through change.

Peer pressure in this instance discourages change. The group can reinforce itself to stay safe by remaining superficial and unwilling to move to more painful subjects. As one member begins to relate a moving and particularly painful incident, other members, uncomfortable with the revelations, sometimes become anxious and move to block the communication by narrowing in, giving advice, or stating how they would have handled the situation better. The group begins to compete for worst story or best solution, ignoring the client's original attempts at meaningful disclosure.

IMPACT OF LEARNING AND EDUCATION ON GROUP PROCESS

Within the group milieu lies a vast potential for learning. As a group begins, usually with members who do not know each other and who are unaware of biological, social, or psychological effects of addiction on themselves, learning plays a key role. Addiction is often called the disease of denial, and education regarding this disease begins to unveil the denial. Therapeutic change commences.

Information about addiction/alcoholism is shared realistically and factually in groups, relieving and erasing irrational fears or fantasy beliefs about the physiology of abuse. A foundation of knowledge is developed staving off further denial. Along with this, education addresses the accompanying beliefs and feelings of shame and guilt imbedded in the member's mind about the inherent weakness of character, or of being a recurrent life failure because he or she is not able to curb the abuse alone.

Education takes on a dimension deeper than simply learning facts and fallacies. In the group setting, members have an opportunity to learn and attempt new coping mechanisms. They practice confrontation, preferably moving away from aggressive, hostile demands and accusations to assertive and clearly stated expressions of feelings and thoughts. As the group allows and accepts individual changes, self-esteem and self-acceptance increase, and self-loathing and ineffective self-rewards concurrently decrease. Group members can see how learning stimulates growth in other members, which impacts positively on the interactions in the group as well as outside the group.

Long-denied or unrecognized feelings come to the fore. Dependence on drug/alcohol or the group or the group leader abates as the sense of autonomy and control rises. Superficial verbalizations are heard less frequently, and sensitive communication develops as interaction skills improve. As the interaction among group members becomes better, the pervasive sense of isolation often accompanying addiction wanes, to be replaced by new life skills and mastery (Khantzian, 1986).

TASKS OF THE GROUP LEADER

Beyond the normal tasks ascribed to a group leader working with addicted populations (Yalom, 1985), a focus has to be directed particularly on the ability to be directive, confrontive, tolerant, and nondefensive. *Directive* means being an active participant in the group by guiding discussion, using appropriate self-disclosure, and maintaining personal honesty with group members. When the group begins energizing toward someone's "war stories," the leader, rather than staying apart and letting members vent and free-associate as they will, must intervene by leading the discussion back to a present, reality-based orientation. A gentle reminder that the group is not a democratic process may be called for. In this same vein, the leader may be required to structure time and experiences in the group, doling out homework as relevant and encouraging reports on learning from previous assignments. Being directive means maintaining the focus and modeling discipline, addressing the need for self-control over low frustration tolerance while dealing with the impulsiveness often ascribed to addicted clients.

Confrontation implies challenging the group or individual members to look beyond surface issues, questioning assumptions and disputing old self-defeating patterns, mannerisms, and beliefs. Confronting can be direct, with the leader attacking the obvious denial, or it can be indirect, with a query toward what underlies the presenting behavior. Confrontation must never be at the expense of the member's sense of self-respect or with injury to the member. This is not a power struggle with the leader as winner. No one wins.

The leader must maintain a *tolerant attitude* toward emotional raging, physical outbursts, and verbal accusations. The pain group members may have could be attributed in part to withdrawing from drug/alcohol, as well as facing deep issues of abandonment, rejection, separation, self-loathing, or intense anger, to name a few. This recognition facilitates respect for another's beliefs or opinions without necessarily agreeing with or accepting them as one's own.

In conjunction with tolerance is an ability to remain *nondefensive* when faced with any of the above more hostile and aggressive behaviors. If active transference is in progress and the group leader is aware of it, he or she can accept that the feelings are directed to a past object rather than to the group leader.

SUMMARY

The format most often used in treating chemical dependency (drugs and alcohol) is the group. Individuals in this specialized group modality are most often referred by the courts or by family and friends who are concerned about the person, so group leaders have to recognize the potential for hostility and resistance inherent in this group form. Third parties (feeders) also are a significant funding source for this type of group, and they therefore may have a large say in the group design and outcomes.

The composition of groups is of critical importance, so screening and assessment should be done thoroughly and carefully to produce a group whose membership is compatible and conducive to intended outcomes. The opposite dimensions of homogeneity and heterogeneity come into play in considering the commonality of purpose, capacity for insight, level of chemical dependency, motivation, age, gender, race, ethnic/cultural background, socioeconomic differences, and the capacity for relationships.

Specific issues for the leader include how to deal with relapsing group members, as well as overriding physiological, psychological/cognitive, and sociological factors. Physiological factors associated with recovering addicts are: lower than normal platelet MAO levels, higher levels of TIQs in the brain, and post acute withdrawal symptoms—with their accompanying characteristic behaviors. These psychological and cognitive behaviors include the tendency toward distaste for boredom, stress and the difficulty in dealing with it, emotional/affective dysfunctions, tendency to be distracted and have short attention spans, exaggerated reactions to stimulation, euphoric recall, and tunnel vision. Sociological factors operating in groups include, in particular, educational background and economic status. If either of these variables is too disparate, group members may have trouble interacting productively.

The two underlying characteristics most counterproductive to group process fall under the umbrella of denial and resistance. Within the rubric of denial are the mechanisms of minimizing, rationalizing, justifying, and projecting. Resistance is typified by hostility. Other dynamics include transference (substituting someone in the present for someone from the past) and countertransference (the leader's feelings toward a group member evoked from the leader's past). The leader has to be aware of all these underlying dynamics in order to fend off possible hostilities, remain in control of self and the group process, and direct members' coping tactics to keep the group on a healthy course. Specific leader techniques include being directive, appropriately confrontive, tolerant, and nondefensive, as well as providing pertinent information to group members in regard to their addiction, typical responses, and recovery patterns.

REFERENCES

Agazarian, Y., & Peters, R. (1981). *The visible and invisible group*. London: Routledge & Kegan Paul.

Brown, S., & Beletsis, S. (1986). The development of family transference in groups for adult children of alcoholics. *Journal of Group Psychotherapy, 36*(1), 97–114.

Carroll, J. F. X. (1986). Treating alcoholics and drug abusers together in residential programs: A question of resident compatibility and staff preparedness. *Alcoholism Treatment Quarterly, 3*(1), 119–131.

Carroll, J. F. X. (1983). *Substance abuse problem checklist*. Eagleville, PA: Eagleville Hospital.

Corey, G., & Corey, M. S. (1982). *Groups: Process and practice*, (2nd ed.). Monterey, CA: Brooks/Cole.

Daley, C., Moss, H., & Campbell, F. (1987). *Dual diagnosis: Counseling clients with chemical dependency and mental illness*. Center City, MN: Hazelton Foundation.

Ellis, A. (1985). *Overcoming resistance*. New York: Springer Publishing.

Flores, P. J. (1988). *Group psychotherapy with addicted populations*. New York: The Haworth Press.

Gorski, T. T., & Miller, M. (1986). *Staying sober*. Independence, MO: Independence Press.

Khantzian, E. J. (1986). A contemporary psychodynamic approach to drug abuse treatment. *American Journal of Drug & Alcohol Abuse, 12*(3), 213–222.

Krippenstapel, P. (1987). A fresh look at relapse. *Alcoholism Treatment Quarterly, 4*(4), 1–17.

Levine, B. (1979). *Group psychotherapy: Practice and development*. Englewood Cliffs, NJ: Prentice Hall, Inc.

Levine, B., & Gallogly, V. (1985). *Group therapy with alcoholics, outpatient and inpatient approaches.* Beverly Hills, CA: Sage. (Human Services Guide, Vol. 40).

McLellan, A. T., Luborsky, L., Cacciola, J., McGahan, P., O'Brien, C. P., & Griffith, J. (1985). *Guide to the addiction severity index.* Washington, DC: Department of Health & Human Services on Drug Abuse.

Monte, C. F. (1980). *Beneath the mask: An introduction to theories of personality* (2nd ed.). New York: Holt, Rinehart and Winston.

von Knorring, L., von Knorring, A., Smegan, L., Lindberg, U., & Edholm, M. (1987). Personality traits in subtypes of alcoholics. *Journal of Studies on Alcohol, 48*(6), 523–527.

Yalom, I. (1975). *The theory and practice of group psychotherapy,* (2nd ed.). New York: Basic Books.

Yalom, I. (1985). *The theory and practice of group psychotherapy,* (3rd ed.), New York: Basic Books.

Zimberg, S., Wallace, J., & Blume, S. B. (1985). Group psychotherapy in the treatment of alcoholism. *Practical approaches to alcoholism psychotherapy,* (2nd ed.). New York: Plenum Press.

IN MEMORIAM

Charles W. Hawes

1945–1991

In fond and loving memory, colleague and friend.

7

Group Counseling for Individuals with Eating Disorders

Mary Lou Frank

*T*he constellation of eating disorders has only recently come into public awareness. Because of the work by Bruch (1973) and Boskind-Lodahl (1976), eating disorders garnered the attention of the psychological and medical communities and precipitated research and theorizing regarding etiology and treatment. Group counseling approaches understandably have been varied in this formative stage. The interpersonal nature of these disorders suggests that group treatment may offer the most potent remedy for individuals with eating disorders.

CLASSIFICATIONS, DEFINITIONS, AND EXPLANATION

Eating disorders were first described by Squire (1983) as existing on a continuum. Since then, others have observed relationships among the primary eating disorders: anorexia nervosa, bulimia nervosa, and compulsive eating (Brownell & Foreyt, 1986; Fairburn & Gardner, 1986; Johnson & Maddi, 1986; Russell, 1979). These three disorders are the anchors for understanding the spectrum of food and weight concerns.*

Anorexia nervosa and *bulimia* were first acknowledged as diagnostic categories in the third edition of the *Diagnostic and Statistical Manual of Mental Disorders* (DSM III) (American Psychiatric Association, 1980). Seven years later, the American Psychiatric Association (APA) changed the name from bulimia to bulimia nervosa, still indicating similarities between the two disorders. The current diagnostic criteria for anorexia nervosa and bulimia nervosa are outlined in the DSM III-R (American Psychiatric Association, 1987, pp. 67–69), with descriptions of both diagnostic categories. Anorexia nervosa and bulimia nervosa share the issues of conflicted body image and overconcern about weight.

---

*For purposes of this chapter, pica and rumination disorders will not be included.

Compulsive eating has not been categorized as a discrete eating disorder. It falls into the DSM III-R category Eating Disorder NOS (not otherwise specified), a classification that exists for individuals with eating disorders who don't meet the other criteria but who nonetheless have a problem with eating (American Psychiatric Association, 1987). Therapeutically, compulsive eating has been a focus of much attention (Bilich, 1983; Chernin, 1985; Orbach, 1978; Roth, 1984). Only diagnostically has it lacked definition. The reason for this noticeable omission seems to be the distinction made between obesity and compulsive eating. Because of the genetic and physiological factors involved in obesity (Brownell & Foreyt, 1986), compulsive eating has been denied a separate diagnosis due to the fear of misdiagnosing a physical problem as a psychological condition. Compulsive eating is differentiated here from obesity according to the following criteria that seem to be emerging in the literature:

1. Recurrent episodes of binge eating (Eichenbaum & Orbach, 1982; Roth, 1984).
2. Dissatisfaction with body size and weight (Eichenbaum & Orbach, 1982).
3. Compulsive eating behavior characterized by a lack of control (Roth, 1984).
4. Eating behavior coupled with emotional or psychological stress (Ganley, 1989; Morley, Levine, & Willenbring, 1986).

Compulsive eating is not singled out to blame individuals for their problems in this area but, rather, to honor their struggle, which is seen as a coping response to emotional neediness. Research on compulsive eating will most likely increase when the psychiatric and psychological associations consider it a separate entity from obesity.

ETIOLOGY

Models for etiology vary slightly for each of the eating disorders, but they seem to have some similar patterns, to differing degrees. The focus of this chapter is not to exhaustively explore predisposing causes of the disorders but, instead, to look at group treatment as a means of addressing the issues that may predispose the disorders. Therefore, the following is not an exhaustive list of causes, merely a summary of themes that have evolved:

1. Developmental deficits include the individual's desire to stay a child (Bruch, 1978; Orbach, 1986), avoid femininity (Lewis & Johnson, 1985), overembrace femininity (Boskind-Lodahl, 1976; Wade, Kegan, Pettinati, & Franks, 1986), lack separation and differentiation from others (Heesacker & Neimeyer, 1990), and characteristically exhibit younger styles of reasoning, such as black-and-white thinking (Garner, 1986).
2. Societal pressures force women to adopt eating disordered behavior to conform to current standards of body size and shape (Boskind-White & White, 1987; Brumberg, 1989; Wooley & Wooley, 1979). The media impose unrealistic standards that women internalize and try to achieve (Garner et al., 1980).
3. Dieting restrains the normal functions that regulate eating behavior and causes dysfunctional eating patterns. Polivy & Herman (1985) saw restraint theory as the main force behind the development of eating disorders.
4. Family systems deficits also have been designated as a precipitant to eating disorders (Sargent, Liebman, & Silver, 1985). Dysfunctional families marked by separation-

individuation difficulties (Friedlander & Siegel, 1990), perfection and chaos (Root, Fallon, & Friedrich, 1986), and over/under involvement (Minuchin, Rosman, & Baker, 1978) may be associated with eating disordered behavior.

5. Several authors (Brumberg, 1989; Carruba & Blundell, 1986; Johnson & Maddi, 1986) have proposed that biological causes should be included in any integrative model.

6. Possibly underlying a number of these factors is the sense of powerlessness (Bepko, 1989).

> Eating disorders are also probably disorders of power, at some level expressing the dilemmas of women who are told to achieve but have only faulty avenues for doing so, who are told they matter but only if they're beautiful. Somewhere along the line they have lost their voices and learned to talk with their bodies. For many the process of therapy requires permission to speak, as well as help in learning how to do so. (Anderson & Holder, 1989, p. 390)

As conveyed in the above quotation, the voice of power has been quieted, hidden in self-directed shame, for many individuals with eating disorders.

A review of the literature indicates that people with eating disorders share similarities and differences. Bulimics and compulsive eaters indulge in binge eating to fill emotional needs (Cauwels, 1983). Bulimia is seen by some (Root et al., 1986) to develop from anorexia, but differences between these two groups exist on "demographic, familial, and behavioral levels that are qualitative rather than quantitative" (p. 18). Because of their complexity, any treatment would best be advised to acknowledge the individuals, their background, and any specific medical complications unique to their situation. Separating the three groups for treatment has some precedent (Cauwels, 1983). While acknowledging that the underlying dynamics across the eating disorders have certain similarities (Heesacker & Neimeyer, 1990), separating them facilitates group homogeneity and connection.

THERAPEUTIC CONSIDERATIONS

Eating disorders are increasing in incidence (Brumberg, 1989; Heesacker & Neimeyer, 1990; Klesges, Mizes, & Klesges, 1987; Rodin, Silverstein, & Striegel-Moore, 1985). Group counseling and techniques used to treat eating disorders have a very short history. Understandably, respectful treatment takes into consideration what is known about this population.

❑ Individuals with eating disorders have many physical complications. Anorexia is the most lethal of all the psychological disorders (Garfinkel & Garner, 1982). After initial group screenings, medical evaluations and support are important to ensure that the individuals are medically stable for outpatient treatment or receiving necessary attention while in inpatient treatment. At the minimum, this includes a physician to do the medical screenings (Brownell & Foreyt, 1986) and a psychiatrist to screen for medication when indicated (Hudson & Pope, 1984). Nutritional (Kempley, 1988) and exercise counseling (Boskind-White & White, 1987) may be a needed adjunct for individuals during treatment. Bauer, Anderson, & Hyatt (1986) and Cauwels (1983) addressed these needs through a multidisciplinary team serving the dual purpose to support and to direct treatment.

❑ Until recently, women were the sole focus of eating disorders research. Men were considered a "puzzling minority" (Cauwels, 1983, p. 147). Yet an estimated 5% of anorectics are men, and 5%–20% of bulimics are men (Cauwels, 1983; Pyle, Mitchell, & Eckert, 1981). For some time, certain sports produced "vocational bulimics," for which men were included (Cauwels, 1983). In an article on eating disordered athletes in the *NCAA News* (Survey on Eating Disorders, 1990), the National Collegiate Athletic Association found that eating disordered behavior is prevalent in male athletes. Because the overwhelming majority of research to date has focused on women, so does much of this chapter. But readers should be sensitive to this bias, which seems to be unfounded. The need for continued research focusing on men with eating disorders cannot be overemphasized. Individuals express the universal needs for intimacy, acceptance, and independence through disordered eating. Men and women share these concerns. Nevertheless, as more men come into treatment, men may best be served by groups separate from women (Cauwels, 1983).

❑ The groups discussed in this chapter are counseling, not support groups, and this is an important distinction, as the two types of groups each have different functions and uses in treatment. Overeaters Anonymous, a support group in the 12-step tradition, has the sole purpose of helping individuals who compulsively overeat. Separate groups for anorexics and bulimics also exist. Many people have gained support from these groups, especially individuals from a 12-step orientation.

The need for a support group versus a counseling group is drawn from the model proposed by Hogg and Frank (in press). From their model, the most appropriate treatment modality depends on the individual's level of emotional neediness. When people have become dependent on food as an external source of selfhood, they would best be referred to a counseling group. When individuals have sufficient ego strength to remain separate when connected with others, a support group is recommended. Support groups are usually helpful in the latter stages of treatment.

❑ Respect for individual and group boundaries is paramount. Some theorists believe that women in treatment need to connect with other women (Boskind-White & White, 1987). Because these clients may hesitate to challenge a male group leader, are less honest with males because they defer to them, and try to please men in the counseling environment, they are advised to seek females for primary treatment needs. Some counselors suggest male-female teams (Andersen, 1986). Thelen, Farmer, McLaughlin, Mann, & Pruitt (1990) suggested that relationships with men should be addressed before counseling is complete. Because of potential issues with incest and abuse from men, women may need to first reconnect with the feminine part of themselves (Brody, 1984). This would also be parallel for men in treatment.

❑ The benefits of having two co-leaders for groups involving these intense issues are apparent. Yalom (1985) suggests that one leader generally is viewed as harmonizing and the other as questioning. Together, they can observe and intervene in the various issues that arise with eating disordered group members.

❑ Individual or family counseling, or both, may have to be maintained as an adjunct to group treatment. Many people realize personal issues (e.g., incest, abuse or shame) in groups, which necessitate more in-depth work than the group alone can provide. For individuals in whom the disorder developed before age 18, family counseling has yielded positive results (Russell, Szmukler, Dare, & Eisler, 1987).

❑ Women in general may share many of the themes and concerns that characterize women with eating disorders (Orbach, 1978; Rodin et al., 1985; Roth & Ross, 1988). Therefore, approaching these issues in a way that does not overpathologize what may be the result of cultural pressures is a delicate process.

❑ Physical considerations may have to be broached before beginning group counseling. Inpatient settings provide the most appropriate environment to treat clients with conditions that are life-threatening. Once the person is medically stable, group counseling may take place in the inpatient setting.

❑ The stability of a group may be a consideration even when offering services on a school or university campus that will last only one term. Individuals with eating disorders often will develop trust within the group and want to continue for additional grading periods or terms. Additionally, consistent group time and place help provide an element of stability and reliability in a person's otherwise chaotic existence.

EATING DISORDERS THERAPY GROUPS

Regardless of the therapeutic orientation, no group treatment for eating disorders has been shown to be superior to any other therapy (Pope & Hudson, 1989). Although many (Andersen, 1986; Barth & Wurman, 1986; Boskind-White & White, 1987; Root et al., 1986; Roth & Ross, 1988) have found benefits to group counseling with individuals who have eating disorders, no one approach has emerged as universally accepted.

Models

Eating disorders groups have until now followed one of three general models: *cognitive* (Lee & Rush, 1986), *process-focused* (Roy-Byrne, Lee-Benner, & Yager, 1984), or a *combination* (Love & Johnson, 1989; Roth & Ross, 1988). Pure cognitive-behavioral approaches focus on decreasing eating disordered behavior and improving affective states, self-esteem, and distorted attitudes (Kempley, 1988; Lee & Rush, 1986; Roth & Ross, 1988). The process model emphasizes "interpersonal relationships and the intrapsychic adaptive function of the eating disorder" (Love et al., 1989, p. 176).

Counselors have had difficulty knowing how to integrate the cognitive approach (challenging dysfunctional thoughts and behaviors), with the process-focused model (addressing group interactions and relationships) (Love et al., 1989; Roth & Ross, 1988). This conflict was reconciled by the suggestion that the groups be run separately (Piran & Kaplan, 1990) or start with cognitive work and end with the group process (Roth & Ross, 1988). The challenge was to combine two models that were inherently at odds.

The model Yalom (1975) devised, based on Sullivan's (1953) interpersonal theory, has the dual capacity of attending to dysfunctional thoughts and behaviors while focusing on interpersonal interactions. In this model the cognitive distortions are not explicitly taught but, instead, are addressed when they are manifest within relationships. Yalom asserts that "there is no need for them to describe their pathology—they will sooner or later act it out before the group's eyes" (p. 29). In accordance with Sullivan's model, the group leader attempts to recognize and address "parataxic distortions" (Yalom, 1985, p. 21)—the misperceptions we have of ourselves and others that can be seen in our interactions. These distortions are changed best by interpersonal comparisons and evaluations (Yalom, 1975).

Characteristics of the Three Groups

An understanding of the distortions that characterize people with eating disorders is essential in order to process them as they emerge in the interpersonal context. Research has yielded the following cognitive distortions characteristic of bulimic, anorectic, and compulsive eater clients:

Bulimic   (Bauer & Anderson, 1989, pp. 416–419)
1. Being or becoming overweight is the worst thing that can happen.
2. Certain foods are good foods; others are bad foods (good food = good person).
3. To feel safe, I must have control over all my actions.
4. I must do everything perfectly or what I do is worthless.
5. Everyone is aware of and interested in what I am doing.
6. Everyone must love me and approve of what I do.
7. External validation is everything.
8. As soon as I _____ I will be able to give up bulimia.
9. To be successful, a woman must combine the traditional values of women with the aggressive career orientation of men.

Anorectic   (Brumberg, 1989; Levenkron, 1982; Orbach, 1982)
1. Fear of being/getting overweight.
2. Feelings of inferiority.
3. Fear of intimacy.
4. Fear of criticism.
5. Fear of achievement.
6. Desire to be independent and powerful.
7. Desire for restraint and silence.

Compulsive Eater   (Orbach, 1978; Roth, 1984)
1. Fear of fat and fear of thin.
2. Fear of being too powerful.
3. Fear of having.
4. Fear of trusting.
5. Overjudging oneself.

By recognizing these underlying fears and thoughts that arise out of developmental needs (Garner, 1986) and societal pressures (Boskind-White & White, 1987), dynamics may be understood and addressed when they are evident in group relationships.

Relationship Patterns

The following interpersonal patterns, reflective of the cognitions, can be seen in groups (Bauer & Anderson, 1989; Brumberg, 1989; Levenkron, 1982; Orbach, 1978; Roth, 1984):

1. *Trust issues:* "If I hear people laughing, I know it's about me"; "I wonder when it's safe to say how I really feel"; "Others in the group are critical of me."
2. *Power issues:* "I must be dependent and subservient to others in the group"; "My needs are not as important as others"; "I'm a failure"; fears of weight: "To be fat is the worst possible, and I will compare myself to other group members"; "I hold myself to standards that I do not hold for others."
3. *Control issues:* "If I get into my feelings, I'll lose control"; "I must do everything perfectly, even be a perfect client here"; "I'll dwell on my mistakes and ignore my successes."

In the relational context these issues can be "actively illuminated" (Yalom, 1975, p. 121) with immediate interpersonal impact. Changing relational patterns within and between individuals with eating disorders becomes the goal of the counseling process.

Curative Factors

In the book, *The Theory and Practice of Group Psychotherapy*, Yalom (1985) lists 11 curative factors necessary in the group process. With an understanding of the symptomology and the parataxic process, these factors should be explored in a process group. Some of the curative factors have already been discussed in relation to eating disordered groups (Love et al., 1989; Root et al., 1986). The 11 factors are (Yalom, 1975, pp. 3–4):

1. Instillation of hope
2. Universality
3. Imparting of information
4. Altruism
5. Corrective recapitalization of the primary family group
6. Development of socializing techniques
7. Imitative behavior
8. Interpersonal learning
9. Group cohesiveness
10. Catharsis
11. Existential factors

Understanding these factors as they relate to eating disordered groups offers the framework for the interpersonal, process-oriented model.

Instillation of Hope   Observing that others in group are in varying stages of recovery provides hope and encouragement. Giving to and receiving from others have also been associated with increasing self-respect (Yalom, 1985). These are crucial elements in treating those who have eating disorders. People who feel little self-worth learn that all is not hopeless (Barth & Wurman, 1986).

Universality   Many individuals with eating disorders suffer because they feel alone and afraid (Johnson & Pure, 1986; Orbach, 1986; Roth, 1984). In a group setting they can come to know that others share these feelings. They are not shamed for their behaviors or thoughts, and others can learn to accept them (Yalom, 1985). Knowing that others have the same problem with food means they are not different and isolated.

Imparting of Information   Information about the processes of counseling and eating disorders is helpful to group members (Orbach, 1986; Roth & Ross, 1988; Weiss, Katzman, & Wolchik, 1986). Explaining the eating disorders, predicting relapse, providing information about the group model, giving information about the process of the disorder, and explaining the physical needs in treatment are addressed through this curative element.

Altruism   The benefit of altruism in groups is highly evident with members who have eating disorders. The example Yalom (1975) uses seems written for the eating disordered group. In this example, when shown hell, a rabbi saw starving people surrounded by adequate food but spoons with very long handles. The length of the spoon handles did not allow the people to feed themselves. Then shown heaven, the rabbi saw the same scene but saw well fed, happy people. The difference was that the people in heaven had learned how to feed each other.

The emotional needs of people with eating disorders have not been met for a long time. They don't yet know how to get their needs met (Bepko, 1989; Love et al., 1989). A group provides a context to learn how to ask and to "get fed." After learning how to metaphorically feed and get fed by others, group members need to develop new tools that can also allow them to feed themselves.

Corrective Recapitulation of the Primary Family Group   Family issues are at the core of working with the eating disordered population, whether this means working with the family (Minuchin et al., 1978) or working through family issues (Chernin, 1985; Levenkron, 1982; Root et al., 1986). Acknowledging that the issues of family are re-created in the group setting (Yalom, 1975) allows the group to be a safe place to deal with these complex issues.

Development of Socializing Techniques   Yalom (1975) asserts that learning how to tune into what is happening with others, to be helpful to others, to resolve conflict, to be less judgmental, and to be more empathic with self and others are potential benefits of participation in a group. Johnson and Pure (1986) identify the same interpersonal elements as vital in the curative process. Developing these socialization skills translates to aspects of healthy relatedness that will help individuals with eating disorders re-relate to themselves and others.

Imitative Behavior   Modeling—not just from group leaders but from other group members as well—is essential. Women listed participant modeling as one of the most helpful factors in eating disorders treatment (White, 1985). Members benefit from watching and learning from others who have shared the same experience and are farther along in the recovery process.

Interpersonal Learning   We learn best in our relationships with others Lerner (1985). Sullivan's theory and Yalom's model both have a strong interpersonal focus. Group counseling is preferred over individual counseling, primarily because the former offers more opportunities for learning (Boskind-White & White, 1987). A "corrective emotional experience" (Yalom, 1975) may entail expressing strong affect, be it positive or negative. People with eating disorders often hold in strong feelings of anger and inadequacy (Bepko, 1989). A group offers its members a safe, supportive place to begin feeling.

Group Cohesiveness   Not only is a support network a source of health and recovery, but it also has been highly correlated with success in weight studies (Brownell and Wadden, 1986). The relationships in a group are facilitative for members who need healthy intimacy and connections (Heesacker & Neimeyer, 1990). Connecting with others in a group also allows individuals to reconnect with the unaccepted/unacceptable parts of themselves.

Catharsis   American society has not supported women in venting thoughts and feelings regarding food and weight (Boskind-White & White, 1987; Orbach, 1978). A group is a good environment for women to express these feelings. Men also benefit from a supportive environment in expressing feelings of loss and shame (Osherson, 1986), and group counseling is unequaled in its potential in this area (Hogg & Frank, in press).

Existential Factors   Few writers have delved into existential issues as related to eating disorders. The universal nature of the constructs of fairness, pain, death, aloneness, and individual responsibility (Yalom, 1975) makes these especially applicable to the eating disordered population. Perhaps these struggles are particularly appropriate to people who struggle with severe, life-threatening illnesses; their shame and guilt fit well into the existential dynamics. Group members need to recognize their responsibility for change (Bepko, 1989; Boskind-White & White, 1987; Chernin, 1985; Orbach, 1978), and by taking responsibility, individuals become empowered.

Group Development

Within the interpersonal, process-focused model, group development requires consideration of several factors, and it moves through certain phases of development. Counseling begins with the group screening and ends with termination of group counseling.

Screening and Composition   Group screenings are critical to eating disorders groups. When group members are motivated and ready for counseling, recidivism seems to decrease. Root, Fallon, and Friedrich (1986) have suggested some guidelines for group screenings:

1. Members should not be using or abusing alcohol or drugs. Addiction to drugs or alcohol should be addressed before eating disorder issues.
2. Members should share commonalities of experience as well as presenting problems (e.g., no males in groups for women and no women in groups for men; anorexics, bulimics, and compulsive eaters in separate groups).
3. Members should show some interest in the group process (e.g., by returning phone calls, by attending the group screening appointment, and by expressing interest and commitment to the group).
4. Members who are willing to wait for membership in a group may be even more motivated to be in the group.

Length   Adhering to a 12-session model (which fits many campus programs), individuals commit to a closed group for this term. Treatment, however, may extend beyond a 12-session group. Some leaders report that individuals benefit from longer term group treatment (Barth & Wurman, 1986; Roth & Ross, 1988). If incest issues arise during treatment, they are best dealt with in individual sessions as an adjunct to the group (Kerr & Piran, 1990). The setting (inpatient, outpatient, or campus) may dictate the duration of group. Yalom's (1975) model suggests that instead of weeks, members work together for months. A 12-session group would not be expected to progress as far as groups of longer duration.

Open groups Open membership in groups is also an option (Love et al., 1989). New members are integrated as others leave. When new members join a preexisting group core, this entails connecting with new members and possible subgrouping (Yalom, 1975). In any group, members may choose to leave prematurely. If someone leaves, the leaders should discuss the issues of loss and the importance of saying good-bye. The group environment provides an optimal opportunity to bring up connectedness and separation—particular concerns of people with eating disorders (Heesacker & Neimeyer, 1990).

Stages The *first stage* of group counseling involves "orientation, hesitant participation, and search for meaning" (Yalom, 1985, p. 301). In the first group session, the leader should explain rules and norms to group members. Individuals with intense shame and guilt need to be in a safe environment. Group boundaries with regard to membership and confidentiality must be discussed in the initial meeting.

Group members with eating disorders often hesitate to say the words that describe their behavior. Group members with bulimia may refer to "it." Those with anorexia may be silent (Orbach, 1986). Most women will talk about their dissatisfaction with the size and shape of their body (Wooley & Wooley, 1979). Compulsive eaters also may exaggerate or hide feelings to protect themselves from pain (Orbach, 1978). The leader should normalize members' need to be hesitant in disclosure and should not encourage or reinforce their need for dependence by providing answers (Yalom, 1985). Even though food may become the topic, food is not the real issue (Orbach, 1978). The leader should also be aware of the natural tendency to parentify the leader, and thus recognize initial transference tendencies (Yalom, 1975). Ethically, the group leader must also discuss the limitations and potential effects of treatment. The tenor of the group begins to develop in the first session.

The search for meaning leads group members to seek out the function of the eating disorder in their lives. This quest may have a broader scope as group members begin to look to their past and their future for needs and fulfillment. In the early phase of group counseling, members begin to notice common patterns and trends. A group setting offers the potential for understanding the universal nature of emotional needs.

The second stage of group development is characterized by "conflict, dominance, and rebellion" (Yalom, 1985, p. 304). Eating disordered groups begin to enter the second phase when they conflict over speaking time and show competitiveness related to attractiveness and success (Love et al., 1989). Parentification continues to surface. This is an important facet of group progress (Yalom, 1975). Though conflict is unpleasant for the parentified leader, group members learn from this conflict to be honest interpersonally, confront "psychodynamic and group dynamic issues" (Yalom, 1975, p. 310), and express anger—important areas to develop. For example, a member may express "I'm always disappointed in my friendships" as, "I'm always disappointed in you" (Kerr & Piran, 1990, p. 35). Cognitive distortions as well as intrapersonal deficits are manifested in these intense interpersonal relationships. The leader can facilitate discussions to help members begin resolving their interpersonal conflicts and connect these deficits to their eating disordered behavior.

The third stage of group treatment features "development of cohesiveness" (Yalom, 1975, p. 311). Out of the conflict and storming of the previous stage evolves group integration, respect, and purpose (Yalom, 1985). A member's hidden shame and fear are potentially released in this safe environment. When group members feel a healthy closeness with others, this connectedness allows them to escape from their isolation (Eichenbaum & Orbach, 1982). By learning to accept and appreciate others, they learn to accept and appreciate themselves.

The more advanced stages of group are difficult to map. During this period "it is no longer possible to describe discrete stages of development" (Yalom, 1975, p. 332). Group members face their own issues as they come up.

Subgrouping may be proposed in this phase—particularly if new members join the group or if extra-group contacts evolve—because group members want to gain more from interpersonal relationships with each other than from the group. The challenges of integrating new members have already been discussed, and group leaders do not always encourage extra-group contacts (Yalom, 1975). Although gaining support from people with eating disorders outside of a group has been viewed as helpful (Hoage, 1989), not all group leaders encourage those connections because subgrouping can promote fragmentation if conflict arises and it is not processed. Group members should be apprised that conflicts outside of a group should be processed in the group for the therapeutic process to continue.

Termination, the final stage of group work, entails dealing with separation and loss again at a personal level in the group. This parting may be the first time individuals in the group have formally said good-bye (Kerr & Piran, 1990). The termination phase generates unresolved losses and separation issues. Group members may discuss each other's progress, feelings toward one another, and their own sadness. Remissions might be expected after the group termination because of this experience of loss (Yalom, 1985). Or progress may continue after a group ends if members effectively work through the termination issues.

Strategies

Because the history of treating eating disorders is relatively brief and no definitive treatment model has emerged, strategies have not stood the test of time and research validity. Several strategies, however, have met with success. Focusing on the group's interpersonal process is at the core of the group counseling process. The following strategies are suggested to supplement and facilitate that dynamic, not supplant it.

1. *Adult nomenclature.* In the group setting, introductions are important, as are the names members use for themselves. In women's counseling groups, when members begin to refer to themselves and female friends as "woman," not "girl," it is empowering. When it comes up, the issue often leads to a discussion of what image members have of a "woman," what they might do if they were women, and the fears associated with growing up. This intervention is simple and has facilitated development, identity, and empowerment—important aspects of healing.

2. *Relaxation and hypnosis.* The use of relaxation and hypnosis with clients who have eating disorders can be a useful strategy (Gross, 1983; Pettinati, Kogan, Margolis, Shrier, & Wade, 1989; Thakur, 1980). Teaching relaxation in the early stages of group counseling gives members another tool to use when they are alone with food. Relaxation has been helpful in creating calmness, "reinforcing a positive self-image, modifying binge eating and purging behaviors, learning sensitivity to hunger, altering body image distortion, and training recognition of involuntary dissociative states" associated with binge eating (Pettinati et al., 1989, pp. 44–47). Bulimia provides a stress-reducing function (Mizes & Fleece, 1986), so teaching clients to relax represents a means to replace the bulimic behavior with a more appropriate response.

Ericksonian hypnosis has also been suggested (Bandler & Grindler, 1982). Because of the control problems of most people with eating disorders (Pettinati et al., 1989), this strategy is suggested only when group members are "briefed" and comfortable with the procedure.

3. *Body image exercises.* Body image work is a necessary adjunct to counseling for eating disorders (Hutchinson, 1985; Wooley & Kearney-Cooke, 1986). Kearney-Cooke (1989) hypothesizes that body image disturbances appear in the first three years of life when parents disapprove of the child's body. In some groups, body image exercises may take the form of imagery exercises before the group session really begins. Other body image exercises might evolve from the counseling process, as members compare themselves with others in the group. Using mirrors to promote self-acceptance and having members trace their image and then their real bodies on paper have also been recommended (Orbach, 1978).

Another intervention applied to the body image disturbances and obsessions that characterize all people with eating disorders involves art, music, or dance as an adjunct to treatment (Hornyak & Baker, 1989). Finally, separate and apart from group counseling, LeBlanc (1990) suggests that therapeutic massage may enable group members to "reclaim and feel great" in their bodies (p. 111). All of these experiential forms of treatment require skill and knowledge before attempting them with a group.

4. *Other imagery exercises.* In recent years imagery has been used increasingly as a therapeutic tool with people who have eating disorders (Kearney-Cooke, 1989). Receiving appropriate training, having members' permission to participate, and offering an ample explanation of the imaging process are imperative for group leaders.

All imagery exercises, especially with eating disordered groups, should begin by creating a safe environment (in a special room, down a path, around the next corner) in the members' imagery world. If images get uncomfortable, the person is able to return to the previously identified "safe environment" to process and work through threatening insights. Although selecting themes that evolve from the group content is best, several themes for imagery are suggested as starting points:

❑ Imagine your mother pregnant. Imagine your parents' reaction to that pregnancy.
   Goal: to explore gender expectations and feeling of worth (Kearney-Cooke, 1989).
❑ Imagine yourself at a party and your body expands and then contracts. *Goal:* to explore how body size impacts interpersonal relationships (Orbach, 1978).

❑ Visualize the bodies of all the other women in the group and see where they fit in the lineup. *Goal:* to investigate competition and comparisons with others in the group (Kearney-Cooke, 1989).

❑ Imagine all the food you have at home or would ever want in the supermarket. *Goal:* to help group members recognize that needs can be filled (Orbach, 1978).

❑ Imagine what would happen if you woke up and you felt good about your body. *Goal:* to address resistance to change (Kearney-Cooke, 1989).

❑ Imagine your ideal self is accessible from the safe environment and compare it to your real self of today. *Goal:* to help create self-acceptance and to integrate ideal aspects into the real self as desired.

❑ Imagine what you would want to take with you from each person in our group as you go on a journey. *Goal:* to recognize strengths in self and others.

❑ Imagine that the group has ended. What other things do you wish you would have said or done to feel completed? *Goal:* to help process termination issues.

5. *Memory of meals in the family of origin.* Families have been drawn at the table, imagined at the table, and dramatized in group settings. Each approach offers aspects of the same dynamic. Exploring the early issues around food offers the individual and the group information about early feelings associated with eating and nurturing behavior in the family. Discussing the types of food associated with childhood, as well as family traditions (or lack thereof), may be useful. From this, members develop a deeper understanding of emotional needs in the family.

6. *Structured eating.* Another exercise that has been used with anorexics and bulimics is structured eating (Hoage, 1989; Sparnon & Hornyak, 1989). Compulsive eaters share similar dynamics. Structured eating is a way to desensitize group members to food and normalize the experience of eating socially. Eating in a group also provides a parallel for the family meal exercises. Whether food is brought every week or as a one-time experience depends on the group and the process issues discussed.

Once food has been discussed in the group, suggest that individuals bring their favorite food or the food they most fear (possibly the same) to the next group session. Once the food is present, have members process it at each level: presence, touch, smell, and taste. A single taste experience can be stretched out to include food texture, taste on different parts of the tongue, feelings as it is swallowed and goes down the esophagus, and the aftertaste. When group members stretch out the eating experience, they have a model for slower, controlled eating they can apply to other situations. After the food has been processed and sampled, some groups want to share their food with one another. Other groups have members who do not want to share; they want to be able to keep their food. The information gained from this exercise gives leaders information about group and individual trust and development.

7. *Contracts.* Behavioral contracts have been recommended as a safety net during treatment. Kaplan (1990) outlined expectations in treatment, expectations concerning weight gain, expectations to give as well as receive feedback in the group, and expectations prohibiting self-harm. The behavioral contract Kaplan (1990) described is verbal.

Written behavioral contracts are used at Arizona State University to provide consequences for students at medical risk with a pattern of manipulating treatment (Bower,
1990). These contracts incorporate the same elements Kaplan suggested, but are more
explicit. The contract carries with it consequences limiting the ability to stay enrolled in
the university. Just as Selzer, Koenigsberg, and Kernberg (1987) believe explicit expectations are necessary for borderline patients, safeguards for eating disordered clients in
denial may be needed. The purpose, as with Kaplan (1990), is to create an "environment
that is controlling, yet empathic" (p. 47). A contract of this nature will obviously impact
group work.

8. *Workshops.* Boskind-White and White (1987) have instituted short-term, intensive group experiences that allow each participant to focus on eating issues. In a workshop format, group development will not progress through the same stages as a longer
term group. In any case, the impact of sharing experiences (seen in the first part of group
development) will be realized and may offer relief for individuals who have never felt
their voice was heard.

Population Specific Considerations

Despite the common threads running through the eating disorders, some specific considerations apply to each of the three populations.

Anorectic Groups   Problems specific to physical starvation have to be considered when
working with anorectic individuals (Boskind-White & White, 1987). Those authors
describe anorectics as apathetic, irritable, younger and less social than bulimics, isolated,
family-dependent, and less prone to eating binges. Levenkron (1982) further describes
them as controlling and manipulative. Group screening procedures have to assure that
their physical needs are being met. In groups, these members have limited social skills
and resist treatment, so they may be challenging for the leaders.

Feminist theorists (Boskind-White & White, 1987; Chernin, 1985; Orbach, 1978)
suggest that the anorectic and bulimic clients are more a byproduct of social pressures
than psychological impairments that would complicate group work. Groups have the
unique ability to provide a contained environment where anorectic members can directly
confront their isolation.

Bulimic Groups   Bulimic group members "rival their anorectic sisters in being difficult
to treat" (Cauwels, 1983, p. 180). They are differentiated from compulsive eaters because
the former compensate for their binge behavior with purging. They, too, have health concerns and should be monitored, but the risk is not generally as great as with anorectics
(Boskind-White & White, 1987). These group members have more social skills than
anorectics, but not without cost.

Wooley and Kearney-Cooke (1986, p. 486) noted that bulimics tend to be compliant
and make others feel at ease, their apparent warmth concealing grave difficulties in sustaining connection, avoiding anger, and preferring isolation. Bulimics may be difficult to
commit to treatment, impatient when they do not recover quickly, competitive with other
group members, and resistant to receiving help from others (Cauwels, 1983). Wooley and

Kearney-Cooke (1986) delineate the goals of a bulimic group as: (a) to be honest emotionally with each other, and (b) to make comparisons between their relationships in the group to relationships outside of the group. Yalom's model sensitively answers these two goals. Helping the bulimic person look at distancing patterns in relationships is not easy, but is crucial for recovery.

Compulsive Eating Groups   Medical problems with the compulsive eater also require attention but, again, do not pose as critical a threat as for the anorectic. Compulsive eaters share an obsession with food but rely on internally directed guilt and shame to compensate. These symptoms may persist longer than for the other eating disordered groups. Years of compulsive eating have layered the shame and guilt that distance them from others. Overeating has been correlated with anxiety and depression and, in some cases, "extreme disruptions of psychological functioning bordering on psychotic episodes" (Striegel-Moore & Rodin, 1986, p. 100). If obesity is also an issue, social discrimination (including educational and employment prejudice) is often aimed against overweight people (Bray, 1986; Richardson, Goodman, Hastorf, & Dornbusch, 1961). Emotional wounds have to be addressed in the group context. A group can initiate working through the layers of shame.

Age Specific Considerations

Mintz and Betz (1988) found that 64% of their college sample had some degree of eating disordered behavior. Much of the research and this chapter have focused on college campuses. Anorexia nervosa has been considered a rare disorder of young adolescents but also may occur in women in their 20s (Garfinkel & Kaplan, 1986). Bulimia has been viewed as a phenomenon of young adult college populations, the mean age of onset being 18.4 years (Agras & Kirkley, 1986). Compulsive eaters may run the gamut. Groups, therefore, have to consider the developmental level of group members.

Addressing younger group members entails understanding their current social situation. Whenever the person is living at home family dynamics come to the fore, and the family should be included to support the work of counseling.

Counseling groups with older people should respect the developmental and social issues unique to that population. Couples and significant others (close friends, children, and so on) may be included in the group or in a separate group (Schwartz & Barrett, 1987). Again, the aim is to help heal the emotional wounds that may be manifest in individuals or systems.

A wide age span among group members sometimes allows the opportunity to speak to intragenerational issues more immediately than in age-homogeneous groups. Transference between "parents" and "children" may be faced directly in the group context. Although diversity has been screened out in the past (Root et al., 1986) to make the groups more homogeneous, it should be a matter of the group leader's preference.

Final Considerations

Individuals with eating disorders elicit various countertransference issues in group leaders. Root et al. (1986) suggest that leaders who work with these groups be experienced, recognize that new issues may arise, and understand the leader's role in the group. Reactions to the binge, purge, or restrictive behavior itself may be strong. Leaders may need to confront their own feelings about competence and authority. Authenticity, considered an important dimension in counseling when women work with women (Brody, 1984), is important for all group leaders who work with this population. Leaders also may have to face their own issues of power (Osherson, 1986). Yalom (1989) described how personal issues can become manifest in counseling with an obese client.

Internalized societal values concerning fatness and thinness have impacted all of us. Perspectives differ on the amount of pathology connected with eating disorders. The perceived difficulty in treating these people sometimes may be less a case of severity than of orientation, perspective, and countertransference.

Leading eating disorders groups is challenging and may be frustrating. It also has the potential to be rewarding. Considering the societal implications, the work may be as empowering for the group leader as for the member, but the path to change is not fully chartered because what works is not fully known. In the labyrinth of the eating disorders group, "there is no substitute for experience, supervision, and intuition" (Yalom, 1975, p. 332).

SUMMARY

In the recently recognized area of eating disorders, three basic classifications have emerged: anorexia nervosa, bulimia nervosa, and compulsive eating. Each has unique characteristics with implications for treatment. Although eating disorders have been earmarked as a female problem, some males are also afflicted, and research is continuing. These disorders may stem from developmental deficits, societal pressures for thinness, improper dieting, family systems deficits, a sense of powerlessness, or biological causes, in any combination.

Eating disorders have health consequences and may be life-threatening. Counseling groups are at the present the preferred modality for treatment because of the perceived values gained interacting with others who share the problem. Within a group setting, no one treatment has been found to be superior than any others; however, an interpersonal approach using Yalom's group model meets the cognitive and emotional needs specific to this population.

At the root of treatment are trust, power, and control issues. Curative factors include instillation of hope, universality, altruism, corrective recapitulation of the primary family group, socializing techniques, imitative behavior, group cohesiveness, catharsis, and existential factors.

Group development follows several stages, beginning with screening and progressing through orientation, conflict, and cohesiveness, to termination. Strategies have included using adult nomenclature, relaxation and hypnosis, body image exercises, imagery activities, recalling eating memories, structured eating experiences, contracts, and workshops.

Interwoven in treatment are population-specific and age-specific considerations. In addition, group leaders are encouraged to learn about the eating disorders, know about the possible medical needs of group members, recognize societal pressures specific to women, and seek supervision or consultation.

REFERENCES

Agras, W., & Kirkley, B. (1986). Bulimia: Theories of etiology. In K. Brownell & J. Foreyt (Eds.), *Handbook of eating disorders* (pp. 367–378). New York: Basic Books.

American Psychiatric Association (1980). *Diagnostic and statistical manual of mental disorders* (3rd ed.). Washington, DC: Author.

American Psychiatric Association (1987). *Diagnostic and statistical manual of mental disorders* (3rd ed., rev). Washington, DC: Author.

Andersen, A. (1986). Inpatient and outpatient treatment of anorexia nervosa. In K. Brownell & J. Foreyt, *Handbook of eating disorders* (pp. 333–350). New York: Basic Books.

Anderson, C., & Holder, D. (1989). Women and serious mental disorders. In M. McGoldrick, C. Anderson, & F. Walsh, (Eds.), *Women in families: A framework for family therapy* (pp. 381–405). New York: W. W. Norton.

Bandler, R., & Grinder, J. (1982). *Reframing.* Moab, UT: Real People Press.

Barth, D., & Wurman, V. (1986). Group therapy with bulimic women: A self-psychological approach. *International Journal of Eating Disorders, 5*(4), 735–745.

Bauer, B., & Anderson, W. (1989). Bulimic beliefs: Food for thought. *Journal of Counseling & Development, 67*, 416–419.

Bauer, B., Anderson, W., & Hyatt, R. (1986). *Bulimia: Book for therapist and client.* Muncie, IN: Accelerated Development.

Bepko, C. (1989). Disorders of power: Women and addiction in the family. In M. Goldrick, C. Anderson, & F. Walsh, *Women in families: A framework for family therapy* (pp. 406–426). New York: W. W. Norton.

Bilich, M. (1983). *Weight loss from the inside out: Help for the compulsive eater.* New York: Harper & Row.

Boskind-Lodahl, M. (1976). Cinderella's stepsisters: A feminist perspective on anorexia nervosa and bulimia. *Signs: Journal of Women in Culture & Society, 2*, 324–356.

Boskind-White, M., & White, W. (1987). *Bulimarexia: The binge/purge cycle* (2nd ed.). New York: W. W.Norton.

Bowen, D. (1990, May). *Physician's role in eating disorders team treatment.* Paper presented at American College Health Association National Convention, San Antonio.

Bray, G. (1986). Effects of obesity on health and happiness. In K. Brownell & J. Foreyt (Eds.), *Handbook of eating disorders* (pp. 3–44). New York: Basic Books.

Brody, C. (1984) Authenticity in feminist therapy. In M. Brody (Ed.), *Women therapists working with women* (pp. 11–21). New York: Springer.

Brownell, K., & Foreyt, J. (Eds.) (1986). *Handbook of eating disorders.* New York: Basic Books.

Brownell, K., & Wadden, T. (1986). Behavior therapy for obesity: Modern approaches and better results. In K. Brownell & J. Foreyt (Eds.), *Handbook of eating disorders* (pp. 180–197). New York: Basic Books.

Bruch, H. (1973). *Eating disorders: Obesity, anorexia nervosa, and the person within.* New York: Basic Books.

Bruch, H. (1978). *The golden cage: The enigma of anorexia nervosa.* New York: Vintage Books.

Brumberg, J. (1989). *Fasting girls: A history of anorexia nervosa.* New York: New American Library.

Carruba, M., & Blundell, J. (Eds.) (1986). *Pharmacology of eating disorders.* New York: Raven Press.

Cauwels, J. (1983). *Bulimia: The binge-purge compulsion.* New York: Doubleday.

Chernin, K. (1985). *The hungry self: Women, eating, and identity.* New York: Harper & Row.

Eichenbaum, L., & Orbach, S. (1982). *Understanding women: A feminist psychoanalytic approach.* New York: Basic Books.

Fairburn, C., & Garner, D. (1986). The diagnosis of bulimia- nervosa. *International Journal of Eating Disorders, 5*, 403–419.

Friedlander, M., & Siegel, S. (1990). Separation-individuation difficulties and cognitive-behavioral indicators of eating disorders among college women. *Journal of Counseling Psychology, 37*(1), 74–78.

Ganley, R. (1989). Emotion and eating in obesity: A review of the literature. *International Journal of Eating Disorders, 8*(3), 343–361.

Garfinkel, P., & Garner, D. (1982). *Anorexia nervosa: A multidimensional perspective.* New York: Brunner/Mazel.

Garfinkel, P., & Kaplan, A. (1986). Anorexia nervosa: Diagnostic conceptualizations. In K. Brownell & J. Foreyt (Eds.), *Handbook of eating disorders* (pp. 266–282). New York: Basic Books.

Garner, D. (1986). Cognitive therapy for anorexia nervosa. In K. Brownell & J. Foreyt (Eds.), *Handbook of eating disorders* (pp. 301–327). New York: Basic Books.

Gross, M. (1983). Correcting perceptual abnormalities, anorexia nervosa and obesity by use of hypnosis. *Journal of the American Society of Psychosomatic Dentistry & Medicine, 30*, 142–150.

Heesacker, R., & Neimeyer, G. (1990). Assessing object relations and social cognitive correlates of eating disorder. *Journal of Counseling Psychology, 37*(4), 419–426.

Hoage, C. (1989). The use of in-session structured eating in the outpatient treatment of bulimia nervosa. In L. Hornyak & E. Baker (Eds.), *Experiential therapies for eating disorders* (pp. 60–77). New York: Guilford Press.

Hogg, A., & Frank, M. L. (in press). Toward an interpersonal model of codependence and contradependence. *Journal of Counseling and Development.*

Hornyak, L., & Baker, E. (Eds.). (1989). *Experiential therapies for eating disorders.* New York: Guilford Press.

Hudson, J., & Pope, G. (1984). *New hope for binge eaters.* New York: Harper & Row.

Hutchinson, M. (1985). *Transforming body image.* New York: Crossing Press.

Johnson, C., & Maddi, K. (1986). The etiology of bulimia: Bio-psycho-social perspectives. *Annals of Adolescent Psychiatry, 13,* 1–10.

Johnson, C., & Pure, D. (1986). Assessment of bulimia: A multidimensional model. In K. Brownell & J. Foreyt (Eds.), *Handbook of eating disorders* (pp. 405–449). New York:Basic Books.

Kaplan, A. (1990). The role of the director. In N. Piran & A. Kaplan, *A day hospital group treatment program for anorexia nervosa and bulimia nervosa* (pp. 42–60). New York: Brunner/Mazel.

Kearney-Cooke, A. (1989). Reclaiming the body: Using guided imagery in the treatment of body image disturbances among bulimic women. In L. Hornyak, & E. Baker (Eds.), *Experiential therapies for eating disorders* (pp. 11–33). New York: Guilford Press.

Kempley, F. (1988). *Effectiveness of an exposure treatment for bulimia.* Unpublished doctoral dissertation, Arizona State University, Tempe.

Kerr, A., & Piran, N. (1990). Comprehensive group treatment program. In N. Piran & A. Kaplan, *A day hospital group treatment program for anorexia nervosa and bulimia nervosa* (pp. 20–41). New York: Brunner/Mazel.

Klesges, R., Mizes, J., & Klesges, L. (1987). Self-help dieting strategies in college males and females. *International Journal of Eating Disorders, 6*(3), 409–417.

LeBlanc, D. (1990). *You can't quit 'til you know what's eating you: Overcoming compulsive eating.* Deerfield Beach, FL: Health Communications.

Lee, N., & Rush, A. (1986). Cognitive-behavioral group therapy for bulimia. *International Journal of Eating Disorders, 5*(4), 599–615.

Lerner, H. (1985). *The dance of anger.* New York: Harper & Row.

Levenkron, S. (1982). *Treating and overcoming anorexia nervosa.* New York: Charles Scribner's Sons.

Lewis, L., & Johnson, C. (1985). A comparison of sex role orientation between women with bulimia and normal controls. *International Journal of Eating Disorders, 4*(1), 247.

Love, S., Lewis, L., & Johnson, C. (1989). Group therapy in the treatment of bulimia nervosa. *Advances in eating disorders* (Vol. 2, pp. 175–195). New York: JAI Press.

Mintz, L., & Betz, N. (1988). Prevalence and correlates of eating disordered behaviors among undergraduate women. *Journal of Counseling Psychology, 35,* 463–471.

Minuchin, S., Rosman, B., & Baker, L. (1978). *Psychosomatic families: Anorexia nervosa in context.* Cambridge, MA: Harvard University Press.

Mizes, J., & Fleece, G. (1986). On the use of progressive relaxation in the treatment of bulimia: A single subject design study. *International Journal of Eating Disorders, 5*(1), 169–176.

Morley, J., Levine, A., & Willenbring, M. (1986). Stress induced feeding disorders. In M. Carruba & J. Blundell, *Pharmacology of eating disorders* (pp. 71–99). New York: Raven Press.

Orbach, S. (1978). *Fat is a feminist issue.* New York: Berkeley Books.

Orbach, S. (1982). *Fat is a feminist issue: II.* New York: Berkeley Books.

Orbach, S. (1986). *Hunger strike: The anorectic's struggle as a metaphor for our age.* New York: W. W. Norton.

Osherson, S. (1986). *Finding our fathers.* New York: Fawcett Columbine.

Pettinati, H., Kogan, L., Margolis, C., Shrier, L., & Wade, J. (1989). Hypnosis, hypnotizability, and the bulimic patient. In L. Hornyak & E. Baker, *Experiential therapies for eating disorders* (pp. 34–59). New York: Guilford Press.

Piran, N., & Kaplan, A. (Eds.). (1990). *A day hospital group treatment program for anorexia nervosa and bulimia nervosa.* New York: Brunner/Mazel.

Polivy, J., & Herman, C. (1985). Dieting and bingeing: A causal analysis. *American Psychologist, 40,* 193–201.

Pope, H., & Hudson, J. (1989). Eating disorders. In H. Kaplan & B. Sadock (Eds.), *Comprehensive textbook of psychiatry* (5th ed.). Baltimore: Williams & Wilkins.

Richardson, S., Goodman, N., Hastorf, A., & Dornbusch, S. (1961). Cultural uniformity in reaction to physical disabilities. *American Sociological Review, 26,* 241–247.

Rodin, J., Silverstein, L., & Striegel-Moore, R. (1985). Women and weight: A normative discontent. In T. B. Sonderegger (Ed.), *Nebraska symposium on motivation, 1984: Psychology and gender* (pp. 267–307). Lincoln: University of Nebraska Press.

Root, M., Fallon, P., & Friedrich, W. (1986). *Bulimia: A systems approach to treatment.* New York: Norton.

Roth, D., & Ross, D. (1988). Long-term cognitive-interpersonal group therapy for eating disorders. *International Journal of Group Psychotherapy, 38,* 491–510.

Roth, G. (1984). *Breaking free from compulsive eating.* New York: New American Library.

Roy-Byrne, P., Lee-Benner, K., & Yager, J. (1984). Group therapy for bulimia. *International Journal of Eating Disorders, 1*(20), 97–116.

Russell, G. (1979). Bulimia nervosa: An ominous variant of anorexia nervosa. *Psychological Medicine, 9,* 429–448.

Russell, G., Szmukler, G., Dare, C., & Eisler, I. (1987). An evaluation of family therapy in anorexia nervosa and bulimia nervosa. *Archives of General Psychiatry, 44,* 1047–1056.

Sargent, J., Liebman, R., & Silver, M. (1985). Family therapy for anorexia nervosa. In D. Garner & P. Garfinkel (Eds.), *Handbook of psychotherapy for anorexia and bulimia* (pp. 257–279). New York: Guilford Press.

Schwartz, R., & Barrett, M. (1987). Couple therapy for bulimia. In J. E. Harkaway (Ed.), *The family therapy collection*. Rockville, MD: Aspen.

Selzer, M., Koenigsberg, H., & Kernberg, O. (1987). The initial contract in the treatment of borderline patients. *American Journal of Psychiatry, 144,* 927–930.

Sparnon, J., & Hornyak, L. (1989). Structured eating experiences in the inpatient treatment of anorexia nervosa. In L. Hornyak & E. Baker (Eds.), *Experiential therapies for eating disorders* (pp. 207–233). New York: Guilford Press.

Squire, S. (1983). *The slender balance*. New York: Pinnacle Books.

Striegel-Moore, R., & Rodin, J. (1986). The influence of psychological variables in obesity. In K. Brownell & J. Foreyt, *Handbook of eating disorders* (pp. 99–121). New York: Basic Books.

Sullivan, H. S. (1953). *The interpersonal theory of psychiatry*. New York: W. W.Norton.

Survey on eating disorders shows significant problem. (1990, September). *NCAA News,* pp. 1,3,4.

Thakur, K. (1980). Treatment of anorexia nervosa with hypnotherapy. In H. T. Wain (Ed.), *Clinical hypnosis in medicine* (pp. 147–153). Chicago: Year Book Medical.

Thelen, M., Farmer, J., McLaughlin, L., Mann, L, Pruitt, J. (1990). Bulimia and interpersonal relationships: A longitudinal study. *Journal of Counseling Psychology, 37*(1), 85–90.

Wade, J., Kogan, H., Pettinati, & Franks, V. (1986, April). *Sex-role self-perceptions in eating disorder patients*. Paper presented at Eastern Psychological Association. New York.

Weiss, L., Katzman, M., & Wolchik, S. (1986). *You can't have your cake and eat it too*. Saratoga, CA: R&E Publishers.

White, W. C. (1985). Bulimarexia: Intervention strategies and outcome considerations. In S. Emmett, *Theory and treatment of anorexia nervosa and bulimia* (pp. 246–267). New York: Brunner/Mazel.

Wooley, S., & Kearney-Cooke, A. (1986). Intensive treatment of bulimia and body image disturbances. In K. Brownell & J. Foreyt (Eds.), *Handbook of eating disorders*. New York: Basic Books.

Wooley, S., & Wooley, O. (1979). Obesity and women: I. A closer look at the facts. *Women's Studies International Quarterly, 2,* 67–79.

Yalom, I. (1975). *The theory and practice of group psychotherapy* (2nd ed.). New York: Basic Books.

Yalom, I. (1985). *The theory and practice of group psychotherapy* (3rd ed.). New York: Basic Books.

Yalom, I. (1989). *Love's executioner*. New York: Basic Books.

8

Group Counseling for People with Physical Disabilities

Hanoch Livneh and Robert E. Pullo

*T*he origins of group work as applied to individuals with physical disabilities can be traced to the pioneering work of Joseph Pratt, a physician at the Massachusetts General Hospital, who, as early as 1905, used group methods with tubercular patients (Gust, 1970; Miller, Wolfe & Spiegel, 1975). Upon noticing the role group members played in positively affecting the emotional adjustment to their illnesses, Pratt later expanded his work to encompass patients with other chronic illnesses (Durkin, 1972). Pratt's approach valued two components embedded in group methods—support and inspiration—of particular importance when considering the feelings of depression and isolation often associated with long-term disabling conditions.

MERITS OF GROUP COUNSELING

Group counseling with individuals who have physical disabilities has much to offer. The advantages of group counseling for those with physical disabilities are many:

1. Groups can help people who strive toward the resolution of some common problem (e.g., accepting functional limitations, dealing with employer's prejudice), through the opportunity to learn from one another by sharing common concerns and problems and generating solutions to obstacles and difficulties (Gust, 1970).
2. Groups offer members a forum for the emotional release of burdensome personal issues in a supportive setting. Realizing that others face similar problems tends to lessen the anxiety and fear that accompany various disabling conditions.
3. The group experience can partially alleviate the stress, pain, and misery often generated by physical disability and further aggravated by social isolation, separation from family and friends, and perceived alienation from one's own body (Chubon, 1982; Jacobs, Harvill & Masson, 1988).
4. The group experience eases the transition into the able-bodied community. Via various socialization and social skill building (e.g., assertiveness, frustration-tolerance) exer-

cises, group members learn and practice how to better deal with the outside community (Chubon, 1982; Gust, 1970).
5. Through the group modality, leaders are able to more fully arrive at an accurate and comprehensive psychosocial assessment of group members (Salhoot, 1977).

NEEDS AND CONCERNS OF PEOPLE WITH DISABILITIES

Group counseling strategies for people with disabilities have been applied to a wide range of physical disorders. Included are groups for those with psychosomatic conditions, such as ulcers, asthma, migraine headaches, and neurodermatitis (Scheidlinger, 1984), sensory disabilities (Seligman, 1982), and neuromuscular and orthopedic impairments (Lasky & Dell Orto, 1979; Seligman, 1982). These groups can be established in inpatient (hospitals and rehabilitation centers) as well as outpatient (community) settings. Hospital-based groups typically focus on the participants' immediate medical concerns and initial reactions to the onset of disability (e.g., dealing with medical staff and procedures and feelings of anxiety and being overwhelmed by daily stress), whereas community-based groups confront concerns such as adverse public attitudes, long-term functional limitations, and prospects of employment.

More specifically, the needs and concerns people with disabilities customarily manifest can be conveniently classified into five major categories:

1. Physical needs (e.g., mobility, activities of daily living, pain control).
2. Psychological needs (e.g., alleviation of anxiety and depression, anger control, frustration tolerance).
3. Social needs (e.g., appropriate interpersonal communication, assertive behavior, managing stigma).
4. Vocational needs (e.g., employment training, job interviewing, job maintenance).
5. Financial needs (e.g., disability benefits, gainful employment).

This wide array of needs and concerns of clients with disabilities has necessitated various therapeutic group formats. Four general group modalities seem to dominate the field:

1. *Educational groups.* These didactic groups impart factual information to participants. For example, the leader discusses and clarifies specific treatment procedures, necessary lifestyle changes, and appropriate vocational pursuits. This type of group is aimed at helping members to make appropriate decisions concerning these life issues.
2. *Social support groups.* Support groups, typically generated from self-help and peer-helper group models, seek to provide mutual support to participants and create a forum for exchanging ideas, concerns, and problem-solving methods.
3. *Psychotherapeutic groups.* The emphasis in psychotherapeutic groups is on the affective domain and increased self-understanding. By providing participants cathartic outlets, these groups directly address pressing emotional issues such as anxiety, depression, anger, and changes in personal identity.
4. *Coping and skill training groups.* These groups are more readily aligned with the cognitive and behavioral camps. Participants are trained to cope effectively with their dis-

ability and its implications. Specific skills are taught during group sessions and later practiced in the external environment.

THERAPEUTIC FACTORS OF GROUPS FOR PEOPLE WITH DISABILITIES

Yalom's (1985) curative factors inherent in group counseling seem to be directly addressed by groups whose members have disabilities (Buchanan, 1975; Jacobs et al., 1988; Mann, Godfrey, & Dowd, 1973; Seligman, 1982). These principles are reviewed only briefly here, in relation to disabilities, as they are more fully explained earlier in the text.

Instillation of Hope

The expectation of recovery or overcoming disability and threat of future bodily deterioration, coupled with observation of gradual progress of other group members, is a powerful motivating force. Participants perceive and vicariously identify with group members who overcome adversity.

Universality

The perception of uniqueness is dispelled in groups. Members are quick to discover that their problems, concerns, and fears are shared by others and that one does not suffer alone. The feeling of commonality tends to decrease social isolation and withdrawal.

Imparting Information

Didactic instruction (e.g., informing participants of new medical procedures; discussing anticipated psychological reactions associated with the particular impairment), as well as advice and suggestions by the group leaders, rehabilitation personnel, or other group members on the availability of health related services, job opportunities, and so on, can reduce client ignorance and anxiety about the unknown future.

Altruism

Participants learn how to be helpful and useful to others. Group members derive many personal benefits from sharing the experiences, suggestions, insights, and reassurances of other members. Veterans and novices alike benefit from the mutual sharing of these experiences.

Corrective Recapitulation of the Primary Family Group

Groups for people with or without disabilities bear certain resemblances to families, both in structure and dynamics. Group leaders and members are capable of eliciting feelings and behaviors that once were directed at parents and siblings. Early family dynamics and conflicts (e.g., dependence-independence, scapegoating) can be relived and corrective feedback applied to faulty perceptions and maladaptive behaviors.

Development of Socializing Techniques

In many instances, preparing individuals with disabilities to go into the community is predicated on their acquiring social skills. Group members role play various social situations with the goal of achieving useful and constructive interpersonal behaviors.

Imitative Behavior

Emulating the behaviors of successful role models has been a cornerstone of the rehabilitation movement. Participants learn how to model their thoughts and behaviors after those of group leaders and other members who have successfully coped with their physical and social environments (e.g., gained independence, secured a job).

Group Cohesiveness

Belonging to a cohesive group produces an attitude of solidarity in the members. During group interactions, members share feelings of acceptance and mutual respect, which, in turn, results in a more positive self-concept.

Catharsis

Groups afford their members the opportunity to ventilate strong emotions (e.g., anger, fear, loss, anxiety, joy). In the supportive social environment of the group, relieving these pent-up emotions constitutes an important curative factor. It may pave the way to gaining insight into one's problems as participants recognize their present emotional reactions and the connection to those experienced earlier with members of the nuclear family.

GOALS OF GROUP COUNSELING FOR PEOPLE WITH DISABILITIES

In reviewing the literature on the purposes and goals of group counseling for people with disabilities, and in considering their problems and needs, three primary group counseling goal categories seem to predominate: affective, cognitive, and behavioral.

Affective Goals

Goals considered under this category pertain to those group approaches that address the client's emotional well-being (Democker & Zimpfer, 1981; Henkle, 1975; Kriegsman & Celotta, 1981; Rose, 1989; Salhoot, 1977):

1. *Provide the opportunity for emotional catharsis.* Offer group members the opportunity to express and share common feelings, experiences, and problems (e.g., depression, despair, helplessness, anger) in a safe environment.
2. *Give members emotional support.* Receiving support from peers and group leaders is a cardinal step in the process of adapting to disability.
3. *Reduce anxiety.* Overcoming initial fear and anxiety is mandatory for successful rehabilitation.
4. *Provide members with the opportunity to recognize that they are not alone.* Group members come to realize that others have similar experiences and emotional reactions.

Cognitive Goals

Cognitive goals are those directed at thought-related or perceptive processes. They are also geared toward the individual's knowledge and understanding of his or her disability and its implications for future functioning. More specifically, these goals are to (Democker & Zimpfer, 1981; Kriegsman & Celotta, 1981; Singler, 1982):

1. *Assist the group member to increase self-acceptance and self-esteem.* The concept of self (self-confidence and personal worth) is intimately linked to acceptance of self with a disability and the subsequent personal adjustment.
2. *Help the person confront reality.* Clients receive opportunities to test reality and form more realistic evaluations of their assets and limitations.
3. *Provide the member with accurate and comprehensive information.* Information might include prognosis of condition, use of medication, available sexual outlets, and other facts to foster a sense of personal control and demystify the nature of the disability.

Behavioral Goals

The primary purpose of behavioral goals is to decrease clients' maladaptive behaviors (e.g., dependency, social withdrawal) and replace them with adaptive ones (e.g., independence, appropriate interpersonal relationships). Accordingly, these goals might be to (Democker & Zimpfer, 1981; Kriegsman & Celotta, 1981; Mannet al., 1973; Miller, Wolfe & Spiegel, 1975; Rose, 1989):

1. Assist dependent group members in overcoming dependence (in a mutually supportive environment).
2. Increase the person's ability to cope more effectively with the disability and its associated functional limitations.
3. Provide a setting wherein group members can safely and gradually practice and rehearse new skills and behaviors.
4. Improve interpersonal communications and socialization skills.
5. Assist members in setting and implementing new and more appropriate, personal, educational and vocational goals.

These do not constitute a complete list of all possible counseling goals of groups for people with disabilities. Rather, they represent the more common types of goals often suggested in the literature. Goals vary with the type of disability and the functional limitations it imposes, the immediate needs and concerns of each member or the group as a whole, and the leader's philosophy, knowledge, and skills (Democker & Zimpfer, 1981; Salhoot, 1977).

PHASES OF GROUP COUNSELING FOR PEOPLE WITH DISABILITIES

Most authors perceive the group process as being composed of two or possibly three essential segments (Kriegsman & Celotta, 1981; Lasky, Dell Orto, & Marinelli, 1984; Mann et al., 1973; Oradei & Waite, 1974; Power & Rogers, 1979). In a three-phase model, the first phase may be construed as one of relationship building. Group members are encouraged to talk about their disability, its etiology, major presenting problems, and so on. The discussion typically evolves around issues related to factual information concerning the disability. When needed, misconceptions pertaining to the disability, its causes, nature, and anticipated progress are clarified. Using methods such as reflection, clarification, self-disclosure, positive reinforcement, role playing, and establishing a relaxed atmosphere, group leaders encourage participants to develop mutual trust, openness, involvement, personal awareness and responsibility, and commitment (Kriegsman & Celotta, 1981).

During these initial sessions, group leaders play a more active role earlier rather than later by initiating topics for discussion, offering support and encouragement, raising questions and, in general, facilitating an active exchange of experiences and ideas. In more structural groups (see, for example, Lasky et al., 1984; Roessler, Milligan, & Ohlson, 1976), individual goal identification, clarification, and planning are paramount.

The second phase is normally geared toward (a) encouraging members to express and explore their feelings regarding the disability, (b) helping participants become aware that others share similar emotions, and (c) based on this gained awareness, developing a mutual understanding and closeness among group members (Oradei & Waite, 1974; Power & Rogers, 1979). During this middle phase, group leaders shift their role from that of active structure providers and discussion guiders to a less overtly leading role in which participants are allowed to ventilate anxieties and fears about their future, and anger and frustration over interpersonal conflicts, and to initiate most discussion topics.

Attention is clearly directed to helping the participant, through ego-supportive feedback, to gain insight into his or her adjustment difficulties, while at the same time providing the opportunity for members to learn from each other's experiences and achieve a more positive outlook on life with a disability (Power & Rogers, 1979). Group leaders, therefore, pay particular attention to exploration of self, interpersonal dynamics and group functioning as a cohesive unit (Lasky et al., 1984; Mann et al., 1973).

The third and final phase of group counseling centers on development of coping and problem-solving methods, with special emphasis on resocialization, future planning, and community reintegration. During this phase, members are assisted in assessing, selecting, and prioritizing their future needs and objectives, and ways of implementing those objectives. Those who are released into the community for the first time since onset of the disability are given emotional support and feedback on their progress. They also receive ample opportunity to practice their newly learned behaviors. Group leaders and veteran participants often model community-based, adaptive behavior to clients who have recently sustained a disability. Lasky et al. (1984) view this final phase as directed toward "life and living," with an emphasis on creating resources that will help members apply their newly acquired skills in daily, community-based activities.

STRATEGIES FOR GROUP SESSIONS

The strategies discussed here pertain to two groups of disabling conditions: (a) sensory (visual and auditory), and (b) neuromuscular (spinal cord injury and cerebrovascular accident, or stroke) disabilities. Cross-disability group strategies developed specifically for rehabilitation settings include (a) structured, coping-based interventions, (b) self-help group methods, and (c) vocational-related (placement-oriented) procedures.

Approaches with Physical Disabilities Groups

The intent of this section is first to acquaint the reader with those relevant functional limitations (i.e., physical and psychosocial) inherent in some of the commonly encountered physical disabilities. Second, specific group strategies and issues directly related to counseling these populations will be presented.

Visual Impairment Groups   The chief difficulties people with visual disabilities encounter include (Keegan, 1974; Lindemann, 1981; Vander Kolk, 1983):

— mobility (restriction of freedom of movement that compromises their ability for independent living).
— dependence on the social environment.
— diminished socialization skills.
— anxiety resulting in avoidance of other people.
— accepting the reality of the disability and altered body image.
— coping with frustration and anger and related lack of assertiveness.

In one of the earlier attempts to use group strategies with people who have visual impairments, Cholden (1953) sought to offer them the opportunity to verbalize and gain insight into their feelings. He argued that blind people have difficulty expressing certain feelings because of their inability to perceive visual and social cues that customarily encourage or hinder the expression of emotions during interpersonal transactions. During group sessions, members were encouraged to express and gain understanding of their personal reactions to the disability. This was followed by discussing the means available for managing and controlling emotions. Cholden concluded that these group experiences fostered and enriched emotional communications in people who are blind.

Herman (1966) discussed the use of group therapy for blind people in rehabilitation settings. Weekly discussion topics included: (a) denial of blindness and its implications, (b) depression and despair following realization of the visual loss, preventing successful adaptation, (c) dependency and low self-esteem that work against the struggle for independence, (d) devaluation of self and guilt feelings, and (e) avoidance of social situations. Based on his clinical impressions, Herman concluded that the group experience was instrumental in bringing about closeness among the members.

Goldman (1970) and Wilson (1972) have further contributed to understanding the psychological reactions of persons with visual impairments and suggested specific strategies for coping with their psychological and behavioral difficulties. Wilson (1972) discussed two types of group therapy. The first, *exploratory group therapy*, delves into interpersonal issues that seem to have caused the problems. The second, *supportive group therapy*, is geared toward providing reassurance, encouragement, education, and advice on how to manage daily problems.

Using what he termed "encounter microlabs" with a group of young people with visual handicaps, Goldman (1970) sought to encourage participants to become aware of their own and others' feelings and their own and others' bodies. Goldman viewed encounter therapy as a multifaceted concept encompassing elements of various therapeutic modalities (e.g., Gestalt, person-centered, psychodynamic) in which action, holism, awareness, and self-growth are underscored. In a comprehensive discussion, he delineated five classes of techniques:

1. *Techniques to reduce initial anxiety.* Exercises involving deep breathing, progressive relaxation, and corpse posture (lying down and "letting your body go").
2. *Techniques to initiate interactions.* Milling exercises (moving randomly around the room, first nonverbally and then verbally, and using touch) and go-around exercises (going around to every person, touching him or her and making an "I feel" statement).
3. *Techniques for trust building.* For initiating real trust, falling and catching (falling backwards into the arms of others), lifting (being lifted up from the floor by others), and blind walk (being paired off with another member designated a "sighted guide" and together exploring the environment).
4. *Techniques for eliciting and working through problems.* A brief lecture, followed by an exercise. The lecture (covering topics such as honesty, openness, directness, and emphasizing the present) is followed by exercises including secret pool (writing down a secret anonymously, and then while the secret is being read by another member, discussing its meaning and providing feedback) and magic shop (being offered the opportunity to purchase anything one desires from a magic shop owned by the group leader).
5. *Guided fantasy techniques.* Exercises to assist in conflict resolution and goal setting, strategies to improve perception of body and physical appearance (e.g., stretching out and relaxing, exploring internal and external body boundaries), fantasizing significant others talking about oneself, and finally, future projection (imagining what the client will be doing in the distant future).

From his studies, Goldman (1970) concluded that these exercises increase self-assertiveness and feelings of independence, in addition to self-awareness and empathy toward others.

Another concern often encountered in group counseling with people who are blind is about sexual matters (e.g., dating, marriage, sex, pregnancy). Employing group therapy with adolescent, multihandicapped girls, Avery (1968) offered participants the opportunity to learn about sexuality issues. Through (a) reflection of feelings, (b) thought clarification, (c) interpretation of emotions and behaviors, and (d) answers to questions on sexual issues, the leader allowed the girls to ventilate emotional concerns in a supportive atmosphere, and provided related factual information.

Still another concern revolves around interactions with sighted people (Cholden, 1953; Welsh, 1982). During these interactions, feelings of hostility and resentment are often evident. Counseling strategies geared toward appropriate assertiveness skills and developing a more positive self-concept are called for under these circumstances (Welsh, 1982).

Another topic frequently encountered is how to cope with the functional limitations the visual impairment imposes. Group members might discuss the impact of these limitations on their ability to independently perform various tasks and activities in the community and how this might affect their self-concept (Inana, 1978; Welsh, 1982). Group leaders seek to facilitate acceptance of the condition, internalization of the concept of personal loss, and the development of a more realistic self-perception.

Finally, groups must attend to personal skill building. These skills may be applied in vocational training programs and in securing appropriate employment. Roessler (1978) reported on a personal achievement skill training program for visually impaired people.

They were taught problem-solving, decision-making, and self-modification skills. Participants engaged in exercises and activities that enabled them to improve their communication skills, to identify and prioritize goals, and to implement and monitor progress of those goals. This group achieved higher levels of goal attainment and self-esteem as compared to a control group.

Group counselors working with clients who have visual impairments should pay particular attention to:

1. *Uses of silence.* Periods of silence are most threatening to blind people (Welsh, 1982). Silence generates discomfort, anxiety, and resentment, and may even lead to paranoid projection by some participants. Leaders must, therefore, be more verbal and directive (e.g., use audible reinforcers, invite participants to speak) rather than rely on more traditional nonverbal methods (e.g., eye contact, head nodding). Co-leadership as a means to bridge periods of silence is also recommended (Keegan, 1974; Welsh, 1982).
2. *Group structure.* When counseling people who are blind, the need for more structure of group sessions is inherent (Welsh, 1982). This is particularly important for members who are congenitally blind.
3. *Trust-building techniques.* Building trust is important in that many blind people often mistrust and resent sighted people, as well as others who are blind. Goldman's (1970) earlier discussed activities (e.g., "fall and catch," "the blind walk") are recommended (Keegan, 1974; Welsh, 1982).
4. *Selection of group members.* In choosing group participants, the factors of degree of visual impairment, its cause, and age of onset should be considered. Also, clients' levels of denial, optimism, resentment, and anxiety are important variables in establishing a well balanced group (Routh, 1957; Welsh, 1982).

Hearing Impairment Groups   The most pervasive difficulties that beset people who have hearing impairments are (Lindemann, 1981; Ostby & Thomas, 1984):

— communication.
— negotiating various environmental features that may directly impact one's personal safety (e.g., inability to respond to a ringing phone, or to react to honking horns or police sirens).
— experiential deprivation and isolation from significant others.
— maladaptive behavioral patterns (e.g., withdrawal, rigidity, suspiciousness, immaturity, denial) that prevent effective social interaction with hearing peers.
— handling frustrations because of inadequate communication and isolation.
— coping with overprotective and dependency-fostering parents and public.

In an earlier effort to apply group counseling strategies to hospital patients who were deaf, Robinson (1965) reported on a group of six participants and a hearing psychiatrist who employed manual communication methods. The group proved successful in offering participants the opportunity to ventilate feelings toward other group members and the therapist. Portner (1981) described a YWCA group for deaf members, related to problems of living, group members' denial of impairment, projection of frustrations and anger toward hearing people, feelings of inferiority, and difficulties in communicating with mates.

As previously mentioned, a common problem of people who are deaf is their experiential deprivation and its subsequent progression into lack of social assertiveness. In an effort to rectify this, Sedge (1982) sought to teach clients with hearing impairments to openly express their feelings and assert themselves in situations where communication barriers exist. Sedge further argued that prior research demonstrated the effectiveness of assertiveness training in (a) increasing assertive behavior, (b) improving self-concept, (c) elevating self-confidence, (d) improving speech fluency, and (e) increasing interactional activities.

Accordingly, Sedge developed an assertiveness training model for hearing-impaired servicemen, employing (a) mini-lectures, (b) modeling, (c) role playing, (d) overt and covert behavior rehearsals, (e) relaxation training, and (f) homework assignments. Training goals were to: (a) discriminate between passive, assertive, and aggressive behaviors; (b) identify and accept personal rights and those of others; (c) exert control in situations where communication is impaired; and (d) communicate more effectively within the environment. The training group demonstrated significant increases in level of assertiveness and in self-concept, when compared to a control group.

Concerns commonly raised and discussed in groups for people who are deaf include (Schein, 1982): (a) feelings of isolation because of a communication handicap (e.g., difficulties associated with accurately perceiving the motives of others); (b) appropriate expression of feelings such as anger and frustration; (c) interpretation of symbolic behaviors, often manifested in nonverbal (e.g., facial) cues and messages (of particular importance in the prelingually deaf population); and (d) appropriate rules and customs regarding dating and sex-oriented issues (more prevalent in individuals with prelingual deafness and those educated in restrictive residential settings).

Schein (1982) further asserted that to successfully manage these (e.g., isolation, lack of effective communication) and similar group-raised concerns, the leader should realize the importance of emotional ventilation. In a group context, it allows members to realize that their problems and frustrations are not unique. Furthermore, mutual expression of feelings and exchange of concerns increase self-esteem, alleviate the expression of anxiety, and reduce interpersonal awkwardness.

When working with deaf and hearing impaired populations, group leaders consider the following:

1. *Arrangement of the physical setting.* In organizing the group setting, the leader should pay particular attention to the participants' seating arrangements (so that members must be able to see each other and the leader at the same time). Barrier-free sightlines must be ensured. Semicircular or rectangular seating patterns are often recommended (Schein, 1982). Lighting must facilitate nonverbal and manual communication, and appropriate acoustics must be ensured for members who use hearing aids.
2. *Interpreter.* Although employing a sign language interpreter is often suggested to facilitate communication in these groups, it is not without difficulties (Schein, 1982). The addition of a "third party" may adversely affect group dynamics by hindering

establishment of relationships and impeding expression of many feelings and thoughts (Portner, 1981). Also, the interpreter cannot attend to more than one person's verbalization at a time, thus placing himself or herself under pressure to keep pace with the messages. Then the group leader has to assume the role of "verbal traffic director" (Schein, 1982).

When interpreters are used, they should be easily visible to all, and preferably seated next to the group leader. Ideally, the leader should be adept at signing, for both practical reasons (speed in communication) and psychological reasons (learning sign language is considered to be a gesture of respect for the person who is hearing impaired) (Riekehof, 1987).

3. *Eye strain.* The leader must be alert to the strain placed on members' vision as a result of their total reliance on this communication modality (Schein, 1982).

4. *Deaf-hearing group mixture.* The ratio of group members who are deaf to those whose hearing is normal (e.g., people with other disabilities, family members, other staff members) partially dictates group communication efforts (choice of modalities for language expression), structure, and content (Schein, 1982). Group leaders should, accordingly, carefully plan the content and structure of sessions, taking into account the participants' oral and manual communication skills, degree of hearing impairment, age of onset (prelingual versus postlingual) and social and emotional maturity.

Approaches with Neuromuscular Injury Groups

Spinal Cord Injury (SCI) Groups   Individuals who sustained spinal cord injury (SCI) are primarily faced with (Crewe & Krause, 1987; Donovan, 1981):

— mobility impairment (i.e., restricted ambulation and often inaccessible environment).
— problems with personal hygiene, dressing, eating and drinking, toileting and writing (specific impairments depend upon the nature and severity of the injury).
— difficulties (particularly in men) in sexual performance.
— feelings of depression, passivity, embarrassment, and helplessness.
— denial of the injury's degree of severity and its permanency, resulting in unwillingness to cooperate with rehabilitation efforts.
— disruption of familial, social, and vocational activities.

Mann et al. (1973) counseled with SCI groups. Specifically, they established four group goals: (a) to help participants increase their self-concepts, to positively impact total rehabilitation efforts; (b) to help dependent members overcome dependency in a mutually supportive environment; (c) to provide a setting wherein interpersonal relations issues could be identified, discussed and, when necessary, resolved; and (d) to modify members' perceptual distortions about other people. The group was structured so participants who had sustained their injuries earlier could assist newer clients in accepting the limitations imposed by, and adjusting to life with, a disability. Feedback and reinforcement related to progress were provided by the group leader and other participants. Group discussion also focused on assisting clients to make maximum use of their strengths and remaining physical functions. Reporting on short-term group counseling with SCI members, Miller, Wolfe and Spiegel (1975) emphasized a more structured, didactic-informative approach. Their group was aimed at providing information on the physiology and associated problems (e.g., sexual, muscular) of spinal cord injuries. Their group members showed positive changes in self-concept, as well as their knowledge and understanding of the impairment.

The concern with sexuality has led several clinicians to establish groups that specifically address this issue (Banik & Mendelson, 1978; Melnyk, Montgomery, & Over, 1979). In these groups, clients were encouraged to talk about their concerns and feelings related to sexual relations. The discussion commonly revolved around fears of rejection by sexual partners when satisfactory functioning was impaired. Using lectures and films, group leaders disseminated specific and technical information on the psychophysiology of sex, to relieve anxiety and avoidance of the issue. In general, group leaders seek to balance the informative coverage of sexual alternatives and means of expression with small-group discussion, role playing, and behavioral rehearsal of effective partner communication, sexual adaptation and other related concerns (Melnyk et al., 1979).

During their group counseling, Melnyk and his co-workers developed the following weekly format: (a) member introduction through "games" and discussion of program goals and member problem areas; (b) small-group work using self-guided imagery for sensuality, and large-group discussion of communication issues; (c) verbal and nonverbal communication followed by discussion of films on sex education and techniques; and (d) discussion of body image followed by discussion of spinal cord injuries and the use of sexual aids.

A comprehensive structured group counseling program for people with SCI was proposed by Roessler et al. (1976). Termed the Personal Achievement Skills (PAS) training program, it strived to (a) develop awareness of their personal values, capacities, and acceptance of other group members, and (b) develop skills in areas such as communication, problem identification, goal setting, and action implementation. Typical member goals included: (a) independent community living, (b) educational-vocational training culminating in successful job placement, (c) identification of recreational and leisure needs and how to meet them, and (d) family counseling focusing on sexual issues.

Counselors who conduct group sessions with clients with SCI, should heed the following considerations:

1. *Appropriateness of physical setting*. The setting for group sessions must be totally free of architectural barriers. The leader may have to ensure physical modifications and arrangements prior to the first session (Seligman, 1982).
2. *Attention to client fatigue*. Because fatigue plays a major role in the lives of individuals with SCI, each session should be limited to a maximum of 2 hours (Roessler et al., 1976).
3. *Knowledge of spinal cord injuries*. The group leader(s) should thoroughly understand spinal cord injuries and their functional implications (Roessler et al., 1976), and be able to recognize and, when necessary, deal with emergency medical situations that might arise.
4. *Personal comfort with sexual issues*. Because a large portion of group work focuses on alternative sexual outlets, sexual aids, and the like, group leaders should become familiar with these topics and personally comfortable discussing these issues in a group format.

Cerebrovascular Accident (CVA) Groups   The major physical and psychosocial difficulties associated with cerebrovascular accidents (strokes) are (Anderson, 1981; Singler, 1982):

— perceptual-spatial deficits (including problems with visual-motor coordination, visual dysfunctions, spasticity and seizures).
— impairment of cognitive functioning (speech and language abilities, learning, abstract reasoning, memory, attention, and concentration).
— deficient affective performance (emotional reactions including anxiety, denial, depression, frustration, agitation, anger, and shame).
— behavioral involvement (increased impulsivity, restlessness, social discrimination).
— communication problems that result from deterioration in cognitive functioning (such as verbal fluency and involvement of the affective domain), causing lower frustration threshold and other emotional lability manifestations.

Because the psychophysiological implications of CVA are many, the counseling goals listed by clinicians address a wide array of concerns, issues, and problems. For example, in their patient-family, hospital-based group sessions, D'Afflitti and Weitz (1974) identified the two major goals as encouraging patients and families to (a) share feelings about the stroke in order to facilitate a better adjustment to the impairment, and (b) use appropriate community resources and supports available to them. As expected, patients and their family members raised numerous issues during the sessions. Among these were (a) loss of control of certain bodily parts and functions and its effect on self-esteem, (b) attempts at denial of impairment, (c) expression of resentment and anger by family upon realizing the magnitude of the impairment and ensuing guilt feelings, and (d) attempts of restitution and resolution of problems by discussing life prior to the disability, accepting the loss, and adjusting to life with a disability.

D'Afflitti and Weitz reported that discussion of the above issues in a group format seemed to be positively associated with facilitating communication between patient and family and creating more realistic expectations about the future, such as return to the community. Similar findings were reported by Oradei and Waite (1974), whose hospital-based stroke unit patients indicated better understanding of their impairment, its functional limitations, and how to better cope with depression and loneliness.

Singler (1982) argues that strategies for clients who have sustained CVA must capitalize on group members' current needs and remaining strengths, such as the need to talk about oneself, the fear of future strokes, and awareness of physical losses and the resultant limitations. In developing her hospital-based group, Singler set the goals of: (a) reducing anxiety and heightening emotionalism through a supportive atmosphere and the opportunity to ventilate feelings, (b) fostering increased self-acceptance, (c) rebuilding damaged self-esteem, and (d) reducing social isolation.

Accordingly, group discussions centered on: (a) providing members with accurate information on strokes, the therapeutic procedures involved, and the hospital setting; (b) sharing experiences and feelings; and (c) identifying and confronting members' most bothersome fears and problems (e.g., fear of subsequent strokes; feelings of depression, isolation, and anger; anxiety over reactions by community members). In earlier sessions, the group leader was directive, guiding members and explaining life-threatening issues.

In later sessions, the group leader made indirect interpretations by questioning, thus allowing members to gain insight into their problems.

An innovative approach to group counseling with stroke and other neurologically impaired clients is illustrated by Evans, Halar, and Smith (1985). Their short-term cognitive therapy was aimed at assisting recently discharged patients to cope with personal issues (e.g., depression, loneliness) and to interact productively with family and friends. Adopting a conference call system permitted nonambulatory participants to engage in discussion from their homes. The group conference took place weekly, and lasted an hour. The group leader directed the flow and exchange of their concerns.

Briefly, the cognitive therapy format espoused task-oriented objectives geared to improving mood or modifying behavior, based on cognitive processes that affect one's attitudes and belief system. Particularly targeted were negative and rigid cognitions leading to depression and loneliness. Leaders provided participants with feedback on circular, faulty, and destructive thought processes. Individually tailored objectives included: (a) providing accurate information on the impairment and its implications, (b) decreasing levels of anxiety, (c) increasing energy levels, (d) precipitating a higher level of personal independence, and (e) generating improved relationships with family.

With CVA groups, leaders should consider the following aspects of structuring and planning activities:

1. *Participants' speech and perceptual abilities*. Because a large number of CVA individuals have speech impairments, in addition to various other perceptual, physical, and cognitive losses, the group leader has to examine the impact of these factors on the group's structure and communication modalities (Singler, 1982).
2. *Individual and group goals*. As a result of the cognitive and verbal impairments and the often observed signs of frustration and anger among participants, group leaders should strive to develop specific and concrete goals to guide future group activities. Explicit, realistic, and attainable goals will most likely result in better attendance, motivation, and progress toward goal achievement.
3. *Handling denial*. Denial of their limitations by people with CVA is a rather prevalent and most disturbing phenomenon. Two strategies commonly mentioned to diffuse the long-term impact of denial are *awareness raising* and *gentle confrontation*. Youngjohn and Altman (1989) reported on a self-awareness group to reduce denial of deficits in a group of stroke and head injury patients attending a rehabilitation day hospital. Patients received explanations of the cognitive and personality changes that often accompany stroke. They also were assisted in identifying their cognitive strengths and limitations by being introduced to a wide range of cognitive tasks. Similarly, confrontational strategies, when applied discretely and cautiously (e.g., pointing out discrepancies between client's present functional abilities and unrealistic future goals), may gradually penetrate the protective shield of denial.

Several other equally important disabilities are not discussed here but can be found in Bilodeau and Hackett (1971) and Subramanian and Ell (1989) on group strategies for survivors of myocardial infarctions (heart attacks); Crawford and McIvor (1985) and Welch and Steven (1979) on group counseling with people who have multiple sclerosis;

Fischer and Samelson (1971) and Rogers, MacBride, Whylie, and Freeman (1977–78) on groups with amputees; and Buchanan (1975) and Hollon (1972) on group counseling interventions with people coping with chronic kidney disorders.

Approaches in Rehabilitation Settings

Three types of rehabilitation-specific group strategies are discussed here. First, Structured Experiential Training: Rehabilitation (SET:R) will be reviewed, followed by the application of self-help and peer helper groups to rehabilitation settings. Finally, mention is made of a vocationally related group model, the Job Club, for people with disabilities.

Structured Experiential Training: Rehabilitation (SET:R)   "Structured Experiential Training (SET) is an eclectic group rehabilitation model which is especially designed to meet the needs of persons with physical disabilities and emphasizes group members' goal involvement, mutual concern, and accountability" (Lasky et al., 1984, p. 317). The SET model synthesizes elements of educational, social support, psychotherapeutic, and coping skills into a systematic framework to benefit people undergoing rehabilitation. Those with disabilities share common concerns in the group. They are afforded the opportunity to capitalize on strengths, benefit from role models, and gain more awareness and sensitivity to issues such as stress and stigma. This communication among group members increases mutual trust and understanding.

Methodologically, SET uses structured experiential learning, the power of the group process, and explicit goal orientation directed at acquiring skills and resolving related therapeutic issues. SET incorporates a variety of structured experiences related to group and personal functioning. The structured experience is an intervention in a group's process that involves a set of specific instructions to participants. The five steps in this process are: (a) experiencing an activity, (b) publishing or sharing reactions or observations about the activity, (c) processing the activity with other participants, (d) generalizing from the experience, and (e) applying this new learning behaviorally.

Group organization   Prospective members are oriented to the expectations of the SET format and are selected based on their potential to gain from the experience as well as their commitment to the SET process and the goals in the initial group contract. A typical group consists of a group leader or co-leaders and six to ten members, who meet once a week for 3 hours. Group composition is limited to people who show the motivation and capability to work toward personally relevant goals. Participants are required to keep a daily record to (a) help raise self-awareness, (b) develop and clarify individual and group goals, and (c) become a more cohesive group.

Phases   The SET process involves three sequential phases (Lasky et al., 1984): personal, group, and life and living.

1. *Personal phase.* This personally oriented stage involves (a) acquainting group members with one another and with the purpose of the group; (b) selecting individual goals, and strategies and steps necessary to attain them; and (c) actively pursuing and implementing these goals.
2. *Group phase.* The group-oriented stage entails (a) convergence, or joint group work to identify a common goal for all members; (b) implicit mutuality, or assessing interper-

sonal relationships and the implications of these relationships; (c) interpersonal feedback; and (d) explicit mutuality, or the demonstration of genuine concern for other group members.

3. *Life and living phase.* The third phase, life and living, calls for (a) utilization or application of new knowledge and experience to daily living; (b) congruence, or the demonstration of consistent integration of thought, feeling, and action; (c) commencement, or the sharing of mutual experiences and future perspectives; and (d) reunion, or the opportunity for group members to come together and share successes and failures.

Specific structured experiential tasks are employed as interventions to facilitate development of the group, completion of each phase, and movement of the members through the SET process.

SET Focus   The consistent themes throughout the SET process are (a) the emphasis on goal involvement, (b) mutual concern, and (c) accountability (any of which may be the focus of any group meeting). Selected goals are expected to be relevant, understandable, performable, measurable, attainable, and time-limited. The concept of mutual concern requires members to extend themselves to others in the group, to learn to rely on the group, and to provide the group support and caring necessary for growth. Accountability takes the form of personal and interpersonal responsibility. Group members are responsible for their behavior and are not allowed to attribute personal problems to external forces.

Self-Help and Peer Helper Groups   Self-help and peer help groups for individuals with disabilities have been flourishing in the past three decades. Most have been spearheaded by citizen and consumer advocacy groups sparked by the Civil Rights movement of the 1960s (Rhoades, 1986). Early groups were initiated by parents whose children had disabling conditions. Now the self-help movement is geared more directly toward people with disabilities. Peer helper programs have been established for those affected by alcoholism, heart disease, stroke, spinal cord injuries, amputations, neurological disorders, cancer, mental retardation, and many other disabling conditions.

These self-governing groups, composed of individuals who share a common condition or experience, offer direct, active, and effective interventions to their participants while avoiding the stigma frequently associated with seeking outside professional help (Lieberman & Borman, 1979). Because the person with difficulty promotes his or her own advocacy, self-help and peer helper groups afford their members a chance at a rightful and equal role in society (Rhoades, Browning, & Thorin, 1986).

The operational principles underlying the self-help philosophy, cogently stated by Jaques and Patterson (1974), are:

❑ Participants have a commonly shared personal problem or condition.
❑ All participants maintain an equal status (i.e., peer relationships).
❑ Peers come together with the expectation of helping themselves and each other.
❑ All participants seek behavioral change.
❑ Peers identify with the particular program developed by the group and actively support this program.

❑ The group process consists of actively relating, owning, and sharing experiences, hopes, and problems; receiving and giving feedback to each other; and providing encouragement and criticism.

❑ Participants are held responsible for themselves and their behaviors.

❑ Group leadership develops and changes from within the group and follows the program's principles and goals.

Self-help groups serve many important functions in the lives of people with disabilities, including:

1. *Accurate knowledge*. Members can gain information (e.g., medical facts, innovative treatment and rehabilitation modalities) about the disability.
2. *Coping strategies*. Members can learn adaptive coping strategies from others who successfully live with the same or similar disability. They also benefit from the social modeling of others who demonstrate successful problem-solving behaviors in the community and from the feedback they provide newer members (Wright, 1983).
3. *Motivation level*. Members can become more motivated by openly sharing and communicating with others who have similar conditions and life experiences. Self-help groups provide a psychosocial support network, creating opportunities for receiving and giving emotional support and solving mutual problems (Gottlieb, 1982).
4. *Social reference group*. Groups offer identification with a social reference group, which gives members a sense of rootedness and belongingness, thereby decreasing feelings of isolation, rejection and alienation (Plummer, 1982).
5. *Self-evaluation process*. Groups can provide members with concrete evidence of self-progress. This evaluative function is closely linked to the type of feedback received from the group leader and other members as the various phases of members' problems and coping efforts unfold (Jaques & Patterson, 1974).
6. *Active participation*. Groups enable members to surrender the role of passive recipient of services to active participant. This action orientation is germane to the rehabilitation philosophy of being responsible consumers who choose among various alternatives and ultimately manage their individual rehabilitation plans and are also accountable for their results (Plummer, 1982).

The Job Club   The job club method exemplifies a behavioral group approach to vocational counseling and job placement. It centers on individual needs and uses reinforcement and peer support "to obtain a job of the highest feasible quality within the shortest feasible time period for all participating job seekers" (Azrin & Besalel, 1980, p. 1).

Each procedure is standardized into a consistent, intensive process for all job seekers (Azrin & Philip, 1979). Group members work together under the instruction and encouragement of a leader who provides support, information, facilities, and supplies. More than 30 procedures and activities are specified by Azrin and Besalel (1980). These include: (a) standard scripts and forms, (b) group support from other job seekers, (c) a buddy system, (d) use of telephone, (e) emphasis on personal skills, (f) interview training, (g) transportation, (h) daily progress charts, and (i) continued assistance.

In the job club model, job search and related activities are scheduled within the club session as much as possible so immediate assistance can be given for activities such as

(a) resume and letter writing, (b) calling friends and former employers for leads and interviews, (c) reviewing job listings in newspapers and other available sources, and (d) planning daily and weekly job seeking activities. The group leader's role requires a commitment to help every member obtain an appropriate job through selective placement; he or she provides job leads, encouragement, and a positive perspective highlighting on the member's assets, not limitations.

Before initiating the job club, an intake group may be to orient members to the job club program, basic hygiene, health and living skills, work behavior and ethics, and the world of work. Typically meeting for 8–10 weeks, once a week, the intake group prepares the person to apply these new knowledge areas and skills in the Job Club. The Job Club itself may meet from 1–5 days per week and is a continuous resource to be tapped by members, who may reenter at any time, usually for only minimal assistance.

The job club approach is efficient because it can address every participant at the same time and reinforce members' behaviors and achievements in the presence of all other members. This encourages others to follow examples of peer success while offering support. It also shows group members how to engage in mutual support endeavors, confront similar problems, share resources and offer peer support. Because many of the demands of work are largely social in nature (e.g., accepting criticism, attending to directions), employers are concerned not only with the person's capacity to work but also with his or her ability to work as a team member (Johnson, Greenwood, & Schriner, 1988). Research on applying the group method to work adjustment and job placement also supports the hypothesis that participants in job seeking groups are seen as more competent overall and better prepared for the jobs (Garvin, 1984; Roessler, 1986).

AGE-SPECIFIC VARIATIONS

An important consideration in groups of people with physical disabilities are the members' age and the age of onset of disability. The latter was noted under "Strategies for Group Sessions." Here, the focus is on present age-related variables.

Considerations with Younger People

Group goals with children and adolescents differ from those for adult clients (Kennedy, 1989; Marshak, 1982), because factors such as levels of psychosocial and cognitive functioning, self-identity, self-insight, social maturity, and attained level of independence. In general, goals should be narrower and should focus on solving present problems and issues (Marshak, 1982). In goals with youth with disabilities, the leader should consider the following strategies and issues:

1. Initiating and maintaining a more active style than that practiced with adults, to counteract the passive or resistant attitude commonly seen in adolescent clients (Bruce, 1975).
2. Being aware of the negative impact of long periods of silence during group sessions (Marshak, 1982). Adolescents seem to react more adversely (e.g., become anxious) to silence and to breakdown in communication. This impedes the group counseling process, especially with participants who have visual and hearing impairments.

3. Self-disclosing personal feelings by the group leader may be a valuable clinical tool in showing members that owning a wide range of feelings, rather than resorting to denying them or being overwhelmed by them, is normal (Marshak, 1982).

4. Making cautious and limited use of interpretations. The aim should be behavioral and functional improvement, and setting and implementating specific and time-bound goals. Berkovitz (1972) and Marshak (1982) further maintain that attempts at in-depth interpretation, and especially interpreting transference in a group setting, can have a negative impact on younger members. Also, members' level of cognitive and social maturity plays a prominent part in deciding on the type and timing of interpretation.

5. Discretely using role playing and psychodrama exercises. Although these strategies are often recommended in the literature (Marshak, 1982; Sussman, 1974), they are not without their pitfalls. Role playing, especially with members who have sensory impairments, is rather common. The group leader who adopts these and similar techniques (e.g., music therapy, movement therapy) should weigh: (a) the member's ability to ambulate (in the case of participants with SCI, muscular dystrophy, etc.); (b) the member's body image (especially young adolescents whose perception of their own bodies is precarious); and (c) the level of group cohesiveness (for example, in open groups, new members with body deformities may find role playing extremely threatening, particularly in early sessions).

6. Paying special attention to the youngster's typical concerns, which, in addition to the visible physical impairment, also include the more age-related concerns of physical appearance, peer acceptance, self-identity, sexuality, emancipation from family, and the like (Kennedy, 1989; Weinman, 1987).

The presence of a disability compromises the resolution of various developmental tasks adolescents face (Manaster, 1977). According to Marshak (1982), the tasks most affected are: (a) acquiring more mature relationships with peers of both genders, (b) acquiring feminine or masculine social roles, (c) accepting one's physique and use of body, and (d) becoming emotionally independent from parental figures. The stresses associated with these age-related developmental tasks, the presence of physical impairment, and attitudes of parents and peers (e.g., overprotection, rejection) should all be given equal consideration when selecting group strategies for adolescents with disabilities.

Considerations with Older Adults

When counseling older adults, the group leader is often required to consider an age-specific set of therapeutic goals (Kalson, 1982). The factors that exert the greatest impact on the lives of older individuals include (Gugel & Eisdorfer, 1985; Kalson, 1982): (a) loss of significant others, (b) disruption of social support systems, (c) loss of independence and control over one's life, resulting from physical deterioration, (d) economic and financial concerns, (e) cognitive changes (e.g., impairment of recent memory), and (f) fear of institutionalization.

The group leader who works with older adults may be affected by time constraints. Long-term goals should be carefully selected with particular attention to setting time limits on goals and their implementation (Kalson, 1982). In group counseling settings, the leader should:

1. Be brief and direct in approach (Kalson, 1982), which will expedite group cohesiveness and development of individual and group goals.
2. Attend to member's organic conditions. Cognitive deficits related to organicity may further exacerbate physical and sensory impairments (e.g., stroke, head injuries). Kalson (1982) recommends that, to assess the level of organic brain involvement, the leader should arrange for tests of the member's general intelligence, short-term memory, orientation as to place and person, and judgment. If organicity is present, the counseling style should be modified to (a) allow the member more time to respond to the leader and other participants, (b) be much more concrete in content, and (c) clearly and slowly present the member with simply worded questions.
3. Be aware of the complex set of transference responses exhibited in this age group. According to Linden (1955), two of the more common types of transference displayed by older adults are *recession* and *sociological transference*. In recession-transference, social unlearning or return to repressed material occurs. This results in a series of reverse steps of psychosexual development, leading to an inversion of the parent-child relationship. The younger leader, then, is perceived in the role of a parent. In sociological transference, the older member manifests signs of self-rejection because of identification with cultural beliefs upholding the value of youth and physical prowess. Group leaders who seek to facilitate the therapeutic effect of transference may heed Linden's (1954) advice to install dual-gender group leadership in an effort to replicate the original family structure.
4. Take a flexible approach in structuring and pacing sessions. Because of the numerous life crises (e.g., impaired mobility, retirement, death of mate, impending death) that beset older people with disabilities, group leaders should be prepared to deviate, when necessary, from planned group topics and address the more immediate needs of individual members.

Many advocate a greater use of therapeutic group programs for people in nursing homes. Gugel and Eisdorfer (1985) say the functional level of older people may be improved by (a) recreation therapy, (b) occupational therapy, (c) reality orientation, (d) remotivation programs, (e) behavior therapy, and (f) environmental (milieu) approaches.

SUMMARY

Group counseling has been applied with a wide range of people who have physical disorders including psychosomatic conditions, sensory (visual and auditory) disabilities, and neuromuscular and orthopedic impairments. The needs and concerns of these people can be generally delineated as physical, psychological, social, vocational, and financial. The four modalities used most often are educational, social support, psychotherapeutic, and coping and skill training groups. Goal setting addresses affective, cognitive, and behavioral areas.

People with visual impairments have concerns generally related to their reduced mobility, dependence on others, limited social skills, anxiety and avoidance of people, altered body image, and coping with the reality and limitations of the disability. Groups for people with hearing impairments focus on communication, negotiating the environment, compensating for experiential deprivation and isolation, adaptive behavior patterns, handling frustrations and overdependency.

Neuromuscular injury groups are often geared toward individuals with spinal cord injury and those who have had cerebrovascular accidents (strokes). The former typically have difficulties with mobility, self-care, sexual performance, and affective aspects. The latter have perceptual-spatial deficits, cognitive impairments, affective problems, behavioral involvement, and communication difficulties. In addressing all these needs, information providing is a fundamental strategy in group settings. Approaches in rehabilitation settings include the Structured Experiential Training: Rehabilitation (SET:R) model, self-help and peer help groups, and the Job Club model, among others.

Groups with younger people and older people are necessarily different because of developmental factors unique to each age. Another important variable is age of onset and whether the disability was present at birth or occurred later.

REFERENCES

Anderson, T. P. (1981). Stroke and cerebral trauma: Medical aspects. In W. C. Stolov & M. R. Clowers (Eds.), *Handbook of severe disability* (pp. 119–126). Washington, DC: U. S. Department of Education.

Avery, C. (1968). Para-analytic group therapy with adolescent multi-handicapped blind. *New Outlook for the Blind, 68*, 65–72.

Azrin, N. H,. & Besalel, V. (1980). *Job Club counselor's manual: A behavioral approach to vocational counseling.* Baltimore: University Park Press.

Azrin, N. H., & Philip, R. A. (1979). The Job Club method for the job-handicapped: A comparative outcome study. *Rehabilitation Counseling Bulletin, 23*, 144–155.

Banik, S. N., & Mendelson, M. A. (1978). Group psychotherapy with a paraplegic group with an emphasis on specific problems of sexuality. *International Journal of Group Psychotherapy, 28*, 123–128.

Berkovitz, I. H. (1972). *Adolescents grow in groups.* New York: Brunner/Mazel.

Bilodeau, C. B., & Hackett, T. P. (1971). Issues raised in a group setting by patients recovering from myocardial infarction. *American Journal of Psychiatry, 128*, 73–78.

Bruce, T. J. (1975). Adolescent groups and the adolescent process. *British Journal of Medical Psychology, 48*, 333–338.

Buchanan, D. C. (1975). Group therapy for kidney transplant patients. *International Journal of Psychiatry in Medicine, 6*, 523–531.

Cholden, L. (1953). Group therapy with the blind. *Group Psychotherapy, 6*, 21–29.

Chubon, R. A. (1982). Group practices in the rehabilitation of physically disabled persons. In M. Seligman (Ed.), *Group psychotherapy and counseling with special populations* (pp. 59–76). Baltimore: University Park Press.

Crawford, J. D., & McIvor, G. P. (1985). Group psychotherapy: Benefits in multiple sclerosis. *Archives of Physical Medicine & Rehabilitation, 66*, 810–813.

Crewe, N. M., & Krause, J. S. (1987). Spinal cord injury: Psychological aspects. In B. Caplan (Ed.), *Rehabilitation psychology desk reference* (pp. 3–35). Rockville, MD: Aspen.

D'Afflitti, J. G., & Weitz, G. W. (1974). Rehabilitating the stroke patient through patient-family groups. *International Journal of Group Psychotherapy, 24*, 323–332.

Democker, J. D., & Zimpfer, D. G. (1981). Group approaches to psychosocial intervention in medical care: A synthesis. *International Journal of Group Psychotherapy, 31*, 247–260.

Donovan, W. H. (1981). Spinal cord injury. In W. C. Stolov & M. R. Clowers (Eds.), *Handbook of severe disability* (pp. 65–82). Washington, DC: U. S. Department of Education.

Durkin, H. E. (1972). Group therapy movement. *Psychiatric Annals, 2*, 14–23.

Evans, R. L., Halar, E. M., & Smith, K. M. (1985). Cognitive therapy to achieve personal goals: Results of telephone group counseling with disabled adults. *Archives of Medicine & Rehabilitation, 60*, 693–696.

Fischer, W. G., & Samelson, C. F. (1971). Group psychotherapy for selected patients with lower extremity amputation. *Archives of Physical Medicine & Rehabilitation, 52*, 79.

Garvin, R. E. (1984). Vocational exploration and job search activities in a group setting. *Journal of Applied Rehabilitation Counseling, 15*(1), 15–17.

Goldman, H. (1970). The use of encounter microlabs with a group of visually handicapped rehabilitation clients. *New Outlook for the Blind, 64,* 219–226.

Gottlieb, B. H. (1982). Mutual-help groups: Members' views of their benefits and roles for professionals. In L. D. Borman, L. E. Borck, R. Hess, & F. L. Pasquale (Eds.), *Prevention in human services: Vol. 1. Helping people to help themselves: Self-help and prevention* (pp. 55–68). New York: Haworth.

Gugel, R. N., & Eisdorfer, S. (1985). The role of therapeutic group programs in a nursing home. *Rehabilitation Psychology, 30,* 83–92.

Gust, T. (1970). Group counseling with rehabilitation clients. *Rehabilitation Record, 11,* 18–25.

Henkle, C. (1975). Social group work as a treatment modality for hospitalized people with rheumatoid arthritis. *Rehabilitation Literature, 36,* 334–341.

Herman, S. (1966). Some observations on group therapy with the blind. *International Journal of Group Psychotherapy, 16,* 367–372.

Hollon, T. H. (1972). Modified group therapy in the treatment of patients on chronic hemodialysis. *American Journal of Psychotherapy, 36,* 501–510.

Inana, M. (1978). You and your body: A self-help health class for blind women. *Journal of Visual Impairment & Blindness, 72,* 399–403.

Jacobs, E. E., Harvill, R. L., & Masson, R. L. (1988). *Group counseling: Strategies and skills.* Pacific Grove, CA: Brooks/Cole.

Jaques, M., & Patterson, K. W. (1974). The self-help group model: A review. *Rehabilitation Counseling Bulletin, 18,* 48–58.

Johnson, A. J., Greenwood, R., & Schriner, K. F. (1988). Work performances and work personality: Employer concerns about workers with disabilities. *Rehabilitation Counseling Bulletin, 32,* 50–57.

Kalson, L. (1982). Group therapy with the aged. In M. Seligman (Ed.), *Group psychotherapy and counseling with special populations* (pp. 77–97). Baltimore: University Park Press.

Keegan, D. L. (1974). Adaptation to visual handicap: Short-term group approach. *Psychosomatics, 15,* 76–78.

Kennedy, J. F. (1989). The heterogeneous group for chronically physically ill and physically healthy but emotionally disturbed children and adolescents. *International Journal of Group Psychotherapy, 39,* 105–125.

Kriegsman, K. H., & Celotta, B. (1981). Creative coping: A program of group counseling for women with physical disabilities. *Journal of Rehabilitation, 47,* 36–39.

Lasky, R. G., & Dell Orto, A. E. (Eds.). (1979). *Group counseling and physical disability: A rehabilitation and health care perspective.* North Scituate, MA: Duxbury Press.

Lasky, R. G., Dell Orto, A. E., & Marinelli, R. P. (1984). Structured experiential therapy: A group approach to rehabilitation. In R. P. Marinelli & A. E. Dell Orto (Eds.), *The psychological and social impact of physical disability* (2nd ed.) (pp. 319–333). New York: Springer.

Lieberman, M. A., & Borman, L. D. (Eds.). (1979). *Self-help groups for coping with crisis.* San Francisco: Jossey-Bass.

Lindemann, J. E. (1981). *Psychological and behavioral aspects of physical disability.* New York: Plenum Press.

Linden, M. (1954). The significance of dual leadership in gerontologic group psychotherapy: Studies in gerontologic human relations III. *International Journal of Group Psychotherapy, 4,* 262–273.

Linden, M. (1955). Transference in gerontologic group therapy: Studies in gerontologic human relations IV. *International Journal of Group Psychotherapy, 5,* 61–79.

Manaster, G. J. (1977). *Adolescent development and the life tasks.* Boston: Allyn & Bacon.

Mann, W., Godfrey, M. E., & Dowd, E. T. (1973). The use of group counseling procedures in the rehabilitation of spinal cord injured patients. *American Journal of Occupational Therapy, 27,* 73–77.

Marshak, L. (1982). Group therapy with adolescents. In M. Seligman (Ed.), *Group psychotherapy and counseling with special populations* (pp. 185–213). Baltimore: University Park Press.

Melnyk, R., Montgomery, R., & Over, R. (1979). Attitude changes following sexual counseling program for spinal cord injured persons. *Archives of Physical Medicine & Rehabilitation, 60,* 601–605.

Miller, D. K., Wolfe, M., & Spiegel, M. H. (1975). Therapeutic groups for patients with spinal cord injuries. *Archives of Physical Medicine & Rehabilitation, 56,* 130–135.

Oradei, D. M., & Waite, N. S. (1974). Group psychotherapy with stroke patients during the immediate recovery phase. *American Journal of Orthopsychiatry, 44,* 386–395.

Ostby, S., & Thomas, K. R. (1984). Deafness and hearing impairment: A review and proposal. *Journal of Applied Rehabilitation Counseling, 15*(2), 7–11.

Plummer, S. J. (1982). Independent living centers: A self-help group model for the severely disabled. In M. Seligman (Ed.), *Group psychotherapy and counseling with special populations* (pp. 117–142). Baltimore: University Park Press.

Portner, D. (1981). Clinical aspects of social group work with the deaf. *Social Work with Groups, 4,* 123–133.

Power, P. W., & Rogers, S. (1979). Group counseling for multiple sclerosis patients: A preferred model of treatment for unique adoptive problems. In R. G. Lasky & A. E. Dell Orto (Eds.), *Group counseling and physical disability: A rehabilitation and health care perspective* (pp. 115–127). North Scituate, MA: Duxbury Press.

Rhoades, C. (1986). Different organizational models for self-help advocacy groups that serve people with developmental disabilities. *Journal of Rehabilitation, 52,* 43–47.

Rhoades, C. M., Browning, P. L., & Thorin, E. J. (1986). Self-help advocacy movement: A promising peer-support system for people with mental disabilities. *Rehabilitation Literature, 47,* 2–7.

Riekehof, L. L. (1987). *The joy of signing* (2nd ed.). Springfield, MD: Gospel.

Robinson, L. D. (1965). Group therapy using manual communication. *Mental Hospitals.* Washington, DC: American Psychiatric Association.

Roessler, R. T. (1978). An evaluation of personal achievement skills training with the visually handicapped. *Rehabilitation Counseling Bulletin, 21,* 300–305.

Roessler, R. T. (1986). Training for vocational coping: A method for enhancing work establishment skills. *Rehabilitation Counseling Bulletin, 29,* 258–265.

Roessler, R. T., Milligan, T., & Ohlson, A. (1976). Personal adjustment training for the spinal cord injured. *Rehabilitation Counseling Bulletin, 19,* 544–550.

Rogers, J., MacBride, A., Whylie, B., & Freemen, S. J. (1977-78). The use of groups in the rehabilitation of amputees. *International Journal of Group Psychotherapy in Medicine, 8,* 243–255.

Rose, S. D. (1989). Coping skill training in groups. *International Journal of Group Psychotherapy, 39,* 59–78.

Routh, T. A. (1957). A study of the use of group psychotherapy in rehabilitation centers for the blind. *Group Psychotherapy, 10,* 38–50.

Salhoot, J. T. (1977). Group strategies with the severely physically handicapped. In M. Seligman (Ed.), *Group counseling and group psychotherapy with rehabilitation clients* (pp. 149–172). Springfield, IL: Charles C. Thomas.

Scheidlinger, S. (1984). Group psychotherapy in the 1980s: Problems and prospects. *American Journal of Psychotherapy, 38,* 494–504.

Schein, J. D. (1982). Group techniques applied to deaf and hearing-impaired persons. In M. Seligman (Ed.), *Group psychotherapy and counseling with special populations* (pp. 143–161). Baltimore: University Park Press.

Sedge, S. K. (1982). Assertiveness training with hearing-impaired persons. *Rehabilitation Counseling Bulletin, 25,* 146–152.

Seligman, M. (1982). Introduction. In M. Seligman (Ed.), *Group psychotherapy and counseling with special populations* (pp. 1–26). Baltimore: University Park Press.

Singler, J. K. (1982). The stroke group: Planning for success. In M. Seligman (Ed.), *Group psychotherapy and counseling with special populations* (pp. 43–57). Baltimore: University Park Press.

Subramanian, K., & Ell, K. O. (1989). Coping with a first heart attack: A group treatment model for low-income anglo, black, and hispanic patients. *Social Work with Groups, 11,* 99–117.

Sussman, A. E. (1974). Group therapy with severely handicapped. *Journal of Rehabilitation of the Deaf, 8,* 122–126.

Vander Kolk, C. J. (1983). Rehabilitation counseling with the visually impaired. *Journal of Applied Rehabilitation Counseling, 14*(3), 13–19.

Weinman, B. (1987). Membership retention in group therapy among adolescents who are physically disabled. *Journal of Rehabilitation, 53,* 52–55.

Welch, G. J., & Steven, K. (1979). Group work intervention with a multiple sclerosis population. *Social Work with Groups, 2,* 221–234.

Welsh, R. L. (1982). The use of group strategies with the visually impaired. In M. Seligman (Ed.), *Group psychotherapy and counseling with special populations* (pp. 163–184). Baltimore: University Park Press.

Wilson, E. L. (1972). Programming individual and adjunctive therapeutic services for visually impaired clients in a rehabilitation center. *New Outlook for the Blind, 66,* 215–220.

Wright, B. A. (1983). *Physical disability—A psychosocial approach* (2nd ed.). New York: Harper & Row.

Yalom, I. D. (1985). *The theory and practice of group psychotherapy* (3rd ed.). New York: Basic Books.

Youngjohn, J. R., & Altman, I. M. (1989). A performance-based group approach to the treatment of anosognosia and denial. *Rehabilitation Psychology, 34,* 217–222.

9

Group Counseling with Victims of Abuse/Incest

Anita Vinson

Group work with adults who have survived the ravages of incest, sexual abuse, and physical and emotional abuse is a complex and delicate process (Finkelhor, 1979; Groth, 1978; Krieger, Rosenfeld, Gordon, & Bennett, 1980; Lesnik-Oberstein, 1983). Every person's abusive history is different; every person's reaction and defended states are unique to that person's characteristics. This uniqueness must not be overlooked. The defending states or creative adjustments to abusive situations propelled them toward physical and emotional survival. From the perspective of the individual's internal world, these defending states have been both useful and functional.

People who have experienced human contact as mostly painful and childhood care-givers as invasive, unseeing, or nonresponsive to their needs will continue to respond as if these past events are still occurring. These people are frequently isolated and suffering from guilt, anger, depression, low self-esteem, and suicidal ideation (Duenas, 1986; Sedney & Brooks, 1984). The range of symptoms includes sexual dysfunction, promiscuity, prostitution, adolescent pregnancy, depression, intense guilt, markedly poor self-esteem, drug or alcohol abuse, anxiety, and somatic complaints. Increased risk of intergenerational incest and abuse can be accounted for by the chronic nature of the psychological disturbance, continuing relationship disturbances, and the possibility of inadvertently continuing a cycle of abusiveness (Gelinas, 1983; Goodwin, McCarthy, & Divasto, 1981).

CONCEPTS OF GROUP WORK WITH VICTIMS OF ABUSE

Obviously, group work can encompass everything on a continuum from structured content to the emergent curriculum of the counseling group. Each approach has its usefulness according to the needs of the agency, the group leader, and the group member (Briere, 1989).

Roberts and Gwat-Yong (1989) and others (Tsai & Wagner, 1978) have written of success with time-limited groups in a format designed to elicit the traumatic events, impart information, and allow the participants to move from feeling isolated and different to seeing that others have also had traumatic events. Longer group work, of a year or more, may also be useful; it can provide an atmosphere in which disclosure can occur at an individualized pace and each member can experience his or her own unique nuances as well as similarities. This is particularly important because of the enmeshment almost always present in the family of origin.

SELECTION OF GROUP MEMBERS

Selecting people for the group may provoke extreme anxiety in individuals with histories of psychological and physical abandonment as well as generalized low self-esteem. In addition to finding out about mental health history, any hospitalization, suicide attempts (recent and past), substance abuse, criminal history, current medication, and medical problems, it is important to find out why the person is coming into group counseling at this particular time and what the person would like the leader to know about the abuse during this initial interview.

The person needs to have some ability to function within this level of questioning and also to gain some information about whether work with this particular leader is possible. Groups of this type are not appropriate for people who are actively psychotic, are suicidal, have a history of violence with low impulse control, are abusing drugs or alcohol, or are so fragmented that they are not coherent (Yalom, 1985). For the person to be accepted into the group, concurrent individual work may be recommended or necessary.

During the initial interview, the leader might actually work with prospective members to help them decide if they want to participate and invite them to ask questions regarding the group process. Frequently, individuals express fears about who will be in the group. The leader may assure prospective members that, though there are no guarantees, he or she can interrupt verbally attacking behavior, and that the focus is on each person's self-exploration with feedback from others as an option.

STAGES OF GROUP WORK WITH VICTIMS OF ABUSE

Beginning Stage

One cannot learn to be a group leader from reading a chapter in a book but additional reading and, more important, experiencing the human processes in counseling and counselor education may contribute to awareness of the potential leader's process and individually appropriate methods that facilitate awareness in others.

In the initial phases of group work with victims of abuse, the leader may have to attend to the major task of establishing the atmosphere of a holding environment within the I-Thou relationship (discussed later) and also to increase the familiar routine by making orienting statements. Orientations might include asking how each member is feeling now, inquiring whether anyone would like to talk about the last week, or if anyone has anything urgent to discuss.

Orienting questions and statements afford each participant the opportunity to respond at a comfortable pace and not allow excessive silence to generate intolerable amounts of anxiety and paranoia. Sometimes this is done by going around the circle and checking in. When queried about whether they want to do this, members often say yes because they hope it will decrease anxiety. If most members want to check in, the leader should to invite them to begin and advise those who do not want to participate to remain silent or state their names only. This allows for separation and differentiation in the beginning stage of the group and permits the group to feel the difficulty and awkwardness of meeting, of becoming cohesive and establishing safety. Acknowledging this difficulty is important.

The pivotal quality of this stage of group work cannot be overemphasized. Although the pacing may seem painstakingly slow, it provides for a fuller experience of the anxiety, paranoia, impatience, fantasies, and fear characteristic of beginning relationships. To diminish or rush this beginning stage undermines the individual's opportunity to learn what happens when a meeting with someone is imminent and possible. Almost everyone who is self-aware has some type of anxiety or feelings or images about beginning to be together. These almost always reflect family-of-origin patterns.

At some point in the orienting process, the leader should state that each person is here to develop self-awareness. In contrast to some other approaches to groups, the primary focus is on each person's work with the leader rather than interactions between group members. The general format requires relatively short pieces of uninterrupted work with the leader.

A member may invite the group's comments following his or her segment. Each member has to know that others' comments may or may not be useful and that he or she does not have to respond to questions asked as a part of the feedback process.

The idea behind this general format is to provide some protection from critical, abusive, and invasive comments, as well as to mediate attempts to merge into togetherness or deny conflict or differences. Providing opportunities for each person to experience, name, and discuss feelings, beliefs, and life events highlights differences, and provides a means to notice and appreciate minute nuances of change.

This initial difficulty of coming together creates beginning cohesiveness. Not only have the participants weathered troubled family-of-origin situations, but they also have battled the personal demons activated during these initial group meetings and survived intact both individually and as a group. The leader has to gain some sense of each person's presenting and primary processes during the initial meeting, to keep the level of risk at a place that allows the anxiety to stay within tolerable limits.

Middle Stage

Although group work almost never follows discrete stages, after several months some participants may begin what can be characterized as the middle stage. The routine of briefly checking in is now established, and participants are usually excited and eager to begin to explore present life or family-of-origin issues. Members are not expected to reveal the details of molestation at this time. In fact, the person is revealing the process of the effects of the trauma from the beginning. Embedded in a member's responses are patterns of avoiding emotional and physical pain that emanate from the past. One way to conceptualize these avoidances is to view them as processes of paranoia, depression, hysteria, and anxiety overlying deeper organizing structures of the individual. These are present in everyone and can be both useful and inhibiting.

Paranoia The member who responds with suspicion may be able to tell of a time when that reaction was useful. As often happens, the paranoia stems from real events and may have generalized into present interactions. When the paranoia rises as a response within the group, the member needs information from the environment. One important intervention would be to help participants recognize how past experiences contributed to the natural formation of paranoia, and to honor this process by seeking information, which might include checking with the group members regarding the accuracy of their perception.

Depression   Likewise, the person who is naive and unwary may have learned, in the family of origin, that "going along with" the circumstance is safer and that questions or protests arising from experienced needs are usually futile. This continual inhibition or denial of needs can create a depressive approach to the environment. A flat affect is often a way to remain in the background. To escape notice could be a way to escape abuse. Also, depression is a way to contain and substitute the experience of numbness rather than feel the impact of the abuse.

Hysteria   Often, members interact in a flighty manner, quickly jumping from one topic to another, and are unable to stay with any experience for very long. This process is based on the anxiety associated with an underdeveloped sense of self. The self is experienced as a series of partial identifications, giving the person a chameleonlike quality. The leader should carefully uncover the roots of the anxiety, slow the process without harming the member, and help the person bridge the fragments of identity.

Anxiety   When a participant is operating from a position characterized by high anxiety, the leader may perceive the exhibition of inability to act because of fear of making the wrong choice and an almost complete lack of sensory awareness. At this point the leader may attempt to explore the usefulness of the anxious behavior. Questions such as, "What might happen if you were not thinking about this so much?" or "What is underneath the need to do it right?" can be useful. Exploring the beliefs supporting the quest for the right decision also may be helpful.

Sometimes the covert issue is the clash between what the person believes is the right or healthy way and that person's needs. Often group members are unaware of subtle ways that past traumas have affected their feelings and beliefs about themselves. In fact, some may describe events with no awareness of the cruelty and viciousness they contain.

Traumatic Events   The middle stage of group work is frequently characterized by greater focus on traumatic events in families of origin or in the more recent past with members' children or partner or, less frequently, with group members. Usually, not all members will have time to work during each session, so the leader should take notice if someone is indicating extreme need or suicidal ideation. If members are also in individual counseling or can schedule extra time with a counselor, the emergency status recedes. Nevertheless, leaders frequently try to structure the session so everyone gets some time. Also, some members may routinely acquiesce to others whom they see in greater need. Certain members may function in parental roles. Others may be passive and activate others to attempt to draw them out. As these interactional processes unfold, the leader may invite a participant to explore his or her behavior. Members may freely accept or reject these invitations. If rejected, the leader may invite the person to explore hesitations.

Organizing Structures   As the work progresses, the leader needs a conceptual framework for responding to the members as they reveal the deeper organizing structures of their persons. Based upon my training years of experience working with this population, one way to conceptualize these deeper organizing structures is to view them as narcissistic, schizoid, and borderline processes. Again, everyone will show these to some extent, but one configuration will probably be more developed than the others in a person (L. Jacobs, personal communication, 1986).

Narcissistic Process   The narcissistic process results from being severely criticized within the family-of-origin, with little attention to needs, including the need to move through childhood egocentricity. Members may talk excessively about themselves, be unable to listen to another's comments without self-referencing, exhibit grandiosity, and be easily harmed. A person in this position needs mirroring, empathy, and understanding. Transition statements and attention to the possibility of harm are vital in working with a person with this primary process.

Schizoid Process   The schizoid process may appear as shyness, woodenness, and inability to function spontaneously. This person has experienced abuse so intensely injuring to the sense of self that he or she must modulate or rehearse any statement to shield the self. This type of process must be addressed in much the same way as the narcissistic process, but the work proceeds much more slowly. The member's pace must be honored. For this person to remain within the group may be an accomplishment, and his or her work, however rehearsed and wooden, requires uncritical acceptance. Subtleties such as offering spontaneous feedback to another, reporting less isolation, and working first may signal important movement.

Borderline Process   A person exhibiting the borderline process may present with extreme anxiety to separateness. For example, he or she may attempt to coerce the leader to offer solutions or agree with the member's viewpoint. Another defense that can be particularly disruptive is *splitting*, which may reveal itself as polarized thinking, either/or positions, or oppositional vacillating feelings. Gently confronting these vicissitudes of thinking and emotions may bring the person into awareness, thereby offering a method of self-observation. A leader might also notice that unintentional harm can be an antecedent to these defenses.

Unintentional Harm   Leaders can unintentionally harm. The delicacy of working with severely harmed victims requires that the leader remain sensitive to this possibility and enable members as much as they can to reveal when and how they have been hurt. Often, the leader's every movement is scrutinized to detect what will please.

In one group, a leader moved from one chair to another to better see the members, causing one member to wonder in silence for two weeks what she had done to provoke the leader to move. Harm will occur, but most of the time it can be explored so resentments and hurt do not build to an intolerable level and cause premature endings for group members.

Confrontation Issues   In the middle and later middle stage of group work (and this might take place for some during the first year, while others would stay in the beginning stage for the first year), members may face the prospect of confronting offenders, setting limits with abusive relatives or others in the person's life, or leaving an abusive relationship. Again, no formula applies. Each person can come to a unique, creative solution, and some may reach no solution. Action can range from confronting the offender and filing a civil suit to no confrontation. Some members decide that no contact with the family of origin is appropriate, while others may continue muted or even frequent contact. The important consideration here is not the solution but, rather, the exploration that takes place and what the client learns about self in deciding what to do or if, in fact, to do anything.

A leader might want to find out what the person believes about confronting the offender or abusive parent. What does the member imagine will happen after the confrontation? What makes this action important to the member? What does the member imagine feeling in the process? How might the confrontation be useful? All of these are not voiced to coerce the client in one direction or another but, instead, to facilitate a fuller understanding of hidden hopes, fears, and expectations. The leader also might suggest that the person confront the offender in fantasy within the group, to uncover other, more intense reactions. This would not be a rehearsal because the actual confrontation is unpredictable but, rather, would result in a deeper self-knowledge about this issue.

Many people have found this useful in gauging the amount of their own internal support. Some have discovered a hopefulness that the abuser will admit and apologize or that the family members will listen and surround the wounded party in nurturing warmth and understanding. These outcomes are rare. Usually the offender remains in denial, accuses and blames the client, or ignores the confrontation.

Families often collude with the offender in denying abuse, especially families that receive no mental health treatment. This sort of confrontation, while not producing the outcome the victim desires, provides opportunities for new awareness of the depth of the abusive behavior and validation that the abuse is real. A parent who attends to the adult child's revelations with no curiosity or understanding or sadness at the events perpetuates the feeling that the child's perspective is superfluous, of no consequence, and not worthy of attention. The harm continues. The victim learns more about the limitation of the family member.

When the leader-member-group relationship is solid and cohesive, the work can move in many directions. As they discover more of their true selves, members may turn from heterosexual to gay or lesbian relationships or the reverse. Some may have never felt close to another person. Others may have more career success. Still others feel the despair and grief at lost childhoods. Life events outside the group, such as deaths of relatives or friends, AIDS-related issues, issues with children and partners, may also become significant. This work has the capability of shaking the foundations of the members' images of themselves, uprooting a whole system perpetuated on resisting abuse. Of course, these defensive skills and patterns will not be lost but can be used more judiciously, and the person's repertoire of responses to others will be enlarged and refined.

Separation and Individuation   Another way to envision this work is as separation and individuation from the family system. Therefore, exploring the abandonment of the person is a major facet of the work and may constitute a connecting thread throughout the group process. Abandonment can be actual physical abandonment or the abandonment by nonresponsiveness to the child's needs, dismissing the pleas for help, or ignoring. Many victims experience not being protected and defended by a parent.

Because many families respond to attempts to separate with abusive behavior, examining how these feelings and actions are played out within the group is important. Members can experiment with saying no to a group member's request or identify the feelings associated with imagining saying no. These feelings are less risky and form the cornerstone of awareness of how one feels when separating, standing out, or standing alone. All of these may be associated with being targeted for abuse.

Group work is by now connecting the historical emotional content to the retelling and that, in fact, the events signal the tip of the iceberg. The issue is promoting the development of individuality that was arrested or diminished by the atmosphere of fear, often terror, and extreme discomfort within the family. One participant described feeling as if she were in a perpetual state of siege, not knowing when or how the next verbal or physical attack would occur.

Interrupted Development   Another way to picture the process is to recognize that the focus in group work is the central disturbance in development (Gillman, 1980) and not eradication of symptoms by persuasion or education. The unexpressed, unfilled needs of childhood are hidden behind a wall of shame and humiliation. The leader, if continuing to harm by attempting to appeal through educational approaches, increases the chances of causing further damage to the individual's self-concept. If, however, the leader can facilitate the member's awareness of the function of his or her grandiosity, social isolation, paranoia, and how the global low self-esteem developed, there can be spontaneous movement to remove the barriers impeding development of the self (Kohut & Wolf, 1978).

At this point, the leader must not allow the content of the client's life to provide the sole and primary focus. Although the events give context and important information, group work also includes attention to the process underlying the content. For example, how the member avoids connecting with others in the group, or avoids feeling pain or joy, or resists seeing and feeling the impact of the past and the impact of group members reveals the member's process. Avoidance will surface in a myriad of ways, each of which is an indicator of past as well as present experiences that operate out of awareness. As the avoidance mechanisms come into awareness, the person begins to perceive choice regarding shifting beliefs, behaviors, or emotions.

One man related that as a child, school was stressful and difficult for him and he needed a break when he arrived home. He usually wanted to play or watch TV. His father demanded that he finish his homework. This seemingly innocuous event illustrates the difficulty his father had in identifying and responding to his needs. As the work continued, the man identified other events of violence and hurt that were rooted in his father's limitations. This opened the door to examining the man's own limits in responding to others' needs, identifying and asking for what he needed, and saying no—all of which created problems in present interpersonal relationships. Embedded in this work, occurring over several years, is the retelling, many times, of these events, the impact on relationship issues, and the difficulties when encounters even remotely resembled his father's behavior.

Family and individual processes, such as not seeing the other's needs or believing that children's opinions and feelings are of little importance, portend abuse. Identifying feelings surrounding unmet needs enables the group members to trust the leader's ability to provide acknowledgement and builds a relationship in which the person can more safely reveal and experience previously buried sensations and feelings connected with abusive incidents.

Abuse is always multifaceted. Parents who viciously attack their children verbally or physically or seek them out for sexual gratification may have a history of abuse (Goodwin et al., 1981), be severely limited, psychotic, extremely narcissistic perhaps to the point of psychopathic, addicted to drugs or alcohol, or, in a few cases, have degenerative organic brain dysfunction. The effects of abusiveness are present from the beginning of the work, and as the person reveals more about self and past history, the fabric of abuse and the client's creative responses to it begin to unfold. A sense of wonder may arise in the leader at the child's creative ability to survive (R. Martin, personal communication, 1989).

Each person in a group of this type is best approached with fresh perspective, fresh eyes, to appreciate that person's unique survival mechanisms. Ongoing weekly case supervision is necessary and useful in keeping this freshness available to group members.

Ending Stage

Although group work with abuse victims is complex, an ending to the group work does come, either because of a time-limited commitment agreed to at the outset or because a member has reached a completion point and needs to end. A 10- or 12-week format would not allow for much unfolding, but a 12-week format in which members could re-register would have some advantages. One member in such a group continued the 12-week segments for 4 years. Obviously, continuity and trust are diminished because of membership fluctuation, but endings in a group of a year or more, in which the bonding is more developed, will promote and can exacerbate the defenses against abandonment.

The leader might see expressions of numbness, acquiescence, sadness, disappointment, regret, or anger. Other possibilities are the longing for continuance, a quiet acquiescing or numbing to the meaning of ending, or denial of the ending and inability to say good-bye.

Taking enough time to address these newly surfacing responses is important. What is enough time—4 weeks, 8 weeks, 12 weeks? One person worked a year on ending and its meaning for her. The leader must be sensitive and allow the emergence of differences. For some, ending of the group will be premature; others may be in varying stages of readiness; and still others may ignore its significance. One member "forgot" that this was the last meeting even though we had talked at length regarding this momentous event for months. Members may attempt to organize telephone lists, social meetings, or otherwise postpone or resist feeling the ending. The leader should not discourage these efforts, as isolated members may need this continued contact. Or the group's end might be explored as another response to the process of ending one of life's events. Noticing the differences in members' responses can create a climate of nonjudgmental acceptance.

CONTEXT AND THERAPEUTIC METHODS

I-Thou Relationship

Gestalt therapy frames the client-counselor relationship in the I-Thou, as described by Martin Buber (Jacobs, 1978), and treats this type of relationship as a necessary condition for the person to experience enough support to gain interpersonal awareness of the effects of past events and how they affect the present. This approach assumes that the group leader has explored traumatic life events and the effects of and feelings surrounding these events. Awareness of one's own grief, sadness, despair, delight, euphoria, fragmentation, sadism, masochism, cruelty, depression, and other states, and how these operate within the internal landscape, are crucial to being able to meet the other in the broad range of human processes.

The Holding Environment

Also useful in treating abuse patterns is "holding"—the group's power as a holding environment for the individual. To paraphrase Winnicott (1965), who is referring to the infant's environment, the holding environment meets the needs, is reliable, protects from insult, takes into account the person's sensitivity, includes a whole routine, and follows the minute changes belonging to growth and development. This holding environment, occurring within the I-Thou relationship, provides the format and background to support each member's work within the group.

Pacing

Groups of six to ten people who have been abused tend to begin very slowly and beginning may take months. The foundation for trust, both in the leader and in the group, has to emerge at a pace that is natural for each member. For example, in weekly group sessions, one person stated only her first name for the first 16 weeks during group work. She was attentive and silent the remainder of the sessions. During the 17th meeting she began to self-disclose, ask questions, and participate fully until the group's ending. When asked about those first 16 weeks, she stated that she was testing the leader to see if she could really do what she needed. This is an example of the group's structure allowing and trusting the client to be ready to move toward more exposure and risk taking.

One can also assume a degree of lack of object constancy (Greenberg & Mitchell, 1983). A member may "forget" or not trust that the leader or group members are whom they seemed last week. For instance, a member may think that, although the leader has not been critical for the past several meetings, this meeting could be different.

The member may come to group not expecting the leader to be there. This lack of trust in the integrity of the environment is a function of the betrayal and chaos within the original family structure. The importance of the group's holding environment, assisted by congruence and authenticity of the leader is obvious. The work follows the member's pace to provide the foundation on which the member can become aware of internal process as well as reactions to the environment, including other group members and the leader.

The Awareness Process

Awareness is being able to name or describe and differentiate feelings, beliefs, memories, sensations, and anything else occurring within the person's internal and external environment. It is associated with noticing sensoric phenomena. The ability to notice or experience when numbness or lack of sensory data occur is also important. According to Polster and Polster (1973), this awareness of sensations and actions is useful in experiencing needs fulfillment, understanding how one operates in relationship to others, and discovering how old experiences impact current thinking, feelings, and behavior. Awareness on intellectual, physical, and emotional levels is the goal and the means of achieving it.

Within the group, many approaches can be taken to facilitate awareness of the individual's process (Briere, 1989; Ogden, 1982):

1. Naming the process or feeling, thereby creating a more solid identifiable place for the member.
2. Mirroring the member (closely listening, responding, tracking the information; acknowledging feelings by repeating with appropriate feeling, tone, and indications of comprehension), thereby facilitating feelings of acceptance and understanding.
3. Asking questions or making statements that elicit self-disclosure.
4. Inviting exploration, to incorporate more personal history and current issues.
5. Imaging an event, to recapture the avoided feelings or as a rehearsal to role playing a family member or event.

Rather than rely solely on technique, the leader should be alert to possibilities within the group that can provide unique and creative opportunities. Even better, the process of facilitation can naturally evolve from the member's work. This does not preclude art media, drawing, dramatization, role play, singing, puppetry or other tools, but the suggestion must be within the member's expressive ability; otherwise the risk of humiliation will interrupt the work. Shame and humiliation must be considered, and the degree to which the members feel these emotions necessitates moving slowly into more expressive modalities.

Members often can be included in designing the group's work. This is also a way to ensure that the risk level is appropriate and congruent with the member's needs.

Intervention

An intervention is anything the leader does that is intended to facilitate awareness in the other. Statements, questions, noncommittal "hm-m-m's," expletives such as "Oh! How hard!" and physical indications such as leaning forward or standing, as well as silence, are examples of interventions (Roberts & Gwat-Yong, 1989). Certainly a leader will do something unintentionally at times with positive results. These are accidents or, some might say, intuitive interventions. But, for purposes of this chapter, an intervention is considered to be an activity performed with intent.

Interruption can be useful when a member's self-disclosure seems premature, potentially humiliating, or moving too rapidly for awareness to occur. For instance, if a person were to begin revealing graphic details of molest during the first group meeting, the leader could interrupt to find out if the member truly wants to reveal this now. The participant may believe he or she should do this, or that this is a way to escape the anxiety of the meeting or some other possibility. At this point, some members will need to self-disclose because they cannot contain their anxiety. But often a member will discover that he or she does not want to continue revealing a story; the self-disclosure is premature.

Interventions should allow the member room to focus, to be taken into account, to have needs responded to, in fact to be seen as a person whose opinions matter, who can participate in decisions regarding personal welfare or who can make group participation work. This participatory flavor ensures that the member is not abused by the leader, recreating the victimization and the experience of not being seen. This latter point is crucial because many victims have learned to hide behind going-along-with, forgetting, agreeing, not challenging, and it may be easy for them to play "good group members."

Self-Disclosure

Recalling, retelling and reremembering one's life events occurs with differing degrees of awareness. Initially it may happen with no awareness of the associated feelings. Each reremembering ideally is connected with rediscovering the layers of feelings and reactions that have been buried for years, sometimes decades. A single episode is commonly worked on for a year or more (Tsai & Wagner, 1978).

One group member presented at each session feelings that she would be "kicked out" or "banished" from the group. This took place for approximately a year. Each time, the leader explored the genesis of her responses, both internally and externally. She was reexperiencing past feeling states based on actual historical events. Her ability to describe her anticipation and fear gave her the opportunity to examine many facets of abuse within her family of origin. Eventually these were no longer issues within that group.

Working through feelings arising from abusive incidents can be painstakingly slow, arduous, and complex. In contrast are those moments when a client leaps to a connection and the working through seems speedy. Solid change, however, often happens slowly over a period of years.

Sameness and Difference

When a group is descriptively titled "incest survivors" or "victims of domestic violence," this implies the building of cohesiveness, a commonality to the participants. For instance, in an incest group, everyone assumes that all of the members have been sexually assaulted. Because the expectations of group members may range from "I thought we would only talk about incest" and "would get down and dirty" to "I had no expectations," precise attention to tracking the expectation and anxiety may elicit differentiation and increased feelings of curiosity, surprise, impatience, and wariness. This gives each participant the opportunity to explore his or her reactions to the unexpected and the new experience of being a member of this particular group.

Allowing the group opportunities to track its awareness in this new environment, and to experience the variety of differences and similarities of reactions to the novel and unexpected beginning, provides the basis for the deeper work to follow. In fact, the process remains the same but the content and self-disclosure become more risk-laden (Stolorow, Brandchaft, & Atwood, 1987).

For some group members, the need to work with past or current family events is more pressing because of crises or an inability to contain anxiety. The same format of exploration is effective with attention to members' awareness of the process. As the member tells about the event in this environment, the leader may invited him or her to notice any feeling or thinking reactions to the events. Sometimes becoming more connected in this way is enough for resolution or integration. If it is not, the incident will surface again.

TRANSFERENCE AND CONCOMITANT FACTORS

Several other factors that naturally occur in these groups and must be addressed include transference and the concomitant factors of introjection and projection, overidentification, and projective identification, as well as handling intergroup conflict and confluence.

Transference

Transference can be thought of as the person producing an important part of life history and acting it out rather than reporting or describing it. In fact, present experience in the group produces symbols or processes that are valid statements of states that extend beyond the therapeutic interaction (Polster & Polster, 1973). Therefore, the primitive defense mechanisms of idealization, splitting, and grandiosity may be seen in the context of transference and also as an accurate response to the leader-member or member-member relationship. These cannot be dissolved too quickly. They will naturally fade, given time and as the client is able to emerge from a defended place to peer out and see the world with more clarity and with less contamination by past traumas.

Because transference issues also can occur with the other group members, the structure of each doing individual work can be crucial. If a person is angered by another group member, the leader invites the offended member to explore how this anger arose without involving the other group member. The similarity of past experiences can also be explored, as can the feelings underneath the anger. This is not to exclude the possibility that harmful statements actually were made within the group but, rather, for the leader to use this as a bridge to explore responses to past hurts and ways to effectively address current difficulties. Perhaps, if the past hurts and humiliations were acknowledged, explored, and finished, the immediate response would have more clarity and less sustained emotional content. Leaders need to be aware that people from extremely abusive backgrounds have little tolerance for continued abuse within the group and will withdraw into more defended states or flee the scene altogether—neither of which facilitates exploration and self-discovery.

Introjection

Closely related to transference is the process of introjection. Introjection is a generic mode of interacting with the environment in which whatever is presented is accepted. For example, a member who accepts the values of parents, school, and society without sorting what fits, or fits his or her life situation, can be said to have introjected these (Polster & Polster, 1973). This is a beginning stage of learning. Ideally, the group member at some point needs to select what he or she does want and can identify with and resist the pressures and influences that he or she does not want.

The leader cannot stop this process of introjecting within the group, but the leader's awareness of how his or her beliefs can be introjected and become a part of the person's idealization is imperative. A group that is too agreeable, never challenging the group leader or offering dissenting opinions, may not be able to support the sorting-through process that is a part of undoing an introject and making it one's own. If this is not happening, the leader may be giving covert messages that it is not permissible to differentiate, or the leader may not be decreasing the risk level sufficiently for the members to be able to examine a possible introject. (This is not to be confused with the leader having certain needs related to beginning and ending times, ways of working, stands regarding appropriate group behavior, and the like).

Introjects often exist outside of awareness and feel like "that's just the way it is" or "that's how I am." The abusive family's system of verbal and nonverbal beliefs and actions contribute to the matrix of introjects that lead to the low self-esteem and depression that are often presenting problems in this work.

Projection

Although introjection is the basis for projection, it is useful to discuss this process also. The projector cannot accept feelings or actions viewed as unpalatable. To resolve this dilemma, the projector attaches that part of self to another person (Polster & Polster, 1973). Feeling seduced by another may be based on the unacceptability of the member's own seductive feelings toward the other person. Often, in an effort to not identify with the abuser, the member may have no awareness and project out cruelty, sadism, anger, and disdain or disgust. One can see how these could reverberate throughout a group as each person projects those disowned parts of self onto the leader as well as other members. As the projection often contains some truth, the leader should take care not to attempt to dissolve the projection too quickly. Projection feels real. Initially it has no "as if" quality. The fact that the experience seems so real often means that the trust between member and leader provides the only impetus to leap into an exploration of the projection as a function of past experiences. What may seem to the member to be manipulation is vital to uncovering the events that provide foundations for projections.

Projective Identification

Projective identification addresses ways that unaware feeling states are created or engendered in the other. The person attempts to contain an aspect of self in this way. Projective identification is a type of defense, a means of primitive communication, and a means toward psychological change. Often the leader is only retrospectively aware of the process, for it has no clear demarcation as in projection, in which the leader experiences separateness from the member's material (Ogden, 1982). In group work, this process can also occur with group members. Scapegoating, not attending to a particular member, eliciting helpfulness or dislike—these may represent signals of projective identification.

Often, victims of abuse are in less danger if they are not seen, and their ability to create this within their environment can also occur within the group. The leader may become angry and frustrated with the member. This can also signal that member feelings of this nature are unallowable and the depth of disintegration and fragmentation that has occurred with the abuse may reverberate within the leader, resulting in his or her feeling scattered, unable to focus, impotent, or guilty. Allowing these parts of oneself to be tolerated, to be seen as another human state that can be named and discussed, can signal the reintegration of past experiences.

From another view, projective identification is a blurring of the distinction between the member and leader or between the self of the member and a perceived tie with the leader. If these states of confusion are a part of undeveloped abilities to distinguish between self and other, their occurring in the group indicates a reliving of this early developmental process.

The leader may have intense reactions. If the leader's self-esteem depends on accepting and not questioning the interventions, he or she may be insufficiently differentiated from the member, who may need protection from any involvement until some spontaneous recovery has set in. To some extent, the leader at times feels impotent, at times frustrated, and at times infuriated, when the member's disagreements, assertions, and primary wishes to have his or her subjective experience understood have not been responded to (Stolorow, Brandchaft, & Atwood, 1987).

AGE-SPECIFIC VARIATIONS WITH CHILDREN AND ADOLESCENTS

In general, the previous discussion of the group counseling process for adult victims of abuse/incest is applicable to child and adolescent victims. Group counseling is a natural way for children to practice relating to their peers and provides a protective, experimental, and experiential environment.

Size of the group has not been specified, but one recommendation is that the younger the child, the smaller the group—perhaps three to six children if under age 8, and six to ten in groups of older children.

The duration depends on the setting and the focus. Some more educationally oriented groups operate in a school setting within a 30- to 60-minute period, and more counseling-oriented groups may specify 90 minutes to 2 hours.

Children may begin with reporting present feelings, awareness, and anything that has happened to them since the last meeting. Generally, sessions with children are structured around a theme or activity that provides a focus. An example of a theme is "sharing" or "words that hurt" (Oaklander, 1978). Structure may take the form of a ball of clay in which "sharing" may emerge as the theme, or games such as jacks, tic-tac-toe, dominoes, pick-up sticks, or checkers, which provide ways to interact. Members may also help establish group rules, usually toward the beginning of the work. Often children need markers, such as passing an object to signal a members's turn to talk. Allowing a finishing time of a few minutes is important and provides a sense of closure. Children may need to say something before ending, and they might voice appreciation or resentment. The session is intended to be a positive experience in which the child should feel attended to, interested, safe, and accepted.

Depending on his or her orientation, the leader may choose to take part in the activities, even storytelling, puppetry, and games, or not to take part. Some leaders prefer to observe and offer reflective or clarifying comments while others join in. One advantage to nonparticipation is that the observer role keeps the line clear between leader and participant. Participation may facilitate more openness if it does not interfere with the response to members' needs. If the leader combines these positions, he or she should make a clear statement to that effect early in the session. Group counseling with children can follow many approaches. These can be reviewed in Landreth (1982), Oaklander (1978), Schaefer (1988), and Schaefer and O'Connor (1983).

Adolescent Groups

The screening process for adolescent groups is similar to the screening process for adult groups. Those who may have trouble benefiting from group work include those presenting a great amount of disorganization and panic, those functioning at a level in which opinions or support of peers is not valued, unsocialized acting-out youngsters, and those who have never shown adequate ability to relate to others or little capacity for affectionate attachment.

Other principles of selection are the parent's permission and encouragement, some interest (or at least mixed interest and anxiety) on the adolescent's part, and social compatibility, which might include socio-economic factors, degree and type of disability, or other social differences to which adolescents are extremely sensitive. A balance of verbally passive and active members and those who tend to act out with those who tend to reflect on solutions is also useful.

In the pre-group work, the leader provides a means to get acquainted, orient the member to how counseling works, and in particular to what he or she may possibly expect, and explain ground rules regarding prohibited physical contact, confidentiality, regular attendance, and the procedure for quitting the group.

Based on the setting, group needs, and the leader's needs, the group may be structured around an initial activity or theme or around an emergent one, or may be guided by the members' verbal interactions. As in adult group work, attention to trust, bonding, and gradations of risk are also important. Depending on the setting, the group may be time-limited, open to taking in new members periodically, or closed with a clear ending date (Meeks, 1986; Oaklander, 1978). Usually, closed groups of some months' duration provide more opportunity to build an environment that will support greater self-disclosure.

Some group leaders consider parental involvement necessary. This may take many forms, from a parallel counseling group for parents to periodic meetings or meetings arranged as needed by the leader or members (Meeks, 1986). The leader has to make clear to adolescent members any guidelines about notifying the parent or agency. These guidelines will reflect ethical and legal issues as well as the philosophy of the organization within which the group takes place.

Work with adolescents often is dictated by the symptom, such as substance abuse, incest and sexual abuse, physical abuse, or the adolescent sex offender. Although information and orientation may be directed toward the specific symptoms, discussion of other topics that seem to be tangential is often useful, with an ear to the resistances and denial that may also be revealed.

Some leaders believe that they should suggest issues surrounding body image and sexuality, because these concerns will almost never surface without the leader's introduction (Oaklander, 1978). Other leaders see these issues as arising naturally after building trust, but in oblique ways such as asking, "When are we going to talk about . . . you know?" or by giggles or innuendoes that allow the counselor to comment directly on the sexual content.

Abused adolescents suffer shame, humiliation, and low self-esteem, with the added factor of often inadequate vocabulary to describe feelings and the inability to disclose. If group work is concurrent with individual counseling, the traumas may require less attention, without seeming to discount or ignore these, and more attention to school- or peer- or parental-related problems. Adolescents have to be able to use the group in whatever way is best.

A CAVEAT

No one can work effectively with adults who were severely physically and sexually abused and neglected as children without some form of case supervision. The tendency to protect oneself from the feelings elicited by group members' work or to merge with the strong needs of the members is too great. The deeply integrated defensive processes that were useful at one time afford formidable tests of endurance, knowledge, and skill for the leader. These individuals have survived and are now, by their entrance into the group, seeking to discover the parts of themselves that were not allowed to develop within the family of origin.

While a part of the member moves toward developing the awareness, emotional range, and openness to experience, the other polarity perpetuates fear, hesitation, and archaic, repetitive patterns. Many of these people enter the group with hopefulness, only to be met with their ability to reorganize the group into an echo of their abusive family. And, often, group members with their own unresolved issues can be abusive. Clearly setting the priorities of individual work within a group setting, identifying and responding to the primary human processes as presented by the members, and attending to the delicate meetings between individuals, which include both being seen and being harmed, can provide a place for members to move toward a real sense of self.

SUMMARY

Abuse is multifaceted and complex, and within the group each victim is unique. Selection of group members requires knowledge of their histories of abuse and mental health. The first group stage entails establishing an I-Thou relationship within a holding environment, and making orienting statements. In the middle phase the leader looks for members' responses that may reveal paranoia, depression, hysteria, anxiety, traumatic events, and organizing structures (narcissistic, schizoid, and borderline processes). Later in the middle stage, the member may start thinking about confronting the accuser. Other issues may include separation and individuation, and interrupted development. The final stage deals with preparing members to leave the group.

Therapeutic methods involve framing the leader-member relationship in an I-Thou relationship that allows the person to feel enough support to gain awareness of the effects of past events on the present. This is done in a holding environment, which meets the individual's needs, is reliable, protects from insult, is sensitive to the person, and follows a specified route related to growth and development. Pacing of a group's development tends to be slow, as awareness comes after being buried under built-up defenses. The leader facilitates awareness through self-disclosure, so members come to recognize their sameness and differences.

Transference means acting out a past event rather than telling about it, engendered by the primitive defense mechanisms of idealization, splitting, and grandiosity. Introjection means that the person accepts values of others without sorting out what fits, and the leader has to encourage this without causing members to introject the leader's beliefs. Stemming from introjection is projection, which attaches a part of self to another person; and projective identification addresses ways that unaware feelings are created or engendered in the other. The leader has to traverse this mass of psychological variables without unintentionally harming the member.

Group counseling with children, a natural way for them to relate to peers, follows the same general principles, but the groups may be shorter in duration and have fewer members. Adolescent groups are often dictated by the symptom, and developmental stage should also be taken into account.

REFERENCES

Briere, J. (1989). *Therapy for adults molested as children*. New York: Springer.

Duenas, M. T. (1986). Impact of long term sexual abuse. *Clinical Gerontologist, 4,* 47–50.

Finkelhor, D. (1979). *Sexually victimized children*. New York: Free Press.

Gelinas, D. J. (1983). The persisting negative effects of incest. *Psychiatry, 46,* 312–332.

Gillman, I. S. (1980). An object-relations approach to the phenomenon and treatment of battered women. *Psychiatry, 43,* 346–358.

Goodwin, J., McCarthy, T., & Divasto, P. (1981). Prior incest in mothers of abused children. *Child Abuse & Neglect, 5,* 87–95.

Greenberg, J. R., & Mitchell, S. A. (1983). *Object relations in psychoanalytic theory*. Cambridge, MA: Harvard University Press.

Groth, A. N. (1978). Patterns of sexual assault against children and adolescents. In A. W. Burgess, A. N. Groth, L. L. Holmstrom, & S. M. Sgroi (Eds.), *Sexual assault of children and adolescents* (pp. 3–24). Lexington, MA: D. C. Heath & Co.

Jacobs, L. (1978). *I-Thou relation in gestalt therapy*. Unpublished doctoral dissertation, California School of Professional Psychology, Los Angeles.

Kohut, H., & Wolf, E. S. (1978). The disorders of the self and their treatment: An outline. *International Journal of Psycho-Analysis, 59,* 413–424.

Krieger, M. J., Rosenfeld, A. A., Gordon, A., & Bennett, M. (1980). Problems in the psychotherapy of children with histories of incest. *American Journal of Psychotherapy, 34,* 81–88.

Landreth, G. (1982). *Play therapy: dynamics of the process of counseling with children*. New York: Charles C. Thomas.

Lesnik-Oberstein, M. (1983). Denial of reality: A form of emotional child abuse. *Child Abuse and Neglect, 7,* 471–472.

Meeks, J. E. (1986). Group psychology of the adolescent. *The fragile alliance* (pp. 194–223). Melbourne, FL: Robert E. Krieger Publishing Co.

Oaklander, V. (1978). *Windows to our children*. Moab, UT: Real People Press.

Ogden, T. H. (1982). *Projective identification and psychotherapeutic technique*. New York: Jason Aronson.

Polster, E., & Polster, M. (1973). *Gestalt therapy integrated*. New York: Random House (Vintage Books).

Roberts, L., & Gwat-Yong, L. (1989). Group therapy approach to the treatment of incest. *Social Work with Groups, 12,* 77–90.

Schaefer, C. E. (Ed.). (1988). *Innovative interventions in child and adolescent therapy*. New York: John Wiley & Sons.

Schaefer, C. E., & O'Connor, K. (1983). *Handbook of play therapy*. New York: Wiley.

Sedney, M. A., & Brooks, B. (1984). Factors associated with a history of childhood sexual experience in a nonclinical female population. *Journal of the American Academy of Child Psychiatry, 23,* 215–218.

Stolorow, R. D., Brandchaft, B., & Atwood, G. E. (1987). *Psychoanalytic treatment, an intersubjective approach*. Hillsdale, NJ: Analytic Press.

Tsai, M., & Wagner, N. N. (1978). Therapy groups for women sexually molested as children. *Archives of Sexual Behavior, 7,* 417–427.

Winnicott, D. W. (1965). *The maturational processes and the facilitating environment*. New York: International Universities Press.

Yalom, I. D. (1985). *The theory and practice of group psychotherapy* (3rd ed.). New York: Basic Books.

10

Group Counseling with Gays and Lesbians

Reese M. House and Virginia Tyler

Being gay or lesbian involves much more than specific sexual behaviors. . . . Indeed, being gay is being different, having a distinct identity, frequently in a way that is felt even before it is sexually expressed. Gayness is a special affinity and a special feeling toward people of the same gender; it is not the inability to love and to relate to others, nor is it a denial of the opposite sex. Rather it is a special capacity and need to love and to express one's love for people of the same gender in all the meanings of the term "love." (Woodman & Lenna, 1980, p. 11)

*T*he counseling profession has been slow to respond helpfully to the mental health needs of gays and lesbians. Until 1973, the American Psychiatric Association labeled "homosexuality" a form of mental illness. The American Psychological Association did the same until 1975. Since that time, the official position of the counseling profession has been to educate counselors to adopt an enlightened stance toward gay and lesbian populations (Iasenza, 1989). Like the culture, however, the counseling profession has a long way to go to overcome the societal stigmatization against gays and lesbians (Dworkin & Gutierrez, 1989). Gay and lesbian counseling groups are like other culturally different counseling groups, and their leaders need special gay and lesbian culture-specific preparation, which most counselor candidates do not receive (Buhrke, 1989; Iasenza, 1989; McDermott, Tyndall, & Lichtenberg, 1989). Not only do group leaders need adequate skill, knowledge, education, and supervision, but also they need to make an effort to accurately understand the values, lifestyles, and cultural norms of gays and lesbians. Also, group leaders need to examine their own belief systems to see whether they can offer unbiased, helpful counseling assistance to people with sexual orientations and behaviors that may be quite different from their own.

This chapter deals with language variables related to the gay/lesbian community, heterosexism, internalized and leader homophobia, gay/lesbian affirmative counseling, general group approaches in the gay/lesbian community, and specific gay/lesbian groups.

A WORD ABOUT WORDS

Language is important for what it communicates as well as what it implies. Gay and lesbian people hear biased and offensive street language such as "queer," "faggot," "homo," "dyke," and "queen" throughout their lives. This language affects self-esteem, stigmatizes gays and lesbians and is just as offensive to them as ethnic slurs are to ethnic populations.

Many consider "homosexual"—the term often used in the media, popular fiction, and professional literature and by psychologists, lawyers, lawmakers, clergy, and educators—to be archaic, imprecise, and misleading (Krajeski, 1986). They reject the label partly because "homosexual" is the term used by the dominant and often oppressing class in our culture. As a label, "homosexual" reflects an inaccurately narrow, clinical focus on sexual conduct (Blumenfeld & Raymond, 1988).

"Homoerotic," used to describe individuals who prefer intimate emotional and physical relationships with people of the same gender (Silberman & Hawkins, 1988), is another clinical term that is similarly narrow. We do not use the terms "homoerotic" and "homosexual" in this chapter because of the limitations of their meaning.

Even gays and lesbians disagree about what constitutes appropriate language. One difference of opinion involves the terms "sexual orientation" and "sexual preference." Preference implies that individuals choose to be gay or lesbian, and orientation suggests that sexual predisposition is innate (Blumenfeld & Raymond, 1988). Evidence is increasing that sexual orientation is biologically intrinsic in each human being (Money, 1987; Ritter & O'Neill, 1989). We use the term *sexual orientation* throughout this chapter to support the concept that sexual orientation is not primarily a matter of choice.

Another area of debate involves using the term *gay* to describe both gay men and lesbians. In this chapter we reject that convention. As women, lesbians contend with both homophobia and sexism. Use of the word *gay* for both genders is a subtle but potent continuation of the protocol that suggests that "man" is an acceptable term for both men and women. The generic use of *gay* tends to make lesbian women invisible, and it may obscure the fact that lesbians and gay men have very real differences (Blumenfeld and Raymond, 1988). For these reasons, we use the term *lesbian* to refer to women and *gay* to refer to men, to avoid the stereotyping that results when *gay* is used to represent both populations.

Group leaders need to be aware of their language choices and directly address the question of terminology with members. It is appropriate to ask: "How do you prefer to have your sexual orientation described?" "What terms would you like the group to use?" "How do you describe yourself?" "Do you refer to yourself as gay or lesbian?" These questions are respectful and imply to members that the leader is sensitive to the importance of language. This sensitivity shows an openness in discussing issues of sexual orientation and sexual behavior.

A CULTURAL OVERVIEW OF GAYS AND LESBIANS IN U.S. SOCIETY

Gay [and lesbian] people who survive and grow strong in the struggle for integrity and freedom from oppression are able to do so by increasing consciousness and developing a sense of community. Increasing one's consciousness is a matter of increasing awareness, alertness or sensitivity to facets of oppression. (Clark, 1987, p. 100)

Surveys suggest that approximately 10% of the U.S. adult population, at least 20 to 25 million people, is exclusively gay or lesbian (Blumenfeld & Raymond, 1988; Kinsey, Pomeroy, & Martin, 1948; Kinsey, Pomeroy, Martin, & Gebhard, 1953). This figure undoubtedly underestimates the number of gays and lesbians in society. Many people behave sexually with both men and women but do not define themselves as gay or lesbian. In addition, many self-identified gay and lesbian people in this country choose to remain an invisible minority (Klein, 1986) to avoid risks associated with disclosing their sexual orientation.

In June 1969, patrons of the Stonewall Inn in New York's Greenwich Village revolted against ongoing police harassment. The Stonewall riots fed a wave of gay and lesbian openness and militancy that was duplicated around the world in places as dissimilar as Sydney, Australia; London, England; Mexico City, Mexico; and Lincoln, Nebraska (Blumenfeld & Raymond, 1988). Since the 1960s, great numbers of gay and lesbian people have "come out" and publicly identified themselves as gay or lesbian. This openness has led to the development of a strong community identity, which, in turn, is an antidote to society's negative reactions.

The increasing openness of gay and lesbian people about their sexual orientation is mirrored by a slowly growing societal acceptance of their lifestyles. Recent surveys suggest that the American public is changing its attitudes toward them. Between 1983 and 1989, the number of Americans who agreed with the statement "homosexuality is unacceptable" decreased from 66% to 48% (Blumenfeld & Raymond, 1988; "A Special Report," 1989). Some businesses, universities, and cities have recently adopted antidiscrimination policies that include sexual orientation. Even though more than half of Americans currently accept gay and lesbian people, and some legal changes are taking place, our culture continues to support heterosexism and perpetuates homophobia in countless ways.

Heterosexism

> Unless we heal the homophobia and heterosexism deep in the hearts and minds of people, legislative efforts alone will not bring about any profound or lasting social change. (Williams, 1990, p. 15)

Heterosexism is a set of political assumptions that empowers heterosexual persons, especially heterosexual white males, and excludes people who are openly gay or lesbian from social, religious, and political power. It is a system that demands heterosexuality in return for first-class citizenship and forces gays and lesbians into silence concerning the majority of their lives (Mollenkott,1985). Heterosexism also occurs when the dominant group pities sexual minorities as poor unfortunates who can't help being the way they are (Blumenfeld & Raymond,1988). Heterosexism is the societal norm in the United States. People assume that teenagers will marry a person of the other sex at some future date. The media portray only heterosexual relationships as positive and satisfying. Teachers talk in class as though all students are straight. These are examples of the subtle and indirect ways heterosexuality is reinforced as the only viable, acceptable life option.

Homophobia

Homophobia, first defined by Weinberg in 1973, is an attitude of fear and loathing toward individuals perceived to be gay or lesbian. Homophobia is a belief system that supports negative myths and stereotypes, and maintains that discrimination based on sexual orientation is justified (Lapierre, 1990). Homophobic people downgrade, deny, stereotype, or ignore the existence of gays and lesbians. Responses range from telling or laughing at "queer" jokes, to condoning, supporting, or participating in violent hate crimes committed against gays and lesbians, popularly referred to as "fag bashing."

Homophobic reactions create a devalued minority in the midst of a hostile society. For example, in 1989, when the *San Francisco Examiner* ran a 16-part series on "Gay in America," letters to the editor included comments such as, "It's not gay to be homosexual, it's disgusting, loathsome, and perverted!" "You can print all the gay-lesbian articles you want, but those of us in mainstream America who find the sordid sexual practices of gays and lesbians repugnant will never change our minds about these deviates." "Long live gay bashers!" (Rizzi, 1989; Warren, 1989; Wett, 1989).

Public figures have fueled the flames of bigotry through their public comments. Jerry Falwell, a fundamentalist Christian, stated that AIDS (acquired immunodeficiency syndrome) was "the judgment of God" on gays for "subanimal behavior." Morton Downey, a television talk show host, stated that he was "turned off by that type of sickness (homosexuality)." Jesse Helms, a Senator from North Carolina, said in testifying against a hate crimes bill, "We have to call a spade a spade and a perverted human being a perverted human being." These homophobic comments reflect a lack of acceptance of gays and lesbians in a society that no longer tolerates racial, religious, and sexist slurs by public figures. These bigoted remarks also perpetuate homophobia by giving it the credibility of public pronouncement without societal retribution (House, 1991).

Homophobia leads to institutionalized discrimination that condemns, punishes, and limits the rights of gays and lesbians (Forstein, 1986). Individuals perceived to be gay or lesbian are discriminated against in employment and housing. Career positions in teaching, the military, police, and public office often are available only to those who pass as heterosexual.

In additional, many religious organizations are openly homophobic. In a 1989 edict, Pope John Paul denounced homosexual activity as "an intrinsic moral evil" and called upon churches to dissociate themselves from gay and lesbian people. Also, gay and lesbian couples are not legally recognized in the United States. This lack of legal standing limits them in a number of significant ways, including health insurance, hospital visitation rights, child custody rights, survivorship and estate benefits, and other rights and benefits available only to married couples.

Internalized Homophobia   Perhaps the most devastating result of the isolation and alienation gays and lesbians experience is internalized homophobia, the internalization of society's negative attitudes and assumptions (Sophie, 1987). Gays and lesbians who internalize the values of otherwise credible sources, including friends, family, church, school, and mass media, experience personal dissonance and low self-esteem, which are major sources of distress for them.

Internalized homophobia manifests itself in a variety of ways, including the total denial of one's sexual orientation, contempt for or distrust of openly gay or lesbian people, attempts to "pass" as heterosexual, increased fear, and withdrawal from friends and families. Acute anxiety attacks, self-destructive use of alcohol and drugs, and missed work or therapy sessions are frequent symptoms of internalized homophobia. At its most extreme, internalized homophobia can lead to suicide (Lapierre, 1990).

Gays and lesbians are not the only ones who have internalized homophobia. We all live in a culture that teaches that same-sex behaviors are morally repulsive, psychologically damaging, or do not exist. No one is totally protected from internalizing these negative attitudes—including counselors.

Counselor Homophobia   Counseling professionals are part of the heterosexist and homophobic culture. Furthermore, many counselors practicing today were trained in an era when homosexuality was classified as an illness. Therefore, it is not surprising, although it is discouraging, that many counselors are homophobic and heterosexist and have not addressed or even recognized their own internalized homophobia. This ignorance and prejudice are manifested in many ways. Despite classification changes almost 20 years ago, many practitioners continue to consider gays and lesbians abnormal, deviant, and in need of change (Klein, 1986).

Some counselors believe the goal of counseling is to reduce or eliminate "homosexual" behavior and substitute "heterosexual" behavior (Coleman & Remafedi, 1989; Herron, Kintner, Sollinger, & Trubowitz, 1985). Some group leaders assume that they will not have any gay or lesbian people in their groups. Others are tolerant of gay and lesbian individuals but uninformed about the gay and lesbian culture and its resources.

Although currently the counseling profession verbally supports a gay-affirmative position, counselor candidates typically receive little exposure to lesbian or gay issues, and thus are not well trained to work with gay or lesbian clients (Buhrke, 1989). In addition, counselor trainees who have limited exposure to gay and lesbian clients show a high degree of homophobia and provide inadequate, improper, and harmful services to gay and lesbian individuals (Moses & Hawkins, 1985).

Counselor trainees must demand that their educators and supervisors help them address gay and lesbian issues (House & Holloway, 1991). To do this successfully, students and supervisors alike may need to confront and overcome their own homophobic and heterosexist beliefs and behaviors. The questions in "Personal Values Assessment: How Homophobic Are You?" can help counselor trainees and their supervisors identify their own biases about sexual orientation (House, 1991).

Gay and Lesbian Professional Counselors

Until recently, it was assumed that heterosexuality was the only suitable orientation for counselors (Rochlin, 1985), but the number of publicly identified gay and lesbian counselors is growing. Gay and lesbian professionals who come out serve as role models, provide security for clients who want to see gay or lesbian counselors, and act as resource consultants in the gay and lesbian community and among professional counselors in the mental health community (Woodman & Lenna, 1980).

Many gay and lesbian individuals prefer to work with gay and lesbian counselors, particularly on issues directly related to sexual orientation (Hall, 1985). One recent study, however, found that although nearly half the gay and lesbian individuals surveyed favored a gay or lesbian counselor, a significant number (39%) thought that a counselor's sexual orientation did not make a difference (McDermott, Tyndall, & Lichtenberg, 1989).

Personal Values Assessment: How Homophobic Are You?

1. Do you stop yourself from doing or saying certain things because someone might think you are gay or lesbian? If yes, what kinds of things?
2. Do you ever intentionally do or say things so that people will think you are nongay? If yes, what kinds of things?
3. If you are a parent, how would you (or do you) feel about having a lesbian daughter or gay son?
4. How would you feel if you discovered that one of your parents or parent figures, or a brother or sister, were gay or lesbian?
5. Are there any jobs, positions, or professions that you think lesbians and gays should be barred from holding or entering? If yes, why?
6. Would you go to a physician whom you knew or believed to be gay or lesbian if that person were of a different gender from you? If that person were of the same gender as you? If not, why not?
7. If someone you care about were to say to you, "I think I'm gay," would you suggest that the person see a therapist?
8. Would you wear a button that says "Don't assume I'm heterosexual"? If not, why not?
9. Can you think of three positive aspects of a gay or lesbian lifestyle? Can you think of three negative aspects of a nongay lifestyle?
10. Have you ever laughed at a "queer" joke?

The following questions apply particularly to counseling, and suggest how easily personal values can infuse the counseling relationship.

11. Do you assume your clients are all heterosexual?
12. If a client says "partner," do you assume he or she is speaking of someone of the opposite sex?
13. If a client uses a derogatory term for a gay or lesbian person, do you let the comment pass unchallenged? What do you do when a client uses a derogatory term for an ethnic minority?
14. If you have a client you know is gay or lesbian, do you assume that all the client's issues are somehow related to sexual orientation? Do you make the same assumption about the sexuality of your heterosexual clients?
15. Do you assume that all of your client's past partners have been the same gender as the current partner is?

It may be as important for counselors to be gay-affirmative as it is for them to have the same sexual orientation as the people they serve.

Gay-Affirmative Counseling

Gay-affirmative counseling is based on six interlocking assumptions (Schwartz & Hartstein, 1986):

1. Being gay or lesbian is not a pathological condition.
2. The origins of sexual orientation are not clearly understood or completely known.
3. Gay and lesbian individuals lead fulfilling and satisfying lives.
4. There are a variety of gay and lesbian lifestyles.
5. Gay and lesbian individuals who come to counseling groups with no desire to change their sexual orientation should not be coerced into doing so.
6. Gay-affirmative individual and group counseling should be available.

Counselors are in a powerful position to help gays and lesbians recognize and accept their sexual identity, improve their interpersonal and social functioning, and value themselves while living in a predominantly heterosexual society (Coleman, 1985). Those who are sensitive to sexual orientation issues, and who have examined and challenged their own heterosexist and homophobic attitudes, can assist all group members, whatever their sexual orientation. Group leaders who are unable to meet these standards are ethically obligated to refer to other professionals.

Gays and lesbians have a right to unbiased and professional counseling services. Group leaders must recognize and address homophobia and heterosexism in themselves, in the counseling profession, in individuals, and in groups they lead. Gay-affirmative group leaders create an atmosphere of tolerance and acceptance so that all clients who wish to explore their sexual orientation can bring up their concerns easily and openly. Group leaders who are sensitive to gay and lesbian individuals address the issues presented and do not make sexual behavior the problem if it is irrelevant to the situation. Gay-affirmative counselors encourage groups they facilitate to openly address sexual orientation issues. They create and model norms of nonjudgmental acceptance and tolerance of everyone in the group. Finally, gay-affirmative group counselors are knowledgeable about the gay and lesbian culture and the resources that exist for gays and lesbians.

THE EMERGENCE OF GROUPS IN THE GAY/LESBIAN COMMUNITY

> Overall, the gay and lesbian community provides a haven for its members. There is love and fun and support. There is self-acceptance and understanding. There is hope and commitment. All these are qualities that any good community would take pride in. (Griffin, Wirth & Wirth, 1986, p. 39)

As gays and lesbians have become more public about their sexual orientation, groups have become more common and more open. Groups offer a counterpoint to the isolation, oppression, and alienation of being gay or lesbian in American society. Groups create a mini-culture wherein the prejudice and homophobia gay and lesbian individuals experience in the general culture are countered by social support and acceptance in a community where their sexual orientation is not an issue.

Gays and lesbians have taken the initiative and created organizations and groups to provide a community of social support in which their sexual orientation is not an issue. Community service centers, which provide speakers' bureaus, hotlines, newsletters, information on community resources, referral, medical services, and other social activities such as dances and potlucks, have emerged because gays and lesbians often have unique and special needs that go unmet in the larger society (Blumenfeld & Raymond, 1988). Local gay and lesbian newspapers list dozens of groups and organizations—groups for women, men, racial and ethnic minorities, youth, older individuals, bisexuals, and couples in mixed orientation marriages (Klein, 1990). Groups address a variety of lifestyle issues, including coming-out, relationships, and parenting. Groups have evolved for the parents of gay and lesbian individuals, their children, and their mates. In addition, there are groups to address issues not directly related to sexual orientation, such as substance abuse and personal growth. All of the existing groups in the gay and lesbian community can be divided into three primary categories: common interest, self-help, and counseling.

Common Interest Groups

> The ultimate reward from developing a sense of community with other gay people is that you are no longer alone. . . . There are people who share your values and lifestyle. There are people to learn from and models to emulate. . . .There is the assurance of people who care and understand—people who can share familiar feelings and offer mutual support. (Clark, 1987, p. 104)

A multitude of common interest groups is available for gays and lesbians. Examples are professional support groups for lawyers, social workers, school teachers, health care providers, academics, business owners, and artists. Organizations on many university and college campuses offer a number of group activities for gay and lesbian students. Also, major religious denominations have groups that allow gays and lesbians a way to participate in religious activities without homophobic overtones. Table 10.1 lists some of these.

Other interest groups are organized around recreational activities, such as hiking, bowling, card games, music, or dancing. Political Action Committees (PACs) are another form of common interest group in which many gays and lesbians are involved. PACs help empower the gay and lesbian community, providing political strength and influence. All of these groups play an important part in the lives of many gay men and lesbian women by providing an opportunity to be together and share common concerns and interests.

Self-Help Groups

> The self-help group functions for its members. It is organized around addressing a common concern. Individuals' separate agendas are transcended. Continual focusing on the common agenda leads to unity and a power base that is collectively sustaining and useful. (Eller & King, 1990, p. 330)

Self-help groups are effective for people who are stigmatized by the culture; they break down the sense of personal isolation caused by an unhealthy condition or habit (Eller & King, 1990; Hall, 1985) and help disenfranchised individuals cope and change. Self-help groups are common in gay and lesbian communities, and they address a variety of issues including alcoholism, drug addiction, incest survival, and eating disorders. Mainstream recovery groups, such as Narcotics Anonymous, Cocaine Anonymous, Alcoholics Anonymous, Overeaters Anonymous, and Al-Anon often have groups specifically for gay and lesbian members. Some self-help groups address issues uniquely part of the gay and lesbian experience, including coming-out groups, groups for children of gay or lesbian parents, and groups for the parents of gay or lesbian children. In the last 10 years, support groups have also developed for people with AIDS (PWAs) and their significant others.

Table 10.1 GAY/LESBIAN GROUPS AFFILIATED WITH RELIGIOUS DENOMINATIONS

Religious Denomination	Gay/Lesbian Organization
American Baptist Churches USA	American Baptist Concerned
Buddhist	Buddhist Association of the Gay/Lesbian Community
Catholic	Dignity
Christian (Disciples of Christ)	Affirming Disciples Alliance
Church of the Brethren	Brethren/Mennonite Council for Lesbian and Gay Concerns
Church of Christian Science	United Lesbian and Gay Christian Scientists
Episcopal	Integrity
Evangelical	Evangelicals Concerned
Jehovah's Witnesses	Jehovah's Witness Gay Support Group
Jewish	Gay Synagogue
Lutheran	Lutherans Concerned
Mormon	Affirmation
Nondenominational	Metropolitan Community Church
Pentecostal	National Gay Pentecostal Alliance
Presbyterian	More Light Churches
Quakers	Friends for Lesbians and Gay Concerns
Seventh Day Adventist	Seventh Day Adventist Kinship and Kinship International
Unitarian/Universalists	Unitarian/Universalists for Lesbian/Gay Concerns
United Church of Christ	United Church of Christ Coalition for Lesbian/Gay Concerns
United Methodist	Affirmation

Counseling Groups

> A therapy group can be a place of refuge, a place to share the most private aspects of oneself, a place to practice social skills, to get support for changing behavior. People go to groups for a variety of reasons, and that provides the diversity which makes groups so productive. (Hall, 1985, p. 68)

Gays and lesbians become participants in counseling groups to address issues such as eating disorders, depression, anxiety disorders, panic attacks, sexual dysfunction, or personality disorders. Other counseling groups focus on personal growth or relationship issues rather than dysfunctional behaviors. Regardless of the specialty, group counseling is particularly effective for gays and lesbians because groups offer a balance to the indifference and hostility of the general culture. The feeling of safety in numbers may be the emotional condition needed to start a positive therapeutic process (Lapierre, 1990). In groups, gay and lesbian members share their experiences and feelings and find out how others cope with similar situations. "Often creative forms of resolution of these kinds of negative feelings can be discovered through the group process" (p. 96).

The first decision gays and lesbians must make is whether to attend groups organized specifically for gay or lesbian membership or groups in which sexual orientation is not the basis for selection. When internalized homophobia is an issue, all-gay or all-lesbian groups are more appropriate for dealing with adjustment difficulties (Conlin & Smith, 1985). Even in groups that do not specifically entail sexual orientation, being gay or lesbian is apt to be an issue in the group. Gay and lesbian individuals who attend mixed groups will have to decide whether and how to come out in the group. Coming out always involves risks. In counseling groups, many members will accept gays and lesbians, but at least one person in the group commonly rejects and abuses gay or lesbian members. Alternately, the group can become engrossed with trying to change the sexual orientation of gay or lesbian members (Schwartz & Harstein, 1986; Yalom 1985).

The distinction between counseling groups and self-help groups is sometimes confusing. One important difference is that counseling groups are almost always led by credentialed counselors who take a more active role in the group. Because counselors are powerful facilitators in counseling groups, they need to be sensitive to the group's attitudes and behaviors about gays and lesbians. Leaders have a responsibility to recognize and confront homophobia and heterosexism among the group's members. Group leaders who fail to intervene on these issues are subtly expressing their own homophobia (Hall, 1985). Gays and lesbians frequently attend groups with a gay or lesbian leader or facilitator. If such groups are unavailable, gay-affirmative facilitators are needed to assist gays and lesbians in mixed orientation groups.

SPECIFIC GAY AND LESBIAN GROUPS

Groups are often advisable for sexual minorities who have had little or no contact with others like themselves. The group functions to "socialize" members. They typically provide a supportive atmosphere for knowledge and skill sharing about how to cope with various life problems. Groups are an important counter to the real and felt isolation which sexual minorities face in the larger social cultural milieu. (Klein, 1986, p. 28)

Groups help gay and lesbian members accomplish developmental tasks. Support and counseling groups are often structured to help participants address and successfully accomplish the age-related and sexual identity developmental tasks that all people face—sexuality, career, relationships, spirituality, parenting, aging. These tasks are not unique to gays and lesbians, but the lack of societal support systems often exacerbates the issues. Groups create a mini-culture in which the ignorance, prejudice, oppression, and homophobia our society directs toward gays and lesbians are countered by support, acceptance, and universality. The group process allows individuals to better understand and accept the issues of being gay or lesbian.

Human development theories identify the development of a distinct identity and a positive construct of self-worth as necessary for growth and development. All people develop and define their identities and sense of self-worth through an interactive process between the individual and his or her environment. As gay and lesbian individuals question "Who am I in this world?' and "How do I relate with others?" they face challenges and controversies directly related to their sexual orientation. Specific groups, such as those discussed below, can help members begin to arrive at answers to these questions.

Coming Out Groups

> Being gay [or lesbian] offers an uncommonly powerful catalyst for personal transformation. If we can stand the heat and give ourselves over to the full scope of the process of coming out, we will learn flexibility in the midst of life's chaos, paradox, and mystery. (Griffin, Wirth, & Wirth, 1986, p. 188)

The process of developing an identity as a gay or lesbian is called coming out. The first step is to acknowledge feelings for the same sex. Then individuals will have to decide whether to share their sexual orientation with others such as parents, friends, children, employers, and co-workers. Coming out is difficult because gays and lesbians typically are not born into gay or lesbian families. They suffer oppression alone, without benefit of advice or emotional support from relatives or friends. Most gays and lesbians have few role models and no self-validating and visible culture on which to pattern themselves (Forstein, 1986). They make statements like: "As I became aware of my attraction for others of the same sex, I thought I was the only one with these feelings."

Individuals may decide to come out at any age. Some have indicated that they knew they were gay as early as age 6 or 7. If people come out during the teenage years, development of sexual identity is congruent with adolescent development. But coming out as a teenager can be particularly difficult because adolescents are most often financially and emotionally dependent on their parents. In addition, parental acceptance and approval are important to young people, and adolescents risk being thrown out of their homes by parents if they identify themselves as gay or lesbian (Silberman & Hawkins, 1988).

Many individuals do not come out until later years and may not "enter their true adolescence until their chronological adolescence has long passed" (Coleman, 1985, p. 36). Some come out as senior citizens. Coming out is an identity crisis, and whenever it occurs, most gays and lesbians will need assistance with coming out issues and developing a positive sense of self.

Each person must decide whether to identify as gay or lesbian. Those who choose to keep their sexual orientation secret are said to be "living in the closet." This supports internalized homophobia, shame, and guilt, and reinforces a negative self-image by implying that certain feelings and aspects of being gay or lesbian are too shameful to disclose to anyone. Closeted gays and lesbians lead constricted lives, constantly monitoring their thoughts, emotions, and responses. Hiding does irreparable harm to their sense of integrity and leaves them in a stressful and dissonant position, which detracts from their mental health and well-being. Stress, depression, and substance abuse are all related clinically to maintaining a secret existence.

The stresses of addressing sexual orientation affect the function and quality of life no matter how far out of the closet gays and lesbians are, or how carefully cloistered and defended about their lifestyle (Riddle & Sang, 1978). Gays and lesbians are under constant, conflicting pressure both to stay in and to come out of the closet; they face decisions about whether to come out every day. For example, when co-workers are discussing what they did on the weekend, do gay and lesbian workers share with whom they spent time, or do they make up appropriate other-gender partners? At holiday times, do gay and lesbian attendees of office parties and family dinners bring their partners or do they go alone and feign being unattached?

Coming out groups may be appropriate for gays and lesbians at any time. The focus of these groups has to be on taking creative responsibility for the way one's life is developing. Because friends, family, and society do not often encourage or support the development of a defined and positive identity, coming out groups are a place for positive support during the coming out process. In groups, members take steps to make connections with others and move away from their isolation and secrecy. Gays and lesbians frequently attend groups to address coming out issues and understand the possible consequences of sharing the fact that they are gay or lesbian.

No matter what stage of development a person is confronting, coming out groups provide a place to bring out daily issues of being gay or lesbian. For example, a 45-year-old who has lived an active and "out" life as a lesbian may find that attending a coming out group with people in different stages is invaluable in assessing her own current issues. Group leaders need to recognize the risks involved in sharing information about being gay or lesbian, and remain sensitive to every member of the group.

Group leaders may wish to familiarize themselves with various coming out models. Several that provide a framework for understanding the process of identity development for gays and lesbians are available (Cass, 1984; Coleman, 1985; Falco, 1987; Lewis, 1984; Sophie, 1987). Leaders of coming out groups, regardless of their sexual orientation, also come out when they lead these groups. Thus, they will have to confront their own homophobia, face the coming out issues in their own lives, and be comfortable discussing sexual issues, including their own sexuality, in the group. Otherwise they may find themselves impeding rather than helping the group process.

Youth Groups

Peer groups are important for all adolescents, and a number of organizations provide teenagers with opportunities to participate in groups. Most school, church, and community groups, however, do not serve the special needs of youth struggling to identify themselves as gay or lesbian (Gerstel, Feraios, & Herdt, 1989). This is unfortunate, as groups can be particularly important in helping gay and lesbian youth accomplish basic developmental tasks. Because most gay and lesbian teens have experienced rejection and discrimination by friends, family, church and teachers, the approval and inclusion that groups provide are essential for appropriate identity development.

Groups give gay and lesbian youth a chance to address issues of identifying themselves as gay or lesbian in society, and to learn from and with other gay and lesbian teens. Gay and lesbian youth typically lack positive role models and friends during their teenage years (Kus, 1990). The chance to compare experiences with other group members who are wrestling with similar identity issues enhances self-esteem and promotes emotional growth in all the participants (Gerstel et al., 1989).

Youth groups also might be described as coming out groups. The paramount issue among adolescents addressing their sexual orientation is whether and how to come out to friends. Family relationships, including the question of whether to come out to family members, is also an important topic, and the group will probably spend considerable time discussing various strategies and approaches. Members can explore their own thoughts and feelings with the group, and get the group's feedback. As members make and implement decisions, and share the reactions of people they disclose to, everyone in the group gains new perspectives on their own choices.

The Horizons Youth Group in Chicago has been meeting since 1978. A typical meeting is described (Gerstel et al., 1989):

> Newcomers are welcomed; anyone attending for the first time is introduced and applauded, which constitutes their intentional recognition by the group. Meetings open with general announcements about events, and new activities are planned and discussed. Youth make announcements regarding events of local interest, such as bake sales and parties. . . . The group offers a choice of topics for discussion that may be taken up in one larger or several small rap groups. The teenagers select the topic that interests them and form small groups of about 10, each of which is led by at least one facilitator. (p. 83)

Establishing and maintaining youth groups in rural areas may be more difficult than in urban areas. School administrators, public officials, and church leaders may be actively hostile to the idea of gay and lesbian groups for young people and create an atmosphere of fear and paranoia in which individuals may hesitate to attend for fear of retribution. In many small communities, groups do not advertise their location; people are asked to phone for time and place of meetings.

Leaders serve a number of different functions in these groups. They offer a stable hub, which is important in a group in which the membership fluctuates. They also reinforce and model the norms of confidentiality and safety within the group. These norms must be explicitly discussed whenever new people attend the group. Leaders also facilitate the group's process during discussions by modeling and reinforcing behaviors such as active listening and nonjudgmental acceptance of each individual. They can encourage linking between group members and can draw parallels between what the members discuss.

Group leaders may find that inevitably they have to address the community's homophobia. This can mean a number of things, from networking with school counselors about gay and lesbian students, to advocating at school board meetings for permission to advertise the group in the high school newspaper, to writing to the Letters to the Editor section of the local newspaper, defending the group's existence. Leaders working with gay and lesbian members often find themselves in the role of activists promoting change on a community level.

Couples' Groups

> Today, gay couples live in every area of the country. They are found in urban settings and rural farm communities. We find men in loving, lifelong relationships with all the romance and passion found in heterosexual marriage. (Silverstein, 1990, p. 205)

> Lesbian couples living in our present culture often believe they have found the best of all possible worlds as women because they are not confined to the traditional woman's role in relationships. (Hall & Stevens, 1990, p. 215)

Most gay and lesbian individuals live with a partner. Weinberg and Williams (1974) found that 71% of the men in their sample were living together as partners, and Bell and Weinberg (1978) reported that 82% of the lesbians they studied were living with a partner. With the advent of the AIDS pandemic, more gay men are choosing to live with partners in a monogamous fashion (Allers & Katrin, 1988). Most often, gay and lesbian couples bring concerns to group counseling that are no different than the issues in heterosexual relationships—differences in socioeconomic and family backgrounds, education, religion or values, communication problems, previous relationships, illness, financial issues, individual emotional problems, sexual dysfunction, and jealousy. Lesbian and gay couples, however, face other relationship problems related to their sexual orientation.

Gay and lesbian couples "do not have the social, legal or moral sanctions that sustain opposite-sex couples. Thus, the development and maintenance of same-sex couples involves a commitment to a difficult process with many destructive internal and external forces in its path" (Forstein, 1986, p. 105). For example, lesbian and gay couples frequently disagree about how open to be about their sexual orientation. One member of the couple may have come out to his or her family while the other has not discussed sexual orientation with his or her parents. Other issues gay and lesbian couples may face are related to the lack of visible role models for their relationship. Gay and lesbian couples frequently express curiosity about how other couples deal with their everyday lives and bring up issues such as finances, outside relationships, families, and sex.

Group counseling gives gay and lesbian couples opportunities to explore these unique relationship issues in a safe, supportive environment. Groups can help couples look at what happens in a relationship when one member of the couple is more out of the closet than the other. Groups also can help couples realize that, although the lack of modeling for gay and lesbian couples creates uncertainty about how to behave as a couple, the absence of strict, societal guidelines for same-sex couples allows for creativity in establishing ground rules for the relationship.

The leader and other group participants provide couples with mirrors of their relationship. The various group members also offer a variety of role models for each couple to consider. The group leader and group members also can suggest books to read, videos to view, and lectures and other community events to attend to help couples explore alternative models of behavior. Because many of the issues facing gay and lesbian couples are related to being male or female in our society, same-gender leaders are apt to be most appropriate for these groups.

Couples also face the effects of societal sex-role stereotypes on their relationships. Gay couples tend to experience competition as a difficulty in relationships, whereas lesbian couples frequently have difficulty with fusion and separation (McCandlish, 1985; Silberman & Hawkins, 1988). Group leaders working with gay couples should know about the developmental model created by McWhirter and Mattison (1984). They developed a six-stage model that describes and identifies the tasks male couples encounter as they progress through predictable developmental stages in their relationship. Leaders might use this model in group counseling with gay couples to assess whether the partners are moving at the same pace or are on different developmental tracks.

Group leaders working with lesbian couples may have to address the serious and widespread problem of violence and battering among lesbian couples (Hammond, 1989; NiCarthy, 1986). Lesbians often have difficulty letting go of relationships. Rather than leave relationships, they frequently fight and vent anger toward their partner. Like other abusers, lesbian abusers batter to exercise power over their partners, and they have learned that violence is effective in getting their partners to comply with their wishes (Hart, 1989).

Battering has a profound impact on the victim. Closeness and equality in the relationship disappear, and fear, mistrust and disillusionment take over. Group leaders must be sensitive to the issues between partners involved in domestic violence while helping to restore the victim's integrity and self-worth. As in all issues of violence, the victim's safety takes precedence over supporting the relationship or taking care of the batterer's current emotional needs (Hammond, 1989).

Parenting Groups

Gays and lesbians are becoming partners, having and rearing children, and challenging society's definition of what "family" means. In the United States, at least one in three lesbians and one in ten gay men have children (Moses & Hawkins, 1982). Sometimes these children are born in heterosexual partnerships. Increasingly, however, gay and lesbian couples are choosing to become parents and are raising their children in redefined families.

Many of the difficulties of gay and lesbian parenting are exactly like the stresses heterosexual parents feel—jealousy, time spent with children, privacy, communication. In blended families, parenting styles and responsibilities are common points of disagreement. Other stresses are unique to gay parents. The gay partner's inability to become a legal stepparent can complicate the attempt to co-parent another's child. Gay couples face difficulty if they wish to adopt children. Many states discriminate against gay individuals in awarding child custody and visitation rights; in some states, gay parents are considered unfit. Other issues that arise for gay parents include concerns about coming out to a wife or husband, to children, and to other family members. Concerns about coming out also affect the children of gay and lesbian parents. Some children choose to hide their parent's sexuality from friends.

Group counseling can help gay and lesbian parents in several ways. Leaders may wish to introduce the group to behavioral techniques that will teach members how to improve their information or skill level. Group members are a circle of supportive people with whom the participants can explore specific parenting topics. The group also can problem-solve and brainstorm about parenting strategies and share information on legal and other professional resources. Groups for gay fathers and lesbian mothers exist in most urban communities and many rural areas. Group leaders should be aware of these resources and refer members to those groups when appropriate.

Parents of gay and lesbian children also face difficult issues in accepting the reality that they have gay or lesbian children. A national organization, Parents and Friends of Lesbians and Gays (PFLAG), exists as a support and information network for these parents. In many communities, PFLAG meetings revolve around issues of guilt, shock, and pain that parents face when they discover they have a gay or lesbian child. These groups assist parents in overcoming the cultural messages of rejection and hatred of gays and moving toward acceptance and peace. "The act of confronting homosexuality [sic] openly and courageously can become a source of freedom and fulfillment in the family," (Griffin et al., 1986, p. 9).

Drug and Alcohol Abuse Groups

Approximately 30–35% of the gay and lesbian population is chemically dependent on alcohol or drugs, and many mental health professionals see alcoholism as the number one health problem among gays and lesbians (Kus, 1987; 1990). Internalized homophobia may account for the high incidence of alcoholism. Gay and lesbian abusers of drugs and alcohol do so to relieve "fears, anxieties, feelings of low self-esteem, feelings of self-hatred and worthlessness, and feelings of not being able to go on with life" (Kus, 1990, p. 94). The issue of being gay or lesbian in society must be attended to in substance-abuse counseling and self-help groups.

Although the substance abuse may originate with internalized homophobia, counselors cannot work on self-image while the client is drinking or using drugs. Accepting oneself as gay or lesbian does not typically happen during periods of abuse. Leaders can work with individuals in groups only after they have successfully treated the substance abuse problem—an approach consistent with that of other substance-abusing populations.

Gay and lesbian individuals who come to treatment groups may be experiencing heightened shame and guilt. Therefore, leaders should ask questions about sexual identity and behavior in ways that indicate all answers are acceptable. "If the question [of sexual orientation] is not posed, gays or lesbians may feel heterosexuality is assumed and homosexuality is possibly unacceptable in this setting" (Finnegan & McNally, 1987, p. 61). Addressing sexual orientation issues in groups as a part of the treatment plan demonstrates sensitivity to gay and lesbian issues. Group leaders working on substance abuse issues should be familiar with local self-help groups and resources and be able to make appropriate referrals, because most gay and lesbian individuals will need to be in both counseling and self-help groups to stay clean and sober. Leaders must encourage group members to attend gay, lesbian, or gay-lesbian Alcoholics Anonymous meetings.

AIDS Groups

The response of the gay and lesbian community to the AIDS pandemic is a striking example of the importance of groups in the gay and lesbian community. AIDS, first identified in 1981, is a usually fatal disease with no known cure or immunization. At first, gay men were the hardest hit group in the United States. Groups in the gay community organized the initial, desperately needed support services, generated the earliest self-help and safer sex materials, and lobbied incessantly about the need for funds for care and research (McLaughlin, 1989). Gay men banded together, at first informally and then with increasing sophistication and organization, to provide and demand adequate, respectful care for their lovers and friends. The lesbian community responded similarly and has also been actively involved in AIDS support services.

Groups were organized to help with transportation, to deliver meals and to run errands. Self-help and support groups began as well: for people who were HIV-positive; for people with AIDS (PWAs); for the friends and families and mates and lovers and grieving survivors of PWAs; for the doctors and nurses and counselors and volunteers and home care aides and neighbors who care for people living with and dying from AIDS. Today, AIDS care continues to be provided by groups that supplement care and in some instances substitute for institutionalized medical and support services that do not exist for people with AIDS.

[AIDS community-based organizations] have provided a way for thousands of volunteers to give countless hours of assistance and comfort to patients, their loved ones, and families. . . . In a larger social sense, these groups have served as bridges between the gay and lesbian and the straight communities, bringing together individuals who share a commitment to humanitarian goals and a refusal to give in to a lethal enemy. (Fineberg, 1988, p. 132)

Leaders are most likely to be involved in support and counseling groups for PWAs, and support groups for friends and family members. As with many of the issues confronting gays and lesbians, group leaders may see the need to extend their involvement to the larger social and cultural factors that affect group members. For example, leaders may choose to advocate for changes in drug experimentation and approval requirements so that PWAs will have access to treatment alternatives.

Support Groups for PWAs   Most mental health professionals and physicians view support groups for HIV-positive people and PWAs as an essential element of optimum care. "Another patient [sic] can do more toward relieving another's nagging fear than a host of health professionals" (Eller & King, 1990, p. 332). Support groups extend the participants' circle of support (Price, Omizo, & Hammet, 1986) and offer a powerful antidote to the isolation and alienation that PWAs often encounter (Morin, Charles, & Malyon, 1984). In support groups, members can discuss problems related to their HIV status and share their feelings and thoughts. In most groups, members spend time discussing their individual reactions to the diagnosis, as well as the reactions of friends and family members.

The AIDS diagnosis may force PWAs, families, and friends to face previously avoided issues such as sexual orientation or drug use. The PWA often tries to keep the AIDS diagnosis a secret from certain family members or from people outside the family, because of fears of rejection, stigma, retaliation, and isolation. Family members may attempt to exclude gay friends or lovers. All of these responses are brought to the group to be shared and addressed. Other group discussions may focus on anger; guilt; and grief over their own loss of health, the deaths of friends and loved ones, and their own approaching death; recurring denial about their illness; safer sex behaviors; and the need for decision making about burial and funeral matters.

Support Groups for Friends and Family of PWAs   Support groups give friends and family members of PWAs the opportunity to vent their anger, frustration, and sorrow at the illness and its effects on their lives in a safe and accepting environment (Martin, 1989). Friends and family often face issues very similar to those confronted by the PWA. In addition, they must deal with the exhaustion caused by physical caregiving, the anxiety of wondering what will happen next, and the stress of financial responsibility for a disease for which long-term costs can run into the hundreds of thousands of dollars (Fineberg, 1988). Support groups for significant others often are led by professionals who act as facilitators or by family members acting as peer facilitators.

Counseling Groups for PWAs   Counseling groups for HIV-positive people and PWAs are usually closed (new participants are not accepted after the group begins) and time-limited (eight to 10 weeks). For people facing life-threatening illness, this model provides stability that reinforces the participants' attempts to become empowered and hopeful. It also offers consistency, which is important in the development of social support, trust, and comfort within the group. A time-limited, closed group is also most likely to maintain a constant membership, given the high mortality rate for AIDS. These groups may look at a number of different questions, including relationship issues, existential issues raised by their illness, the challenge of making lifestyle changes, or their own death and dying.

Aging Groups

Older lesbians and gays are a large, usually ignored, minority (Berger, 1982). There are, by conservative estimates, nearly a million gay men over age 65, and more than a million lesbians in that age group (Kimmel, 1978). Although they fit into two groups—the elderly and the nonheterosexual—they are often overlooked by other gays and lesbians, and by those working with the elderly. Little research has been done on these populations (Berger, 1982; Robinson, 1979; Wolf, 1978), and services geared to their special situations rarely exist. The older gay and lesbian population is a silent, often hidden one, whose needs remain largely unassessed and generally unmet. Part of the problem is that older gay and lesbian individuals are much less likely than their younger counterparts to take advantage of the support of the gay and lesbian community. They are less involved in civil rights organizations, social clubs, bars, self-help groups, or counseling groups than are younger people (Berger, 1982). As a result, older gays and lesbians are often isolated and alone, and younger gays and lesbians are deprived of valuable role models for aging.

Older gays and lesbians face issues relevant to this stage of their lives. Some are related to aging, including the aging process and physical changes of aging, sensible nutrition, sex as an older adult, issues of ageism, misconceptions about older gays and lesbians, bereavement overload, and combating loneliness. Other problems are more specifically related to aging as a gay or lesbian, such as the lack of recognition as a surviving mate when a partner dies, the lack of financial security, conflicts with family members over care and decision making during illness, sexual changes, and unique medical needs.

Gay and lesbian couples may have to make financial plans so that if one partner dies, the other will not lose possessions and property the two purchased together. Gay and lesbian elderly people are much less likely to have children to provide care and help with decision making. Other arrangements, such as power of attorney and hospital visitation agreements, have to be considered, discussed with family and lovers, and instituted.

Recently, groups for older gay men and lesbians have emerged to provide a therapeutic environment in which to approach aging issues. These groups offer older gay and lesbian members opportunities for peer sharing, socialization, and social activities. Groups also help members feel less isolated and alone. Urban areas often have groups or programs that focus on the particular needs of the older gay and lesbian population. The Gay Community Services Center in Minneapolis, with its "Affectional Preference and Aging" program, the Gay Forty Plus Club in San Francisco, and Senior Action in a Gay Environment (SAGE) in New York City are examples of programs in which groups are used as a way to reach out to older gays and lesbians (Berger, 1982). In less populated areas, these issues may be encompassed in the context of a mixed-age group.

Personal Growth Groups

> Gay [and lesbian] growth experience groups are growing in strength and membership. We are beginning to understand that our loneliness is not required as the only alternative to conformity or self-destruction. (Clark, 1987, p. 100)

Many gays and lesbians experience loneliness, depression, anxiety, guilt, anger, and suicidal thoughts as a result of the conflicts they confront in their childhood and throughout their lives. In some ways, these conflicts are like those of many people in contemporary society, but with a depth of feeling and the absence of hope of resolving the conflicts that do not exist for most people (Fortunato, 1983). Great anxiety and loneliness sometimes result when people realize that they may never receive support from parents, siblings, family members, or loved ones. Life can be extremely painful for gays and lesbians who have lost friends or a job or their church membership because of their sexual orientation.

Gays and lesbians who remain closeted and secretive frequently have feelings of paranoia and may abuse alcohol or drugs. They may recognize societal oppression but refuse to deal with it. Individuals who are in extreme denial and live totally in the closet isolate themselves from other gays and lesbians and have minimal social and sexual contacts. These individuals have ingested the fear of being gay or lesbian and internalized the oppression of society. They bargain with themselves about being gay or lesbian, make excuses for their behavior, and deny their sexual orientation. They are caught in a co-dependent phase, making excuses for their behavior and defending the people who are oppressing and rejecting them.

Gays and lesbians, however, do not have to live lives of loneliness and depression. Personal growth groups represent one place where they can confront their denial and direct their attention to the source of their oppression. In groups, members share their feelings of guilt and internalized homophobia. They learn to take responsibility for themselves rather than blaming society and the people in their life for the awful state of "their world." Growth groups help members deal with the anger they feel toward society. Group members who learn to express their anger in positive ways are more likely to avoid the inward expressions of anger often associated with loneliness, substance abuse, or suicidal ideation.

As research is indicating that sexual orientation is not a matter of choice, gays and lesbians need to stop asking the question "Why me?" and begin to affirm their sexual orientation. The group should encourage self-affirmative statements that will allow members to embrace being gay or lesbian. Such honest discussion in groups is liberating and lays the foundation for honest and direct interaction with other people. The ultimate reward of developing this sense of community within gay and lesbian personal growth groups is learning that "you are no longer alone" (Clark, 1987, p. 103).

SUMMARY

Professional groups have been slow to respond to gay and lesbian individuals and their unique concerns, mirroring the attitudes of the American public, which continues to favor heterosexism. As a product of homophobia, some gays and lesbians have internalized society's negative attitudes and deny their own sexual orientation. Some counseling professionals have adopted heterosexist and homophobic attitudes.

What is needed is gay-affirmative counseling, in which leaders create an atmosphere of tolerance and acceptance, are sensitive to gay and lesbian concerns, openly address sexual orientation issues, and create and model norms of nonjudgmental acceptance and tolerance of all group members. Some groups, particularly couples groups, might best be led by gay or lesbian professional counselors.

Types of groups include common-interest groups, self-help groups, and counseling groups. The latter is differentiated by virtue of their leadership by a credentialed counselor, who takes a more active role in facilitating group processes and goals. Specific gay and lesbian groups include coming out groups, youth groups, couples groups, parenting groups, drug and alcohol abuse groups, and AIDS groups. Self-help and support groups have developed for HIV-positive individuals; for people with AIDS (PWAs); for families and mates and lovers and grieving survivors of PWAs; for doctors and nurses and counselors and volunteers and home care aides and neighbors, as nonprofit, community-based organizations.

A special needs population still largely ignored is that of older lesbians and gays. And a final type of group is the personal growth group, which endeavors to help members deal with underlying issues and move ahead in the process of human development.

REFERENCES

Allers, C. T., & Katrin, S. E. (1988). AIDS counseling: A psychosocial model. *Journal of Mental Health Counseling, 10,* 235–244.

Bell, A. P., & Weinberg, M. S. (1978). *Homosexualities: A study of diversities among men and women.* New York: Simon & Schuster.

Berger, R. M. (1982). *Gay and gray: The older homosexual man.* Boston: Alyson.

Blumenfeld, W. J., & Raymond, D. (1988). *Looking at gay and lesbian life.* Boston: Beacon Press.

Buhrke, R. A. (1989). Incorporating lesbian and gay issues into counselor training: A resource guide. *Journal of Counseling & Development, 68,* 77-80.

Cass, V. C. (1984). Homosexual identity formation: A concept in need of definition. *Journal of Homosexuality, 10,* 105–126.

Clark, D. (1987). *The new loving someone gay.* Berkeley, CA: Celestial Arts.

Coleman, E. (1985). Developmental stages of the coming out process. In J. C. Gonsiorek (Ed.), *A guide to psychotherapy with gay and lesbian clients* (pp. 31–43). New York: Harrington Park.

Coleman, E., & Ramafedi, G. (1989). Gay, lesbian and bisexual adolescents: A critical challenge to counselors. *Journal of Counseling & Development, 68,* 36–40.

Conlin, D., & Smith, J. (1985). Group psychotherapy for gay men. In J. C. Gonsiorek (Ed.), *A guide to psychotherapy with gay and lesbian clients* (pp. 105–112.) New York: Harrington.

Dworkin, S. H., & Gutierrez, F. (1989). Introduction to special issue. Counselors be aware: Clients come in every size, shape, color and sexual orientation. *Journal of Counseling & Development, 68,* 6–8.

Eller, M., & King, D. J. (1990). Self-help groups for gays, lesbians, and their loved ones. In R. J. Kus (Ed.), *Keys to Caring* (pp. 330–339.) Boston: Alyson.

Falco, K. (1987). *Psychotherapy with lesbian clients: A manual for the psychotherapist.* Unpublished doctoral dissertation, Oregon Graduate School of Professional Psychology, Pacific University, Forest Grove.

Fineberg, H. V. (1988). The social dimensions of AIDS. *Scientific American, 259,* 128–134.

Finnegan, D. G., & McNally, E. B. (1987). *Dual identities: Counseling chemically dependent gay men and lesbians.* Center City, MN: Hazelden Educational Materials.

Forstein, M. (1986). Psychodynamic psychotherapy with gay male couples. In T. S. Stein & C. J. Cohen (Eds.), *Contemporary perspectives on psychotherapy with lesbians and gay men* (pp. 103-137). New York: Plenum Press.

Fortunato, J. E. (1983). *Embracing the exile: Healing journey of gay Christians.* New York: Seabury.

Gerstel, C. J., Feraios, A. J., & Herdt, G. (1989). *Widening circles: An ethnographic profile of a youth group.* In G. Herdt (Ed.), *Gay and lesbian youth* (pp. 75–92). Binghamton, NY: Haworth Press.

Griffin, C. W., Wirth, M. J., & Wirth, A. G. (1986). *Beyond acceptance: Parents of lesbians and gays talk about their experiences.* New York: St. Martins Press.

Hall, M. (1985). *The lavender couch: A consumer's guide to psychotherapy for lesbians and gay men*. Boston: Alyson.

Hall, J., & Stevens, P. (1990). The coupled lesbian. In R. J. Kus (Ed.), *Keys to caring* (pp. 215–223). Boston: Alyson.

Hammond, N. (1989). Lesbian victims of relationship violence. In E. D. Rothblum & E. Cole (Eds.), *Lesbianism: Affirming nontraditional roles*. New York: Haworth Press.

Hart, B. (1989). Lesbian battering: An examination. In K. Lobel (Ed.), *Naming the violence: Speaking out about lesbian battering*. Seattle: Seal.

Herron, W. G., Kintner, T., Sollinger, I., & Trubowitz, J. (1985). Psychoanalytic psychotherapy for homosexual clients: new concepts. In J. C. Gonsiorek (Ed.), *A guide to psychotherapy with gay and lesbian clients* (pp. 177–192). New York: Harrington Park.

House, R. M. (1991). Counseling gay and lesbian clients. In D. Capuzzi & D. R. Gross (Eds.), *Introduction to Counseling: Perspectives for the 1990s* (pp. 323–394). Boston: Allyn & Bacon.

House, R. M., & Holloway, E. L. (1991). Empowering the counseling professional to work with gay and lesbian issues. In S. H. Dworkin & F. Gutierrez (Eds.), *Counseling gay and lesbian clients* (pp. 288–306). Washington, DC: American Association for Counseling and Development.

Iasenza, S. (1989). Some challenges of integrating sexual orientations into counselor training and research. *Journal of Counseling & Development, 68*, 73–76.

Kimmel, D. C. (1978). Adult development and aging: A gay perspective. *Journal of Social Issues, 34*(3), 113–130.

Kinsey, A., Pomeroy, W. B., & Martin, C. E. (1948). *Sexual behavior in the human male*. Philadelphia: W. B. Saunders.

Kinsey, A., Pomeroy, W. B., Martin, C. E., & Gebhard, R. H. (1953). *Sexual behavior in the human female*. Philadelphia: W. B. Saunders.

Klein, C. (1986). *Counseling our own: The lesbian/gay subculture meets the mental health system*. Renton, WA: Publication Service.

Klein, C. (1990). Gay and lesbian counseling centers: History and functions. In R. J. Kus (Ed.), *Keys to Caring* (pp. 312–320). Boston: Alyson.

Krajeski, J. P. (1986). Psychotherapy with gay men and lesbians: A history of controversy. In T. S. Stein & C. J. Cohen (Eds.), *Contemporary perspectives on psychotherapy with lesbians and gay men* (pp. 9–25). New York: Plenum Press.

Kus, R. J. (1987). Alcoholics Anonymous and gay American men. *Journal of Homosexuality, 14*, 253–276.

Kus, R. J. (1990). *Keys to caring: Assisting your gay and lesbian clients*. Boston: Alyson.

Lapierre, E. D. (1990). Homophobia and its consequences for gay and lesbian clients. In R. J. Kus (Ed.), *Keys to caring* (pp. 90–104). Boston: Alyson.

Lewis, L. A. (1984). The coming out process for lesbians: Integrating a stable identity. *Journal of the National Association of Social Workers, 29*, 464–469.

Martin, D. J. (1989). Human immunodeficiency virus infection and the gay community: Counseling and clinical issues. *Journal of Counseling & Development, 68*, 67–72.

McCandlish, B. M. (1985). Therapeutic issues with lesbian couples. In J. C. Gonsiorek (Ed.), *A guide to psychotherapy with gay and lesbian clients* (pp. 71–78). New York: Harrington Park.

McDermott, D., Tyndall, L., & Lichtenberg, J. W. (1989). Factors related to counselor preference among gays and lesbians. *Journal of Counseling and Development, 68*, 31–35.

McLaughlin, L. (1989). AIDS: An overview. In P. O'Malley (Ed.), *The AIDS epidemic: Private rights and the public interest* (pp. 15–35). Boston: Beacon Press.

McWhirter, D. P., & Mattison, A. M. (1984). *The male couple: How relationships develop*. Englewood Cliffs, NJ: Prentice-Hall.

Mollenkott, V. R. (1985). *Breaking the silence, overcoming the fear: Homophobia education*. (Available from the Program Agency, United Presbyterian Church, U.S.A., 475 Riverside Drive, Room 1101, New York, NY 10015)

Money, J. (1987). Sin, sickness, or status? Homosexual gender identity and psychoneuroendrocrinology. *American Psychologist, 42*, 384–399.

Morin, S., Charles, K., & Malyon, A. (1984). The psychological impact of AIDS on gay men. *American Psychologist, 39*, 1288–1293.

Moses, A. E., & Hawkins, R. O. (1982). *Counseling lesbian women and gay men: A life-issues approach*. Columbus, OH: Charles E. Merrill.

Moses, A. E., & Hawkins, R. O. (1985). Two-hour in-service training session in homophobia. In H. Hidalgo, T. Peterson, & N. J. Woodman (Eds.), *Lesbian and gay issues: A resource manual for social workers* (pp. 152–157). Silver Spring, MD: National Association of Social Workers.

NiCarthy, G. (1986). *Getting free: A handbook for women in abusive relationships*. Seattle: Seal.

Price, R. E., Omizo, M., & Hammett, V. L. (1986). Counseling clients with AIDS. *Journal of Counseling & Development, 65,* 96–97.

Riddle, D. I., & Sang, B. (1978). Psychotherapy with lesbians. *Journal of Social Issues, 34*(3) 84–100.

Ritter, K. Y., & O'Neill, C. W. (1989). Moving through loss: The spiritual journey of gay men and lesbian women. *Journal of Counseling & Development, 68,* 9–15.

Rizzi, D. (1989, June). It's repugnant. [Letter to the editor]. *San Francisco Examiner,* p. 15.

Robinson, M. K. (1979). *The older lesbian.* Master's thesis, California State University of Dominguez Hills.

Rochlin, M. (1985). Sexual orientation of the therapist and therapeutic effectiveness with gay clients. In J. C. Gonsiorek (Ed.), *A guide to psychotherapy with gay and lesbian clients* (pp. 21–29). New York: Harrington Park.

A Special Report: Gays in America. (1989, June). *San Francisco Examiner,* pp. 1–78.

Schwartz, R. D., & Hartstein, N. B. (1986). Group psychotherapy with gay men: Theoretical and clinical considerations. In T. S. Stein & C. J. Cohen (Eds.), *Psychotherapy with lesbians and gay men* (pp. 157–177). New York: Plenum Press.

Silberman, B. O., & Hawkins, R. O., Jr. (1988). Lesbian women and gay men: Issues for counseling. In E. Weinstein & E. Rosen (Eds.), *Sexuality counseling: Issues and implications* (pp. 101–113). Pacific Grove, CA: Brooks/Cole.

Silverstein, C. (1990). The coupled gay. In R. J. Kus (Ed.), *Keys to caring* (pp. 204–214). Boston: Alyson.

Sophie, J. (1987). Internalized homophobia and lesbian identity. *Journal of Homosexuality, 14,* 53–65.

Warren, S. (1989, June). Shame — Shame! [Letter to the editor]. *San Francisco Examiner,* p. 15.

Weinberg, G. (1973). *Society and the healthy homosexual.* Garden City, NY: Anchor.

Weinberg, M. S., & Williams, C. S. (1974). *Male homosexuals: Their problems and adaptations.* New York: Oxford.

Wett, A. (1989, June). Long live bashers! [Letter to the editor]. *San Francisco Examiner,* p. 15.

Williams, R. (1990). Studying sex in Sweden . . . or how I spent my summer vacation. *Christopher Street, 13*(4), 11–15.

Wolf, D. G. (1978, November). *Close friendship patterns of older lesbians.* Paper presented at convention of the Gerontological Society, Dallas.

Woodman, N., & Lenna, H. (1980). *Counseling with gay men and women.* San Francisco: Jossey-Bass.

Yalom, I. (1985). *The theory and practice of group psychotherapy* (3rd ed.). New York: Basic Books.

11

Group Counseling with Couples and Families

Max Hines

Group counseling with couples and families is unknown territory for many group leaders. The two main types are multiple family group counseling (MFGC) and couples group counseling. As commonly practiced, group counseling has involved work with individuals, not couples or families. Group counselors typically do screening interviews with individuals. After pre-group screening, the individual is placed in a group composed of other individuals, all of whom were strangers to one another prior to joining the group. Although group counseling can and often does address each group member's underlying relationship issues that directly affect that member's significant other and family, people often come for counseling specifically identifying their problem as a couple or family problem.

In an extensive survey, Parad and Parad (1968) found that participants described more than 75% of their presenting problems as either relationship problems (37%) or problems posed by another family member (39%). In many situations, people are hesitant or simply unwilling to enter into traditional group counseling with strangers and without their significant other or family with whom they are experiencing the problems for which they have sought counseling. In light of their view of the problem, these people are often much more willing to join a group that fits well with the nature of the presenting problem as they see it (e.g., a couples group or a group composed of families with similar problems).

MULTIPLE FAMILY GROUP COUNSELING

Laqueur (1976) is usually regarded as the founder of multiple family group counseling (MFGC). Multiple family group counseling has been promoted as a useful treatment modality in a wide range of clinical settings including inpatient treatment of schizophrenics (Anderson, 1983) and outpatient treatment at family agencies (Gritzer & Okun, 1983). Reiss and Costell (1977) point out that multiple family groups closely resemble members' everyday social settings or communities. MFGC thus provides a context in which members can simulate their intrafamilial and extrafamilial patterns of interaction.

Indicators and Contraindicators

Based upon clinical experience, MFGC has been recommended as especially useful for families of physical or emotional abuse, for families in which parenting is an issue, for socially isolated families (O'Shea & Phelps, 1985), and for families dealing with an impending death within the family unit (Greaves, 1983). Multiple family group counseling is reportedly contraindicated for chaotic families, families in which an important fact remains secret (Leichter & Schulman, 1974), and families with an actively psychotic member (Parker, Hill, & Miller, 1987). Sigman, John, Levinson, and Betts (1985) identify MFGC as a useful adjunct to inpatient treatment.

Multiple family group counseling allows the treatment team an opportunity to identify disturbed family interactions that inhibit a person's recovery. In addition, MFGC provides families an opportunity to see and reflect on their own difficulties as mirrored by other families.

Sigman et al. (1985) suggest that multiple family group counseling in connection with hospitalized psychiatric patients:

— avoids the patient's premature discharge due to family anxiety.
— enhances the autonomy of individual family members.
— begins to improve couples and parent/offspring relationships.
— serves as a bridge between hospital and home.

Lansky, Bley, McVey, and Brotman (1980) also report success using MFGC to minimize relapse when inpatients are about to be or already have been discharged from the inpatient unit.

All of these recommendations and statements favoring multiple family group counseling are essentially practitioners' impressions that have yet to be empirically tested. The MFGC literature is noticeably lacking in rigorous empirical outcome studies. Most of the MFGC literature consists of descriptive and anecdotal reports essentially based upon the untested opinions of counselors who have experience in multiple family group counseling.

Counseling Procedures

The counseling procedures used in forming a multiple family group are in many ways similar to those used in forming any other group except that families are the treatment unit. Instead of meeting with an individual for an intake interview, the professional meets with a family for the pre-group intake interview. Just as intake interviews help prepare individuals for the group experience, intake interviews facilitate a smooth transition for families as they enter the group. During the pre-group interview, goals and expectations can be clarified with the family. In forming a multiple family group, O'Shea and Phelps (1985) recommend homogeneity regarding presenting problem(s). Cassano (1989) also recommends homogeneity as to age range of children, thereby encouraging peer interaction in the group.

The number of families suggested for a multiple family group has typically been three to four (Parker, Hill, & Miller, 1987; Raasoch, 1981; Singh, 1982), although Reiss and Costell (1977) report working with as many as 13 families in one group. Cassano (1989) recommends including three families in the group to provide for more opportunities for interaction across families. O'Shea and Phelps (1985) suggest that each partici-pating family should have present for all or most of the sessions at least two family mem-bers representing at least two generations in the family. As do counselors in most other group counseling contexts, multiple family group counselors commonly ask participating families for a commitment to regular attendance.

Dynamics

In multiple family groups, social interaction can occur at many levels. The social process may be within families or across families. Interaction within families might be mate to mate, parent to child, or sibling to sibling interchanges. Interaction across families might be within a generation (e.g., parent to parent or adolescent to adolescent) or across gener-ations (e.g., parent in one family to child in another family). Group members might address another individual, a dyad, an intrafamilial subgroup (three siblings, for exam-ple), a family, an extrafamilial subgroup (perhaps the mothers), or the group as a whole. Add in leader interactions with each of the aforementioned, and the interaction permuta-tions expand exponentially.

In short, leaders of multiple family groups are challenged to decide at which level to attend. The leader might attend within or across families, to an individual, a dyad, a fam-ily, a subgroup, or the entire group. Leader attention might be to a level of interaction independent of the leader, between co-leaders, or between group and leader.

Stages of Group Development

Cassano's (1989) developmental model for the multiple family group can provide struc-ture and guidelines for the counselor with little or no experience in MFGC. Cassano's *beginning stage* is a time when participants rely upon the leader for support and direction. Hence, interaction between the leader and individual group members is more frequent. Intrafamily interaction is also more frequent, and interfamily interaction is relatively infre-quent. During the beginning stage of a multiple family group, the group may be best served by leader acceptance of more frequent leader/individual and intrafamily interaction. A central issue for the leader is the extent to which interfamily and group level interaction can be productively encouraged and promoted. The leader might be inclined to push too hard and too fast for interfamily or group level interaction. If the group is not ready for these levels of interaction, the leader may be more productive in fostering group develop-ment by first accepting and validating individual/leader and intrafamily interaction.

During the *middle stage*, intrafamily interaction occurs more spontaneously, and interfamily interaction can be especially promoted, encouraged, and validated. Gould and DeGroot (1976) found that interfamily interaction in MFGC initially took the form of mothers talking more to other mothers and fathers talking mostly to children or to other fathers. To more actively involve adolescents, the leader can promote adolescent interac-tion across families. Cassano (1989) notes that during the middle stage children often request an opportunity to play with each other. Parents then establish further links with other parents while enabling their children to get together outside the group.

In short, the middle stage is a time for the leader to foster interfamily interaction. Gradually a sense of identity and bonding occurs at the group level. During the latter part of the middle stage, the leader can more actively emphasize and foster interaction at the group level.

During the *ending stage* the interaction sequence commonly proceeds in the reverse order. The primary level of interaction generally has the following sequence: group, interfamily, intrafamily, and then individual/leader. Participants typically talk about their thoughts, feelings, and experience in and about the group, then address the same at the interfamily level. This is followed by processing within families and at the individual/leader level.

Research by Cassano (1989) provides empirical support for this developmental model for multiple family groups. In what is probably the most rigorous research to date on the stages of group development in MFGC, Cassano collected data through structured observation and audiotapes from a time-limited multiple family counseling group that met for ten 90-minute weekly sessions. The group consisted of three families and one group leader. Each interactive sequence in the group was coded into one of the following six major classes of interaction: (a) professional (leader/group member); (b) peer intrafamily; (c) peer interfamily; (d) nonpeer intrafamily; (e) nonpeer interfamily; and (f) group as an entirety.

The results indicated that over time the interactive sequences within families (intrafamily interaction) decreased while interaction across families increased. Furthermore, group leader involvement decreased over time. Initially group leader responses were frequent, but they decreased as intrafamily and then interfamily responses increased in frequency. In summary, Cassano's study provides evidence that the primary level of interaction in MFGC follows this sequence:

1. Individual/leader.
2. Intrafamily.
3. Interfamily.
4. Group.

Using this model, the group leader can support and validate interaction at the appropriate level and at the same time encourage interaction at the next level in the sequence.

Co-Facilitation

In my experience, co-leadership is almost a necessity when facilitating a multiple family group. Multiple family groups require considerable leader presence and influence to effectively develop group cohesiveness and establish therapeutic norms during the beginning phase of the group. A co-leader can be beneficial in this process. I have found that a co-leader is markedly less important for other kinds of groups (e.g., a mixed group, an adolescent group, or a men's group). Anecdotal accounts such as this, however, have notoriously poor generalizability.

The Smiths sought help "to put our family back together." Bob Smith (age 42) had just completed a 28-day inpatient alcoholism treatment program. While Bob was in chemical dependency treatment, Sue Smith (age 41) and the two Smith children participated in the family program at the chemical dependency treatment facility. The family worker at that treatment facility referred the Smith family for multiple family group counseling as part of Bob's aftercare treatment plan. The aftercare plan also included twice weekly Alcoholics Anonymous meetings for Bob and once weekly AlAnon meetings for Sue.

During the screening interview Sue stated that she did not think Sara (age 15) and Jerod (age 13) were dealing in a healthy way with Bob's returning home. Bob himself acknowledged feeling guilty, wanting to develop a better relationship with his children, but not knowing how to proceed. Sara seemed sad, hurt, and withdrawn. She cried during the intake and said, "Dad, I just don't know if I want you back home or not." Jerod presented himself as aloof, not caring, yet subtly angry, "I don't know" and "I don't care" were his standard answers whenever the counselor or his parents asked him a question. By the end of the screening interview, the Smiths were deemed suitable for multiple family group counseling and committed themselves to regular attendance for 10 weeks with assessment and possible recontracting at that time.

During their first 2 weeks in the multiple family group, Sara and Jerod remained quiet while Bob and Sue each took turns interacting individually with the group leaders. The group leaders began working to facilitate increased communication within the Smith family. For example, when Bob stated to the group leaders that he felt guilty of having hurt Sara and Jerod during his drinking days, the group leaders asked him to "talk to them now about this." Bob did so, and communication between Bob and his children steadily grew in the group.

The group leaders also facilitated increased peer group interaction across families. For example, when Sara said she hesitated to be honest and open with her parents "Because I might hurt them or get hurt myself," the group leaders directed her to ask the other adolescents in the group if they ever felt a need to protect themselves or their parents. This led to a rich and meaningful exchange between the adolescents and subsequently to an equally rich and meaningful dialogue between the parents. The other parents were able to take the risks involved in providing Sue with feedback about how helpless and fragile she presented herself in the group. Bob received feedback about how frightening and intimidating some of the other parents in the group experienced him to be.

With this lead and group support, Sara and Jerod both told their father directly that at times in the past they had felt frightened and intimidated by him. Bob then asked if they felt this way just when he was drinking or at other times as well. Through an honest and forthright dialogue, the Smith children expressed themselves openly to their parents for the first time ever. Sara and Jerod received much encouragement and support as they opened up in the group about their feelings and experiences as members of the Smith family. Jerod told his parents that his acting as if he did not care was just a way to protect himself. Maintaining direct eye contact with both of his parents, Jerod said, "When you two were yelling, it hurt so much for me to hear it that I just wanted to get away."

After 10 weeks, the Smiths recontracted for another 6 weeks. After 16 weeks, the family decided to terminate from the group. Bob and Sue reported believing that they still needed help, but that what they needed to do next was to work on their marriage. The couple made plans to do so in a couples group co-facilitated by one of the leaders of the multiple family group.

COUPLES GROUP COUNSELING

The leader presence and impact needed in multiple family group counseling are also needed in couples group counseling to help develop group cohesiveness and establish therapeutic norms during the beginning phase of the group. Again, co-therapy is highly recommended. The potential modeling inherent in a good relationship between the co-leaders can also be a rich and powerful component in a couples group.

Why, one might ask, is a cohesive, working couples group more difficult to develop than, for example, a similarly cohesive mixed group? The answer, of course, relates to the preexisting pairs in a couples group. The power of the couple dynamic is poignantly depicted by D. H. Lawrence (1949) as follows:

> The hot narrow intimacy between man and wife was abhorrent. The way they shut themselves into their own exclusive alliance with each other, even in love, disgusted him. It was a whole community of mistrustful couples insulated in private homes or private rooms, always in couples, and no further immediate, no disinterested relationship admitted: a kaleidoscope of couples, disjoined, separatist, meaningless entities of married couples. (p. 226)

In essence, couples group members commonly enter the group expecting that the relationship with their partner will be the only focus. With time, the spread of themes from one couple to another helps participants identify with other group members. Gradually group members experience the group itself as a valued, protective environment in which relations with the group leader and other group members become vehicles for constructive feedback and change in their partner relationship as well in other relationships. The group as a whole then begins to develop an identity and power of its own, providing group members a rich opportunity to learn more about self in relation to others.

Indicators & Contraindicators

Neiberg (1976) suggested that a couples group is the treatment of choice for couples with longstanding interpersonal conflict, a commitment to staying together, and a commitment to achieving change. A couples group offers participants an opportunity for an intimate experience in which they are in their dyadic relationship and simultaneously able to get outside the stormy intensity of that relationship. Sometimes couples counseling with just the couple and the counselor present can amplify the couple's already intense, negative, repetitive interaction pattern without providing a context for change. In a couples group, on the other hand, participants have an opportunity to stabilize and deescalate as they connect more meaningfully with others in the group.

The limited research to date on couples group counseling suggests that this is a relatively effective treatment modality. Barlow, O'Brien, and Last (1984) compared the results of group counseling in which agoraphobic women were accompanied in treatment by their husbands versus group counseling without husbands present. Results at posttesting indicated a substantial advantage to the group with husbands present when compared on measures of agoraphobia. In another study, Wilson (1986) found couples group counseling and conjoint couples counseling to be equally effective, and both conjoint and couples group counseling were found to be effective modalities for resolving marital dysfunction.

In my experience, however, closed, emotionally isolated couples do especially well in a couples group, whereas couples who are less emotionally isolated do equally well in a couples group or conjoint couples counseling. The "hot, narrow intimacy" (Lawrence, 1949, p. 226) can become less negatively hot and narrow via participation in couples group counseling.

Counseling Procedures

Coche and Coche (1990) recommend screening interviews to select couples who have a definite commitment to their relationship. They suggest a heterogeneous group in regard to group members' age, diagnosis, and the severity of marital problems. Morrison (1986) describes the couples group as a particularly fertile setting for projective identification because of the number of personalities and relationships available as recipients of participants' projections. Group heterogeneity is necessary so that a couples group can offer a diversity of group members of each sex and a number of different dyadic relationship patterns as objects for projective identification.

On the other hand, a certain degree of homogeneity regarding group composition can help facilitate group cohesiveness early on. As in groups with nonrelated individuals, the group leader has to find the balance between heterogeneity and homogeneity that works best. If the couples are quite heterogeneous, the leader probably will need to more actively facilitate group cohesion early in the group. I recommend maximizing heterogeneity while maintaining enough homogeneity to be able to effectively develop a cohesive working group.

Coche and Coche (1990) recommend four couples as the ideal group size. A group with three couples often does not provide the strength, vitality, and diversity desired, and a group with five couples often feels crowded and less intimate.

Dynamics

The nature of the group dynamics in a couples group depends, at least to some extent, upon the leader's conceptual orientation and approach. Coche and Coche's (1990) five-stage model is essentially based on a psychodynamic orientation. Many other theoretical orientations are commonly applied in MFGC. From an object relations perspective, for example, group members are encouraged to grope with the disavowed, unconscious aspects of their own personhood that they find objectionable, intolerable, or bad (Dicks, 1967) and have projected onto their partner. From a structural family therapy perspective, boundaries and hierarchy become the focus of attention and the avenue for change toward a more functional dyadic relationship (Minuchin, 1974). From a communication skill training perspective, the core work involves couples' learning to utilize effective communication skills to address the intense, conflictual issues that have precluded a more satisfying couple relationship (Guerney, 1977; Miller, Wackman, Nunnally, & Miller, 1988).

Family systems counselors commonly emphasize complementarity, mutual escalation, and other systems concepts. Given the large number of theoretical orientations currently available, the group leader is faced with the challenge of selecting one or more orientations that fit best for the group leader and the specific couples group.

Stages of Group Development

Coche and Coche (1990) describe a developmental model, involving the following five stages, for couples group counseling:

1. Joining.
2. Beginning work.
3. Group crisis/dissatisfaction.
4. Intensive work.
5. Termination.

During *joining,* participants show much concern about being accepted, and they fear rejection by other group members. Participants may be more reluctant to share openly than if they were alone. This reluctance might have a variety of reasons including (a) loyalty to one's partner (e.g., a protective response for fear of being the worst couple), (b) a silent agreement between partners not to wash their dirty linen in public, and (c) a taboo for the couple regarding certain topics. During the joining stage, group members often seem highly dependent upon the group leader. Typical member behavior includes pleasantries, social graciousness, diplomacy, and compliance with perceived expectations. "Looking good" is important, and participants tend to operate so as to look good as a couple.

During the *beginning work stage*, participants shift from "pleasant couple" identity to personal identity. Group members begin to share as individuals. Other group members who were initially seen only as partners in a dyad are now seen as individuals with their own problems, pain, means of coping, and interpersonal style.

The *group crisis/dissatisfaction stage* may take the form of intensified blaming, scapegoating, or counterdependence that turns into a full battle. One group member might lose his or her temper and blow up at another group member. A couple might threaten to leave the group if the "nonsense" does not stop. One or more couples may turn on the leaders, questioning the leader's competency or whatever they perceive as the leader's vulnerability.

Out of his own frustration and fear, a group member once said to me, "Our marriage isn't getting any better, so as a leader of this group, you must not know what you're doing here." My response was, "I can appreciate your frustration with your relationship with your wife not improving. If you really want to hold me 100 percent responsible for that, though, I suggest you say it's because I'm not very likable or lovable. I'm much more vulnerable there. My dad helped me feel competent at a very early age." This led to a shift toward increased openness and self-responsibility by the previously closed, blaming group member.

This shift typifies the *intensive working stage,* during which group members are able and willing to talk about their own contribution to their problematic relationship. Group members actively seek understanding of the ways in which they perpetuate their own relationship problems. Other group members become a resource for feedback that participants find difficult to hear from their partner. Once group members become conscious of their own defenses, they often surrender to the underlying pain. If the partner is not able to respond appropriately when a group member has surrendered to his or her own pain, this too can be processed in the group.

The altruism, group cohesiveness, universality, and other therapeutic factors in the group during the intensive working stage provide a context in which growth and constructive change can occur for couples. Couples reenact their relationship in many ways and at various levels in the group (Yalom, 1985), and the group becomes a safe context for participants to learn about the powerful, though often subtle, ways they contribute to the conflict with their partner.

Termination in couples group counseling is in many ways similar to termination in other counseling groups. Couples are asked to give 2 weeks' notice to the group. Termination is a time for giving and receiving feedback, assessing progress and plans, and drawing closure. During this process, the focus is upon the couple and the relationship between the two. Assessment and feedback center upon the couples' relationship, the contribution of each to the satisfying and unsatisfying aspects of their relationship, the progress made in improving their relationship, and how the couple will not only maintain the gains made in the couples group but also how they will proceed to further enhance their relationship. Sometimes this involves further counseling and sometimes it does not. Invariably, validating each partner's relationship strengths and their efforts and progress during their time in the couples group is important.

Co-Leadership

From my perspective, having a co-leader in some counseling groups is unnecessary. In other groups a co-leader is a definite help, though one leader is often sufficient. In process-oriented couples group counseling, however, a co-leader might be a necessity, for at least two reasons.

First, couples groups are similar to multiple family groups in that the preexisting subgroupings make it more difficult to establish group cohesion and to set and maintain effective group norms. An engaging, influential leader presence is required, and often the group simply will not give the necessary power to a single leader. Couples and the same sex alliances that so rapidly develop in couples groups can be powerful, undermining the single group leader in a covert process of which the leader becomes aware after the fact, often far too late to fully recoup and be able to provide effective leadership.

Second, couples benefit enormously from a good co-leader relationship. Acknowledging that the co-leaders' relationship is important in most process groups, it is even more important in couples group counseling. Some call this an *isomorphism*; others call it *transference*. Essentially, the process is one in which the co-leaders' relationship mirrors the issues and dynamics of couples in the group. Hence, the co-leaders' resolution of their own relationship issues frees them to facilitate the couples' resolution.

A question the co-leaders need to consider is whether to address their relationship issues as they arise within the group or to do so outside the group. Generally, when the co-leaders can successfully do so in a limited time within the group, the couples in the group benefit significantly from witnessing the process. If the co-leaders have a secure and good working relationship with a demonstrated ability to resolve their differences, addressing this as they arise in the group can be effective. If, however, the co-leaders, for whatever reason, are even the slightest bit unsure as to whether they can effectively work through their relationship issues as they arise within the group, doing so outside the group may be more advisable. Either way, the co-leaders' relationship serves a central, catalytic role in couples group counseling.

The more Bob and Sue Smith made progress in resolving their parenting and family problems, the more they talked about needing to work on their marriage. Sue repeatedly said, " I've stored up a lot of anger toward Bob during all the years he was drinking." Sue's stated goal in the couples group was to deal with all of her stored-up feelings as related to her marriage. Bob acknowledged feeling guilty, and he reported somehow feeling hopelessness regarding the possibility of having an alive, vital marriage. Bob contracted to address these feelings in the couples group. Sue summed up their marriage as follows: "We're tired of fighting. It just doesn't get us anywhere." The Smiths committed to regular attendance for a minimum of 16 weeks, with 2 weeks' notice when they would feel ready to terminate from the group.

Given their prior experience in multiple family group counseling, the Smiths' joining process in the couples group proceeded more rapidly than is often the case for other couples. In multiple-family group counseling, the Smiths had already openly acknowledged their marital difficulties. Also, their experiences in Alcoholics Anonymous and AlAnon probably helped them to more quickly progress toward seeing themselves as individuals in their marriage.

Both Sue and Bob responded readily to group facilitator leads shifting from a focus upon their partner to a focus on self in relation to partner. For example, when Sue talked in the group and essentially said, "Bob did this, and Bob didn't do that" with implicit, unexpressed dissatisfaction and frustration, the group leaders and some of the more senior group members asked Sue how she felt about each of these things that Bob was or was not doing. Sue readily shifted into an expression of self, a process probably facilitated by her ongoing involvement in AlAnon.

The crisis that apparently served as a turning point for Bob and Sue in the couples group occurred during their fourth session. Bob came in presenting as markedly despondent, quiet, and withdrawn. When approached, he responded curtly. Upon being asked what was going on for him, Bob initially denied being even the slightest bit troubled. The group leaders then asked other group members to give Bob their reactions and feedback about how he was coming across. Sue and the other group members told Bob that he looked and acted bothered, frustrated, depressed, and removed. Many of them said they reacted by wanting to keep their distance from him. Others confessed to having the urge to fight with him.

Then Bob said, "All right. All right. If you really want to know, I'll tell you, even though I don't think you're gonna like hearing it." All group members including Sue reassured Bob that they really did want to hear what he had to say. Bob proceeded as follows:

"Well, to be honest, I don't think this group is helping me much. It's too surfacey; there's too much going through the right motions but not really getting anywhere. My problem is I don't even know if I should be in this group because I don't know for sure if I want to stay in my marriage. I can't see this marriage going anywhere. Sue's always focusing on me. Even when she's not criticizing me, she's still looking for her happiness through me. I just wish she'd have a life of her own. It feels like a gigantic responsibility for me to have to make her happy. I think it's a set-up for us to fail."

As might be expected, Sue was hurt and furious. She said, "You're blaming me again, Bob! You always end up saying I'm to blame! Well, I'm not the one who spent all our money on booze. I didn't come home all tanked up and pass out on the living room floor. Wake up, Bob! It's not all my fault!"

During the post-crisis processing in the group, other group members expressed their acceptance, support, understanding, and respect to both Sue and Bob, whom they described as having been courageous enough to be real in the group. The Smiths subsequently settled into the work phase. Each week they took time in group. Sue told Bob that one of the reasons she maintained a low profile and did not express herself was because she was afraid he would get mad and maybe even go away (i.e., divorce her). Other women in the group gave Bob feedback about what they perceived and experienced as a judgmental, controlling, sexist attitude on his part.

Bob took this feedback well, even though he said it was painful to hear and accept. Bob later challenged Sue for making him responsible for her not developing a life of her own. "You say I'm blaming you a lot. Well, this blaming stuff is going both ways, Sue! Take a look at it, Sue!"

Sue did, and in many ways both Sue and Bob were leaders in the group. Their willingness to take the risks involved in being honest, open, and vulnerable helped other couples take similar risks. During the last 6 to 8 weeks of their 24-week stay in the group, the Smiths gave consistently high-quality feedback to others in the group. The group leaders interpreted the markedly improved quality of the Smiths' feedback as an indication of the progress they had made.

Termination for the Smiths was a time of laughter and tears. Bob and Sue were able to laugh at how easily they used to fall into "the blame game." Their tears were grounded in gratitude, joy, and grief in letting go and saying goodbye to the group. After terminating from the couples group, Bob continued with weekly Alcoholics Anonymous meetings and monthly individual counseling sesions, which Bob described as being for maintenance and personal growth. Sue stayed with her weekly AlAnon group, saying "That's exactly what I need for myself, and I know it." The group acknowledged Sue and Bob for all the work they had done and thanked them for giving so much of themselves in the group.

GROUP COUNSELING VERSUS FAMILY COUNSELING

Couples counseling and multiple family group counseling might both be thought of as counseling modalities that simultaneously involve group counseling as well as couple or family counseling. On some level, this physical union of group and couple/family counseling presupposes an ongoing working relationship between the two treatment modalities. In real life, however, group and family counseling have had little association with one another. Group counseling texts rarely mention family counseling, and family counseling texts essentially ignore group counseling.

This is a bit surprising in light of the common ground these two interpersonal disciplines share. Both consider the etiology and curative components to be interpersonal. Both group and family counseling developed, at least to some extent, as a counterreaction to the relative dearth of interpersonal considerations within the traditional, individual counseling approaches that predominated. Yet, each continues to essentially ignore the other, acting as though no other interpersonal approach exists. Little dialogue occurs across disciplines. Given the disappointing nature of this reality, I will engage in a fantasy in which the relationship between group and family counseling differs from the stark reality.

Once upon a time, not so very long ago, there lived two bright, competent, warm, caring, dynamic, and attractive counseling disciplines, Group Counseling and Family Counseling. Although they had the same last name, Group and Family were not related by blood. Group grew up in the 1950s and 1960s and was a few years older than Family. Both grew up with parents who were Individuals and who insisted that Group and Family be Individuals, too. As it turned out, however, to actually be individuals, Group and Family needed room to think and behave differently than did Individuals. In both cases, their parents essentially rejected Group's and Family's ways of thinking and acting. Their adolescences were, therefore, relatively long and stormy. Both were rejected by many members of the extended families of Individuals in which they grew up.

The pain and anger for each lasted many years, but eventually both Group and Family grew up and entered adulthood. They each even began to see that Individual Counseling was well intended and might have some redeeming qualities after all.

During their childhood and adolescent years, Group and Family had barely known one another. When they became young adults, each was preoccupied with the process of establishing itself in the professional world. Then, one warm and lovely spring day, Group and Family happened to meet. Some would call their meeting coincidental; others would call it fate. Be that as it may, upon meeting, Group and Family were thoroughly intrigued by one another. Group loved Family's systemic thinking, charisma, and dynamic way of interacting. Family adored Group's egalitarianism, patience, and attention to subtleties. Each was truly enthralled and captivated by the richness of the other.

Both had been single young adults for a while and, therefore, had much to share with the other. Their romance was wonderfully rapturous, invigorating, validating, and just plain fun. Their wedding was an extravaganza. Music Therapy played a moving medley, and Dance Therapy performed a piece abounding in dyadic symbolism. The couple chose to honeymoon at a kibbutz.

Group and Family were very happy together, and they continued to enthusiastically share and learn from one another. Their firstborn was named Multi-Family Group Counseling; their secondborn, Couples Group Counseling. Then Group and Family decided that a physical union between them was simply insufficient. Their resultant union at the theoretical, emotional, social, and spiritual levels led to the birth of numerous Creative and Integrative Counseling approaches. The multilevel union of Family and Group was indeed vital and prolific. Each of their offspring grew up in an atmosphere of collaboration coupled with acceptance, respect, and intrigue for that which is different. The Counseling community was invigorated by the vital and creative energy that had now become a multigenerational norm long since established when Group and Family got together. Group and Family will long be remembered by the millions of people whose lives are happier and more productive as a result of the marvelously effective counseling that resulted from that now infamous union of Group and Family Counseling.

SUMMARY

Group counseling with couples and with families is unknown to many group leaders. One modality, multiple family group counseling (MFGC), has been used most often in clinical settings, especially with families of physical or emotional abuse, families with a problem in parenting, socially isolated families, and families dealing with an impending death. Screening procedures and intake interviews pave the way for entering the group, which usually consists of three or four families.

In MFGC, social interaction may occur between mates, parents and children, siblings within a family, or any combination of these outside the family, including cross-generational and subgroup interactions. These tend to follow a sequence throughout the group's life from individual/leader, to intrafamily, then to interfamily, and, finally, group. Co-leadership is strongly recommended because of the complexities of the relationships and dynamics.

A co-leader format is also urged for the second modality, couples group counseling, to facilitate group cohesiveness, establish therapeutic norms, and provide mirroring of relationship models. The couples group may be the treatment of choice for couples with longstanding interpersonal conflict, a commitment to stay together, and a commitment to achieving change. In a couples group, participants are more able to get outside of their own intense relationships and connect meaningfully with other group members.

Group composition is recommended to be heterogeneous as to age, diagnosis, and severity of marital problems, although some homogeneity can foster earlier group cohesiveness. Stages of the group are called joining, beginning work, group crisis/dissatisfaction, intensive work, and termination.

Although group and family counseling are two disciplines that share much in common and have much to offer each other, to date each has essentially ignored the other. This author fantasizes on the potential richness of a closer union between the two.

REFERENCES

Anderson, C. A. (1983). A psychoeducational program for families of patients with schizophrenia. In W. W. McFarlane (Ed.), *Family therapy in schizophrenia*. New York: Guilford Press.

Barlow, D. H., O'Brien, G. T., & Last, C. G. (1984). Couples treatment of agoraphobia. *Behavior Therapy, 15*(1), 41–58.

Cassano, D. R. (1989). Multi-family group therapy in social work practice. In D. R. Cassano (Ed.), *Social work with multi-family groups* (pp. 3–39). New York: Haworth Press.

Coche, J., & Coche, E. (1990). *Couples group psychotherapy: A clinical practice model*. New York: Brunner/Mazel.

Dicks, H. V. (1967). *Marital tensions*. New York: Basic Books.

Gould, E., & DeGroot, D. (1976). Inter- and intrafamily interaction in multifamily group therapy. In H. Grunebaum & J. Christ (Eds.), *Contemporary marriage: Structure, dynamics, and therapy* (pp 65–73). Boston: Little, Brown.

Greaves, C. C. (1983). Death in the family: A multifamily therapy approach. *International Journal of Family Psychiatry, 4*(3), 247–261.

Gritzer, P. H. & Okun, H. S. (1983). Multiple family group therapy. In B.B. Wolman & G. Stricker (Eds.), *Handbook of family and marital therapy*. New York: Plenum Press.

Guerney, B. G., Jr. (1977). *Relationship enhancement*. San Francisco: Jossey-Bass.

Laqueur, H. P. (1976). Multiple family therapy. In P. J. Guerin (Ed.), *Family therapy: Theory and practice* (pp. 405–416). New York: Gardner Press.

Lansky, M. R., Bley, C. R., McVey, G. G., & Brotman, B. (1980). Multiple family groups as aftercare. *Advances in Family Psychiatry, 2*, 425–436.

Lawrence, D. H. (1949). *Women in love* (with a forword by the author). New York: Modern Library.

Leichter, E. & Schulman, G. L. (1974). Multi-family group therapy: A multidimensional approach. *Family Process, 13*, 95–110.

Miller, S., Wackman, D., Nunnally, E., & Miller, P. (1988). *Connecting with self and others.* Littleton, CO: Interpersonal Communication Programs.

Minuchin, S. (1974). *Families and family therapy.* Cambridge, MA: Harvard University Press.

Morrison, A. P. (1986). On projective identification in couples' groups. *International Journal of Group Psychotherapy, 36*(1), 55–73.

Neiberg, N. (1976). The group therapy of married couples. In H. Grunebaum & J. Christ (Eds.), *Contemporary marriage: Structure, dynamics, and therapy* (pp. 401–410). Boston: Little, Brown.

O'Shea, M. O., & Phelps, R. (1985). Multiple family therapy: Current status and critical appraisal. *Family Process, 24*, 555–582.

Parad, H. J., & Parad, L. G. (1968). A study of crises-oriented planned short-term treatment. Part I. *Social Casework, 49*, 346–355.

Parker, T., Hill, J. W., & Miller, G. (1987). Multiple family therapy: Evaluating a group experience for mentally retarded adolescents and their families. *Family Therapy, 14*(1), 43–51.

Raasoch, J. W. (1981). Multiple family therapy. In R. J. Corsini (Ed.), *Handbook of innovative psychotherapies* (pp. 515–524). New York: John Wiley.

Reiss, D., & Costell, R. (1977). The multiple family group as a small society: Family regulation of interaction with nonmembers. *American Journal of Psychiatry, 134*, 21–24.

Sigman, M., John, R., Levinson, E., & Betts, L. D. (1985). Multiple family therapy with severely disturbed psychiatric patients. *Psychiatric Journal of the University of Ottawa, 10*(4), 260–265.

Singh, N. (1982). Notes and observations on the practice of multiple family therapy in an adolescent unit. *Journal of Adolescence, 5*, 319–332.

Wilson, G. L. (1986). The comparative efficacy of alternative treatments in the resolution of marital dysfunction. *Dissertation Abstracts International, 47*(7), 3129–3130B.

Yalom, I. D. (1985). *The theory and practice of group psychotherapy* (3rd ed.). New York: Basic Books.

12

Group Counseling: Career and Lifestyle Issues

Art Terry

*I*n the past 40 years the phenomenal growth in group counseling is recognized as much needed and helpful. The premise has been well documented in many books and articles such as Cohen (1969), Corey and Corey (1987), Gazda (1984), George and Dustin (1988), Luft (1970), Moreno (1962), and McAuliffe and Fredrickson (1990). Although these authors have discussed special types of groups, group counseling for the purpose of enhancing career development and launching adult students into the job market has received little attention. Even so, group process is a valuable tool in assisting people with career decisions and transitions.

DEFINITION OF CAREER GROUP COUNSELING

Career can be defined as the sequence of major positions a person accepts throughout his or her pre-occupational, occupational, and post-occupational life. It includes all work-related positions, such as those of student, employee or self-employed worker, and pensioner, together with complementary avocational, familial, and civic positions. "Careers" exist only as persons pursue them; they are person-centered (Super, 1976).

ELEMENTS OF CAREER GROUP COUNSELING

Individuals have three primary needs in career group counseling: (a) input about occupations, (b) assessment data about self (abilities, interests, skills, and values), and (c) exploration of personal meaning, identification and examination of subjective aspects of the self, feedback from others, and trying on roles (Tolbert, 1974). This third component is what distinguishes career group counseling from group guidance. A synthesis of group counseling and career group counseling establishes an environment of acceptance and openness in which group members have the freedom and opportunities to try out and integrate information about themselves and the world of work. Within this environment, they practice and develop decision-making skills that will enable them to implement decisions.

The major differences between group counseling and career group counseling are the use of information and the emphasis on decision making.

Use of Information

Career group counseling makes use of information that usually is generated externally. The goal is to assist members in understanding information and gaining insight about themselves and the world of work. Thus, career group counseling combines external information with personal insight development (Pyle, 1986). In this context, career group counseling is every bit as complex as group counseling, and possibly more so because of the added dimension of information processing.

Decision-Making Process

Most theorists of career counseling consider the skills of decision making as the core of career group counseling. Group techniques that combine decision-making concepts have been shown to stimulate occupational information-seeking behavior (Krumboltz, 1989; Gati, 1990). Gelatt, Varenhorst, and Corey (1972) set forth a decision-making strategy built around the following steps:

1. *Purpose*. A decision has to be made based on at least two options.
2. *Information*. Information about the options is identified or obtained.
3. *Possibilities*. All of the possible courses of action are identified.
4. *Results possible*. Possible consequences of each alternative are examined.
5. *Results probable*. The likelihood of each consequence is predicted.
6. *Values*. The personal desirability of each consequence is assessed.
7. *Decision*. A choice is made, either seminal or investigatory.
8. *Feedback and Evaluation*. The suitability of the decision is judged by the counselee, and the counselor evaluates the effectiveness of his or her help.

A number of career group counseling models use decision-making concepts to facilitate career and lifestyle planning and to improve decision making (Chick, 1970; Hansen, 1981; Martin, 1970; Savickas. 1989; Wrenn, 1988). Decision making, a major component of career group counseling, will be discussed later in this chapter.

Rationale for Career Group Counseling

Groups offer many advantages in the career process. These relate to and include: (a) the enhancement of career counseling outcomes; (b) the support of group members; (c) the use of time, efficiency, and cost-effectiveness; (d) the enhancement of feedback; (e) the personalizing of information; and (f) the enhancement of enjoyment and variety (Pyle, 1986).

All counselors are interested in achieving the outcomes generally prescribed for the career counseling process. These include helping an individual with a career decision, developing decision-making skills, and, in general, adjustment (Montross & Shinkman, 1981; Savickas, 1990). All of these goals can be met in career group counseling because peers are a major part of the process and can assist with adjustment concerns. The group setting is particularly conducive to the second goal, support of group members. By hearing others' concerns and problems, the tendency to see oneself as the only person with a career problem diminishes. Clients need to feel that their problems are not unique and that they share with others the frustrations, anxieties, and experiences of being human. The simple process of empathizing and sharing with one another is beneficial to life functioning as well as occupational functioning. Group counseling takes on added dimensions when seen from the perspective that people are social, decision-making beings whose actions have a social purpose (Dreikurs & Sonstegard, 1968).

A group also allows more than one person's needs to be met within the same time frame. This, too, has implications for cost-effectiveness and the effective use of counselor time.

Feedback enhancement is another benefit of career group counseling. The group leader can call upon others to help a member understand a certain aspect of self or use information from others. The group presents a broader perspective and mirror of a person than a counselor alone could provide. It enables people to see themselves both in others and in their own feedback comments. The leader, therefore, has the resources of the diverse and varied personalities within the group to call upon and use in the learning process.

In an age of career information, people need assistance in personalizing information. Career counseling incorporates external information, such as assessment results and computer-assisted information, and group members have the advantage of hearing others' assessment or computer-created results. This helps them put the information in perspective and draw appropriate conclusions. By using techniques that enhance the affective domain, the leader can assist in personalizing the information. The group makes personalization even more powerful because of the influence of peers' comments, feedback, and support.

The combination of affect and information needs is one of the major aspects of working with groups (Pyle, 1986; McDaniels, 1989). All of us have heard the phrase, "high-tech, high-touch," which suggests that the affective domain should be enhanced within the increasing bombardment of technology. Cold and impersonal information can be placed in the "high-tech" category, but the group leader can draw upon the humanness of the group to enhance understanding of that information. Group support, too, is usually far more significant than a counselor's suggestions and comments alone.

Because of the complexity of career development, more than one session is necessary. Three to four sessions may be required to adequately process a career development concept. Retention is usually higher with a group format, and something about the personalization process of a small group motivates members to return.

Finally, research indicates that counselors generally prefer groups over individual counseling and that group counseling decreases the possibility for counselor burnout (Gazda, 1984).

Dinkmeyer and Muro (1979) pointed out that groups meet a variety of needs at one time:

1. The need to belong, to find a place, and to be accepted as one is.
2. The opportunity for affection, to be loved and to be able to provide love; to be a part of the helping process while receiving assistance.
3. The opportunity to interact on meaningful developmental topics related to one's growth and development.
4. The opportunity to receive help in seeing that one's problem is not unique.

5. The opportunity to develop feelings of equality and acceptance without feeling that one has to "prove" himself or herself to belong.
6. The need to look at one's identity as it relates to the various social and career tasks of life.

CAREER GROUP COUNSELING RESEARCH AND PROGRAMS

Literature in career counseling is generally organized around the areas of: (a) computer-assisted guidance; (b) family systems; (c) career maturity, self-concept, and attitudes; (d) goal setting and peer group support; and (e) comparative studies with individual and self-help counseling.

Computer-Assisted Guidance

The computer has vastly increased our knowledge of the possibilities of assessment measuring careers, jobs, information, and life choices. Counselors are using computers to organize information. As the counseling profession approaches two decades of experience with computers, counselors, as a group, clearly need to demonstrate basic skills in computer use. Commercially developed computer-assisted career guidance programs are a growing feature of counseling programs, although still relatively small in actual numbers. In the future, use of computers in counseling may have the following features:

1. Greater attention to careful and systematic planning for computer use in counseling.
2. An increasing interrelationship of various counseling components with computer use (i.e., a group counseling, computerized assessment and self-management learning model used in an organized, systematic approach).
3. More imaginative and innovative uses of computers in counseling.

Cianni-Surridge (1983) recommends that microcomputers be used to provide assistance in the decision-making process, that computerized files of occupational information be established, and that telematics be used in the placement process by allowing out-of-work people to be interviewed in their own homes or in the placement office.

Family Systems

Career counseling may well be more powerful if the counselor, while working with young adults, acknowledges the family as an important antecedent influence on the young person's career development. Lopez and Andrews (1987) say a systems perspective is essential in career decision making because young adulthood entails the other major developmental tasks of adult identity formation and psychological separation from the family. These three factors—family career values and roles, adult identity formation, and separation from the family—have to be integrated in working with young adults.

Young adults often come to a group with a safe presenting issue like "career." In many cases, the issue may not be just career, however safe that might seem. Career counseling is complex, and in many instances the individual also needs to process self-esteem, denial, transition, identity, risk, and dreams. Career counseling requires a family systems approach and, if one or all of the above issues are part of career indecision, these issues have to be dealt with before career counseling.

Career Maturity, Self Concept, and Attitudes

A number of studies have identified career group counseling as the vehicle to improve career maturity, self-concept, and attitudes toward career and jobs. Significant change in any of these areas is possible after treatment time of at least 8 weeks.

In a study designed to determine the effects of group counseling on the career maturity of ninth graders, Nichol (1969) found no significant differences between group counseling and the control group, as measured by a structured interview and the Attitude Scale of the Career Maturity Inventory. The treatment period was 8 weeks in duration.

Jackson (1971) found positive movement but no significant differences, as measured by the Career Maturity Inventory or a career maturity scale, between a control group and subjects participating in small-group counseling. The treatment in this study was defined only as "group counseling."

Gilliland (1966) showed increased career maturity, academic achievement and occupational aspiration in 14 black adolescents participating in group counseling for 36 weeks. The results were positive, but the time investment may be a problem.

In a short-term study (6 weeks), Flake, Roach, and Stenning (1975) significantly increased career maturity attitude scores of 10th grade students. The researchers concluded that career maturity as a developmental process can be measured and facilitated through group counseling.

Catron (1966) examined changes in self, ideal self, and "ordinary person" perceptions of high school students after exposing the students to a College and Career Planning Group. The counseling took place in 14 small-group sessions of 1½ hours each. The 54 students were involved in test interpretation, listening to tapes and free discussion. Their perceptions of self changed significantly to more positive images, although ideal self and "ordinary person" perceptions were unchanged. Similarly, Garrison (1972) reported that career development counseling over an 8-week period assisted college students in attaining a positive change in self-concept.

Glaize and Myrick (1984) researched the possibilities for melding computer-assisted guidance (CAG) and group counseling. They compared the impact on counselees' career maturity and decidedness when separating CAG from group counseling. All interventions were beneficial, but the group approach was more powerful.

Goal Setting and Peer Group Support

De Rosenroll's (1988) research was directed at combining goal-setting techniques and groups. After career goals, and ways to attain them, have been established, support groups can monitor progress, rework and rewrite goals, and give and receive feedback.

In the literature on adult students, the need for peer group support has been documented (Goldberg, 1980; Hughes, 1983). This need fits well with job search support groups as aids to employment assistance. Bolles (1985), Figler (1979), and Krannich (1983) all recommended joining a support group when job hunting. Wegman (1979) noted that institutes of higher education are starting to offer job search workshops. Trimmer (1984) identified the following common elements for job search support groups:

❑ Exploring the hidden job market.
❑ Developing cohesive relationships to maintain momentum during the job search.

❏ Returning individual responsibility for the search.
❏ Enhancing the self-image of job seekers.

Comparative Studies

Kivlighan, Hageseth, Tipton, and McGovern (1981) examined career counseling and found several approaches, including individual, group, and self-help methods, to be effective. Holland (1973) and Bruch (1978) specifically suggested the use of Holland's typology of persons and environments in matching those receiving career counseling and treatments.

APPLICATIONS TO CAREER GROUP COUNSELING

As mentioned, external information processing differentiates career group counseling from group counseling. Therefore, some of the process and content of the group stages are different, and career group counseling has a number of informational/cognitive goals in addition to affective goals. The end result is that in general career group counseling tends to be more structured than group counseling (Pyle, 1986) and, because of the additional goals, group size has to be fairly small. This allows the group leader time to interact individually with members as necessary and provides more time for group interaction in each of the stages.

A number of specialists in group counseling have identified stages that counseling groups go through (Gazda, 1984; Pyle, 1986; Yalom, 1985). Although these range from three to seven stages, the characteristics of each stage are similar in that the amount, the kind, and the timing of intervention relate to the stage of a group's development. I suggest a four-step sequence for career group counseling, with goals for each stage.

Stage One

Getting acquainted is the high priority of the initial stage. The group leader outlines the group rationale and approach, and basic group rules are agreed upon. The emphasis is on members' participating and assisting one another.

Stage Two

Most career specialists call this the transition stage. The newness of the group wears off, and the leader's major role is to keep the group on task, committed, and participating. Group members self-disclose and open up new possibilities that exist for them.

Stage Three

During this stage members bring problems to the group in a confident manner. The focus is on assisting others to work out problems, so in essence the leader does not have to be as directive to bring about participation and self-disclosure. In that high-energy stage, members identify, synthesize, and realistically consider the variety and amount of information that has been generated.

Stage Four

During the final stage of career group counseling, members are ready to take action on insights and ideas. They engage in activities aimed at gathering further information, or integrating what they have already learned, to aid them with their career development. Members are more deeply aware of and more accepting of self, and they experience a feeling of empowerment.

Some career specialists call this a termination or ending phase (Gazda, 1984), and others (Johnson, 1990; Pyle, 1986; Yalom, 1985) call it an action stage because it is when members are motivated to continue their learning independent of the group.

APPROPRIATE COUNSELING SKILLS

One of the major differences between career group counseling and group counseling is the need to help members understand and personalize information related to the world of work. Each member needs to acquire certain levels of information to help him or her make good decisions to correct misconceptions or myths that are inhibiting career development. Leader skill can help these goals to be realized.

Certainly all of the micro-counseling and helping relations skills are essential. In addition, the career group leader should have counseling skills related to experiential information providing and information processing.

Experiential Information Providing

Experiential information providing is based on guided imagery and imaginal rehearsal. Rather than lecturing on occupational stereotypes, the leader might engage group members by asking them to describe what images they see after certain occupations are mentioned. By using stereotypical careers such as teacher, nurse, social worker, accountant, doctor, or pilot, the leader can help members realize their own internalized stereotypes and can lead a discussion on the problems inherent in such limited perspectives.

- ❏ Where did the image come from?
- ❏ To what extent does the stereotype limit the member?
- ❏ What scripts about the occupation play in the member's mind?
- ❏ How powerful is the self-concept in determining an occupation?

These are just a few of the questions that can help the group leader build awareness and insight. The critical skill here is helping group members develop insight rather than simply telling them what they should know.

Information Processing

In this age of information, one of the most important skills to a group leader is information processing. Carkhuff (1967) indicates that processing, learning and thinking skills are the critical skills of the future for counselors, and not knowing how to process all the data available will overwhelm counselors (Anthony, 1985). Within a career group format, information processing skills can be broken down into three components (Pyle, 1986):

1. Exciting and motivating counselees to the information at hand, which in turn will help them to attend to the information.
2. Helping counselees conceptualize and break down the information by asking them open-ended questions. For example: "Select five careers from your list of 25 that you might seriously consider, and two that you have no interest in whatsoever. What makes you want to retain or discard the career area?"
3. Helping counselees act upon the information by motivating them to use the information appropriately: "What does this mean to you now? What do you need to do to act upon the information you now have?"

PROCESS, COMPONENTS, AND TECHNIQUES FOR CAREER GROUP COUNSELING

To accomplish the stages and apply the skills, an overall process for career group counseling is needed. A limited number of career counseling processes have been conceptualized. The components and techniques to fit the ages and developmental levels of individuals as they work through the process are numerous and diverse. The process described next uses components and techniques specifically for adult career group counseling, but it can be applied to other ages and developmental levels as well.

Career counseling groups of adults should be aimed at helping members break away from their own rigid standards and outdated self-concepts and to recognize their ability to make new autonomous choices at any time. Integral to this approach is the idea that one never "arrives," but is always "on the way." Careers for adults should be seen as reflections of development phases in the life span.

Mezerow (1978) developed a theory of "perspective transformation" that explains the need for the maturation process in adults to be "transformative." According to this theory, adults in transition need to be liberated from previously held roles in order to frame new perspectives and live with a greater degree of self-determination.

Gould (1979) cautioned that adulthood is not a plateau; it is a dynamic and changing time for all. Adults who come to career groups are considering what life has been and what it could be. Forced to see the need to create ones' own life rather than just live out destiny, adults become progressively freer to determine their own lives. The commitment to nurture self-growth demands an ever increasing match of talent to career while balancing the needs for security and freedom.

Career groups can no longer limit their goals to helping members make new career and educational decisions. They must recognize that adults in career transition need a new dynamic self-view resulting from their transformation.

A Process for Career Group Counseling

Career group counseling focuses on four major areas: self-assessment, career exploration, decision making and taking action. The process consists of seven 2-hour sessions and a 1-hour individual counseling session. The participants are directed to focus upon:

1. *Self-awareness.* Group members are encouraged to examine how they feel about their lives and their work/life accomplishments. Participants ask themselves specific questions to stimulate new ideas for realizing their career potential.

2. *Self-assessment.* Interest inventories, values clarification tools and personality assessments are used to help participants develop a sense of identity and define their career interests, work values and personality preferences.

3. *Skills assessment.* Instruments and exercises help participants learn how to identify the skills they possess, how to transfer their skills to other occupations, and how to identify new skills they need to enter or change careers.

4. *Strength bombardment.* Specially prepared checklists, self-appraisal forms and feedback in the group setting help members become aware of and gain confidence in their abilities and strengths. These exercises help them realize that they can bring their skills to many jobs. Group members also learn how to describe their positive attributes to potential employers.

5. *Career exploration.* Career and educational resource materials help participants gain a better knowledge of the world of work and the variety of options open to them. Participants gather information about work settings, the nature of the work, and job opportunities and earning potential in several career fields of interest.

6. *Decision-making.* As participants begin to focus on a career field or a job to pursue, they are shown how to consider and weigh their interests, work values, skills, and preferences. Decision-making strategies and risk-taking behaviors are examined.

7. *Goal-setting.* Group members are encouraged to establish tentative career goals. They learn to establish short- and long-range goals.

8. *Job-hunting.* Members learn how to conduct a successful job hunt. Networking and job search methods are covered. Participants complete sample job applications, resumes, and simple cover letters. They also learn to obtain, prepare for, and participate in employment interviews. Role playing and videotaping focus on effective communication and presentation.

9. *Reinforcing action plans.* Groups conclude by reinforcing the ability of participants to carry out the career action plans they have made.

Career Group Counseling Components

Initiating Counseling   During the first session or initial stage of any session, each person should feel included in the group. The participant should leave the first session confident of the possibility of resolving problems and moving toward self-fulfillment. To assist in this process, the group leader could say to each member, "So, what brings you here?" or "I understand you're looking for help in deciding about what kind of work you'll do in the future." The leader is direct, confident, nonjudgmental, and ready to help the group members help themselves. Participants should be encouraged to take charge of career decisions and move toward self-realization in the world of work.

Determining the Member's Expectations   If a member's expectations for career counseling differ from the leader's, the counseling process will not proceed well. The leader needs to know what each group member is really seeking. To work toward accomplishing this goal:

❏ Be frank and straightforward.
❏ Describe the type of counseling provided.

❑ Explain your role in the process.
❑ Explain the member's role—what the member will be expected to do.
❑ Talk about the group process.

If the above is done correctly, the leader should be able to ask at any point, "What has this got to do with what we set out to achieve?"

Establishing the Structure for Counseling   The leader discusses the need for confidentiality and makes absolutely clear who will have access to information generated in the group, who will use it, and how it will be used. The process is not haphazard; it is planned. Members play a part in structuring counseling time, at least to the extent of setting priorities. The leader can always intervene if a member has to be refocused.

Setting Goals   The leader always thinks in terms of goals. When setting goals for counseling:

❑ Define present behavior.
❑ Discuss new behaviors that will replace old behavior.
❑ Choose goals that mean something to the members.
❑ Select goals that members can attain or partially reach.

The counselor may ask:

❑ Will the goals the members are setting allow for some early, specific successes?
❑ Can I help a member set his or her goals without giving the impression that I am setting them?
❑ Will the members be able to differentiate short-term and long-term goals?

Summarizing and Evaluating   In reviewing each group session, the leader refers to member's expectations, explains the importance of various discussions, interprets members' behavior during the session, recapitulates the goals that were set, and provides a process analysis of the session. Each participant should leave each session with a clear sense of what he or she is going to accomplish before the next session. This builds a firm connection between the counseling process and the rest of the person's daily life. The leader may assign specific tasks as homework, such as conducting informational interviews, researching certain organizations at a career center, or meeting with career contacts.

In the closing remarks the leader should reinforce a sense of purpose. For example: "We'll talk again next week at eight o'clock. I hope you will have done some work on the matters we discussed so we will have some concrete information."

The leader is careful not to develop attitudes and behavior that sustain the dependency of people in career transition. The leader always works to empower individuals to be responsible for themselves, their choices, and their actions.

Career Group Counseling Techniques

Characteristics of group counseling were covered in an earlier chapter. These are basically the same for career and lifestyle counseling. In addition, some techniques are essential for group counseling focused on work history, job expectations, and work values.

Clarifying Feelings   When appropriate, the leader should identify, clarify, and draw attention to members' feelings: "Were you aware that you had difficulty talking about changing jobs?" "Perhaps you could tell us in more detail what feelings you have when you think about changing jobs."

Interpreting Behavior   The leader should try to notice significant behavior, whether active or reactive. At times, drawing the group's attention to this behavior and its meaning will advance the counseling process: "I notice that David is smiling. Does that mean, David, that you agree with what Margaret is saying when she talks about family career expectations?"

Encouraging Independent Thinking   One goal of career group counseling is to help members think independently. Clearer, more rational thinking will result in more productive emotions and more responsible behavior: "We seem to be identifying things about transferable skills for each other rather than helping each person to identify skills for himself or herself more effectively."

Questioning   The leader should evoke only material that is appropriate to group goals. Merely being "provocative" in a haphazard way, without offering encouragement or interpretation, is more threatening than helpful. The group will move along more effectively if a question is addressed to an individual rather than to the whole group.

Examples:

"What did you get out of being upset because you didn't finish college?"

"Give us an example of what you mean, Mary, when you say that no one understands you."

"What exactly do you mean when you say you don't have time to look for a new job?"

"Randy, did you notice that Alan and Sally expressed concerns very similar to yours?"

The leader continues to be accepting, supportive, and nonjudgmental but must also, at times, confront members with inconsistencies in their thinking, emotions, and behavior. The objective is to point out inconsistencies, evasions, and self-defeating behavior in a way that shows concern for the member's growth.

Information Giving   Valid and reliable information is crucial in career counseling. It can be provided by the leader or by any member of the group. When questions come up about businesses, training, referrals, skills, or counseling procedures, the leader has to decide whether to answer immediately or after the session, to refer the member to another information source (e.g., computer, data base, periodical), or to turn the question over to a member of the group who has some knowledge in the matter.

Through words, inflection, gestures, posture, and facial expressions, the leader can be effective, reassuring, and encouraging to members who must deal with painful issues. Though ultimately each member grapples with these issues alone, the leader's empathy and understanding make the task bearable.

Effective counselor statements include:

"Mary, some of the success myths and stereotypes that society perpetuates can be defeating for a woman returning to the workplace, can't they? Perhaps interviewing several women you consider successful in their careers might help destroy those myths."

"Robert, it's terribly difficult for you to talk about the plant closure, isn't it? You've kept all your deep feelings to yourself for a long time, and examining them here in the group is tougher than you thought it would be. You've shown how strong you are in many ways, and how deep some of the anger was. You can use this strength to deal with the past and prepare yourself for future successes. I recognize the pain this is causing you, and I respect your strength in grappling with it."

Closing and Evaluating   When further attention to an individual or to a specific issue is unlikely to be helpful, or when a discussion has become repetitive or irrelevant, the leader helps the group to move on. First, however, the leader gives a summary and sense of closure to the person who has the group's attention: "Joe, you have a firm understanding of what you've been doing that you'd like to change, and you have specific goals to work on between now and next week."

A session should not end abruptly simply because time has run out. The leader should anticipate the end of the session and provide closure by summarizing, reminding members of the homework that has been agreed upon, and creating a sense of continuity and expectation for the next session.

Closure for the final meeting of the group ties up loose ends, appraises achievements, and allows participants to decide on developmental plans:

"We've looked at a lot of information about ourselves and the world of work and tried to understand it in terms of a career direction. I appreciate the hard work you've put into the process and hope it pays dividends for you and your future. In completing this process you are aware that there is no final answer to career and lifestyle development. It is an ongoing process."

TRENDS IN CAREER GROUP COUNSELING

In looking to the future, the adult career group counseling process can be applied to a number of environments and conditions. Because work makes up such a major part of our lives, the need to enhance a person's career choice and a person's work will have to be addressed creatively in schools and universities, the workplace, and the community.

Schools and Universities

Elementary- and middle-school children need exposure to the world of work, to begin to develop an accurate picture of what work is and how it relates to them (Tolbert, 1974). The emphasis in grades K–8 is self-awareness and career awareness. This encompasses the personal and social significance of work and the broad range of career opportunities.

Career groups in the early high school years are directed toward career exploration and career orientation including visits to career sites; evaluation of interests, abilities, values, and needs in relation to life careers; a more detailed study of occupations; and the beginning of skill development in specific career areas. Group counseling should focus on selecting career specialties that will provide direction for further exploration and skill building.

Groups in the later high school and university years provide a forum for more detailed study of occupations, skill development in various career areas, and how to access, interpret, and use career information. Counseling emphasizes decision making and selecting career specialties that will promote skill building, further exploration, and job seeking skills.

Career group counseling can be shaped for each of these levels. Within the career group counseling format, students have the opportunity to process information and enhance their thinking through the leader's appropriate facilitation.

The Workplace

Career counseling and planning programs, long offered in schools and universities, are a fairly recent phenomenon in the workplace (Brown, Brooks, & Associates, 1984; McDaniels, 1989). A variety of forces have provided the impetus for this recent interest. Special programs for women and minorities, for example, have been instituted in response to affirmative action and equal opportunity legislation. Company programs have evoked greater interest in promoting from within and the accompanying need to develop employees to fill human resource needs. Other programs, arising from requests from employers, undoubtedly reflect greater awareness of adult development in general and adult career behavior in particular. Lancaster and Berne (1981) observed that organizations are interested in increasing employee productivity and decreasing attrition, and they view career planning programs as possible sources of assistance.

Career group counseling in the workplace centers on placing the person in an experimental situation where group participants can rehearse new skills (such as job interviewing and selling one's ideas), can find models to imitate, and can be motivated by the stimulus of other participants.

Career development, and the career group counseling approach, has at least five possible applications in the workplace: (a) entry-level professionals; (b) mid-career workers or managers; (c) individuals preparing to leave the organization because of a cut-back, firing, or retirement; (d) enhancement of the worker's present job situation; and (e) employee assistance programs (EAPs).

The Community

Research on work consistently points out that people are looking for meaning, for what their lives and directions mean for them. In his extensive interviews that resulted in the book *The Seasons of a Man's Life*, Levinson (1978) found that "finding meaning" was a continual need and interest of participants in his study. Studs Terkel (1972) found the same in his research for *Working*, and Gail Sheehy (1976) in her studies that resulted in *Passages*.

The career group counseling model has the potential to help people sort out their identities and look at the meaning of their work and how it does or doesn't make sense.

The meaning of one's existence and its relation to how one spends 8 to 10 hours a day are important questions that community groups can address through volunteer work, membership in clubs, the church, and the family. The family is that climate that one "comes home to," and it is the network of sharing values and goals and commitments to one another over time that most accurately describes the family unit, regardless of blood, legalities, adoption or marriage (Ferguson, 1980).

SUMMARY

John Naisbitt (1982) states that we are living in a time of parenthesis, the time between eras. In the time of parenthesis, people have extraordinary leverage and influence—individually, professionally, institutionally—if we can only get a clear sense, a clear conception, a clear vision of the road ahead.

When done effectively, career group counseling can act as a support group for all people in most environments. The counseling profession can enrich the career and lifestyle process for people by providing the means by which dialogue, reflection, focusing, and feedback can take place.

Although group counseling has grown enormously in the past 40 years, little attention has been given to the idea of career counseling in groups. Among the advantages of this format are the enhancement of career counseling outcomes, the support and encouragement of fellow members, efficiency in terms of time and cost, enhanced feedback, more personalizing and sharing of information, and the variety a group affords.

Career group counseling offers members input about occupations, assessment data about one's abilities, interests, skills, and values, and exploration of personal meaning, identification, and examination of subjective aspects of the self, and feedback from others. Career group counseling has a central theme of decision making, with a number of models to facilitate career and lifestyle planning. Computers have greatly enhanced the potential of career counseling through assessment measures, data bases, career information, and the opportunity to organize information meaningfully.

Career group counseling can be the vehicle to improve career maturity, self-concept, and attitudes toward career and jobs. This type of group generally follows the steps of getting acquainted and knowing the group rules, self-disclosing and opening up to new possibilities, problem solving and exploring, and acting on insights and ideas gained.

The group leader has to be able to provide experiential information and facilitate information processing in group members. To do this, participants are encouraged to focus on self-awareness, self-assessment, skills assessment, strength seeking, career exploration, decision making, goal setting, job hunting, and reinforcing action plans. The leader's techniques include clarifying feelings, interpreting behavior, encouraging independent thinking, questioning, and information giving.

REFERENCES

Anthony, W. A. (1985). Human and information resource development in the age of information: A dialogue with Robert Carkhuff. *Journal of Counseling & Development, 63*, 372–376.

Bolles, R. N. (1985). *What color is your parachute?* (13th ed). Berkeley, CA: Ten Speed Press.

Brown, D., Brooks, L., & Associates (1990). *Career choice and development*. San Francisco: Jossey-Bass.

Bruch, M. A. (1978). Holland's typology applied to client-counselor interaction: Implications for counseling men. *Counseling Psychologist, 7*, 26–32.

Carkhuff, R. R. (1967). Do we have a theory of vocational choice? *Personnel & Guidance Journal, 46*, 335–345.

Catron, D. W. (1966). Educational-vocational group counseling: The effects on perception of self and others. *Journal of Counseling Psychology, 13*, 202–207.

Chick, J. M. (1970). *Innovation in the use of career information.* Boston: Houghton Mifflin.

Cianni-Surridge, M. (1983). Technology and work: Future issues for career guidance. *Personnel & Guidance Journal, 61*, 413–422.

Cohen, A. R. (1969). Communication discrepancy and attitude change: A dissonance theory approach. *Journal of Personality, 27*, 386–396.

Corey, G., & Corey, M. S. (1987). *Group counseling: Theory and practice* (3rd ed.). Monterey, CA: Brooks/Cole.

de Rosenroll, D. (1988). *Goal attainment scaling: A vehicle for group support in career and life issues exploration.* Paper presented at 14th Annual Meeting of National Consultation on Vocational Counseling, Ottawa, Ontario, Canada, January 26–28.

Dinkmeyer, D. C., & Muro, J. J. (1979). *Group counseling: Theory and practice* (2nd ed.). Itasca, IL: F. E. Peacock.

Dreikurs, R., & Sonstegard, M. (1968). Rationale of group counseling. In D. C. Dinkmeyer (Ed.), *Guidance and counseling in the elementary school: Readings in theory and practice* (pp. 37–49). New York: Holt, Rinehart & Winston.

Ferguson, M. (1980). *The Aquarian conspiracy.* Boston: Houghton Mifflin.

Figler, H. E. (1979). *The complete job-search handbook.* New York: Holt, Rinehart & Winston.

Flake, M. H., Roach, A. J., & Stenning W. F. (1975). Effects of short term counseling on career maturity of tenth-grade students. *Journal of Vocational Behavior, 6*, 73–80.

Garrison, R. K. (1972). *The measurement of change in self-concept and personal adjustment as the result of brief career development counseling sessions.* Unpublished doctoral dissertation, University of Northern Colorado, Greeley.

Gati, H. (1990). Interpreting and applying career decision-making models: Comments on Carson and Mowsesian. *Journal of Counseling Psychology, 37*(4), 509–514.

Gazda, G. (1984). *Group counseling* (3rd ed.). Dubuque, IA: Wm C. Brown.

Gelatt, H. B., Varenhorst, B., & Corey, R. (1972). *Deciding.* New York: College Entrance Examination Board.

George, R. L., & Dustin, D. (1988). *Group Counseling—Theory and Practice.* Englewood Cliffs, NJ: Prentice Hall.

Gilliland, B. E. (1966). *An evolution of the effects of small group counseling with black adolescents.* Unpublished doctoral dissertation, University of Tennessee, Knoxville.

Glaize, D., & Myrick, R. (1984). Interpersonal groups or computers? A study of career maturity and career decidedness. *Vocational Guidance Quarterly, 32*(3), 168–176.

Goldberg, J. D. (1980). Counseling the adult learner: Selective review of the literature. *Adult Education, 30*, 67–81.

Gould, R. L. (1979). *Transformations: Growth and change in adult life.* New York: Simon & Schuster.

Hansen, L. S. (1981). New goals and strategies for vocational guidance and counseling. *International Journal for the Advancement of Counseling*, 21–34.

Holland, J. L. (1973). *Making vocational choices: A theory of careers.* Englewood Cliffs, NJ: Prentice Hall.

Hughes, R. (1983). The non-traditional student in higher education: A synthesis of the literature. *NASPA Journal, 20*, 51–63.

Jackson, L. D. (1971). *The effect of a formal program of career exploration on the vocational maturity of college freshmen.* Unpublished doctoral dissertation, University of Georgia, Athens.

Johnson, D. (1990). Indecisiveness: A dynamic, integrative approach. *Career Development Quarterly, 39*(1), 34–38.

Kivlighan, D. M., Jr., Hageseth, J. A., Tipton, R. M., & McGovern, T. V. (1981). Effects of matching treatment approaches and personality types in group vocational counseling. *Journal of Counseling Psychology, 28*, 315–320.

Krannich, R. L. (1983). *Recareering in turbulent times: Skills and strategies for success in today's job market.* Manassos, VA: Impact Publications.

Krumboltz, J. D. (1989, August). *The social learning theory of career decision making.* Paper presented at Annual Conference of American Psychological Association, New Orleans, LA.

Lancaster, A. S. & Berne, R. (1981). *Employer-sponsored career development programs.* Columbus, OH: ERIC Clearinghouse on Adult, Career, and Vocational Education.

Levinson, D. J. (1978). *The seasons of a man's life.* New York: Random House.

Lopez, F., & Andrews, S. (1987). Systems perspective. *Journal of Counseling & Development, 65*, 304–306.

Luft, J. (1970). *Group processes: An introduction to group dynamics* (2nd ed.). Palo Alto, CA: National Press.

Martin, A. M. (1970). *The theory and practice of communicating educational and vocational information.* Boston: Houghton Mifflin.

McAuliffe, G., & Fredrickson, R. (1990). The effects of program length and participant characteristics on group career-counseling outcomes. *Journal of Employment Counseling, 27*(1), 19–22.

McDaniels, C. (1989). *The changing workplace: Career counseling strategies for the 1990s and beyond.* San Francisco: Jossey-Bass.

Mezerow, J. (1978). *Education for perspective transformation.* New York: Columbia University, Teachers College, Center of Adult Education.

Montross, D. H., & Shinkman, C. J. (1981). *Career development in the 1980s: Theory and practice.* Springfield, IL: Charles C Thomas.

Moreno, J. L. (1962). Common ground for all group psychotherapists. What is a group psychotherapist? *Group Psychotherapy, 15*(3) 263–264.

Naisbitt, J. (1982). *Megatrends.* New York: Warner.

Nichol, J. S. (1969). *The use of vocational discussion in small groups to increase vocational maturity.* Unpublished doctoral dissertation, Arizona State University, Tempe.

Pyle, R. (1986). *Group career counseling: Principles and practices.* Washington, DC: U.S. Office of Educational Research and Improvement.

Savickas, M. (1988). Annual review: Practice and research in career counseling and development. *Career Development Quarterly, 38*(2), 100–134.

Savickas, M. (1990). The career decision making course: Description and field test. *Career Development Quarterly, 38*(3), 275–284

Sheeny, G. (1976). *Passages.* New York: E. P. Dutton.

Super, D. E. (1976). *Career education and the meanings of work.* Washington, DC: U.S. Government Printing Office.

Terkel, S. (1972). *Working.* New York: Avon Books.

Tolbert, E. L. (1974). *Counseling for career development.* Boston: Houghton Mifflin.

Trimmer, H. W., Jr. (1984). Group job search workshops: A concept whose time is here. *Journal of Employment Counseling, 21*, 103–116.

Wegman, R. G. (1979). Job-search assistance: A review. *Journal of Employment Counseling, 16*, 197–226.

Wrenn, C. (1989). The person in career counseling. *Career Development Quarterly, 36*(4), 337–342.

Yalom, I. (1985). *The theory and practice of group psychotherapy* (3rd ed.). New York: Basic Books.

13

Group Counseling for Issues Related to Suicide

Ardis Sherwood-Hawes

Suicide is a universal phenomenon. The act of killing oneself transcends differences in race, gender, age, economic status, and ethnic background, and its devastating consequences can ubiquitously impact any family, any community, and any society.

Adolescents and older adults are the populations most at risk for suicidal behavior. In 1988 the suicide rate for adolescents was 13.1 per 100,000, and the rate for adults who are older was 21.5 per 100,000 (Osgood & Brant, 1990).

The suicide rate in adolescents and children has increased by 300% over the last 30 years (Gilliland & James, 1988), and suicide is now the second leading cause of death in the United States for adolescents between ages 11 and 24 (Capuzzi & Gross, 1988). These data do not include children who attempt suicide or who manifest self-destructive ideation. More than 25,000 children under age 12 are hospitalized annually because they are at risk for suicide (Stiles & Kottman, 1990).

The rate of suicide is even higher among people ages 65 and older (Osgood & Brant, 1990; Saul & Saul, 1988). The ratio of completed suicides for women over 65 is double the rate for the United States population, and for men over 65, the ratio is four times the national average (Gilliland & James, 1988). More attempts at suicide are made by adolescents (ages 15–24) and women (ages 25–64), but older adults and men (ages 25–64) have more successful completions of suicide and choose more lethal ways to die (Henry, 1987; Saul & Saul, 1988; Vidal, 1989). People who attempt suicide are at greatest risk for a repeat attempt during the first two-year period following the original attempt, and adolescent attempters have a high rate of repeating the attempt during the first few months after attempting suicide. Despite this dire prognosis, suicide attempters are seldom referred for further psychological services (Curran, 1987).

Considering that suicide attempts and suicide completions are significantly underreported, the national statistics are even more alarming (Allberg & Chu, 1990; Gutstein & Rudd, 1988; Saul & Saul, 1988; Stefanowski-Harding, 1990).

A number of researchers note that mortality data contain intentional cover-ups by physicians or family members or misclassification as accidental death when evidence of suicide is insufficient. It has been suggested that a more accurate picture might be revealed by multiplying given statistics two- maybe threefold. (Gutstein & Rudd, 1988, p. 5)

ASSESSMENT OF SUICIDE RISK

Assessment or identification of a propensity toward suicidal behaviors is a complex and difficult task. A vast amount of research has been directed at identifying common denominators that cause suicidal behavior, but these investigations have failed to establish any outstanding characteristics manifested by all people who attempt or complete suicide. Researchers have agreed, however, on a number of interactional factors that are correlated with suicidality (Capuzzi & Gross, 1989; Gilliland & James, 1988). Suicide is considered to be a process and suicide attempts and completions are the climax of this process (Bogdaniak & Coronado, 1987). A comprehensive approach that incorporates psychological, behavioral, social and situational factors, and examines the interaction among these factors, can enable professionals to comprehend the common clues and patterns associated with suicidality and facilitate a competent estimation of the risk for suicide.

Suicide is rarely precipitated by a single factor. Depression is the major predictor of suicidal behavior, and vulnerability increases when both depression and impulsiveness are present (Capuzzi & Gross, 1989; Garfinkel et al., 1988). There are also significant correlations between feelings of hopelessness, depression and suicidal behavior (Asarnow, Carlson, & Guthrie, 1987). The emotional features of depression (e.g., sadness, low self-esteem, feelings of helplessness, lack of control over situations and self, despair, self-degradation) can affect the way depressed people view the world. These feelings and beliefs can produce a frame of reference that can generate certain dysfunctional and debilitating coping mechanisms (e.g., withdrawal and isolation, anhedonia, low tolerance for frustration, dependent behaviors, inept problem-solving and communication skills, cognitive rigidity, anxiety). Depressive behaviors can (a) reduce the ability to develop solutions to troublesome situations and amplify feelings of hopelessness; and (b) elicit negative reactions and rejection from other people, further diminishing weakened emotional bonds.

Inadequate coping skills lessen the chance that people who are depressed will experience positive events and receive environmental reinforcers, and lack of these skills increases the probability of aversive reinforcement. Alienation and negative experiences reinforce the nullifying emotions and concepts. The devastating effects of episodes of depression on the life circumstances of people who are depressed can lead to lasting maladaptive compromises in personal adjustment, and these perverse accommodations, which increase with successive episodes, intensify the risk of suicide. Losses (e.g., divorce, status, death, emotional ties) compound this risk (Garfinkel et al., 1988). Often, individuals who are prone to suicide have difficulty expressing their thoughts, feelings, and needs, and they are consequently unable to discuss and resolve issues that surround disappointments and losses (Capuzzi & Gross, 1989).

Research (Capuzzi & Gross, 1989; Garfinkel et al., 1988; Gutstein & Rudd, 1988; Henry, 1987; Morgan, 1981) identifies the following crucial variables that can denote potential suicidal behavior:

❑ Depression.
❑ Psychological pain.
❑ Difficulty with interpersonal relationships.
❑ Inability to adjust and cope.
❑ Cognitive constriction (rigidity in thinking).
❑ Low self-esteem.
❑ Social isolation.
❑ Anxiety and distress.
❑ Hostility and rage.
❑ Poor communication skills.

Counselors who are assessing suicidal risk must be able to identify the warning signs of suicidality and competently determine the severity of the behaviors and clues.

Certain precipitating behaviors, events, and life circumstances increase the probability that suicide-prone individuals will actively initiate the climax of the suicide process. One of the best predictors for determining suicidal risk is a history of *previous attempts at suicide* (Garfinkel et al., 1988). Another major clue to the probability of overt suicidal behavior is the *severity of depression* the person manifests (Hatton, Valente, & Rink, 1977a). Counselors who are assessing the possibility of suicidal risk in an individual should investigate:

— the seriousness of the crisis.
— the person's coping strategies and current ability to problem solve.
— any prior history of suicide ideation.
— the individual's direct statements or indirect hints of intent to die.
— present affective or mental status.
— social resources.
— personal resources.
— specificity of the suicide plan.

In addition, the following factors indicate future danger of suicidal risk (Bogdaniak & Coronado, 1987; Capuzzi & Gross, 1989; Garfinkel et al., 1988; Gutstein & Rudd, 1988; Hatton, Valente & Rink, 1977a):

— Excessive use of alcohol and/or drug dependency.
— Poor impulse control.
— History of acting out behaviors.
— Prolonged depression.
— Dramatic personality changes.
— Acts of making final arrangements.
— Family conflicts and stressors.
— Sudden mood reversal.
— Intense desire to die.
— Tendency for suicide attempts to increase on days significant to client.
— Family history of suicide.

When people at risk for suicide are given the opportunity to openly discuss and explore the possibility of suicide, they feel relieved and have less suicide ideation (Capuzzi & Gross, 1989).

SUICIDE INTERVENTION GROUPS

Although the group method has been used extensively with a wide variety of mental health concerns, the traditional treatment for suicidal clients has followed the individual model (Hipple, 1982). Despite numerous indications of the positive benefits of the group approach for supporting and treating suicidal populations (Motto, 1979), counselors have been advised not to select individuals who are severely depressed or suicidal for groups (Frey, Motto, & Ritholz, 1983). This reluctance to use the group model for suicidal clients has been attributed to (a) administrative resistance (Frey, Motto, & Ritholz, 1983; Robertson & Mathews, 1989), (b) concerns about professional competency when working with suicidal clients and (c) fear of legal liability in case of a suicide (Motto, 1979; Robertson & Mathews, 1989). In addition, Kaplan and Sadock (1972) suggest that counselors may have a tendency to avoid working with these groups because some of the themes typically dealt with in the group, such as death and dying, can evoke anxiety reactions in the group leader.

During the 1970s, a movement began toward using the group approach as a remedial intervention for people who were depressed and at high risk for suicide (Asimos, 1979). Although the effectiveness of this treatment modality has been widely documented (Robertson & Mathews, 1989), most of these reports have been descriptive, and impressionistic, lacking the controlled clinical trials necessary to impartially assess the therapeutic effect of group work with suicidal people (Frey, Motto, & Ritholz, 1983). The literature has also seriously neglected research reports describing how to use group treatment as a primary format for suicide intervention (Hipple, 1982). The infrequent reports of controlled studies that have investigated the effectiveness of group work with suicidal clients indicate that this treatment modality is a potent intervention for people at risk for suicide.

An epidemiologic study by Billings (in Frey, Motto, & Ritholz, 1983) compared various treatment modalities (individual therapy, traditional group therapy, day treatment centers, inpatient therapy, no treatment) and found that the special suicide group was the most effective intervention for reducing mortality rates in suicidal persons. In a study designed to further clarify the causal relationship between treatment and outcome, Frey, Motto, and Ritholz (1983) researched the influence of a special group therapy program for people at high risk for suicide, and also reported a significant reduction in mortality rates among therapy group members when compared to outpatient services or no treatment at all. Patsiokas and Clum (1985) measured the effectiveness of three modes of intervention for suicidal persons: (a) a problem-solving focused group, (b) a cognitive-restructuring focused group, and (c) a nondirective control group consisting of 10 individual unstructured therapeutic sessions. Suicide ideation scores were not lowered in the control group, they dropped 43% in the cognitive-restructuring group, and they were reduced by 60% in the problem-solving group.

Counselors who use the group therapy model as their primary treatment program for suicidal individuals are positive in their assessment of the efficacy of this approach (Asimos, 1979; Comstock & McDermott, 1975; Frey, Motto, & Ritholz, 1983; Motto, 1979; Robertson & Mathews, 1989). Reports repeatedly mention the special curative factors of suicide groups, such as the social support network of the group treatment and its reparative impact for persons who feel of hopeless, helpless, and isolated (Asimos, 1979). Comstock and McDermott (1975) further state that:

> Group therapy offers appropriate means for dealing with many problems commonly found among suicidal patients, including poor impulse control, lack of future orientation, feelings of sadness and low self-esteem, inability to recognize areas of competence, and failure to accept personal responsibility. (p. 44)

The protective atmosphere of the group provides a unique environment where members can (Robertson & Mathews, 1989):

— satisfy their need to belong, to be accepted, and to give and receive love.
— become more socially integrated as group members exchange offers of support, understanding, and hope.
— disclose information about themselves and receive feedback from other group members.
— improve communication and coping skills.
— learn problem-solving techniques.
— recognize and practice positive thought patterns.
— come to understand that their concerns are not unique, and they are not alone.

In addition, the group offers an unparalleled social resource for corrective influence (Dinkmeyer, 1975). Suicide intervention groups can:

— focus on practical issues of the problems of daily living.
— eliminate the customary resistance to treatment programs (Robertson & Mathews, 1989).
— give group members an opportunity to express emotions and to vicariously experience the feelings of other group members (Goldman, 1986).
— provide a here-and-now experience that allows group members to observe each others' attitudes and behaviors (Dinkmeyer, 1975).
— be informational and educational, and motivate members to attempt new, action-oriented coping strategies (Poey, 1985).

Because the group offers many positive experiences to the suicidal person, Hipple (1982) suggests that counselors for suicidal clients seriously consider this modality as an option for treatment.

GUIDELINES FOR GROUP LEADERS

Characteristics of the Group Leader

Potential counselors for groups that will focus on issues related to suicide should be grounded in the basic theories of group counseling, be thoroughly trained in the fundamental principles of group dynamics, and be knowledgeable about group processes and procedures. Prospective counselors also must have received extensive training on the fundamentals of working with suicidal or depressed people, and be able to recognize the signs and symptoms of the presuicidal syndrome (Robertson & Mathews, 1989). Basic counselor qualities should include:

— emotional maturity.
— an exceptionally high level of self-awareness.
— accurate listening and responding skills.
— poise.
— nonjudgemental demeanor.
— a stable self-concept.
— the ability to analyze and accurately diagnose potential problems.

In addition, the following qualifications are recommended for group leaders of special suicide groups:

1. Leaders are knowledgeable about the ethical and professional issues specific to working with suicide-related groups, recognize their own individual moral beliefs, and comprehend how these values can relate to the issues of autonomy and responsibility (Clements, Sider, & Perlmutter, 1983).
2. Leaders have had personal therapy and have explored and appreciate any personal issues, biases, or unfinished business that might limit their ability to function optimally as a group leader.
3. Leaders maintain current knowledge of new research in group work and suicidality.
4. Leaders are licensed, certified, and covered by professional liability insurance.
5. Leaders obtain personal group experience by participating as a group member in a self-exploration or counseling group.
6. Leaders have the ability to effectively co-facilitate a group. Because working with suicidal people can be emotionally and physically exhausting, Hipple (1982) suggests that the group should be led by two professional counselors. Ideally, three counselors should be assigned to the group, to ensure that at least two co-facilitators are present at each group session.
7. Leaders are confidant in their ability to correctly diagnose an individual's degree of lethality and are willing to make an instantaneous, decisive intervention (e.g., involuntary hospitalization).
8. Leaders have a high tolerance for dependent behavior because suicidal individuals can become extremely needy and demanding during emotional crises. In addition, because a suicide crisis can occur at any time, counselors ideally have flexible schedules so they can be present in times of crisis (Gilliland & James, 1988; Klein, 1985; Motto, 1979; Robertson & Mathews, 1989).

Role and Function of the Group Leader
Suicide intervention group members need a particularly safe milieu to talk about their feelings, concerns, thoughts and behaviors, and suicide-related groups must provide participants with an environment of unconditional acceptance and complete support. To cre-

ate a nonthreatening atmosphere for the group, leaders should introduce to the group as few formal expectations as possible (Hipple, 1982). These groups deal primarily with issues of life and death, and group leaders have to sensitively facilitate the group in an active, directive, and gentle confrontive style. Leaders must be comfortable in energetically managing the group process. When a member has a crisis, (a) the condition must be discussed immediately, (b) problem-solving techniques have to be implemented quickly, and (c) alternative behaviors must be promptly rehearsed and adopted.

Short-Term Group Approach

The group approach as an intervention for suicidal people is generally initiated as a short-term method of treatment. This model typically ranges from 6 to 60 sessions, rarely uses psychodynamic exploration, and customarily focuses on a specific theme or treatment modality (Poey, 1985). The short-term approach is considered to be an effective intervention during and after the crisis phase of suicidal behavior. Frey, Motto, and Ritholz (1983) found that the strongest beneficial changes occur within the first five group sessions, and suggest that the early treatment programs are crucial in preventing additional suicidal behaviors. They further propose that "the special suicide group appears to support the natural and oftentimes slow healing that occurs after a suicide crisis" (p. 291).

Throughout this acute crisis period, the person may be out of control, disoriented, and unable to make appropriate choices. Individuals in crises may have frequent suicidal thoughts and manifest overt suicidal behaviors. They may have a limited capacity to tolerate anxiety and may not have the resources necessary for doing psychological group work. The support-oriented short-term group, directed predominately on symptomatic relief, social maintenance from other group members, understanding the precipitating events, and developing and implementating adaptive coping strategies, more effectively meets the needs of individuals who have suicidal impulses (Hipple, 1982).

Short-Term versus Long-Term Approach

The purpose of short-term groups is to meaningfully identify core conflicts and begin to examine personal implications of those issues. It is not designed to extensively explore deep-seated emotional conflicts, or to achieve a lasting structural change in personality (Klein, 1985). Comstock and McDermott (1975) advocate a two-step approach for group intervention for suicidal clients:

1. Short-term crisis intervention is necessary to confront the suicidal behaviors, and to facilitate exploration of dysfunctional emotions and actions.
2. Because the crisis interventions of the short-term approach may have a limited effect on individuals who are prone toward suicide, the additional strategies of the long-term approach are necessary to alter the self-destructive tendencies that result from ongoing, submerged psychological problems.

Suicide can be defined as a crisis situation, and suicidal behaviors are then considered to be manifestations of that crisis (Hatton, Valente, & Rink, 1977b). Crisis is a state in which intolerable barriers obstruct life goals and aspirations are perceived as no longer attainable. These obstacles, which exceed the person's resources and coping mechanisms, can arise from both developmental and situational events, and unresolved crises can generate chronic and long-term dysfunctional modes of behavior. Often the original crisis and its accompanying discomfort will disappear, and the person may feel the crisis has been resolved. In some cases, memory of the crisis may be repressed from awareness and, during times of stress, may resurface in self-destructive behaviors such as suicide attempts. Individuals may seek help during a suicidal crisis and may seem to achieve a sense of equilibrium during the counseling sessions, but unless the original crisis is resolved, the primordial trauma will often emerge the moment new stressors are presented, and the person will again have sudden, extreme anxiety, agitation or pathology (Gilliland & James, 1988).

As individuals move out of the crisis period, their issues will change, and they will need to explore deeper levels of emotions and underlying personality disturbances. Group leaders can either gradually make the transition toward the processes of the long-term approach (e.g., examination of unconscious material, less effort to avoid anxiety-provoking interactions, exploration of negative effect, less directive leadership), or they can refer the member to appropriate treatment programs (Hipple, 1982). The methods and practices of the long-term approach are beyond the scope of this chapter, and the focus will be on the procedures and processes of the short-term approach.

Structure of the Short-Term Approach

Treatment groups use both the traditional group format of a closed group and the nontraditional format of an open-ended or "drop-in" group (Motto, 1979). The closed group model does not allow new members to join after the original group has been formed. Closed groups are preferable for insight-oriented groups because they promote a stable, consistent environment that encourages the disclosure process and feelings of solidarity among group members. The open group format allows new members to join the group at any time and often gives participants the option of choosing when and how often they will attend group sessions (Motto, 1979).

Many professionals prefer the open group format for the crisis-oriented, short-term process (Asimos, 1979; Comstock & McDermott, 1975; Motto, 1979; Robertson & Mathews, 1989). The acute phase of suicidal behavior is generally short in duration, and during this interval the more intense therapeutic processes of exploration in the closed group may heighten the person's feelings of anxiety and depression (Asimos, 1979). The open model also ensures that anyone who is having suicidal impulses will get the opportunity to immediately join a group and benefit from it.

Asimos (1979) declares that people will feel less threatened if there is a "deemphasis on contractual agreements and imposed expectations regarding attendance and participation in suicide intervention groups. Rather, group members are told to come when they want to, and need to, and there are no guilt feelings if they miss a meeting because they have broken no contract" (p. 110). She further asserts that the open group format offers a benign environment of unconditional acceptance in which members learn that they are worthy of love, and thus, gradually come to understand that they can safely share their negative thoughts and emotions without loss of self-esteem or fear of rejection.

Selection of Group Members

Recruiting and selecting members for a suicide intervention group can be a formidable and complicated task. Hipple (1982) says:

> A common myth about starting such a group is that not enough appropriate clients are available at any given time to warrant the beginning a such a special group. It is my contention that many agencies are not aware of how many clients who might profit from such a group experience are on the case role at any given time. (p. 247)

He suggests that if the group has an open, continuous format, it can be initiated with as few as two or three members. Group members then can be progressively enrolled and terminated throughout the group's existence group.

When forming a group, one of the first issues that counselors face is choosing between a heterogeneous or a homogeneous group composition. The heterogeneous group is composed of people who do not share a specific symptom or circumstance. Group members are dissimilar in their problems, ages, gender, personality traits, strengths, limitations, and socioeconomic backgrounds. The heterogeneous group promotes self-disclosure and has a greater potential to influence personality change and behavior modification (Klein, 1985).

In contrast, the membership of a homogeneous group shares a common condition, and the group focus is toward alleviating that condition. Homogeneous groups tend to be more didactic, and members are prone to superficially interact and self-disclose (Klein, 1985). In groups with a common focus, however, the members are more apt to (a) identify with each other, (b) quickly unite and bond to other group members, (c) attend more meetings, and (d) offer more support to other group members. The rapid development of cohesion among group members enables the group to work efficiently and effectively, and it facilitates a prompt reduction of debilitating symptoms common to members of suicide prevention groups.

Establishing a truly homogeneous group composition is extremely difficult, and leaders of suicide-related groups must remain flexible in their thinking about group composition. Group members will have different histories, unique personalities, special environmental situations, and individual responses to treatment (Frey, Motto, & Ritholz, 1983; Robertson & Mathews, 1989). Robertson and Mathews suggest that selecting members according to gender is desirable in adolescent groups because the same-sex group composition accentuates members' commonality of problems and facilitates disclosure within the group. Hipple (1982) maintains that, in adult groups, a mixture of sexes is ideal, although groups may have more women than men because of the higher incidence of suicide attempts by women.

Other guidelines for group leaders to consider during the screening process include (Frey, Motto & Ritholz, 1983; Hipple, 1982; Robertson & Mathews, 1989):

1. Potential group members should have a moderate to high rating of lethality. Those with a low risk for suicidal behavior may be adversely affected by the intense emotions and acting out behaviors of more lethal group members.
2. People who are psychotic or those who are prone to violence are generally disruptive to the group process and are considered inappropriate for a suicide intervention group.

3. Individuals who are actively involved with alcohol or drugs should be excluded from the group. Suicidal ideation and suicidal behaviors have to be the primary psychological issues for group members.

Group Limitations

During the initial group session, the co-leaders can discuss the goals and objectives of the group, define the rules of confidentiality, survey the members' expectations toward the group experience, and take care of other "housekeeping" tasks (e.g., meeting time, place, attendance guidelines). In addition, Hipple (1982) sets out ground rules specific to suicide intervention groups:

1. *Rule of no secrets*. Group members are encouraged to obtain assistance from people outside the group, and all interactions of external support must be shared within the group.
2. *Physical safety rule*. Group leaders advocate the release of emotions and communication about pernicious behaviors, but prohibit acting out those behaviors in the group. Members are allowed to be angry during the group session but are not authorized to hurt themselves, threaten other group members, or destroy property. As members learn that they can vent intense emotions without indulging in physical demonstrations, they become more self-confident in their ability to be self-controlled and will generalize this more appropriate response to external environments.
3. *Confidentiality rule*. Leaders must inform group members that when they believe a member has a high probability of suicidality, it is the leader's ethical and legal responsibility to ensure the safety of the member through immediate intervention, and to report the possibility of the suicidal behavior to authorities and family members.
4. *Record-keeping issues*. Leaders of suicide-related groups should keep accurate and complete records because of the legal risk involved in facilitating this type of group. Members should be informed of any record-keeping procedures.
5. *Contract*. Leaders of special suicide groups often stipulate that a signed formal contract, in which the client agrees to stay alive, is a precondition for entry into the group. This contract also serves as a powerful intervention for reducing suicidal behaviors.

Goals and Functions of the Short-Term Approach

The primary goal of the short-term approach is to confront and prevent suicidal ideation and destructive behaviors in group members. Leaders (and members) should actively respond to the immediate needs and crises of group members and should encourage expressing feelings and acquiring different, more functional behaviors (Comstock & McDermott, 1975; Robertson & Mathews, 1989). Subsequent group goals may be:

1. *Reduction of distress*. Group members with a potential for suicidal behavior are often depressed and angry. The group leader should support and assist them in expressing their intense emotions and rage. Furthermore, the leader should encourage members to realistically identify the source of their anger. This insight can help thwart internaliza-

tion of the rage, which often precipitates suicidal behaviors (Comstock & McDermott, 1975; Klein, 1985). Internal tension is relieved by expressing emotional feelings when the group member (a) has a conscious awareness of the angry feelings; (b) is aware of the reasons for suppressing the feelings of rage; and (c) does not fear rejection or loss of self-esteem by venting these threatening feelings (Robertson & Mathews, 1989).

2. *Encouragement of self-disclosure.* Group leaders seek to promote a nonthreatening, supportive group environment that enables members to share personal information about themselves. Leaders model appropriate interpersonal communication skills and guide group members to reveal experiences and concerns occurring in the here and now. Personal disclosure facilitates (a) a sense of group cohesion (members feel less isolated and lonely); (b) a milieu of belongingness (members can perceive a commonality in problems and difficulties); (c) feelings of acceptance and empathy toward other group members; (d) social interest and involvement with other individuals (Dinkmeyer, 1975); (e) self-awareness; and (f) feelings of support. Self-disclosure also allows members to absorb, practice and adopt competent interpersonal communication skills (Hipple, 1982).

3. *Encouragement of self-responsibility and self-management.* Group members are encouraged to become aware of, focus on, and monitor their thoughts and emotions, and then connect these internal processes to their external behaviors. Insight into the relationship between thoughts, feelings, and actions can influence tendencies toward impulsive movement and can enable individuals to control dysfunctional behaviors. Members can practice new coping skills in the group and generalize them into their everyday living situations through homework assignments (Comstock & McDermott, 1975).

4. *Enhancement of self-concept.* People who are in a suicidal crisis have a tendency to focus on their negative attributes, and they fail to recognize their positive qualities. Group interactions challenge these preoccupations with the negative aspects of life and emphasize the positive essence of participants. Members are exhorted to discuss their strengths and favorable attributes within the group and are given homework assignments that highlight propitious characteristics (Hipple, 1982).

5. *Consideration of future goals.* Group members are encouraged to develop action plans with a positive and optimistic orientation toward the future.

6. *Development of external support systems.* Initially, the group leaders and other members may be the primary sources of support for participants. The group leaders can immediately begin to orient clients toward reaching out and seeking support from significant others, thus reducing members' dependency on the group. Members can learn by observation and practice to directly communicate their need for assistance, and homework assignments can help them achieve this external support system.

7. *Motivation of clients in the pursuit of extended therapy.* Suicidal people often manifest the dysfunctional symptoms of ongoing personality disturbances, and long-term therapeutic interventions are necessary to alter self-destructive tendencies. As members become capable and willing to tolerate the heightened anxieties of a more intense therapeutic process, group leaders should encourage them to seek and commit to an appropriate extended treatment program (Comstock & McDermott, 1975).

INTERVENTIONS FOR SUICIDE GROUP THERAPY

Problem-Solving Techniques

Feelings of hopelessness, helplessness, and deficiencies in interpersonal problem-solving skills are highly correlated with suicidal behaviors (Asarnow et al., 1987; Patsiokas & Clum, 1985). People who attempt suicide may perceive their problems as insurmountable and may regard the act of suicide as the only solution to their predicament. The inflexible thinking process often manifested by suicide-prone individuals can negate the ability to recognize alternative possibilities.

Through a process of education and practice, group members learn problem-solving skills such as (a) identifying the problem, (b) investigating the facts related to the problem, (c) concentrating on the important aspects of the situation, (d) exploring possible solutions to the problem, and (e) testing these solutions for effectiveness. The study by Patsiokas and Clum (1985) indicates that when individuals who are prone to suicide understand and practice appropriate methods of problem solving, their sense of hopelessness is reduced and they have a more optimistic visualization of the future. In addition, as people acquire effective behavioral skills, their sense of self-efficacy increases and their tendency to experience extreme, dysfunctional emotional arousal during periods of distress is diminished (Lawrence & Ureda, 1990).

Cognitive Restructuring

Because depression is highly correlated with suicidal impulses (Asarnow et al., 1987; Garfinkel et al., 1988), many counselors use cognitive restructuring approaches designed to reduce depressed states in suicide-prone individuals. These interventions are based on the premise that self-defeating thinking processes are determinants in the manifestation of depression. For example, themes of suicide ideation often involve irrational beliefs about the self, life events, and how the suicide attempt will evoke favorable life changes (e.g., significant others will alter unwanted perceptions or feelings about the person) (Patsiokas & Clum, 1985).

The goal of counseling is a cognitive restructuring of erroneous, invalidating, and self-defeating perceptions, and group leaders will provocatively question, gently confront, and challenge members to relinquish and change the dysfunctional beliefs that underlie these faulty cognitions. During the entire procedure, the leaders make a conscious effort to teach and encourage members to develop self-generated rational thinking processes (Grieger & Boyd, 1980).

Self-Observation

Group members are encouraged to monitor and record overt and covert behaviors, and to reflect on the recorded behaviors (e.g., question motives, accurately identify emotions). Self-observation interventions are effective for two reasons. First, they increase the person's ability to understand and control behaviors, and they encourage self-responsible actions. Second, the act of monitoring brings these behaviors into conscious awareness and, thus, can decrease the frequency of the behavior.

Action Plans

Suicidal people are often consumed with negative expectations about the future, and they commonly think about problems that have occurred in the past. This orientation toward hopelessness makes it difficult for suicidal people to have positive expectations about their existence in the future. Group members are encouraged to develop action plans that focus on future events. During periods of crisis, these agendas may have to identify day-to-day activities, and as the person reestablishes emotional equilibrium, the plan of action can be extended into weeks, and then months.

CHALLENGES FOR COUNSELORS

Several areas of potential difficulty seem to be common to groups with suicidal and depressed populations. These include shared depressed affect in the group setting and the attempted or completed suicide of a group member.

Depressed Atmosphere

Many people who are suicidal have feelings of depression. The communication of depressive symptoms (e.g., hopelessness, helplessness, apathy, despair) can be contagious, and group members may come to project a shared sense of futility that damages the therapeutic process of the group. Leaders must be able to effectively intervene and interrupt the propensity for negativism in the group (Comstock & McDermott, 1975).

Attempted Suicide

When group leaders assess that a group member has a high risk for suicide, they must be prepared to make a swift intervention and ensure the safety of the member. Leaders should establish a network of reliable emergency resources that are available during a suicide crisis (e.g., medical, family support system) and research the local requirements for involuntary hospitalization (Hipple, 1982).

Suicide of a Group Member

If a group member commits suicide, the surviving group members may have feelings of denial, guilt, anger, grief, hopelessness, and fear. Members frequently review past group interactions and ask "what if" questions. The group leader's honest disclosure of personal reactions and emotions about the suicide can encourage members to experience and express their own feelings and apprehensions.

Leaders may have to work on the grieving process for several weeks, while gradually guiding the group back to the here-and-now processes of constructive group work. Focusing on the present will allow members to become aware of how survivors are victims of suicide and how they can avoid similar self-destructive behaviors (Comstock & McDermott, 1975; Motto, 1979).

SUICIDE POSTVENTION GROUPS

Public and professional education about issues and facts related to suicide is a fairly recent phenomenon. Only during the last few decades has research has been directed toward establishing commonalities in suicidal behavior and empirically evaluating the effectiveness of treatment programs. The steady and dramatic increase in suicide rates in certain populations has pointed up the intense need for suicide-related literature to explicitly describe programs that can prevent suicide, intervene with people who are suicidal, and assist survivors of suicide (those who have gone through the suicidal death of a friend or loved one) (Wrobleski, 1984). In the last few years, many books and articles have been written about prevention and intervention, but little attention has been directed to the aftermath effects of a suicide. Despite a critical need for assistance programs for survivors of suicide, postvention is a seriously neglected component in the study of suicidality (Constantino, 1989; Valente, Saunders, & Street, 1988).

Bereavement is the slow process through which survivors acknowledge a death and strive to create some meaning out of the death. Mourning a death by suicide is the most difficult type of bereavement because the loss is premature and unexpected (Valente et al., 1988). Immediately after a suicide, survivors often are obsessed with a multitude of noxious emotions. Grief, horror, shock, shame, guilt, and bewilderment are thrust upon them as they simultaneously attempt to deal with the method of death (Shelaman, 1981). This unhealthy complex of disturbing and intrusive emotions can result in depression, psychological distress, social isolation, and suicide ideation.

In comparison to survivors of other types of death, suicide survivors experience (a) a more encompassing distress reaction, (b) a greater number of clinical symptoms, and (c) a higher intensity level in these symptoms (Constantino, 1989). Symptoms manifested by survivors of suicide include (Constantino, 1989; Wrobleski, 1984):

— deeper resentment and anger.
— phobias.
— debilitating fears (about death, possible harm befalling other family members).
— nightmares and dreams about the suicide.
— self-recriminations.
— excessive guilt.
— apathy.
— loneliness.
— greater risk of physical illness.
— difficulty in concentration.
— acute shame (from social stigma).

Wrobleski (1984) asserts that social stigma is the legacy the lack of education has given suicide survivors. Suicide may be viewed as a cowardly behavior, a mortal sin, a revengeful act, or a desperate attempt of a victim who has been wronged by significant others. Many people consider suicide to be a moral rather than a mental issue, and insurance companies have policy limitations that allow them to deny benefits to survivors of a death by suicide (Constantino, 1989). Issues of social stigma aggravate the problems of suicide survivors. Although survivors have a tremendous need to communicate their feelings, they may avoid discussing the suicide with natural sources of support because they feel shame or anticipate societal blame. Family and friends may feel threatened by the suicide and may be unable to reach out and comfort the survivor.

The subject of suicide is often avoided, and the death by suicide may be treated as a non-event. Consequently, suicide survivors can be socially isolated, and their chances of effectively coping with the crisis are diminished (Constantino, 1989; Wrobleski, 1984).

> The availability of external support systems is one of the most critical factors differentiating individual vulnerability from invulnerability; that is, separating individuals who survive a crisis with no harm from those who experience lasting damage. (Carter & Brooks, 1990, p. 379)

Competent programs of postvention can provide the necessary support for survivors of suicide, and can strengthen previously existing resources (Carter & Brooks, 1990).

Suicide survivors typically experience shock and denial. They sometimes are unaware of their need for assistance. The social-emotional alienation phenomenon reduces their ability to mourn and develop coping mechanisms, and they frequently need the structure of professional counseling to vent their feelings. They may not seek counseling, however, because they may be distrustful of postvention (Constantino, 1989). Carter and Brooks (1990) suggest that crisis counselors initiate postvention by actively pursuing survivors.

Postvention can follow several approaches, and intervention can be initiated through individual or group counseling using the formats of:

— short-term consultation (1 to 3 sessions of emergency support).
— intermediate-convergent (10 to 12 sessions focused on crisis resolution and restoration of pre-crisis functioning).
— long-term counseling (intensive therapy revolving around on insight, adaptation, primary personality change, and increased level of psychological health) (Carter & Brooks, 1990).
— grief support groups (emphasizing common problems of suicidal death, alleviation of emotional distress, acceptance, and adaptation) (Wrobleski, 1984).

Whichever format is chosen, the group approach is the preferred method of postvention in helping survivors of suicide cope with psychological distress (Carter & Brooks, 1990; Constantino, 1989; Wrobleski, 1984).

Adolescent Postvention Group

Carter and Brooks (1990) perceive postvention as an opportunity for change toward positive developmental growth. For their school-based postvention program, they use an intermediate-convergent structure with a group counseling format. They advocate this approach because it (a) yields short-term psychological adjustments, (b) reaches multiple survivors, and (c) provides ample time to assess risk and to strengthen and expand external and internal support systems. They also recommend that potential group leaders be trained in issues related to suicide and are qualified to work with postvention groups. Their procedure is to immediately offer postvention services to school administrators and faculty members in the event of a student suicide. After the initial staff meetings, they conduct a rapid assessment of school resources, suicide survivor risk, and need for further interventions.

The first intervention involves students whom school staff members have identified as close friends of the deceased student, as well as other students who are highly distressed by the suicide. The primary purpose of this first intervention is to prevent additional deaths among the student survivors by (a) assessing the emotional needs of the survivors, (b) providing immediate emergency support, and (c) establishing options for further therapeutic support. The goals of the first session are:

— to create a safe, accepting environment in which students can openly express feelings of anger and sadness.
— to offer unconditional acceptance and validation of these intense emotions.
— to assess students' support systems.
— to evaluate students' plans for obtaining support.
— to schedule additional postvention sessions.

Students who are at risk are proactively encouraged to attend the second session. If necessary, a formal postvention group is formed during the first meeting. This group might be composed of students who are survivor-victims, or can be a multifamily group including parents, students, and other family members. Generally, the predominant theme of the group is remaining psychologically sound while coping with uncontrollable losses. The group process centers on disclosure of intimate feelings. Topics might include:

— fears surrounding the conflict between self-protection and commitment to an interpersonal relationship.
— past and future losses (e.g., divorce, death, relocation, developmental milestones).
— communication difficulties in interpersonal relationships.
— holidays and special anniversaries.
— problem solving tactics.

Auxiliary support is crucial for counselors of postvention groups. Working with a group of adolescents suicide survivors requires a tremendous amount of responsibility, and a consultant who is not emotionally involved with the group can objectively evaluate its proceedings and increase the effectiveness of the group process.

The Suicide Survivors Grief Group

Suicide survivors have an inordinate need to verbalize their feelings, and this need to talk about the suicide lasts longer than family and friends are willing to listen (Wrobleski, 1984). The Suicide Survivors Grief Group (SSGG) gives people the opportunity to receive important emotional support from others who share a similar experience and, thus, begin the process of acceptance and recovery.

The SSGG (Wrobleski, 1984) is an open, ongoing postvention group that meets twice a month for 2 hours per session. People can choose their own attendance schedules, and the average number of meetings attended is six, over a period of 3 to 6 months. The open group format is advantageous because new members can benefit from experiences of veteran survivors. People who are recovering from their grief model behaviors that reassure new members that there is hope for overcoming the intense distress reactions to the suicide.

The group leader commences each session by requesting that all members introduce themselves, and state who died and how and when the death occurred. This important function of the group serves two purposes:

1. Shared experiences promote group bonding and feelings of empathy.
2. As members repeat and reproduce the narration, they gradually become desensitized to stigmatized words that surround death by suicide.

Desensitization enables them to talk more freely about the suicide, teaches them to use literal terms when they speak of suicide (e.g., killed themselves, bled to death), and promotes acceptance of the death. Leaders of SSG groups are empathetic (yet emotionally uninvolved to avoid burnout), are nondirective, and participate minimally in the group interaction.

The group's focus is on the common problems of suicide, and there is no agenda or predetermined topics at meetings. In an accepting and nonjudgmental milieu, people discuss the needs and problems they are dealing with that day. "The greatest need of suicide survivors is reassurance that what they are going through is 'normal'" (Wrobleski, 1984, p. 175). Disclosure, and the sharing of similar experiences, feelings, and ideas, encourages people and enables them to learn effectual ways to cope with suicide.

AGE-SPECIFIC VARIATIONS FOR ADULTS WHO ARE OLDER

Americans ages 65 years and older comprise the population group with the greatest risk for suicide completion (Osgood & Brant, 1990; Saul & Saul, 1988). Adults over age 65 initiate fewer attempts at suicide, but the percentage of successful suicide completions increases significantly as people become older (Achté, 1988; Gilliland & James, 1988; Saul & Saul, 1988). This disproportionate vulnerability toward suicide escalates even further among people 75 years and older. Men and women over age 75 commit suicide three to four times more often than younger adults do (Saul & Saul, 1988).

Researchers have uncovered several factors that may possibly explain why a person who is older is more likely to succeed in the attempt to take his or her own life. A study by Achté (1988) revealed that only 34% of unsuccessful suicide attempters under age 25 really wanted to die, whereas 76% of adults over age 65 expressed genuine regret that the attempt had been inefficacious. This earnest desire to die is reflected by the fact that, in comparison with younger adults who attempt suicide, adults who are older use more violent and lethal methods to attempt suicide. Selecting a means that is more certain to elicit death suggests that older suicide attempters have given the matter of suicide long and careful consideration and seriously intend to die (Achté, 1988). In addition, older suicide attempters are more secretive about their intention to end their lives and are less apt to use a suicide attempt as a way to gain attention or as a disguised cry for help. Consequently, when older adults attempt suicide, they are usually successful (Saul & Saul, 1988).

Many professionals are concerned that the seriousness of the risk of suicide for adults who are older is vastly underestimated because the possibility strongly exists that the rate of suicide among people age 75 and older may be underreported and some suicidal behavior may go undetected. Research data do not include the numbers of suicides from indirect life-threatening behaviors (Saul & Saul, 1988).

Osgood and Brant (1990) define life-threatening behavior as "repetitive acts by individuals directed toward themselves, which results in physical harm or tissue damage and which could bring about a premature end of life" (p. 115). This covert form of suicide can include refusal to eat or drink, rejection of medications, propensity toward serious accidents, self-mutilation, and swallowing foreign substances or objects. Their study of suicidal behavior in long-term care facilities points to (a) a fairly high incidence of suicidal behavior among adults who are institutionalized, (b) some frequency of cases of suicide through life-threatening behavior, and (c) often unreported overt and covert suicides.

Saul and Saul (1988) conducted an extensive search for statistical information pertaining to the incidence of suicide in long-term care facilities. Their research revealed "a striking lack of information" (p. 239) and, furthermore, that long-term care facilities are often reluctant to report possible suicides or attempts at suicide. Those authors proposed that the facility may feel vulnerable to punitive repercussions when a suicide is reported because:

— family members often feel guilty when placing a relative in an institution and may, through projection, blame the institution for inadequately caring for the loved one.
— because of lack of public funding, long-term care systems have many inadequacies and social guilt may be directed toward the institution.
— the institution may actually be responsible for the death because the staff neglected the resident physically, psychologically, or emotionally.

Issues Related to Suicide Behavior in Adults Who Are Older

Separation and Loss   As people grow older, they often face an incessant series of significant losses (Leszcz, 1990). These major privations can include (Achté, 1988; Saul & Saul, 1988):

— mandatory retirement and loss of professional and social status.
— reduced sources of income.
— diminished influence among friends and within the community.
— impaired physical and mental capabilities (particularly, loss of hearing or eyesight; loss of speech or ability to walk) (Osgood & Brant, 1990).
— loss of home and separation from family, friends, and other emotional environment.
— gradual deterioration of the body and subsequent changes in physical appearance.
— loss of personal freedom and the opportunity to control one's life.

With each loss, the older individual must strive to regroup, endeavor to adjust, and attempt to adapt to the change to achieve psychological equilibrium (Achté, 1988; Leszcz, 1990). The pervasive series of deprivations, especially restrictions on freedom and sense of control, can lead to a severely damaged or altered sense of identity, a drastic loss of self-esteem, and feelings of emptiness, worthlessness, and depression (Achté, 1988; Leszcz, 1990).

Depression Epidemiological evidence indicates that the incidence of depression does not increase with age, but depression is common among people who are older because of the major life changes in this population (Achté, 1988; Leszcz, 1990). A projected 12% to 18% of older people have a clinically significant depression, and many professionals believe the incidence of major depression is underestimated and misdiagnosed in the elderly. Older adults who are depressed are seriously at risk for suicidal behaviors. A correct diagnosis of depression and referral to treatment is extremely important because even minor depressive episodes and periods of bereavement can be life-threatening to older people (Achté, 1988; Kermis, 1986).

Groups for Adults Who Are Older

Older adults benefit greatly from peer experiences. Even though reports in professional literature neglect the prevalence and positive effects of group work with this population (Capuzzi & Gross, 1980; Goldfarb, 1972; Zimpfer, 1987), the homogeneous group format has evolved as the principal model for counseling older adults (Kaplan & Sadock, 1972; Zimpfer, 1987).

Groups constitute an excellent means to provide services for older people. Group counseling is, of course, less expensive than individual counseling, but, more important, the special qualities of group work seem to precisely suit the requirements of older adults. Older people often suffer from loneliness, and they have fewer opportunities for social interactions. Groups furnish that social contact and offer the friendships that can thwart loneliness and rejection and, thus, help repair injuries to self-esteem.

Moreover, groups can circumvent isolation by presenting the opportunity for participants to share beliefs, information, and feelings, and to receive feedback from others in similar circumstances. Groups can decrease depression in older populations by promoting mental and physical activity. Groups allow the grieving process to happen in a supportive environment, and they facilitate a structured atmosphere in which members can learn problem-solving and coping skills. Being exposed to positive modeling and practicing new skills can help older people adapt to life's changes (Leszcz, 1990; Saul & Saul, 1988; Zimpfer, 1987).

Groups for Depression Leszcz (1990) advocates an eclectic approach, incorporating psychodynamic, developmental, and cognitive-behavioral models of group, for treating depression in older populations. The main goal of this integrated model of group is to restore a sense of mastery, competence, and purposefulness in each group member, and ultimately repair the damaged sense of self. The simultaneous homogenization of these strategies generates a more powerful approach to counseling. Laszcz maintains that certain behavioral modifications are necessary for optimal treatment of older people who are depressed. When these models are synthesized, the cognitive-behavioral interventions that promote the acquisition of specific skills advance the desired goal of psychological mastery, strengthen the psychodynamic and developmental approaches, and facilitate regeneration of the injured sense of self.

1. *Psychodynamic concerns.* Proponents of the psychodynamic approach postulate that the sense of self is strongly influenced by each individual's unique abilities, capacities, achievements, interpersonal relationships, and resources. Losses that can be associated with aging (e.g., loss of personal capability, relationships, functions, and roles) "may result in an impoverished sense of self with feelings of depletion, worthlessness, depression and helplessness" (Leszcz, 1990, p. 381). A group atmosphere that promotes belonging, cohesion, disclosure, support, and grieving can facilitate the restoration of lost self-esteem.

2. *Developmental concerns.* People who are older undergo a natural "life review" process, during which they explore, organize and evaluate life events, and reach a personal resolution regarding the positive and negative aspects of their past behaviors (Robert Butler, in Bledsoe & Lutz-Ponder, 1986). A structured group approach aimed at this reminiscent process (a) promotes a cohort effect among participants, (b) allows them to share significant events, (c) facilitates the resolution of interpersonal conflicts, and (d) renews feelings of self-worth through the verbalization of past achievements and personal successes (Bledsoe & Lutz-Ponder, 1986). Furthermore, reminiscing about former accomplishments can reduce apprehension and insecurities about hermetic future occurrences (Leszcz, 1990).

Reminiscence therapy groups facilitated by a nondirectional leader have a tendency to evolve into an arena in which participants become fixated on the past, and group members may generate and reinforce feelings of guilt about irreversible transgressions. Leaders can halt this harmful occurrence by consistently guiding the reminiscent process back to the here-and-now experience of the group (Leszcz, 1990).

3. *Cognitive-behavioral concerns.* Cognitive-behavioral group approaches adapt behavioral and cognitive strategies to the group setting. The major goal of this approach is to identify, challenge, and change dysfunctional attitudes and irrational beliefs that promote feelings of depression. Insight is considered to be a preliminary contingency for the working-through process, but it is not a sufficient condition for constructive change. The maladaptive cognitions that constitute the core of an individual's disturbance are usually so well practiced, reinforced, and deeply ingrained into the behavioral system that simple awareness of the situation will rarely be enough to elicit a significant modification of behavior (Leszcz, 1990).

As group members gain insight into their feelings and behaviors, their irrational beliefs can be transformed when they engage in repeated, energetic, and multimodal efforts to refute those beliefs. The group leader should (a) provocatively question and challenge the validity of the participants' depressogenic behaviors and cognitions, (b) assist members in formulating more adaptive beliefs, and (c) encourage participants to develop self-generated rational thinking processes (Grieger & Boyd, 1980).

AGE-SPECIFIC VARIATIONS FOR CHILDREN AND ADOLESCENTS

During the past decade, while the projected life spans of most Americans were increasing, the life expectancy rates for adolescents and children were decreasing (Kalafat, 1990; Vidal, 1989). Accidents are typically listed as the primary reason for adolescent and childhood deaths, but many professionals believe suicide is now the leading cause of death in younger populations (Allberg & Chu, 1990). It is estimated that, in the United States, a child attempts suicide every 90 seconds and an adolescent dies from the act of suicide every 90 minutes (Capuzzi & Gross, 1989).

Data imply that adolescent attempts at suicide are increasing, and the age of childhood attempters grows progressively younger each year. National surveys of schools reveal that 10% to 15% of student body members have attempted suicide. This is an extremely disturbing statistic because the probability of a completed suicide is profoundly magnified among adolescents who have attempted suicide (Kalafat, 1990). The puzzling and frightening phenomenon of cluster suicide, in which the suicide of one teenager triggers "copy-cat" behaviors in other teenagers, further jeopardizes the adolescent population (Garfinkel et al., 1988).

The reports on childhood and adolescent suicide behavior have shocked and disheartened adults. "No matter how often the topic is reported or discussed, it always arouses dismay, disbelief and confusion, because it defies comprehension why some adolescents choose to end their lives, and when it happens, why it creates such a ripple effect on other teenagers" (Allberg & Chu, 1990, p. 342).

Public concern has stimulated extensive investigations into suicidality in children and adolescents. This research has produced various possible explanations related to the increases of adolescent suicide but has not identified specific conditions, situations, or stressors that cause suicidality in younger populations (Kalafat, 1990). Research has established, however, that certain variables (e.g., depression, dysfunctional family environment, separation and loss, environmental pressures, peer problems, low self-esteem, family history of suicide), when presented in a cluster of symptoms, are significantly correlated with adolescent suicide. An examination of the relationship among these factors will augment the understanding of adolescent suicide and facilitate the development of effective prevention and intervention programs.

Issues Related to Suicidal Behavior in Children and Adolescents

Childhood suicidal behavior usually evolves through a three-phase process. In the first stage the child encounters a stressful situation (e.g., marital conflict, illness or death in family, feelings of abandonment or rejection). During the second stage the sensations of distress intensify, and the child develops feelings of helplessness and hopelessness. In the final, crisis stage, the child perceives a profound threat to his or her well-being and becomes highly vulnerable to self-destructive behavior (Stiles & Kottman, 1990).

Most children and adolescents who show suicidal tendencies are reacting to some type of loss (Henry, 1987; Stiles & Kottman, 1990). One of the most common precipitating events for childhood suicidal behavior is the loss of a significant other through divorce, death, or chronic illness. In a vulnerable child or adolescent, even the loss of a pet can become a precursor to suicidal behavior (Capuzzi & Golden, 1988; Henry, 1987). These losses can lead to a diminished self-esteem, feelings of hopelessness and helplessness, and depression (Stiles & Kottman, 1990).

Children and adolescents who have demonstrated suicidal behavior typically share the symptom of depression (Allberg & Chu, 1990). Very young children can be depressed, and children as young as age 5 have been diagnosed as having an affective disorder (Stefanowski-Harding, 1990). Diagnosing childhood and adolescent depression is extremely important because younger people who are depressed make more frequent and lethal attempts at suicide (McWhirter & Kigin, 1988). Complications in assessment can arise, however, because depression is often expressed differently in young people (Allberg & Chu, 1990; Alexander, 1988; Stefanowski-Harding, 1990). Depressed children and adolescents often do not exhibit the obvious symptoms of depression (e.g., sadness, apathy, withdrawal) and may manifest this disorder through destructive or unrealistic play or attention-getting or acting out behaviors.

Other behavioral disturbances that can mask childhood depression include: (a) anorexia nervosa, (b) learning disabilities, (c) psychosomatic illnesses, (d) antisocial behavior, (e) school failure, and (f) alcohol and drug abuse (Allberg & Chu, 1990; Capuzzi & Gross, 1989; McWhirter & Kigin, 1988; Stefanowski-Harding, 1990; Stiles & Kottman, 1990). Most teenage suicide attempters habitually use chemical substances, and many professionals believe this destructive behavior is an attempt to self-medicate themselves against the debilitating effects of severe depression (Allberg & Chu, 1990).

Depression is directly correlated with deficiencies in strategies for coping with life situations. Many children are not nourished by a stable and functional family atmosphere that provides support and encouragement, and in which significant others model positive communication and effective coping and problem-solving skills. When parents in dysfunctional families do not demonstrate adequate or successful ways to deal with distressful events, their children may perceive their own situation as hopeless and fail to develop the necessary skills of survival (Allberg & Chu, 1990). In addition, children and adolescents who have not been exposed to self-sustaining skills may become overwhelmed by the stressful circumstances of maturation and development and may perceive suicide as a way to escape distress (Capuzzi & Gross, 1989).

Groups for Children and Adolescents

Children and adolescents benefit from most of the same advantageous conditions that are generated by adult groups (Clouser, 1986; Robertson & Mathews, 1989), and the group model, with some modifications, is effective in the prevention, intervention, and postvention of suicidal behavior in children and adolescents (Robertson & Mathews, 1989). Children express much of themselves through play, and groups that include variations of play activities are extremely productive for children who may have difficulty expressing themselves verbally. Activities involving art, storytelling, poetry, and drama have been successfully combined with a behavioral format to (a) teach children appropriate ways to deal with destructive thoughts, (b) promote social, problem-solving and coping skills, and (c) elevate self-esteem through reinforcement and reward systems (Clouser, 1986; Stiles & Kottman, 1990).

Developmental Counseling Groups

Groups can help reduce self-destructive behavior in children and adolescents. Fairchild (1986) promotes the use of school-based prevention-oriented developmental counseling groups to facilitate (a) self-awareness, (b) interaction with the environment, and (c) assimilation of positive and efficacious methods of coping with internal and external pressures. A major goal of these groups is to enable students to develop self-responsible behaviors, identify personal resources, and develop strategies for coping with potential life crises. Students are invited to join these groups and select the topics they wish to discuss. The group format is generally a function of the maturity of group members. Older adolescent groups are given more responsibility for the content and process of the group, and leaders usually need to provide more structure for younger groups of children.

Groups for Children and Adolescents Dealing with Divorce-Related Issues   Goldman (1986) and others have designed a school-based group intervention program for children and adolescents who have feelings of anxiety, anger, loss, and rejection that are frequently associated with the crisis of divorce. These time-limited (they meet once a week for 50–75 minutes over a 6–12 week period) activity groups collaborate with administration, faculty, and parents, and have a significant and positive impact on creating constructive changes for children and their family systems. The goals of these groups are to (a) provide a safe environment where children can develop skills that will enable them to adjust to family changes, (b) diminish feelings of isolation and shame, and (c) emphasize supportive aspects of the school environment. Students are referred to these groups by counselors, teachers, administration and other school personnel, and an effort is made to keep groups as age-homogeneous as possible. The group model is also offered to students with long standing school-related difficulties and no recent family change, but Goldman states that participants who have had a recent (within 2 years) family transition benefited more from the short-term group intervention format.

At the onset of the group, children are given a journal and encouraged to write about their concerns and feelings. This creates a sense of continuity between sessions. To introduce the concept that each child is a unique individual, participants are given a photograph of themselves to place on the cover of the journal. Photographs also are incorporated into the group's termination process, and during the group's farewell party members are given a picture of the entire group.

Activities that involve art, play, and drama facilitate discussion about divorce-related issues and encourage group members to work through conflicted emotions (e.g., guilt, rage, despair, feelings of abandonment). Goldman (1986) provides an example of the group structure and the types of interventions used at each session.

First session: Drawing of good and bad changes. The concept of change is introduced and discussed. Then participants are asked to draw a picture of a good change, and one of a bad change and present these picture to the group.

Second session: Feeling charades. The group members are each given a card with a feeling written on it (e.g., happy, sad, angry, jealous) and encouraged to act out this feeling until other group members guess it.

Third session: Family change drawing. Various issues surrounding family change are introduced to the group, and children are asked to draw pictures that depict a good change and a bad change within their families over the past year.

Fourth session: Family wish drawings. Participants are asked to draw and share a picture that discloses something they wish would change in their families over the next year.

Fifth session: KKID radio broadcast. A mock radio broadcast (question-and-answer format) facilitates discussion of the children's concerns about issues related to separation and divorce.

Sixth and seventh sessions: Visitation skits. The group is separated into subgroups each of which is asked to write and develop two skits apiece that pertain to good and bad custodial visitations. After the skits are presented, the group leaders help children think of changes that might produce a more pleasant visitation situation, and ways the children might facilitate those changes.

Eighth session: True-false game. The group leaders present prepared true-false statements to group members to (a) assess what participants have learned about divorce and (b) address unresolved issues.

Ninth session: Coping skills diplomas. During the last group meeting, children are given a diploma that has a coping skill written on it. An example of a coping skill could be "When your parents are fighting, you can visit a friend, ride your bike, read a book, or go outside and play ball."

Individual evaluations are conducted a month after the group has ended, to evaluate participants' subjective response to the group, discuss specific school and family problems in more depth, and offer further assistance to the child and his or her family. An additional follow-up interview is suggested to take place 9 or 10 months after the group intervention, to reassess the child's risk and, if necessary, make referrals to appropriate treatment programs.

SUMMARY

Suicide is the ninth leading cause of death in the United States and the populations most at risk for suicidal behavior are children, adolescents, and adults, age 65 and older. The act of killing oneself is rarely precipitated by a single factor, and the phenomenon of suicide is considered to be a process. Suicidal behavior is the result of a culmination of the interaction among various psychological, behavioral, environmental, social, and situational factors.

Depression is identified as the major predictor of suicidal behavior and the emotional and behavioral features of depression (e.g., feelings of low self-esteem, helplessness, hopelessness, and despair; external locus of control; dependency; inadequate coping and problem-solving skills; poor communication skills; and withdrawal) increase the probability of negative experiences (e.g., rejection, reduced social support network) and reduce the ability to generate workable solutions to problems and adopt effective ways to cope with life events.

The group counseling approach is recommended as a treatment modality for people who are depressed and/or suicidal. It is further suggested that a short-term, homogeneous, open group format better suits the special needs of people who have suicide-related issues. The benefits of a group approach are many and include (a) reduction of feelings of loneliness, isolation, and hopelessness, (b) satisfaction of the need to belong, to be accepted, to give and receive love, and to be socially integrated, (c) opportunity to disclose concerns and receive feedback, and (d) provision of a safe arena where members can learn and practice new effective ways to communicate, problem solve, cope, and adapt to life situations.

It is suggested that group leaders co-facilitate special suicide groups, and leaders should be thoroughly trained in (a) psychological assessment, (b) the basic theories of group counseling, (c) the fundamental principles of group dynamics, (d) the processes and procedures of group work, and (e) the application of these maxims to therapeutic work with persons who are suicidal or depressed.

The primary goal of short-term, intervention-oriented group counseling is the confrontation and prevention of suicidal ideation and destructive behaviors in group members. Subsequent goals include (a) reduction of stress, (b) encouragement of self-disclosure, (c) encouragement of self-responsibility and self-management, (d) enhancement of self-concept, (e) consideration of future goals, and (f) development of external support systems.

Adults, age 65 and older, comprise the population group with the greatest risk for suicide completion. Groups are an excellent and practical method of providing mental health services for adults who are older. This population is often isolated and lonely, and groups provide peer experiences, social contact, and opportunities to receive feedback, and share beliefs, information and feelings. In addition, groups (a) restore a lost sense of mastery and competence, (b) help repair injuries to self-esteem, (c) decrease depression, (d) allow the grieving process to occur in a supportive environment, and (e) facilitate adaptation to life's changes through the acquisition of problem-solving and coping skills.

Many professionals believe that suicide is now the leading cause of death in younger populations. Moreover, the current trend for childhood and adolescent suicide is an increased number of attempters and more attempts by younger children. The fact that the probability of a completed suicide is significantly increased among adolescent attempters compounds the seriousness of this problem. Children and adolescents benefit from most of the same advantages offered by adult groups, and the group model, with some modifications, is an effective method of providing mental health services for younger populations. Groups that incorporate play activities, such as art, storytelling, and drama are appropriate for children, and when combined with a behavioral format (a) teach children effective ways to deal with destructive thoughts, (b) promote productive social, problem-solving and coping skills, (c) facilitate discovery of self, and (d) elevate self-esteem.

The increasing rate of suicide is creating another population that is at extreme risk for suicidal behavior, the survivors of suicide. Suicide attempts and completions may adversely affect the lives of over 12 million Americans annually. Postvention groups allow the grieving survivors to express their emotions, receive support from people who share a similar experience, work toward the resolution of the bereavement process, and achieve positive growth.

REFERENCES

Achté, K. (1988). Suicidal tendencies in the elderly. *Suicide and Life-Threatening Behavior, 18*(1), 55–63.

Alexander, K. (1988, March 28–April 1). *Communicating with potential adolescent suicide through art and poetry*. Paper presented at 66th Annual Convention of Council for Exceptional Children, Washington, DC. (ERIC Document Reproduction Service No. ED 300 984)

Allberg, W., & Chu, L. (1990). Understanding adolescent suicide: Correlates in a developmental perspective. *School Counselor, 37*(5), 343–350.

Asarnow, J., Carlson, G., & Guthrie, D. (1987). Coping strategies, self-perceptions, and perceived family environments in depressed and suicidal children. *Journal of Consulting & Clinical Psychology, 55*(3), 361–366.

Asimos, C. (1979). Dynamic problem-solving in a group for suicidal persons. *International Journal of Group Psychotherapy, 29*(1), 109–114.

Bledsoe, N., & Lutz-Ponder, P. (1986). Group counseling with nursing home residents. *Journal for Specialists in Group Work, 11*(1), 37–41.

Bogdaniak, R., & Coronado, M. (1987). *Suicide prevention in special populations.* Paper presented at 20th Annual Meeting of the American Association of Suicidology and International Association for Suicide Prevention, San Francisco, CA. (ERIC Document Reproduction Service No. ED 291 026)

Capuzzi, D., & Golden, L. (1988). Adolescent suicide: An introduction to issues and interventions. In D. Capuzzi & L. Golden (Eds.), *Preventing adolescent suicide* (pp. 3–28). Muncie, IN: Accelerated Development.

Capuzzi, D., & Gross, D. (1989). "I don't want to live": Suicidal behavior. In D. Capuzzi & D. Gross (Eds.), *Youth at Risk: A resource for counselors, teachers and parents* (pp. 271–304). Alexandria, VA: American Association for Counseling and Development.

Carter, B., & Brooks, A. (1990). Suicide postvention: Crisis or opportunity. *School Counselor, 37,* 378–389.

Clements, C., Sider, R., & Perlmutter, R. (1983). Suicide: Bad act or good intervention. *Suicide and Life-threatening Behavior, 13*(1), 28–41.

Clouser, W. (1986). Abused and neglected children. In T. Fairchild (Ed.), *Crisis intervention strategies for school-based helpers* (pp. 158–197). Springfield, IL: Charles C Thomas.

Comstock, B., & McDermott, M. (1975). Group therapy for patients who attempt suicide. *International Journal of Group Psychotherapy, 25*(1), 44–49.

Constantino, R. (1989, April). *Nursing postvention for suicide survivors.* Paper presented at 22nd Annual Association of Suicidology, San Diego, CA. (ERIC Document Reproduction Service No. ED 312 548)

Curran, D. (1987). *Adolescent suicidal behavior.* New York: Hemisphere.

Dinkmeyer, D. (1975). Adlerian group psychotherapy. *International Journal of Group Psychotherapy, 25*(2), 219–226.

Fairchild, T. (1986). Suicide intervention. In T. Fairchild (Ed.), *Crisis intervention strategies for school-based helpers* (pp. 321–369). Springfield, IL: Charles C Thomas.

Frey, D., Motto, J., & Ritholz, M. (1983). Group therapy for persons at risk for suicide: An evaluation using the intensive design. *Psychotherapy, Theory, Research & Practice, 20*(3), 281–293.

Garfinkel, B., Crosby, E., Herbert, M., Matus, A., Pfiefer, J., & Sheras, P. (1988). *Responding to adolescent suicide.* Bloomington, IN: Phi Delta Kappa Educational Foundation. (ERIC Document Reproduction Service No. ED 301 813)

Gilliland, B., & James, R. (1988). *Crisis intervention strategies.* Pacific Grove, CA: Brooks/Cole.

Goldfarb, A. (1972). Group therapy with the old and aged. In H. Kaplan & B. Sadock (Eds.), *Group treatment of mental illness* (pp. 113–131). New York: E. P. Dutton.

Goldman, R. (1986). Separation and divorce. In T. Fairchild (Ed.), *Crisis intervention strategies for school-based helpers* (pp. 22–69). Springfield, IL: Charles C Thomas.

Grieger, R., & Boyd, J. (1980). *Rational-emotive therapy: A skill- based approach.* New York: Van Nostrand Reinhold.

Gutstein, S., & Rudd, M. D. (1988). *Adolescents and suicide. Restoring the kin network.* Austin, TX: University of Texas Hogg Foundation for Mental Health. (ERIC Document Reproduction Service No. ED 298 409)

Hatton, C., Valente, S., & Rink, A. (1977a). Assessment of suicidal risk. In C. Hatton, S. Valente, & A. Rink (Eds.), *Suicide: Assessment and Intervention* (pp. 39–61). New York: Appleton-Century-Crofts.

Hatton, C., Valente, S., & Rink, A. (1977b). Theoretical framework. In C. Hatton, S. Valente, & A. Rink (Eds.), *Suicide: Assessment and intervention* (pp. 20–38). New York: Appleton-Century-Crofts.

Henry, C. (1987, November). *Adolescent suicide and families. A review of the literature with applications.* Paper presented at 49th Annual Conference of National Council on Family Relations, Atlanta. (ERIC Document Reproduction Service No. ED 292 015)

Hipple, J. (1982). Group treatment of suicidal clients. *Journal for Specialists in Group Work, 7*(4), 245–250.

Kalafat, J. (1990). Adolescent suicide and the implications for school response programs. *School Counselor, 37*(5), 359–369.

Kaplan, H., & Sadock, B. (1972). Introduction. In H. Kaplan & B. Sadock (Eds.), *Group treatment of mental illness* (pp. ix–xii). New York: E. P. Dutton.

Kermis, M. (1986). The epidemiology of mental disorder in the elderly: A response to the Senate/AARP report. *Gerontologist, 26*(5), 482–487.

Klein, R. (1985). Some principles of short-term group therapy. *International Journal of Group Psychotherapy, 35*(3), 309–330.

Lawrence, M., & Ureda, J. (1990). Student recognition of and response to suicidal peers. *Suicide and Life-Threatening Behavior, 20*(2), 164–176.

Leszcz, M. (1990). Towards an integrated model of group psychotherapy with the elderly. *International Journal of Group Psychotherapy, 40*(4), 379–399.

McWhirter, J., & Kigin, T. (1988). Depression. In D. Capuzzi & L. Golden (Eds.), *Preventing adolescent suicide* (pp. 149–186). Muncie, IN: Accelerated Development.

Morgan, L. (1981). The counselor's role in suicide prevention. *Personnel & Guidance Journal, 59*, 284–289.

Motto, J. (1979). Starting a therapy group in a suicide prevention and crisis center. *Suicide and Life-threatening Behavior, 9*(1), 47–56.

Osgood, N., & Brant, B. (1990). Suicidal behavior in long-term care facilities. *Suicide and Life-Threatening Behavior, 20*(2), 113–122.

Patsiokas, A., & Clum, G. (1985). Effects of psychotherapeutic strategies in the treatment of suicide attempters. *Psychotherapy, 22*(2), 281–290.

Poey, K. (1985). Guidelines for the practice of brief, dynamic group therapy. *International Journal of Group Psychotherapy, 35*(3), 331–354.

Robertson, D., & Mathews, B. (1989). Preventing adolescent suicide with group counseling. *Journal for Specialists in Group Work, 14*(1), 34–39.

Saul, S. R., & Saul, S. (1988). Old people talk about suicide: A discussion about suicide in a long-term care facility for frail and elderly people. *Omega, 19*(3), 237–251.

Shelaman, E. (1981). Postvention: The care of the bereaved. *Suicide and Life-Threatening Behavior, 11*, 349–359.

Stefanowski-Harding, S. (1990). Suicide and the school counselor. *School Counselor, 37*(5), 328–336.

Stiles, K., & Kottman, T. (1990). Mutual storytelling: An intervention for depressed and suicidal children. *School Counselor, 37*(5), 337–342.

Valente, S., Saunders, J., & Street, R. (1988). Adolescent bereavement following suicide: An examination of relevant literature. *Journal of Counseling and Development, 67*(3), 174–181.

Vidal, J. (1989). *Student suicide: A guide for intervention.* Washington, DC.: National Education Association. (ERIC Document Reproduction Service No. ED 311 334)

Wrobleski, A. (1984). The suicide survivors grief group. *Omega, 15*(2), 173–185.

Zimpfer, D. (1987). Groups for the aging: Do they work? *Journal for Specialists in Group Work, 12*, 85–93.

14

Group Counseling: Loss

Ann Vernon

Although we typically equate loss with death, loss is a prevalent theme throughout our lives, a theme intricately tied to change and growth. According to Judith Viorst (1986), "We lose not only through death, but also by leaving and being left, by changing and letting go and moving on" (p. 15). She notes that losses include separations and departures from loved ones, as well as loss of dreams, expectations, power, and freedom. Thus, whether the loss is a person, a job, an ability, or one's health, looks, or status, these losses are inevitable. Despite the pain, losses are necessary because "we grow by losing and leaving and letting go" (p. 16).

Loss involves adjusting to new patterns, relationships, roles, and events (Margolis et al., 1985). The impact of a loss depends on whether it is temporary or permanent, the nature of the loss and how it occurred, social and historical variables, and the psychological makeup of the individual involved. Notwithstanding these variables, each loss encompasses a period of immediate grief, a transition and adjustment period, and a new beginning (Worden, 1982; Margolis et al., 1985).

Although grieving a loss is a natural and necessary process, support and specific intervention can help resolve the pain of loss. Given the decline of family and religious institutions, counselors can play a significant role in helping clients deal with loss. One of the most effective approaches is group work (Norberry, 1986; Cebollero, Cruise, & Stollak, 1987; Murphy & Perry, 1988; Sanders, 1989; Yalom & Vinogradov, 1988).

The topics of this chapter include the mourning process, feelings associated with loss, support needs, coping skills, strategies for group work, and age-specific variables related to loss.

THE MOURNING PROCESS

The impact of a loss relates to the degree of attachment one feels about the object or situation that is lost (Bowlby, 1980). Attachment implies the need for security and safety, and when this is threatened, as in a loss, grief-like behavior ensues. Bowlby's theory provides a perspective for assessing the degree of mourning associated with a loss: The greater the attachment or dependency (for safety or security), the greater is the sense of loss.

Engel (1980–81) notes that mourning is an adaptation to loss, and it involves four basic tasks: accepting the reality of the loss, experiencing the pain of grief, adjusting to a new "environment," and withdrawing and reinvesting emotional energy.

Accepting the Reality of the Loss

Whether the loss involves a person, self-esteem through rejection, ability to function, or relocation, the first task of mourning is to accept the reality of the loss. This is often difficult to do, and denial is common: denying the facts of the loss, denying the meaning of the loss by making it seem less significant than it really was, or denying that the loss is irreversible (Worden, 1982). Working through this denial is essential before a person can experience the pain of grief.

Experiencing the Pain of Grief

Although not everyone has the same intensity of pain or feels it in the same way, no one can lose someone or something without some pain. Unfortunately, society is often uncomfortable with grieving and may subtly send the message that "you don't need to grieve" (Worden, 1982, p. 13). This may lead to denial of the need to grieve, manifested by repressing feelings or thinking only pleasant thoughts about the loss as a way to protect oneself from the discomfort.

Bowlby (1980) notes that grieving is necessary. He says, "Sooner or later, some of those who avoid all conscious grieving break down—usually with some form of depression" (p. 158).

Adjusting to a New "Environment"

Depending on the degree of attachment to the person or object of loss, adjusting to a new environment means different things and may be a multifaceted process. In the case of death, loss of a partner may mean loss of a companion, a sexual partner, a financial provider, or a housekeeper, depending on the roles this person played. With a terminal illness, critical adjustments have to be made to effects of new medications, limited physical stamina, probable loss of employment at some point, and reactions of family and friends.

When people are unable to adapt to a loss, they may promote their own helplessness, withdraw, or be unable to develop coping skills for the new environment. These non-adaptions make the outcome of mourning more difficult. As Bowlby (1980) notes, "On how he achieves this [third task] turns the outcome of mourning—either progress toward a recognition of his changed circumstances, a revision of his representation models, and a redefinition of his goals in life, or else a state of suspended growth in which he is held prisoner by a dilemma he cannot solve" (p. 139).

Withdrawing and Reinvesting Emotional Energy

This task involves withdrawing from the person or object of loss and moving on to another relationship or situation. For many people, particularly after loss from death or divorce, this difficult process is often associated with the fear of reinvesting emotions in another relationship and risking another loss (Worden, 1982). With other types of loss as well, a person has to successfully work through the withdrawal stage to live fully in the here and now.

Mourning can be a long-term process. Worden (1982) contends that it is impossible to set a date by which mourning should be accomplished. The acute grieving is over only when the tasks of mourning are completed and a person is able to go on with life.

FEELINGS ASSOCIATED WITH LOSS

Depending on the nature of the loss, a sense of unreality and numbness generally help the person temporarily disregard the loss (Worden, 1982). But accepting the loss is important, and the person must be encouraged to talk about it and to identify and express feelings commonly associated with most types of loss: anger, guilt, sadness, anxiety, helplessness, frustration, and depression (Stern, 1985; Worden, 1982).

Anger

Feeling angry over a loss is normal, but people have trouble admitting this anger because they feel ashamed (Worden, 1982). In the case of death of a mate, survivors may be angry particularly because they are left with many responsibilities, limited finances, and necessary painful changes. At the same time, they may feel guilty because they know their mate suffered and did not want to die. In these instances, the anger may be turned inward and experienced as depression. Stern (1985) notes the importance of talking through the guilt and acknowledging the anger so it can be set aside.

With other types of loss, the anger may be more clearly directed toward the person or situation causing the anger: at the ex-mate in the case of divorce, at the employer in the case of job termination or loss of job status; or at the doctor who cannot find the cure for a terminal illness (Sanders, 1989).

Sometimes identifying the anger or determining the target may be more difficult, as in life transitions. In these situations, the anger may be displaced to other people who look younger or have more physical stamina, or it may be turned inward, resulting in depression at one's personal loss (Sanders, 1989).

Guilt

Guilt plays a major role in most types of loss: "If only I had done this, had not done that, had tried harder, had tried more things. . . ." (Stern, 1985, p. 60). Helplessness often accompanies guilt and leaves people feeling they are not in control of the situation.

Guilt arises from many sources. A lot of guilt is irrational, and counselors should help people reality-test their "if only" statements (Worden, 1982). People may need to see all they did and to reconcile the fact that they cannot change the situation.

Sadness

Some degree of sadness goes along with all types of loss. It may be accompanied by tears and an awareness of how much is missed. The sadness is generally in direct proportion to the amount of attachment felt and the meaning attributed to the person or situation (Stern, 1985; Worden, 1982).

Counseling professionals can support people with losses by encouraging them to express their feelings, legitimizing and normalizing these feelings, and helping them understand the meaning of the loss. Counselors also can convey the expectation that even though the situation is difficult, the person will be able to tolerate it and at some future time will have less pain and more pleasure (Rando, 1986).

Anxiety and Helplessness

After a loss, anxiety often develops, stemming from fear of the unknown and the inability to see how one will manage without support of a partner or the security of a familiar situation or way of being (Worden, 1982). Anxiety is part of the vulnerability and uncertainty associated with loss (Rando, 1982).

Anxiety is to be expected, and individuals may have to be helped to identify the uncertainties and sources of anxiety, as well as to recognize ways they managed situations prior to the loss and how, with some adjustment, they can do so again. In the case of death or disability, survivors also become increasingly anxious about their own death or disability and must be able to articulate these fears.

Frustration

According to Sanders (1989), frustration results "when the bereaved is deprived of the things that heretofore have been expected, needed, and cherished, and when there is no hope of retrieving these resources. . ." (p. 66). Accompanying the frustration is a sense of disappointment and emptiness that things will not be the same again. Regardless of the type of loss, individuals will be frustrated as they attempt to adjust to new situations. Although some degree of frustration is natural, counselors have to help individuals deal with the *demand* that things shouldn't be frustrating or require adaptation.

Depression

Depression is another necessary process of a loss in facilitating the expression of grief (Rando, 1986). Often, depression is connected to what is lost from the past, what one misses in the present, and what anticipated future losses may be. Many symptoms accompany depression, such as sleep difficulties, weight loss or gain, social withdrawal, apathy, feelings of despair, and feelings of being overwhelmed and out of control (Rando, 1986). To help individuals work through depression, they should be encouraged to express feelings, and to identify and mourn the actual loss and the symbolic losses such as opportunities, meaning, beliefs, hopes, and expectations (Rando, 1986).

Even though loss involves a great deal of pain, Viorst (1986) maintains, "Throughout our life we grow by giving up. We give up some of our deepest attachments to others. We give up certain cherished parts of ourselves. . . . Passionate investment leaves us vulnerable to loss" (p. 16). Looking at loss as it relates to growth and change can facilitate the healing process.

LOSS SUPPORT GROUPS

Lipinski (1980) posits that any type of loss disrupts familiar patterns and relationships. The series of losses we encounter throughout our lives has consequences for our self-esteem, general sense of well-being, and emotional integrity. Whether the change is dreaded or welcomed, accidental or planned, people need to adapt to the loss. This often results in anxiety or ambivalence.

Many of these needs resulting from a loss can be addressed effectively within a group setting. Support groups allow people to share common problems and provide mutual aid, thus helping people develop new social support systems (Norberry, 1986; Yalom & Vinogradov, 1988). Norberry notes that groups provide emotional and educational support, characteristics that have a direct relationship to problem solving. In addition to receiving encouragement and relief, learning about resources, and mastering burdens, group members benefit from the opportunity to help others gain strength.

Zimpfer (1989) identified five purposes for loss groups. These are: support, sharing of feelings, developing coping skills, gathering information and education, and considering existential issues.

Support

Perhaps the most important function groups provide is the support that comes from meeting with others who share a similar experience. Depending on the type of loss, people frequently feel a sense of isolation and are often reluctant to divulge this feeling with their usual support system. The mourner may feel a need to protect others from the pain, or mourners think others won't understand because they haven't had the same experience. Meeting with people who have had a similar experience can create a certain bonding as group members share reactions they all readily understand. Members' support comes through encouragement and helping others mobilize their inner resources to gain strength to heal and to continue life. In the group setting, members feel safe to bring up issues without avoidance, disapproval, or patronization.

Sharing Feelings

Many negative feelings appear after a loss: anger, confusion, shame, guilt, helplessness, anxiety, and depression. Within the group setting, negative feelings can be ventilated, enabling members to develop more stability and make clearer decisions (Zimpfer, 1989).

Group leaders need to help members understand how normal their feelings are. This is extremely important because many people believe they shouldn't feel the way they do or that they shouldn't express feelings—they should "be strong" for others. As Zimpfer (1989) notes, these "shoulds" often result in increased stress and more negative side effects.

Developing Coping Skills

The coping skills needed to survive a loss vary greatly depending on the loss. In most cases, however, adjustment relates to finances, social and family relationships, independence and dependence, employment, disfiguration or physical stamina, and day to day living issues.

Because the coping skills needed are so varied, some group member probably will have dealt successfully with at least one of the problems and can share experiences and offer suggestions. As the group member raising the concern hears that others have managed, this restores a certain sense of control and instills a more positive outlook.

Information and Education

Again, depending on the type of loss, group members may need to be educated about issues connected with the loss: how to arrange for a funeral, how to cope with side effects of treatment, how to manage routine tasks if in a wheelchair, or where to look for a new job. Many times new role behaviors must be learned. Duhatschek-Krause (1989) notes the significant role that group members play in providing knowledge and assurance in all of these areas, making adjustment easier after people know how to proceed and what to expect. The group leader or resource personnel also may be good sources of information because they can be objective and draw from experiences in previous leadership roles (Zimpfer, 1989).

Existential Considerations

Whether the loss involves death, dismemberment, serious illness, or change in status, loss often leads to the realization that the present is very temporary. People begin to see that ultimately they have responsibility for their lives and happiness (Zimpfer, 1989). This realization brings several results: recognizing the importance of living each day to the fullest, clarifying what is important and meaningful in life, and learning the importance of not having things left unsaid (Yalom & Vinogradov, 1988).

A group leader can facilitate discussion about the nature of loss, the *meaning* of the loss, and how it affects one's future. Dealing with these existential issues can help members grapple with the present loss and with its future impact. Understanding these issues can lead to positive growth and change.

CONSIDERATIONS IN CONDUCTING GROUPS

Members of all loss groups share the common experience of some sort of loss for which they are seeking emotional relief and a supportive atmosphere where they can discuss problems. Because group members are often at different points in grieving the loss, modeling is important as participants share feelings and describe how they are coping with the particular loss. In all loss groups, leadership and membership issues must be addressed.

Leadership

Leadership can be facilitative or instructional. In groups that are basically *informational*, the leader tends to be more instructional. He or she will have expertise or experience in the specific area of loss and can dispense appropriate information as well as structure discussion or activities around predetermined topics (Zimpfer, 1989).

In *facilitative* leadership, the goal is to encourage people to share feelings and skills that enable them to cope more effectively with the loss. The facilitative leader is less likely to provide information. These groups typically do not have as much structure, nor do they have a predetermined agenda. Topics for discussion emerge from the group members, and the leader facilitates the exchange (Zimpfer, 1989).

Because people experiencing loss need information and support, both styles of leadership are often found in groups, with the dual focus of helping participants take control of their lives through problem solving and emotional support. Regardless of style, the leader has to actively set the tone for mutually sharing and exploring feelings. Norberry (1986) stresses the importance of encouraging group members to raise emotional or informational issues that can be addressed by the leader, by members, or by both.

Leaders should *model* respect, acceptance, nonjudgmental attitudes, and encouragement (Norberry, 1986). Group leaders also must work actively to remain open to the members' losses, avoiding the tendency to placate or protect.

Empathy is another essential leadership skill. Corazzini (1980) contends that empathy has two parts: (a) to experience the state of the person mourning the loss, and (b) to communicate awareness of this loss to group members. Conveying empathy encourages further disclosure, exploration, and release of feelings.

The group leader also can encourage mourners to *reminisce*. Reminiscing is vital to the grieving process and can be facilitated through photos, scrapbooks, and other mementos. "Telling the story" helps relieve the pain and provides necessary catharsis.

Group leaders should continue to help members *acknowledge the truth:* This loss did occur. By avoiding this, the grief process will be prolonged and, perhaps, incomplete (Corazzini, 1980).

Membership

Membership in loss groups may be open or closed (Zimpfer, 1989). In a closed group, the same members attend for a series of sessions, which generally results in more cohesiveness. Open groups, on the other hand, tend to continue indefinitely, with members rotating in and out depending on their needs. Open membership may offer more opportunity for modeling and sharing because of the wide range in stages of grief that are seen as new people join and others leave.

Group members may join the group in response to a recommendation by a physician, a pastor, the hospice organization, or a mental health clinic. Others may be self-referred. Yalom and Vinogradov (1988) suggest that the group leader meet with potential members to orient them to the group's purpose and to assess their readiness for participation.

Most experts recommend heterogeneous group membership, and authorities on loss groups say that this may not be much of an issue because of the natural bonding based on the need for support. Participants in loss groups tend to be at different stages of grief, some better able to share then others (Nahmani, Neeman, & Nir, 1989; Norberry, 1986), so sharing may have to be encouraged.

TYPES OF GROUPS

Although the bereavement process involves common feelings and stages, group members get the most benefit from a group that addresses their specific kind of loss. Two of these types of groups are: loss of a mate and loss resulting from the transition to late adult years.

Loss Group: Death of a Mate

Death of a mate is the number one stressor of all losses, according to Holmes and Rathe (1967). Because of the bonds established within a marital relationship, Sanders (1989) maintains it is difficult to clearly understand what is being grieved because the tasks and needs the mate provided could be endless.

Sanders (1989) emphasizes the debilitating effects of the partner's death on the survivor and recommends support and intervention as a means of preventing mortality or clinical depression of the bereaved mate. Sanders notes, "Everyone needs support and social contact to deal with the frightening aspects of grief. Loss leaves the individual feeling small and empty. Social support can begin to help rebuild the person again" (pp. 218–219).

Stroebe and Stroebe (1987) cite three important functions of support groups for widows and widowers: (a) instrumental support—help with the funeral, household tasks, and so on; (b) emotional support—helping the mourners accept the reality of the death; and (c) validational support—helping the mourners know what to expect during the period of grief and reassuring them that what they are experiencing is normal.

Specific Issues   In addition to providing a place for catharsis and for normalizing and dealing with the feelings of anger, guilt, anxiety, helplessness, sadness, and depression, the loss group can address the following specific issues:

1. *Loneliness and aloneness.* After the death of a mate, the mourner loses the daily intimacies of having someone special to share significant events with and the sense of being the most important person in someone else's life. Being single rather than being a couple is also a difficult transition, as is the realization that part of the mourner's "history" died with the mate (Yalom & Vinogradov, 1988).

2. *Sense of deprivation.* According to Sanders (1989), the sense of deprivation following the death of a mate is particularly acute. Widowers and widows may feel deprived financially, socially, sexually, physically, and emotionally, in any combination. Role redefinition becomes a major task that is frequently painful and frustrating. To fill roles the mate had assumed or to learn to do them oneself is often overwhelming. Survivors with children have an even greater sense of deprivation and struggle with their own issues of grief in addition to the children's.

3. *Freedom and growth.* Despite the negative impact of loss, mourners inevitably find an awareness of freedom and the potential for change. Viorst (1986) emphasizes that losses are linked to gains; loss can result in "creative transformations" (p. 326).

Helping group members recognize the strength that comes from facing and surviving a loss and coping effectively with adversity is an important step in recovery. Encouraging participants to look at the potentials of independence and freedom is also essential. Frequently, participants enjoy the freedom of not having to adhere to a schedule, prepare meals, watch certain shows on television, or do things to please a mate (Yalom & Vinogradov, 1988). Along with this sense of freedom comes a sense of choice and greater awareness of "Who am I?" and "What do I enjoy?" (Yalom & Vinogradov, 1988).

4. *Change.* Following the death of a partner, the survivor usually has to learn new behaviors that result in personal change: learning to cook and care for a house and children, handling repairs and financial responsibilities, making decisions alone (Yalom & Vinogradov, 1988). A major lifestyle change, such as relocation or starting a job, also may accompany loss. Even though these changes can be positive, stress and readjustment are to be expected.

5. *New relationships.* Forming a new relationship may signify readiness to put the past aside and move ahead, but this aspect of change is often difficult. Yalom and Vino-

gradov (1988) note that widows and widowers often feel as if they are betraying their marriage or diminishing the love for the deceased mate by entering into a new relationship. Group leaders should point out the fallacy of this type of thinking and encourage participants to accomplish the necessary grieving before forming another relationship.

Leader Techniques   Unless it is a self-help support group, a loss group generally spans 8 to 12 weeks, with each session ranging from 1½ to 2 hours (Marmar, Horowitz, Weiss, Wilner, & Kaltreider, 1988; Yalom & Vinogradov, 1988). Typically a group has eight to twelve members, who may be referred or who join voluntarily. They will probably be in various stages of the grief process. Sessions may be facilitated by either a co-leader team or by one leader.

Yalom and Vinogradov (1988) report that widows and widowers frequently want human contact because of their recent loss, and, therefore, have a high degree of openness from the beginning. This sense of openness frequently results in spontaneous sharing and has implications for the degree of structure imposed on the group.

In a group setting participants should have the opportunity to (Marmar et al., 1988):

— share what bothers them instead of holding it in and trying to "be strong."
— gain insight about what they have experienced by asking questions and listening to others share their similar circumstances.
— receive support for the way they are handling their lives.
— receive advice and help with decision making on issues such as finances, how to carry out responsibilities by the deceased partner formerly had, how to deal with friends, children, and relatives, and how to manage and settle an estate.

The following is a sample outline for an 8-week group session on the loss of a mate. This outline is only one of several group approaches that could be used to deal with loss.

Session 1. Group members introduce themselves, and the leader facilitates a discussion on the group's purpose, soliciting participants' hopes and expectations and stressing confidentiality. The leader points out that this is a safe atmosphere for sharing painful issues and that part of the focus will be on helping members move ahead despite the pain.

During this session members are invited to describe their situation involving loss of their mate. Because participants are usually eager to share their story with others who have gone through a similar experience, the leader usually does not have to introduce any more structure during this initial session. The sharing of experiences will most likely evoke a good deal of emotion, so the group leader will want to carefully monitor the process and intervene if a member becomes too emotional, checking to see if he or she needs to stop talking or needs other support.

Session 2. The concept of loneliness and aloneness can be introduced to continue the grieving and expression of feelings from the first session. Depending on the group's degree of openness, the leader may ask participants at the end of the first session to bring in scrapbooks or photos to stimulate discussion during the second session. Whether the discussion is more open-ended or is introduced by sharing photos, the focus may be on memories, what participants miss most (and least) about the deceased mate, and what being a single person in a couple-oriented society is like. The group leader encourages expression of feelings and helps members recognize the commonality of experiences.

Session 3. Depending on what issues arise during the second session, the leader may determine whether further exploration of loneliness and aloneness is necessary, or if the theme of deprivations should be introduced during this session. If the group is cohesive and the sharing is spontaneous and open, a simple invitation may be sufficient to start participants talking about ways in which they feel deprived. If this is not the case, a structured activity like the following could be introduced:

Give each member an index card and ask him or her to write the word "deprivation" across the top. Next, briefly discuss the concept of deprivation and brainstorm as a group the different kinds of deprivation that widows and widowers might experience. Following this, the leader invites group members to identify two types of deprivation, to briefly identify when they experienced these, and how they feel about them. Depending on the group's cohesiveness, participants can begin either by sharing some of the ideas on their card with their neighbor or by making this activity a total group sharing process. Debriefing should focus on the feelings and how participants have dealt with these deprivation experiences.

Session 4. The first three sessions were directed more at the past, offering an opportunity to share common feelings, concerns, and experiences as an important stage in the grief process. Likewise, looking to the future and entering the healing and renewal phase are important. As a transition, the topic of freedom and growth can be introduced.

Generally, by this session little structure is needed because participants have bonded and may even have contacted each other outside of the group (Lieberman & Videka-Sherman, 1986). If they are still hesitant, the leader might introduce the following activity:

On a large sheet of newsprint, write, "What I can do or am learning to do now that I didn't or couldn't do before." Then invite group members to do some brainstorming on this topic, sharing examples of different types of freedoms they are experiencing or things they are learning to do that contribute to their growth. In debriefing this activity, help participants see that growth comes through pain and that, despite the loss, this may be an opportunity to become a more fully developed person.

Session 5. The fifth session also focuses on change and growth, but with more emphasis on some of the pragmatics of change. Because a partner assumes so many roles and responsibilities, the survivor may need to learn new behaviors to carry out these functions. By this stage, group cohesiveness will probably allow participants to share information and advice on new roles and responsibilities such as finances, child care, household responsibilities, settling an estate, or disposing of personal effects. The group leader may also supply information on community resources relative to these concerns.

Session 6. As widows and widowers work through the stages of grief, the concept of life changes and new relationships may have to be addressed. If the group is open, the leader may simply invite participants to share reactions, feelings, and experiences about this topic. Or the subject could be introduced through the following activity:

Give each member an index card and ask participants to project into one of three future periods: a month from the present, 6 months from now, and a year from the present. After identifying the time period, participants are to project what their life might be like in relation to: (a) where they might be living, (b) how they might be spending their time, (c) who they might be spending time with, and (d) what kinds of feelings they might have about these changes. Then invite participants to share responses, focusing on feelings concerning change and new relationships. Specific issues might include guilt about getting involved with another person, how to enter the single world, how society views new relationships, how new relationships may be a way of avoiding grief, and anxiety about change in general.

Session 7. This session may allow group participants to continue exploring issues and feelings carried over from the previous one. Because members enter the group at different places in the grieving process, they are also ready to make changes and enter into new relationships at different points. Encouraging discussion about anxieties and concerns may offer group members the opportunity to clarify issues and support each other in these transitions.

During this session the group might wish to discuss the meaning of life in general, because many participants probably had marriages that provided them with a basic sense of purpose. Yalom and Vinogradov (1988) suggest a structured exercise in which participants are asked to think about how they would like to be remembered and to write an obituary and share it with the group.

Session 8. In this last session, members have to deal with what has been left unsaid or unasked, and what regrets they expect to have after the group is over. This process could be loosely structured by inviting members to express an appreciation and a regret statement about what the group has meant to them. An exercise like this evokes powerful feelings and reinforces the idea that support from others is vital. The leader may want to encourage post-termination meetings for periodic support.

Loss from Life's Transitions

Life is a series of transitions: from dependence to independence, from childhood to adulthood, from single to married, from work to retirement, from life to death. Transitions may involve major or minor changes, and they may be anticipated or unexpected (Golan, 1981). Transitions involve "a bridging period, often marked by feelings of anxiety, loss, and upset, which sometimes erupt into states of active disequilibrium" (p. 4). This transition period is followed by a new, more stable, identity. Golan notes that shifts in thinking, feeling, and behaving are involved in this period of reorganization and adaptation.

Bridges (1980) contends, "Every transition begins with an ending. We have to let go of the old thing before we can pick up the new—not just outwardly, but inwardly, where we keep our connections to the people and places that act as definitions of who we are" (p. 11). People often make external changes before recognizing that they haven't dealt with the endings. Not until the endings have been resolved can a person move to the second phase of transition, which Bridges identifies as the "lostness and emptiness" (p. 17), and continue to the third stage, a new beginning.

Golan (1981) identifies three ways to categorize transitions: by time periods, by role shifts, and by marker events. *Time periods* refer to passages from one chronological stage to another. *Role shifts* involve taking on new roles and relinquishing old ones. *Marker events* are those events that initiate the transition. Regardless of the category, the actual impact of the transition relates to whether it was gradual or sudden, permanent or temporary, reversible or irreversible, or voluntary or involuntary. The impact of the transition also depends on how relationships, routines, roles, and assumptions are affected (Scholssberg, 1984).

To successfully deal with the transition, Golan (1981) says people need to accomplish material (instrumental) tasks and psychosocial (affective) tasks. The *material tasks* include:

— recognizing the need to do something about the old situation.
— exploring solutions, looking at options, weighing alternatives.
— making a choice and taking on the new role.
— functioning under the new circumstances.

Psychosocial tasks involve:

— dealing with the loss and the lack of security.
— coping with anxiety, frustration, pressure, ambivalence.
— handling the stress of taking on the new role or adjusting to the new situation.
— adapting to shifts in status or position, which may result in feelings of inferiority, lack of satisfaction, or lack of appreciation from others.
— learning to live with the different reality, which may involve adjusting to new standards and levels of satisfaction.

The transition to late adult years is described here in further detail, with specific suggestions for incorporating this information into a 6-week group sequence, each session lasting 1½–2 hours.

Group work to help people deal with transitions has increased tremendously in the past several years, primarily because members can receive social support, factual information, and emotional interaction to cope more effectively with transition periods that can pose problems (Golan, 1981; Sanders, 1989).

Although the transition to late adult years is one of the normal life cycle changes, this stage differs because it involves continuously adapting to decreased abilities and relinquishing social roles (Eisdorfer & Lawton, 1973). The multiple physical and emotional adjustments of this period present a challenge that individuals respond to in different ways depending on their life experiences and personalities.

According to Golan (1981), ages 60 to 65 are normally considered to be the transition period to late adulthood, but the transition may start before this as individuals realize they have now lived longer than they will live in the future. At this point, people think more about what their life includes and its meaning. The following areas may be of concern:

1. Declining health and limited physical stamina.
2. Adjusting to retirement.
3. Role shifts/identity issues.
4. Changes in living conditions/arrangements.
5. Changes in looks/physical appearance.

Session 1. The group leader begins by welcoming participants and explaining that this group will explore issues surrounding the sense of loss in the transition to late adult years. The leader explains ground rules and confidentiality. Because group members may not be in crisis as with the death of a mate, participants probably will not show as much spontaneous openness and bonding. If that is the case, the leader should instill more structure to facilitate discussion.

After group members introduce themselves, the following activity is suggested:

Give each member a sheet of paper divided into four squares. In the first square, each participant identifies a positive aspect about this transition, followed by a negative aspect in the second square. In the third space, each member describes why he or she chose to participate in the group and what he or she hopes to get out of it, and in the last square, something about himself or herself that others can't tell by looking at the person. After sharing their responses with a partner, have the partners introduce each other to the group by sharing one thing they've learned about the other person related to this transition to late adult years.

Following this sharing, lead a total group discussion about the positive and negative words from squares one and two, to elicit the range of topics that might be brought up in subsequent sessions. Record the responses on newsprint. End the session with a discussion of hopes and expectations for the group.

Session 2. The leader posts the list of positive and negative aspects of this transition generated during the first session. Group members are invited to identify one of the negative issues that poses the greatest problem for them and to discuss this with a partner.

After this discussion, distribute the following questions and have partners analyze their concern in relation to these:

1. Does this area of concern represent an ending?
2. If so, is this ending positive or negative?
3. If this does represent an ending, is it necessary? Is it a choice? Or is it a myth or a tradition (such as not being as sexual during this period of life or having to retire at a certain age)?

Encourage sharing in the total group, and challenge participants to look at what will change, how much control they have over this change, and how endings also signify beginnings.

Session 3. In this session the leader addresses the issue of loss. Because the loss is not always associated with chronological transitions as is death or divorce, the leader challenges participants to think about this idea and begin to identify feelings associated with the loss.

To stimulate discussion, write the following categories on newsprint and invite participants to brainstorm actual or possible losses in each area:

1. Physical health.
2. Relationships.
3. Work.
4. Housing.
5. Roles.
6. Appearance.

After the lists are generated, invite discussion about how members have dealt with the actual losses and what information, resources, and support they need to deal effectively with the possible losses.

Session 4. As a follow-up to the previous session, the leader focuses on feelings associated with loss. By this time, the group likely is cohesive and members openly discuss their feelings. If the leader senses that more structure is needed, he or she can invite members to pick one of the six categories identified in session 3 and write several feelings describing their reaction to the loss, which then can be shared with the total group.

Many of the feelings may be the negative ones typically associated with loss, such as anger, guilt, depression, sadness, frustration, anxiety, and helplessness. On the other hand, some people may feel relief, anticipation, or other positive feelings because this transition involves giving up some responsibilities and simplifying a lifestyle. Hearing both the positive and negative sides helps participants clarify personal feelings and, perhaps, develop a different perspective.

At this point, the leader may introduce a discussion about where feelings come from, drawing from rational-emotive therapy (Dryden & DiGiuseppe, 1990), to show group members that feelings come from thoughts about the event.

Point out that negative feelings associated with the loss and change are the result of thinking that the event is awful, that it shouldn't happen, that it is impossible to accept, or that it somehow implies older adults are not as worthwhile. As a specific example:

Event: Having to retire.
Feeling: Very upset, frustrated.
Thoughts: I won't be able to stand this; I won't have anything to do; life will be boring, and that will be awful.

The degree of intensity of the upsetting and frustrating feelings could be diminished if the person were to think: How do I know I'll be bored? Isn't there anything else I could do now that I'll have free time? Lots of other people seem to like retirement, so isn't it possible that I will also?

Helping group members understand where feelings come from may give them a better sense of control and a different perspective.

Session 5. This session looks at change. To introduce this concept, the leader distributes the following piece for members to read:

To everything there is a season, and a time to every purpose under the heaven;
A time to be born, and a time to die;
A time to plant, and a time to pluck up that which is planted;
A time to kill, and a time to heal;
A time to break down, and a time to build up;
A time to weep, and a time to laugh;
A time to mourn, and a time to dance;
A time to cast away stones, and a time to gather stones together;
A time to embrace, and a time to refrain from embracing;
A time to seek, and a time to lose;
A time to keep, and a time to cast away;
A time to rend, and a time to sew;
A time to keep silence, and a time to speak;
A time to love, and a time to hate;
A time for war, and a time for peace. (*Ecclesiastes*, 3:1–8, in Golan, 1981, p. viii)

After participants have finished reading, give each a sheet of paper with the following phrase across the top: "It's a time in my life to. . . ." Allow several minutes for them to complete the sentence as many times as they can. Invite discussion, highlighting the concept of endings and beginnings.

Session 6. The final session is a continuation of the fifth, emphasizing the ability to take charge of the transition. The leader refers to the instrumental and psychosocial tasks involved in transitions, as identified by Golan (1981). Instrumental tasks involve recognizing the need to do something about the old situation, exploring alternatives and solutions, choosing to function differently, and making the change. The psychosocial tasks entail dealing with the loss, coping with the feelings, handling the stress of change, adapting to change, and learning to live with the different reality.

To facilitate this sharing, divide the group in half. Give one half a sheet listing the instrumental tasks and the other half, the psychosocial tasks. Have each group discuss how these tasks relate to the life changes made or anticipated. Following this discussion, ask each group to summarize the issues and present them to the total group. Finally, invite each participant to identify one task that he or she would like to work on and to discuss with a partner strategies for doing this.

In closing the session, encourage members to relate something they have learned from participating in the group and how this will help them handle the transition.

AGE-SPECIFIC VARIATIONS

Children process information differently than adults. Group leaders must be aware that although children have many of the same feelings that adults do concerning loss, they may not be able to articulate those feelings as effectively. Instead, they may reflect the feelings in misbehavior or in causal reaction (Worden, 1982).

Death

Children under age 2 have little conception of death (Worden, 1982). Between ages 2 and 5, children are likely to see death as reversible and to assume that the loss occurred because of their bad behavior (Bertoia & Allan, 1988). They also may express concern for the physical well-being of the person who has died, because they don't understand the reality of the death (Betz & Poster, 1984). By the time children reach age 5 to 7, they have a better understanding of the finality of death, so they begin to fear death. They try to avoid it or personify it as a monster. A child may assume the dead person can see or hear everything and, as a result, tries to be perfect (Gardner, 1983). The group leader must keep this information in mind in developing age-appropriate group experiences.

In conducting group sessions, the leader should use concrete techniques incorporating fairy tales, role playing, art activities, photographs, bibliotherapy, and puppetry, to deal with the child's fears, anger, sadness, and guilt (Matter & Matter, 1988). Because many children have not had a chance to say goodbye to the deceased, Bertoia and Allan (1988) suggest writing a letter, making a tape, drawing a picture, or using imagery to mentally tell the person things that were left unsaid. Children also may need facts about what happens during a funeral, how the body is prepared for burial, and so forth. Information of this sort can help alleviate fear and anxiety.

Life Transitions

Like adults, children go through many chronological transitions: starting school, entering middle school or high school, becoming an adolescent, and leaving home after graduation. They also experience marker events such as moving, changing schools, parental divorce and remarriage. The usefulness of group work to facilitate these transitions is well documented (Gumaer, 1986; Masterman & Reams, 1988; Rossiter, 1987; Sheridan, Baker, & Lissovoy, 1984).

In setting up a transition group, the leader has to provide adequate structure and use concrete illustrations and activities to help children understand. Preschoolers, for example, need a lot of play activities to help them deal with separation anxiety and to gain control of a transition, such as starting school. Older students may benefit from bibliotherapy, journaling, role playing, or structured activities and games geared to the specific transition issues.

Group sessions can facilitate the grief process. When designing loss groups for children, developmental issues should be considered along with the feelings, adjustments, and meaning of the specific loss.

SUMMARY

Life entails a series of losses, which Viorst (1986) describes as necessary, with "subsequent gains" (p. 366). Although loss is inevitable, it is accompanied by grief, and people need varying amounts of support. The usefulness of groups to assist in adjustment and grieving is well documented, and groups can play a vital role in helping people of all ages effectively deal with loss (Murphy & Perry, 1988; Nahmani, Neeman, & Nir, 1989; Norberry, 1986; Yalom & Vinogradov, 1988; Zimpfer, 1989).

The mourning or grief process relates to the degree of attachment to the object or situation lost; the greater the attachment or dependency, the greater the sense of loss. Mourning involves accepting the reality of the loss, experiencing the pain of grief, adjusting to a new environment, and withdrawing and reinvesting emotional energy. Feelings associated with loss include anger, guilt, sadness, anxiety and helplessness, frustration, and depression.

Many of the needs resulting from a loss can be addressed within a group setting, which allows people to share common problems, provide mutual aid, and develop coping skills. The leader can play an important informational and educational role, as well as facilitating the discussion and helpful activities. The leader should model respect, acceptance, nonjudgmental attitudes, and encouragement, and be empathetic. The leader also encourages group members to reminisce and to acknowledge the truth of the loss.

Death of a mate is the number one stressor of all losses because of the bonds established in a marital relationship. The survivor faces loneliness, a sense of deprivation, the possibility of freedom and growth, change, and new relationships. Another type of loss group deals with life transitions marked by time periods, role shifts, and marker events that initiate the transition. People in these groups have to accomplish material, or instrumental, tasks and psychosocial, or affective, tasks. The transition to late adult years is one of the most difficult because it involves adapting to diminished abilities and relinquishing social roles.

Children experience loss somewhat differently according to their developmental stage. Therefore, counseling professionals have to recognize children's conceptions of loss and their manifestations. Techniques incorporate games, role playing, puppetry, and other means to help the child deal with fears surrounding losses, probably most strongly felt by death or divorce or separation.

REFERENCES

Bertoia, J., & Allan, J. (1988). School management of the bereaved child. *Elementary School Guidance & Counseling, 23*(1), 30–39.

Betz, C. L., & Poster, E. C. (1988). Children's concepts of death: Implications for pediatric practice. In J. Bertoia & J. Allan, School management of the bereaved child. *Elementary School Guidance & Counseling, 23*(1), 31.

Bowlby, J. (1980). *Attachment and loss: Loss, sadness and depression* (Vol. 3). New York: Basic Books.

Bridges, W. (1980). *Transitions*. Reading, MA: Addison-Wesley.

Cebollero, A. M., Cruise, K., & Stollak, G. (1987). The long-term effects of divorce: Mothers and children in concurrent support groups. *Journal of Divorce, 10*(1–2), 219–228.

Corazzini, J. G. (1980). The theory and practice of loss therapy. In B. M. Schoenberg (Ed.), *Bereavement counseling* (pp. 71–86). Westport, CT: Greenwood Press.

Duhatschek-Krause, A. L. (1989). A support group for patients and families facing life-threatening illness: Finding a solution to non-being. *Social Work with Groups, 12*(1), 55–69.

Dryden, W., & DiGiuseppe, R. (1990). *A primer on rational-emotive therapy*. Champaign, IL: Research Press.

Eisdorfer, C., & Lawton, M. P. (Eds.). (1973). *The psychology of adult development and aging*. Washington, DC: American Psychological Association.

Engel, G. L. (1980–81). A group dynamic approach to teaching and learning about grief. *Omega, 11*, 45–59.

Gardner, R. A. (1983). Children's reactions to parental death. In J. E. Schowalter, P. R. Patterson, M. Tallmer, A. H. Kutscher, S. V. Gallo, & D. Peretz (Eds.), *The child and death* (pp. 104–123). New York: Columbia University Press.

Golan, N. (1981). *Passing through transitions: A guide for practitioners*. New York: Free Press.

Gumaer, J. (1986). Working in groups with middle graders. *Elementary School Guidance & Counseling, 33*(3), 230–238.

Holmes, T. H., & Rahe, R. H. (1967). Social readjustment rating scale. *Journal of Psychosomatic Research, 11,* 213–218.

Lieberman, M. A., & Videka-Sherman, L. (1986). The impact of self-help groups on the mental health of widows and widowers. *Journal of Orthopsychiatry, 56*(3), 435–449.

Lipinski, B. G. (1980). Separation anxiety and object loss. In B. M. Schoenberg (Ed.), *Bereavement counseling* (pp. 3–36). Westport, CT: Greenwood Press.

Margolis, O. S., Raether, H. C., Kutscher, A. H., Klagsbrun, S. C., Marcus, E., Pine, V. R. & Cherico, D. J. (1985). *Loss, grief and bereavement.* New York: Praeger.

Marmar, C. R., Horowitz, M. J., Weiss, Wilner, N. R., & Kaltreider, N. B. (1988). A controlled trial of brief psychotherapy and mutual-help group treatment of conjugal bereavement. *American Journal of Psychiatry, 145*(2), 203–208.

Masterman, S. H., & Reams, R. (1988). Support groups for bereaved preschool and school-age children. *American Journal of Orthopsychiatry, 58*(4), 562–570.

Matter, D. E., & Matter, R. M. (1982). Helping young children cope with the stress of relocation: Action steps for the counselor. *Elementary School Guidance & Counseling, 23*(1), 23–29.

Murphy, P., & Perry, K. (1988). Hidden grievers. *Death Studies, 12,* 451–462.

Nahmani, N., Neeman, E., & Nir, C. (1989). Parental bereavement: The motivation to participate in support groups and its consequences. *Social Work with Groups, 12*(2), 89-98.

Norberry, L. P. (1986). Divorce over 50: A program of support. *Journal for Specialists in Group Work, 11*(3), 157–162.

Rando, T. A. (1986). *Loss and anticipatory grief.* Lexington, MA: Lexington Books.

Rossiter, A. (1988). A model for group intervention with preschool children experiencing separation and divorce. *Journal of Orthopsychiatry, 58*(3), 387–396.

Sanders, C. M. (1989). *Grief: The mourning after.* New York: John Wiley.

Scholssberg, N. K. (1984). *Counseling adults in transition.* New York: Springer.

Sheridan, J. T., Baker, S. B., & Lissovoy, V. (1984). Structured group counseling and explicit bibliotherapy as in-school strategies for preventing problems in youth of changing families. *Elementary School Guidance & Counseling, 32*(2), 134–141.

Stern, E. M. (1985). *Psychotherapy and the grieving patient.* New York: Haworth Press.

Stroebe, W., & Stroebe, M. S. (1987). *Bereavement and health.* New York: Cambridge University Press.

Viorst, J. (1986). *Necessary losses.* New York: Simon & Schuster.

Worden, J. W. (1982). *Grief counseling and grief therapy: A handbook for the mental health practitioner.* New York: Springer.

Yalom, I. D., & Vinogradov, S. (1988). Bereavement groups: Techniques and themes. *International Journal of Group Psychotherapy, 38*(4), 419–446.

Zimpfer, D. G. (1989). Groups for persons who have cancer. *Journal for Specialists in Group Work, 14*(2), 98–104.

PART THREE

Professional and Ethical Issues in Group Counseling

As noted by the authors of Chapter 15: Group Counseling: Cross-Cultural Considerations, until 25 or 30 years ago, the counseling and human development profession showed little interest or concern for racial, ethnic, and other minority groups. Counseling in a variety of settings usually concentrated on the needs of the "average" person. Minority people, by virtue of their skin color, physical characteristics, and socioeconomic status, were simply seen as disadvantaged in a world designed for White, middle-class people.

Chapter 15 begins by defining terms including "acculturation" and "cultural sensitivity" and then stimulates group leaders to examine their own cultural awareness by recognizing culturally biased assumptions. Perspectives of the Afro-American, Hispanic, Asian/Pacific Islander, and American Indian groups are discussed to enhance the sensitivity and respect with which group leaders can approach culturally diverse groups. When the leader and group members come from different cultural backgrounds, barriers to communication are likely to develop, causing misunderstandings that interfere with rapport and with the effectiveness of counseling.

To address potential areas of misunderstanding, the authors cover acculturation, language, cultural identity, generational factors, cultural custom styles, geographical location and neighborhoods, family constituency, psychohistorical and religious traditions, and individuality. The chapter concludes with subsections on leader awareness and group composition as related to groups with members whose culture and experience differ from those of the group leader.

Another issue facing group leaders is: why study ethical and professional issues? The answer to this question forms the basis for the final chapter. Chapter 16: Group Counseling: Ethics and Professional Issues, begins with information about the purposes of ethical guidelines, ethical guidelines for group leaders, and case study applications. The authors evaluate ethical decision making using the moral principles inherent in ethical guidelines and existing ethical decision-making models as points of departure. Because group leaders have to be aware of professional issues that may have potential legal or ethical overtones, the topics of privileged communication, confidentiality, administrative faculty and staff support, permission to participate, knowledge of the topic, multicultural issues, and purpose are all carefully presented in the context of group work.

15

Group Counseling: Cross-Cultural Considerations

Betty J. Newlon and Miguel Arciniega

*T*he United States contains more ethnically diverse and regional subcultures than any nation in history. The many physically identifiable minority groups, and others not so apparent, make the United States a complex, heterogeneous society. This complexity has not heightened the ability to tolerate, much less understand, cultural differences. Society continues to see the nation as a melting pot, which has devalued cultural diversity. The move to homogenize society and encourage common norms has blinded us to ways that capitalize and encourage the development of the culturally diverse groups (Pedersen, 1988).

The most readily identifiable minority groups in the United States are Asian Americans, Americans of African descent, Hispanic Americans, and American Indians. These groups have all witnessed exclusionist legislation and discriminatory practices. Ethnic groups that have come from other countries or were here before "colonization" of the United States have been thrust, voluntarily or by force, into a dominant majority culture that routinely has subordinated non-White people.

Each minority group has a unique cultural heritage making it distinct from other groups. Cultural distinction, however, has often been interpreted erroneously as evidence of cultural conformity, which has tended to result in a monolithic view of minority group attitudes and behaviors. Clearly, uniformity of attitudes and behaviors is no more true for minority individuals than for members of the dominant culture. Not only do intragroup differences exist, but attitudes and behaviors within individuals also can fluctuate greatly as their identification with one culture or another changes.

Until the mid 1960s the counseling profession showed little interest or concern for the status of racial, ethnic, and other minority groups. Counseling was directed toward the needs of "average" people. Minority clients, by virtue of their skin color, physical characteristics, and socioeconomic status, were seen as disadvantaged in a world designed for White, middle-class people.

In both overt and covert ways equal access to counseling and psychological care has been denied. Until recently, training of counselors and psychologists has not weighed the special needs of unique cultural and ethnic groups. Even now, few training programs include institutionalized multicultural approaches (Casas, Ponterotto, & Guiterrez, 1986). Schools and mental health agencies have not been sufficiently prepared to be culturally responsive to the large and increasing ethnic populations (Padilla, 1980). Hence, many of the diverse cultural groups are being underserved because of lack of training, understanding, and awareness.

Considering the demographic realities and the rapid growth of minority groups, counselors cannot operate without cultural information and awareness. They have to understand the culture of those they are serving, including their history, beliefs, values, and behaviors. Counselors need to develop an awareness not only of the cultural factors and their effect on the counselee but also the effects of the counselee's interaction with the dominant culture. Rather than demanding that a person adapt to the counselor's culture, the counselor has to learn to adjust to and work within the culture of those he or she serves. This adjustment means that group leaders who come from the dominant culture must recognize that their own values have been shaped by a particular cultural environment, and that this environment is significantly different from the cultural environment of group members.

Cultural considerations have to be integrated into a systematic process as a basis for effective group leadership with members from minority cultures. The process of cultural integration involves (Arciniega & Newlon, 1981):

— confronting and challenging personal stereotypes held about cultural groups.
— acquiring knowledge and appreciation of the group's culture and, more important, the heterogeneous response of the group.
— understanding the effects of institutional racism and stereotypes on minority people.
— understanding the traditional, institutional interaction of the dominant society with minorities, and vice versa.
— acquiring firsthand experience with minority groups.
— challenging normative traditional counselor approaches and understanding their cultural implications for minority groups.
— utilizing a culturally pluralistic model in its counseling approach.

Unless group leaders follow a process incorporating the above factors, they will not be effective with minority groups.

This integrative process is not easy, as it requires, beyond a cultural knowledge base, a shift in thinking—a cultural paradigm shift toward broader thinking. The influences of institutional mindsets conditioned over a lifetime by mainstream institutions have made a major impact on counselors' thinking, at conscious and unconscious levels alike. This mindset has shaped the frame of reference—the historically evolved mainstream paradigms, the maps of how counselors perceive other groups. These paradigms are the source of attitudes, values, beliefs, and behaviors that are difficult to modify and change.

If counseling professionals are to act with integrity and commitment to a changing profession, they must begin to take specific steps to shift the existing cultural paradigm. This will take careful study and examination of a body of knowledge at both cognitive and experiential levels. We propose, in this chapter, to introduce a body of knowledge and a process by which to begin the shift to integrate cognitive understanding with experiential application. This knowledge and process has particular impact in the area of group counseling. Because of the potential for cultural diversity in groups, this format represents an excellent vehicle for group leaders and members to come to a greater understanding of cultural differences.

DEFINITIONS

Acculturation: the degree to which minority individuals incorporate, add, or synthesize the dominant culture's values, customs, language, beliefs and ideology with their own.

Cultural sensitivity: the ability to integrate ethnic and racial paradigms other than one's own in a way that conveys understanding.

Culture: the values, beliefs, and practices shared by groups identified by variables such as ethnicity and gender.

Ethnic group: a body of people who think of themselves as alike by virtue of their common ancestry, real or fictitious, and who are regarded so by others.

Ethnicity: a group classification in which members share a unique social and cultural heritage that includes similarities of religion, history, and common ancestry.

Minority: an ethnic group receiving differential and unequal treatment because of collective discrimination.

Multicultural counseling: a situation in which two or more people with different ways of perceiving their social environment are brought together in a helping relationship (Pedersen, 1988).

Race: a pseudobiological system of classifying people by a shared genetic history or physical characteristics such as skin color (Pedersen, 1988).

DEVELOPING CULTURAL AWARENESS

Developing cultural awareness is a process that addresses stages, characteristics, assumptions, and biases. The group leader who is interested in developing cultural awareness proceeds from (a) more awareness of a person's culturally learned opinions, attitudes, and assumptions to (b) more knowledge and relevant facts and information about the culture in question, and finally to (c) better skills for making integrative changes and taking appropriate measures (Lopez et al., 1989).

Culturally aware group leaders begin by assessing their own values, beliefs, and personal strengths and weaknesses. Awareness means the ability to accurately judge a cultural situation from one's own as well as the other's cultural viewpoint and to be able to describe a situation in a culture so that a member of that culture will verify the counselor's perception. Cultural awareness has the following characteristics (Pedersen, 1988):

1. Ability to recognize direct and indirect communication styles.
2. Sensitivity to nonverbal cues.
3. Awareness recognition of cultural and linguistic differences.
4. Interest in the culture.
5. Sensitivity to the myths and stereotypes of the culture.

6. Concern for the welfare of people from another culture.
7. Ability to articulate elements of one's own culture.
8. Appreciation of the importance of multicultural teaching.
9. Awareness recognition of the relationships between cultural groups.
10. Accurate criteria for objectively viewing functional and dysfunctional factors in the other culture.

For the group leader to be able to accurately reflect or paraphrase a situation, these factors must have a basis in knowledge and awareness. In addition, the group leader needs specific knowledge about diverse historical experiences, adjustment styles, role of education, socioeconomic backgrounds, preferred values, typical attitudes, honored behaviors, inherited customs, slang, learning styles, and ways of thinking (Pedersen, 1988).

Basic assumptions determine how people see the world, and each person sees the world more or less differently. Knowledge of one's basic assumptions, values, and beliefs is the first step in clarifying one's perceptual paradigm. People tend to see evidence that supports the assumptions more clearly than evidence that challenges those assumptions. Awareness of nonverbal communications, such as gesture, posture, tone of voice, and timing, are often perceived differently by other groups whose perceptual paradigm is different (Pedersen, 1988).

Recognizing Western cultural biases in our conventional thinking has little to do with geography and a great deal to do with social, economic, and political perceptions. The consequences of these unexamined assumptions are institutionalized racism, ageism, and sexism.

Culturally Biased Assumptions

Some of the unexamined institutional assumptions that group leaders should critically evaluate are (Pedersen, 1988):

1. There is a single measure of "normal" behavior.
2. The individual is the basic component of society.
3. Problems are defined by mainstream society.
4. Everyone will understand our abstractions.
5. Independence is desirable and interdependence is undesirable.
6. Individuals are helped more by formal counseling than by natural support systems.
7. All people depend on linear thinking to understand the world around them, where each cause has an effect.
8. Group leaders need to change individuals to fit the system and not the system to fit the individual.
9. History is not relevant for a proper understanding of contemporary events.
10. We already know all of our assumptions, and they are correct.

Group leaders need to challenge not only the assumptions and the content of what they are thinking but also the way and process by which they handle that content. Perhaps the biggest struggle for group leaders who attempt to consider cultural factors is to know when to apply specific norms for a particular group member and when to apply universal norms. This conflict has been identified as the etic-emic conflict: *Etic* refers to universal norms, and *emic* to group-specific norms (Draguns, 1981). Group leaders sometimes err on the side of assuming that certain behaviors have the same meaning for all people, when in fact the meaning of these behaviors is quite different for certain cultural group members.

Group leaders must vigorously assess both their own view and the group members' views in regard to supposed culturally normative behavior. The process of developing cultural awareness involves balancing different norms and constantly testing alternative hypotheses with the group.

CULTURAL GROUPS

This chapter does not attempt to provide a comprehensive analysis of all minority groups. Rather, it presents a brief overview of information and cultural considerations of four minority groups: Afro-American, Hispanic, Asian/Pacific Islander, and American Indian. An annotated bibliography of additional cross-cultural readings is given at the end of this chapter.

Afro-American Culture

To understand the Afro-American experience before initiating intervention approaches, group leaders have to know the history of this group. It includes knowledge of historical figures; omissions and bias of books; the social, political, and economic climate; development of the militant movement of the 1960s and 1970s; and evolution of demographic data of the Afro-American population.

Group leaders must recognize that (a) no prescriptive approaches can be applied in dealing with Afro-American members, and (b) the myth that the problems of Afro-American members are their own sole responsibility is indeed a myth. Group leaders must incorporate a systemic view, one that views all of the interacting systems in the individual's life to gain a more comprehensive understanding of the Afro-American individual's history with self, family, institutions, and economic and political factors. As with all groups, cultural stereotyping is endemic, and group leaders must exercise caution to separate the culture of poverty from the culture of the group itself.

The following *general* characteristics of Afro-American group members may help group leaders develop a systemic view (Vacc & Wittmer, 1980):

1. Afro-Americans, as contrasted with White people, have differential access to the resources of society.
2. Several forces keep the Afro-American cultural system intact; one is the group of internal factors operating within the Afro-American community to maintain cohesiveness.
3. Older Afro-Americans are treated with respect—often addressed as "uncle" or "aunt."
4. Turning the head and putting the hand over the mouth when laughing, or averting the eyes and perhaps even the face when speaking to elders or other respected persons, are considered marks of respect.

5. The Afro-American mother must prepare her child to take on appropriate gender and age roles as well as the racial role.
6. The African ethos is "survival of the tribe" and "oneness with nature." The cultural values associated with this world view are cooperation, interdependence, and collective responsibility.
7. A strong achievement orientation is a strength of Afro-American families.
8. The church offers a kind of extended family fellowship, providing significant adults to relate to the children, as well as materials and human resources for the family.

Although these characteristics are general, group leaders should understand the progression of ramifications: Afro-American group members may come from situations in which they feel powerless, hostile, and lacking specific direction. The systems and institutions that undergird problems for Afro-American group members are often insensitive and unresponsive to change. Therefore, Afro-American members may want concrete responses from the group leaders much like they would receive from respected family members or friends.

Hispanic Culture

Perhaps the first step in effectively counseling Hispanic individuals from a culturally relevant perspective is to acknowledge the group's tremendous intracultural diversity. The many Hispanic groups have distinct differences as well as similarities. The Spanish language is the most common cultural artifact even though it, too, varies widely in its dialect and linguistic nuances. Other similarities include religious and family values and some traditions. But major historical differences are present among as well as within the various groups.

For example, the history of the Mexican American is tied to the history of the land; some Mexicans were already present in the Southwest whereas others migrated later when the Anglo-Americans arrived in the East. Other Hispanic groups, such as Cubans, immigrated to the United States later, for political or economic reasons. Puerto Ricans' uniqueness comes from their territorial relationship with the United States. Puerto Ricans have retained their cultural ties to preterritorial days.

Many Hispanics have chosen to remain identified with their own ethnic group rather than to be categorized under the aggregate Hispanic/Latino label. To understand the diversity of Hispanics, each group must be examined historically.

When the Spanish explorers came to the North American continent in the early 16th century, they intermarried with the Indians and produced the Mestizo. In Puerto Rico, the Spaniards also intermarried with many of the native peoples. In Cuba, some cultural fusion occurred with imported African slaves, and some Spanish colonists maintained their European lineage. The same phenomenon is true for many of the Central and South American countries. Thus, the population labeled Hispanic is heterogeneous and diverse.

Because of this diversity, common characteristics of Hispanic group members are often difficult to determine. The group leader must be cautious in acknowledging the distinctness of each Hispanic group. Keeping in mind the strong loyalty tied to ethnic identification, many of the Hispanic groups share the following characteristics to various degrees (Ruiz & Padilla, 1977):

1. More than 50% of Hispanics report that Spanish is their native language.
2. The extended family structure is still an important factor in Hispanic group members' backgrounds. They place a high value on the family over the self.
3. The concept of respect is a value, particularly for authority figures.
4. Unwavering love and respect for the mother, who is a unifying force in the family, is a prominent feature.
5. Formalized kinships, such as the compadrazgo "godfather" system, operate to varying degrees.
6. Loyalty to the family takes precedence over loyalty to social institutions. The family fosters a spirit of cooperation, as contrasted with competition with siblings and relatives. Hispanic people learn to share.
7. Sex roles traditionally have been more rigid, but this norm is currently undergoing some change.
8. The concept of "personalismo" for personal contact is a preferred relating style.

In attempting to understand these characteristics, group leaders must recognize how the concept of acculturation affects each member. Rather than assume the above characteristics are static, each member's perceptions must be acknowledged individually and the heterogeneity of the Hispanic population kept in mind. Acculturated Hispanics, second and third generation and so on, will more likely respond to regular group counseling approaches, whereas the traditional immigrants, or first generation, are going to be more hesitant to accept participation in group approaches that rely on individual responsibility and abstract thinking. They will more likely respond to the group leader as an authority figure who will help interpret the system (Newlon & Arciniega, 1983).

Asian/Pacific Islander Culture

The Asian American population in the United States consists mainly of people from China, Japan, Korea, Malaysia, Burma, Cambodia, Indonesia, Thailand, the Philippines, Samoa, and Vietnam. Most are from Japan and China.

Like the Hispanics, the diversity among Asian American groups is vast. Each group has its own cultural norms, values, language, and traditions.

The first Asian American group to immigrate to the United States was the Chinese, in the 1840s. This immigration resulted from the discovery of gold in California, and many Chinese people came with the idea of returning home once they had made their fortune. These Chinese immigrants who came to work as laborers in the gold mines and the railroads were subject to massive acts of discrimination (Sue, 1973).

Japanese immigration began in the late 1800s. These Japanese people filled a demand for cheap agricultural labor and were not initially treated with the same anti-Oriental disrespect that the Chinese were. The Japanese people's success in agriculture, however, antagonized the White citizens, contributing to the threat of "yellow peril." By the beginning of World War II, acts of racism toward Asians had increased and were fanned by the press. This resulted in more than 110,000 Japanese being sent to relocation camps (Daniels, 1971).

The Chinese and Japanese cultures have many similar values and traditions. Scholars have found similar psychological characteristics for these Asian Americans. Following is a synthesized list of some of the psychological characteristics of Japanese and Chinese Americans (Atkinson, Morten, & Sue, 1983):

1. Chinese and Japanese people feel a great sense of obligation toward the family and parents.
2. Family expectations of obedience produce problems when exposed to White values.
3. Asian Americans tend to evaluate ideas on the basis of practical application. Consequently, they are apt to be more intolerant of ambiguities.
4. Asian Americans seem to be more obedient, conservative, conforming, and inhibited than their White counterparts.
5. They tend to exhibit the cultural values of emotional restraint, dependence on family, and formality in interpersonal relations.
6. Asian Americans generally feel more comfortable in structured situations.
7. They are more reluctant to self-disclose than are their White counterparts.
8. Because of their minority status and potential discrimination from White society, Asian Americans may be suspicious of people who are not Asian.
9. Asian Americans seem to have a need to feel guilty and accept personal blame when things go wrong.
10. Asian Americans seem to be less verbal about their feelings with non-Asians.

Cultural differences of Southeast Asians (people from Burma, Cambodia, Indonesia, Laos, Malaysia, Philippines, Singapore, Thailand, and Vietnam) include time orientation, role of the family and its individual members, value system, and social behavior (Fernandez, 1988).

1. *Time orientation.* In their time orientation, Southeast Asians tend to stress the past and the future; they see the present as a transitory period. Although individuals are perceived as in control of their "destiny," lineage and familial background are extremely important in establishing an individual's sense of honor and character (Sue, 1981).
2. *Role of the family and its individual members.* The family is the basic foundation in the lives of most individuals. The continuous affective and social bonds with immediate family members validate individuals' self-esteem and secure their future. Social control is exerted through shame and guilt. Clearly specified roles for family members dictate demands that have to be met to ensure that the family network functions. The father is the head of the family; the mother is the emotionally devoted, nurturant parental figure. Children are socialized into a network in which filial piety and deference to elders are stressed (Shon & Ja, 1982).
3. *Value system.* The primary emphasis in the Asian ethical system is upon social obligation. The family is the fundamental unit of society, and the major emotive support. This society disapproves of individual independence and autonomy. Family needs supersede those of the individual (Sue, 1981; Shon & Ja, 1982).
4. *Social behavior.* Asian cultural emphasis on formality in interpersonal relations versus the much more informal and spontaneous nature of Americans often make Asians uncomfortable when relating to Americans (Sue, 1981).

Southeast Asians are conservative and reticent about their personal problems because of their fear of being looked down upon. Openness, genuineness, and honesty may be construed by Southeast-Asian group members, who value reserved and modest self-disclosure, as an invasion of privacy or as an affront to their dignity (Church, 1982). Asians have an external locus of control because of their perception of being just a part of the larger whole. Expecting individuals to make decisions independent of their families would go against their disposition (Sue & Morishima, 1982).

When Southeast Asians seek group counseling, "they desire a guidance-nurturant oriented intervention." They want the leader to take an active, directive role and give them explicit directions on how to solve problems and bring immediate relief from disabling distress. They are looking for straightforward solutions to concrete and immediate problems that are generating stress in their lives. Asian group members value modesty and are ashamed to admit having any problems. They view group leaders as experts and authorities. They do not initiate conversations and are comfortable with silence. They do not maintain much eye contact because it is considered rude to stare (Fernandez, 1988).

Though this list is limited, it does provide some information regarding Asian Americans. Again, group leaders must exercise caution. All of the characteristics do not apply to all individuals.

American Indians

One of the most neglected areas in the counseling literature has been the American Indian. The literature that does exist has been limited largely to historical or philosophical treatises. This neglect may be attributed to several causes (Newlon & Arciniega, 1983):

1. The monolithic tradition of Western training is prevalent in most counselor training institutions, leaving little room for other world views.
2. Limited information is available about the psychology of the American Indian. More important, there are few Indian counselors and psychologists to assist in interpreting counseling information.
3. The number of tribes, over 200, each with its own language and customs, increases the complexity of developing this counseling area.

Of all the minority groups, leaders often have the most difficulty working with American Indian members, partially because of the strong existing stereotypes, and most Western modes of group counseling are not compatible with the traditional Indian cultures. Further, many American Indians have become bicultural or have acculturated within the dominant society. The process of acculturation is a major counseling factor with all minority groups, and group leaders will encounter American Indian group members on all points of the acculturation continuum (Newlon & Arciniega, 1983).

To gain some understanding of the American Indian group member, the cultural origin must be examined. The following list, compiled from the traditional American Indian cultures, provides some basic guidelines and information potentially helpful to the group leader (Vacc & Wittmer, 1980):

1. The concept of sharing is a major value in family life.
2. Time is secondary to people and is seen more as a natural phenomenon.

3. Nature is part of living and is part of happenings such as death, birth, and accidents.
4. Acceptance of life is a style of being in harmony with the world.
5. Family, including extended family, is of major importance, and the tribe and family to which one belongs provide significant meaning.
6. The basic worth of the individual resides in his or her family and tribe. Individual responsibility is only a part of the total responsibility concept.
7. Harmony and cooperative behavior are valued and encouraged.
8. Tradition is important; it adds to the quality of life in the here and now.
9. Assertive or aggressive behavior is seen as impinging on others' dignity.
10. Respect for elders is valued, and the elders play an important part in family life.

American Indian history is replete with failures of intervention programs. Before considering group counseling with the American Indian, group leaders must develop an understanding of the culture itself, what occurred between Indian cultures and United States society, and, more important, what effect culture, history, economics, and politics have had on the American Indian. Leaders also must be aware of the erroneous institution mindset that has permeated the literature about "Indian problems" rather than the inability to understand a distinct and different view of the nature of the world.

As with all minority groups, a generic understanding of American Indian cultures is essential. Of equal importance is learning about the differences between each member, family, and tribe. Counseling as it is now in the United States has not been successful with traditional Indian cultures. Therefore, group counseling will have to assume a contextual frame of reference compatible with the view of the individual American Indian group member. Only through increased awareness of cultural influences and expanded counselor education can effective group counseling with American Indians become a reality.

Cultural expectations and values that American Indians may reveal in a group counseling situation include the following (Sanders, 1987):

1. American Indians tend to speak softly and slowly.
2. They avoid the speaker or listener.
3. They interject less.
4. American Indians use fewer "encouraging signs" (umm, nod head).
5. They treat auditory messages differently, giving delayed responses.
6. They use nonverbal communication.
7. They are cooperative.
8. They consider group needs more important than individual needs.
9. American Indians consider present goals important; they accept the future as it comes.
10. They value harmony with nature.
11. They try to control selves, not others.
12. American Indians distribute discipline among many; no one person takes the blame.
13. The orientation is to the present time.
14. American Indians encourage sharing, keeping only enough to satisfy present needs.
15. They participate only after observation and when they are certain of their ability to do so.

16. They value privacy and noninterference.
17. They emphasize self-discipline both in body and mind.
18. They value emotional relationships.
19. Physical punishment is rare.
20. They encourage patience and allowing others to go first.

CROSS-CULTURAL FACTORS

Much of the criticism of minority group counseling has been directed at the interactions between the group counselor and the members. Counseling is seen as a process of interpersonal interaction and communication requiring accurate sending and receiving of verbal and nonverbal messages. When the group counselor and the member come from different cultural backgrounds, barriers to communication are likely to develop, leading to misunderstandings that destroy rapport and render counseling ineffective.

Several cultural factors that should be noted in group counseling include acculturation, language, cultural identity, generational issues, cultural custom styles, geographical location and neighborhoods, family constituency, psychohistorical and religious traditions, and individuality. The group leader should take these factors into account when gathering information and should integrate them into the group counseling process (Newlon & Arciniega, 1983).

Acculturation

Acculturation is a multifaceted phenomenon encompassing many dimensions such as values, ideologies, beliefs, and attitudes. In addition, it incorporates language, ethnic identity, cultural customs, practices, and ethnic interaction. This phenomenon is complex and multifaceted. It might be best understood in terms of the extent to which minority individuals uniquely assume, incorporate, add, or synthesize the values, customs, languages, beliefs, and ideology of the dominant culture with their own.

The group leader needs an understanding of this complex issue because it has vast implications in terms of the member's identity, style of communication, and interactional world view. The group member's identity is tied historically to his or her culture of origin. Though some view it as a continuum from traditional culture of origin to a nontraditional dominant culture, it demands far more than a linear explanation.

Many minority group members assume a contextual identity that depends on the social circumstances. Thus, they may manifest behaviors and language from their culture of origin to a totally "Americanized" style and language or to a mixed synthesis. The group leader needs some understanding of contextual identity and where and how it operates with the members. To facilitate groups more effectively, group leaders need to be aware of the nature of acculturation and the manifestations of members' behaviors.

Language

In group counseling with minority members who still use their language of origin, understanding the language is still not enough. Language must be understood for both content and contextual meaning. In addition, the leader must be able to assess the language abilities of the various group members; all members may not have the same degree of fluency in the language of origin or in English. Group leaders must be cognizant of the fact that the language of origin is where much of the affect is first learned. Although members may be fluent in English, the affect of the English words may have a different meaning than they did in the language of origin.

Code switching—mixing and combining words in new and creative expressions that operate from a distinct cultural base—occurs when two languages come in contact. The linguistic style of symbolic meaning and cadence and familial context are factors that need attending.

Cultural Identity

Group leaders must be aware of the self-referent labels that members choose. Self-referent labels are a sensitive issue for many people and may be different even for various members of a family. For example, identifiers for individuals of Mexican or Latin American descent may be Mexican American, Hispanic, Chicano, Americans of Mexican descent, or Latinos. For members of African descent, these may be Afro-American, Negro, Black, or West Indian. For American Indians, identifiers may be Indian, Native American, Red, or even more important tribal names. For Asian Americans, the identifiers may be Asian, Asian American, Oriental, or the specific country of origin.

Generation

Group leaders should consider generational factors (first, second, third generations in this country) to assist in assessing the extent of acculturation that might have taken place. First-generation members may have more ties to the traditional culture, and these ties may be reflected in the nuclear and extended family dynamics. The acculturation process is unique for each minority person. Contrary to some current beliefs, as members become acculturated, they do not drop their former cultural ways but, rather, add new ones and creatively synthesize the new and the old.

Cultural Custom Styles

In addition to the obvious cultural customs of foods, dress, and traditions, several cultural styles of responsibility and communication have to be considered. For example, the Mexican, American Indian, and Asian cultures emphasize the responsibility of the oldest child to younger siblings. Oldest children assume this responsibility as part of tradition. As another example, the Asian family's expectations of unquestioning obedience may produce problems when exposed to American values emphasizing independence and self-reliance in group counseling.

The style of communication in traditional American Indian and Mexican American people stresses patience and personal respect. Group members from traditional families may show respect by looking down and not looking into the eyes of the authority figures. When doing group counseling with members from these groups, the verbal question/answer approach is often ineffective in obtaining behavior cues. This may also be true when using confrontational group counseling approaches. Cultural contextualizing (or cultural interpretation) by a group member who is more bicultural may provide much needed information. Respect is the key to sensitive probing with these groups.

With Afro-American group members, verbal interaction moves at a faster pace, and sensitive confrontation is accepted more readily than with traditional Hispanics, American Indians, and American Asians. Group leaders need to be aware of their own interactional style to determine any contradictory difference in the interaction.

Geographical Location and Neighborhoods

Ethnic groups from different geographical locations have distinct geocultural traditions and customs. Group leaders cannot assume that the same customs apply to seemingly similar cultural groups. An Afro-American family from the South manifests that culture in a different way than an Afro-American family from the West Coast. This concept of geographical differences also applies to Asian American, Hispanic, and American Indian groups. The group leader should also note rural and urban influences in the group member's present situation within the family history.

Neighborhoods where the minority group members reside have a great deal to do with how they see themselves. Minority members living in a totally ethnic area have a different view than members living in an integrated neighborhood or members living in a neighborhood in which theirs is the only minority family.

Family Constituency

In most minority families kinship networks help to satisfy important cultural needs for intimacy, belonging, and interpersonal relations. Extended families, in which more than one generation lives in the same household, with formalized kinship relations, are common among minority groups. The culturally sensitive group leader must be able to comprehend this concept within each culture. In many Hispanic and American Indian families, significant adults may extend to uncles, grandparents, cousins, close friends, and godparents. These adults often play a significant part in child rearing and perhaps should be considered in identifying the significant adult models in the group counseling process.

Family occupies a special place with most minority group members. Love, protection, and loyalty to the family are pronounced, creating an environment in which members can develop strong feelings of self-worth despite the lingering effects of discrimination and racism. In some instances, minority families function as buffers against society's attempt to impose a negative self-image, and effective group leaders have to be aware of this dynamic.

Psychohistorical and Religious Traditions

The history of the ethnic groups' origin and of the ethnic group in the United States is essential information for group leaders. Minority members reflect the psychohistory of the family through child rearing practices. Many facets of child rearing are rooted in the history of minority groups and are distinct from the dominant culture in which the members presently live.

Spiritual and religious practices traditionally have been strong within most minorities. These, too, affect group dynamics. Religion provides the medium through which minority group members deal with forces and powers beyond their control. It also provides a basis for social cohesion and support. Historically, the church has been a resource for personal counseling, and a refuge from a hostile environment. Group leaders must take this factor into account in working with individuals who are more traditionally bound in their religion.

Individuality

Minority groups view the concept of individual responsibility differently than the majority does. American Indians, for instance, judge their worth primarily in terms of whether their behavior serves to better the tribe. Tribal culture places a high value on the harmonious relationship between an individual and all other members of the tribe. The concept of cooperation within certain ethnic groups has been documented (Kagan & Madsen, 1971).

Group leaders must be wary of assuming that individual responsibility is primarily at the expense of cooperation already manifest in these people. Responsibility to the family is a major value found in minorities and should be considered and encouraged. Individual responsibilities are of secondary value, after the family.

COUNSELOR AWARENESS

Why should group leaders attempt to understand minority groups and their cultures? The number and variety of individuals whom group leaders impact, especially in today's world, is staggering. Projected demographics, especially in the Southwest, show a major and significant increase in the minority population. Subsequently, the world of work and all societal institutions, including mental health services, will be greatly affected. Thus, group leaders have a special and unique responsibility to understand the cultural frame of reference of group members and to become more acutely aware of their own views and beliefs.

Currently, most group leaders are White and middle class. In addition to cultural differences, group leaders and members may have class differences in attitudes, behaviors, beliefs, and values. The impact of social class differences on counseling in general acquires added significance when considering that existing group counseling techniques are middle- and upper-class based (Singleton, 1982).

Group leaders frequently impose their own cultural values upon minority members in ignorance. For example, one of the most highly valued strategies for group cohesion entails self-disclosure. Self-disclosure may be contrary to the basic cultural values of some minorities. Chinese American clients who are taught at an early age to restrain from emotional expression feel threatened by direct and subtle demands for self-disclosure. Hispanic and Native American group members have reported similar conflicts.

Stereotyping

Stereotyping is a major problem in all forms of group counseling. It may be defined as rigid preconceptions applied to all members of a group or to an individual over time, regardless of individual variation. Stereotypes are often institutionalized, and group leaders have to be conscious of this process. Most counselor training institutions do not train group counselors from a culturally pluralistic model. Therefore, a process is lacking for confrontation and sensitive awareness of self and institutional stereotypes.

The preconceived notions group leaders have about group members who differ ethnically, racially, and socioeconomically affect their reactions to these members. Leaders may unwittingly act upon these beliefs, approaching members from a monolithic, dominant point of view. In an attempt to avoid stereotyping and treat members as just another human being, leaders may demonstrate "color or culture blindness." This "blindness" shows a lack of respect in acknowledging that their culture is an inherent part of their personhood. The leader may avoid discussing identity, and the content of the group counseling disavows their uniqueness. The content of the counseling may also be restricted by the group leaders' fear that the member will detect conscious or unconscious stereotyping on their part.

Self-Concept

Group counseling inherently deals closely with members' self-concepts. Leaders should be aware that the development of minority members' self-concepts has distinct characteristics not found in the self-concept development of people in the dominant culture. The unique cultural values of minority members are part of their identity and part of their self-concept. These are cognitively and affectively learned through interaction of the family culture and the dominant group environment. Thus, a bicognitive self-concept (concept of self within family and concept of self in relation to the dominant group) may become evident and may be manifested in cultural conflict. Group leaders should be aware of this issue so they can provide a place of acceptance, confirmation, and encouragement to resolve this conflict and enhance healthy minority self-concept development.

Attributes of Effective Counselors

Some studies have shown that the ethnicity of counselors is not always the significant variable in determining the efficacy of their counseling. Counselors who facilitate positive interaction with minority groups (Newlon & Arciniega, 1983):

— personally acknowledge that cultural diversity exists within the United States and that diversity implies difference, not inferiority.
— confront and resolve personal cultural diversity through learning about themselves.
— increase knowledge of cultural variation through study and interpersonal contact.
— examine the historical and present interaction between minorities and the dominant culture.
— expand interactions with people from minority and dominant cultural groups.

Characteristics of culturally sensitive group leaders also include (Sue, et al., 1982):

— the ability to generate a wide variety of verbal and nonverbal responses. The wider the repertoire of responses, the greater the chances are for understanding the presenting problems.
— the ability to send and receive verbal and nonverbal messages appropriately. Some ethnic groups have a high regard for subtlety and indirectness of communication; others prize directness and confrontation. To respond appropriately, the group leader must understand the communication style of an ethnic member.

— the ability to exercise appropriate institutional intervention skills on behalf of the group member. This sensitivity requires a perspective that views many problems and barriers to member success as problems of the institutional system's inability to respond appropriately.

GROUP COMPOSITION

Several areas of consideration have to be addressed in the composition of a group. The group leader needs to consider race and ethnicity, gender, and socioeconomic status when convening a group.

Race and Ethnicity

Race and ethnicity affect not only the assumptions drawn about others but also the comfort levels experienced in interpersonal relationships. Individuals are often most comfortable with people who are racially and ethnically similar and are most likely to be anxious with around individuals who are dissimilar. To reduce this interpersonal dynamic in mixed groups, the leader should make a deliberate and sensitive effort to address this issue.

Gender Considerations

The gender composition of a group seems to influence members' attraction to that group. Males and females prefer different sizes of groups depending on whether they are mixed- or single-gender groups. In general, members of both genders seem to view the other sex more favorably in situations where gender balances are equitable.

Gender affects the dynamics of small groups by influencing the extent to which groups are cooperative or competitive. In general, males are more competitive than females in groups, and males tend to be more competitive in all-male groups than in mixed-gender groups. This is even more apparent in traditional minority groups.

Because women significantly outnumber men as recipients of social and mental health services, group leaders must understand the clear role of social gender roles when they attempt to address women's problems. In group and family situations, gender roles influence members' communication, expectations, and evaluations of one another (Davis & Proctor, 1989).

Socioeconomic Status

Contrary to popular opinion, minority individuals who participate in group counseling may be from varied socioeconomic groups. The question as to whether groups should be heterogeneous or homogeneous with respect to socioeconomic status (SES) is as important as their ethnic and racial makeup. Inherent in this consideration is the need for group leaders to be aware of the differences in the "culture of poverty" and the culture of ethnicity and race. Many professionals advocate against including only one person of a particular SES group in an otherwise homogeneous SES group. The solo status places that single individual in a deviant status that requires him or her to become a representative of his or her income group (Davis & Proctor, 1989).

Research literature suggests that groups composed of individuals of different SES are at great risk for communication problems. Difficulties in communication spring from a lack of common experiential base and a difference in social status. Therefore, balanced group communication might be difficult to achieve in groups consisting of individuals from different status groups (Davis & Proctor, 1989).

SES seems to be more important to group composition when the group's purpose requires that members have some *a priori* understanding of the values and customs of the other members.

SUMMARY

In the most ethnically and culturally diverse nation, four minority groups are illustrated here: Asian Americans, Afro-Americans, Hispanics, and American Indians. In leading groups with members of any cultural group, effective leaders have to be aware of the differences and actively seek to understand them. Leaders have to recognize direct and indirect communication styles, be sensitive to nonverbal cues, recognize cultural linguistic differences, have an interest in the culture, be sensitive to the myths and stereotypes surrounding the culture, appreciate and have concern for the well-being of people from other cultures, recognize the relationships between cultural groups, and apply accurate criteria when viewing function and dysfunction. In doing this, leaders have to search out and face attitudes in themselves that may detract from their effectiveness.

Differences exist not only between cultures but within cultures, related to language, cultural identity, customs, family makeup, geography and neighborhood, psychohistorical and religious traditions, views on individuality, and generational differences and acculturation. In group composition, the leader has to consider race and ethnicity, gender, and socioeconomic status.

Developing cultural sensitivity is an ongoing process that requires a respectful dialogue of mutual education. For this to take place, group leaders need to take the necessary steps to continue this dialogue by sharing their questions, thoughts, and feelings about cultural issues with supervisors, colleagues, and, to some extent, their group members. Willingness to face these issues openly will likely lead to a reduction in the stereotypes, misunderstandings, and prejudices that can adversely affect the quality of group counseling. Genuineness and respect, above all, have to be part of the attitudinal makeup of group leaders. Although this perspective is not different in theory from that for any group, the focus and process with minorities requires a perceptual shift in how this is communicated.

As group counselors cross cultures, they must realize that the theories, techniques, and the profession itself are cultural phenomena reflecting the majority culture's history, beliefs, and values. Without this awareness, in the process of trying to respect and be sensitive to different cultures, we will likely end up destroying differences or being totally ineffective.

The challenge for group leaders who want to be sensitive to cultural pluralism in group counseling settings is to accurately clarify their own values, acquire knowledge of several cultural groups, and learn the systems and helping strategies applicable to or designed for those groups. This task is by no means easy. It takes courage to venture outside one's habitual ways of construing and interpreting events, and time to learn about different cultures, which entails more than reading articles and participating in workshops. Ideally, one should be actively and purposely involved in relationships within other cultures, trying new methods, making mistakes, and correcting errors, to learn what is necessary to be a culturally sensitive helper.

REFERENCES

Arciniega, M., & Newlon, B. (1981). A theoretical rationale for cross-cultural family counseling. *School Counselor, 29*(2), 89–96.

Atkinson, D., Morten, G., & Sue, D. (1983). *Counseling American minorities: A cross-cultural perspective.* Dubuque, IA: Wm C. Brown Publishers.

Casas, J. M., Ponteretto, J. G., & Gutierrez, J. M. (1986). An ethical indictment of counseling research and training: The cross-cultural perspective. *Journal of Counseling & Development, 64,* 347–349.

Church, A. T. (1982). Sojourner adjustment. *Psychological Bulletin, 91,* 540–572.

Daniels, R. (1971). *Concentration camps, USA.* New York: Harper & Row.

Davis, L. E., & Proctor, E. K. (1989). *Race, gender, and class: Guidelines for practice with individuals, families, and groups.* Englewood Cliffs, NJ: Prentice Hall.

Draguns, J. G. (1981). Counseling across cultures: Common themes and distinct approaches. In P. Pedersen et al., (Eds.), *Counseling across cultures* (rev., pp. 3–21). Honolulu: East-West Center.

Fernandez, M. S. (1988). Issues in counseling Southeast-Asian students. *Journal of Multicultural Counseling and Development, 16*(4), pp. 157–166.

Kagan, S., & Madsen, M. (1971). Cooperation and competition of Mexican, Mexican American, and Anglo American children of two ages under four instructional sets. *Developmental Psychology, 5,* 32.

Lopez, S., Grover, K., Holland, D., Johnson, M., Kain, C., Kanel, K., Mellins, C., & Rhyne, M. (1989). Development of culturally sensitive psychotherapists. *Professional Psychology: Research and Practice, 20*(6), 369–376.

Newlon, B., & Arciniega, M. (1983). Counseling minority families: An Adlerian perspective. *Counseling & Human Development, 16*(4), pp. 1–12.

Padilla, A. M. (1980). The role of cultural awareness and ethnic loyalty in acculturation. In A. M. Padilla (Ed.), *Acculturation: Theory, models, and some new findings.* Boulder, CO: Westview Press.

Pedersen, P. (1988). *A handbook for developing multicultural awareness.* Alexandria, VA: American Association for Counseling and Development.

Ruiz, R., & Padilla, A. (1977). Counseling Latinos. *Personnel & Guidance Journal, 7,* 401–408.

Sanders, D. (1987). Cultural conflicts: An important factor in the academic failures of American Indian students. *Journal of Multicultural Counseling and Development, 15*(2), 81–90.

Shon, S. P., & Ja, D. Y. (1982). Asian families. In M. McGoldrick, J. K. Pearce, & J. Giordano (Eds.), *Ethnicity and family therapy* (pp. 208–228). New York: Guilford.

Singleton, D. K. (1982). *Counseling approaches for enhancing self-esteem of minorities.* Ann Arbor: University of Michigan, School of Education, ERIC Counseling and Personnel Services Clearinghouse.

Sue, D. W. (1973). Ethnic identity: The impact of two cultures on the psychological development of Asians in America. In D. Sue & N. Wagner (Eds.), *Asian-Americans: Psychological Perspectives.* Palo Alto, CA: Science & Behavior Books.

Sue, D. W. (1981). *Counseling the culturally different.* New York: Wiley.

Sue, D. W., Bernier, J. E., Durran, A., Feinberg, L., Pedersen, P. B., Smith, E. J., & Vasquez-Nuttall, E. (1982). Cross-cultural counseling competencies. *Counseling Psychologist, 10*(2), 45–52.

Sue, S., & Morishima, J.K. (1982). *The mental health of Asian Americans.* San Francisco: Jossey-Bass.

Vacc, N., & Wittmer, J. (1980). *Let me be me: Special populations and the helping professional.* Muncie, IN: Accelerated Development.

ADDITIONAL CROSS-CULTURAL READINGS

American Indian Studies Center. (1979). *Multicultural education and the American Indian*. Los Angeles: University of California.

> Although this is not a "counseling" book, it does provide the reader an understanding of American Indian philosophy and its relationship to multicultural education.

Asante, M. K., Newmark, E., & Blake, C. A. (Eds.). (1979). *Handbook of intercultural communication*.

> This book provides theoretical and conceptual considerations in the field of intercultural communications. Interdisciplinary in approach, the text reviews multicultural issues from several perspectives useful to the practitioner. The text also contains training designs, specific case examples, and methods.

Atkinson, D. R., (1985). A meta-review of research on cross-cultural counseling and psychotherapy. *Journal of Multicultural Counseling & Development, 13*, 138–153.

> This article examines crosscultural research and provides organizational strategies and objective analysis of research outcomes across ethnic groups, research designs, and research setting. It lists a collective set of major conclusions of the studies and makes recommendations for future studies.

Atkinson, D. R., Morten, G., & Sue, D. W. (1983). *Counseling American minorities: A cross cultural perspective* (2nd ed.). Dubuque, IA: Wm C. Brown.

> Intended to sensitize counselors to the life experiences of culturally distinct populations, this book focuses upon the unique needs and experiences of minority individuals. The traditional counseling role is examined and new directions suggested.

Brislin, R. W. (1981). *Cross-cultural encounters—Face to face interaction*. New York: Pergamon Press.

> Concepts useful in analyzing all forms of crosscultural interactions are defined. Individual attitudes, traits, skills, and thought processes are discussed as a basis for understanding reference groups, organizational conflict, and the process of adjustment. Productive crosscultural encounters are proposed as possible solutions to misunderstandings and conflicts.

Brislin, R. W., Cushner, K., Cherrie, C., & Young, M. (1986). *Intercultural interactions—A practical guide*. Beverly Hills, CA: Sage.

> This is one volume in a series by Sage that is especially useful for practitioners. Interpersonal interactions in crosscultural settings are examined by a critical incident technique: appropriateness of interpretation, underlying reasons for social-psychological principles, and development of different ways to evaluate responses. A series of case studies and vignettes provides a discussion of alternative actions. The book contains a wealth of practical information.

Heath, A. E., Neimeyer, G. J., & Pedersen, P. (1988). The future of cross-cultural counseling: A delphi poll. *Journal of Counseling & Development, 67*, 27–30.

> In this study addressing the future of crosscultural counseling over the next 10 years, opinions of groups of recognized experts were solicited to obtain a consensus in the areas of theory and research, training and preparation, and social organization. Many probable changes were indicated, and these make for fascinating reading. Top programs, journals, and books in the field are nominated.

Helms, J. C. (1988). Expanding racial identity theory to cover the counseling process. *Journal of Counseling Psychology, 33*, 82–84.

> Helms reviews the Racial Identity Attitude Scale and its use in practice and research. The author critiques previous studies and findings to assess racial identity. The article determines that scale reliability and interpretation problems can be lessened by use of multiple variables that reflect the complexity of racial identity, particularly when studying the counseling process.

Henderson, G. (Ed.). (1979). *Understanding and counseling ethnic minorities.* Springfield, IL: Charles C Thomas.

> This collection of readings, broken down by ethnic groups (Blacks, American Indians, Chinese Americans, Mexican Americans, Puerto Ricans, and Japanese Americans), addresses patterns of family life, language, customs, and aspects of social environments. It is intended for school counselors and school psychologists concerned with understanding the lives of ethnic minority individuals. This is a classic reference text.

Henkin, W. A. (1985). Toward counseling the Japanese in America: A cross-cultural primer. *Journal of Counseling & Development, 63,* 500–503.

> Henkins offers pragmatic observations about and insights into counseling Japanese-Americans. A brief subcultural history gives background information and distinguishes between the "quiet therapies" of Japan and Western "talk-therapies." The precise suggestions may help counselors distinguish between client behaviors that are individualistic and those that are cultural.

Hernandez, C., Haug, M., & Wagner, N. (Eds.). (1976). *Chicanos: Social and psychological perspectives* (2nd ed.). St. Louis: C. V. Mosby.

> This book gives readers an overview of the current issues and research on Chicanos in the United States. It includes information about family, history, relationships with the majority society, personality assessment, and mental health.

Herr, E. L. (1987). Cultural diversity from an international perspective. *Journal of Multicultural Counseling & Development, 15,* 99–109.

> The United States is described as a land of immigrants, including the American Indian who has a diverse cultural background. Ethnic traditions and international roots persist over time and have effects that span generations, behaviors, and interrelationships. One set of approaches will not adequately address the needs of all counselors. Rather, a macroenvironment exists in which all counseling approaches and assumptions must be validated against cultural pluralism.

Horowitz, D. L. (1985). *Ethnic groups in conflict.* Berkeley: University of California Press.

> This book provides an overview and insight into the importance of ethnic conflict on a global level. It addresses the importance of ethnic affiliation, sources of conflict, party politics, military politics, and interethnic accommodation. It presents the concept of democratic multiethnic politics as a measure of success in interhuman relations and as a means of reducing ethnic conflict.

Ivey, A. E., Ivey, M. B., & Simek-Downing, L. (1987). *Counseling and psychotherapy: Integrating skills, theory, and practice* (2nd ed.). Englewood Cliffs, NJ: Prentice Hall.

> One chapter in this foundation text deals in depth with individual and cultural empathy. Goals, broad constructs, and examples of cultural and group differences are set forth clearly, enabling the reader to understand techniques that work with one group yet may be offensive to another.

Jones, R. (Ed.). (1972). *Black psychology.* New York: Harper & Row.

> A series of writings by Black psychologists and behavioral scientists, this book gives psychological perspectives and research on Blacks. The range of writings includes psychological assessment, personality and motivation, counseling education, and community perspectives.

LeVine, E., & Padilla, A. (1980). *Crossing cultures in therapy: Pluralistic counseling for the Hispanic.* Monterey, CA: Brooks/Cole.

> Currently the most comprehensive book in the area of counseling Hispanics, this book provides facts, research, and a basic understanding of Hispanic groups in the United States. In addition, it gives specific recommendations on counseling approaches.

McGoldrick, M., Pearce, J. K., & Giordano, J. (Eds.). (1982). *Ethnicity and family therapy*. New York: Guilford Press.

> This book examines the manner in which ethnocultural factors affect family relations and suggests how counselors can assess, communicate, and treat subgroups more effectively by being aware of cultural roots. It discusses a systems approach to more than 23 subgroups and provides a wealth of information about cultural profiles as well as specific therapeutic suggestions.

Parker, W. M. (1988). Becoming an effective multicultural counselor. *Journal of Counseling & Development, 67*, 93.

> This article relates the first-year counseling experiences of a young Black man trained to work with middle-class White clients. Parker discovers a lack of ability to work with ethnic minority clients. Through study and effort, he gains an awareness of his own attitudes, changes negative habits, and develops crosscultural counseling skills.

Pasteur, A. B., & Toldson, I. L. (1982). *Roots of soul: The psychology of Black expressiveness*. Garden City, NY: Anchor Press/Doubleday.

> This book presents a broad range of Black expressive forms and a discussion on how feelings and emotions affect folkways, customs, and personal relationships. It offers a theoretical position with practical provisions for helping Blacks and others attend to interpersonal development and mental health needs.

Pedersen, P. (1988). *A handbook for developing multicultural awareness*. Alexandria, VA: American Association for Counseling and Development.

> This book is called "an ideal handbook for teaching cross-cultural counseling." Pedersen provides a practical guide for improving communication skills and cultural awareness. Role-playing techniques and simulation exercises help readers identify and overcome learned stereotypical behavior and responses. Stages of multicultural development are outlined and offer readers the opportunity to develop their own multicultural identity.

Pedersen, P., Draguns, J. G., Lonner, W. J., & Trimble, J. E. (1981). *Counseling across cultures* (rev. ed.). Honolulu: University of Hawaii Press.

> This valuable text examines the impact of cultural differences on mental health priorities in counseling, specific counselor interventions, and dominant-system values that lead to cultural bias. The authors demonstrate the way in which differences in culture, age, gender, lifestyle, and socioeconomic status can affect communication between counselor and client. This is a well referenced and highly regarded text in the field of multicultural issues.

Ponterotto, J. G. (1987). Counseling Mexican-Americans: A multi-modal approach. *Journal of Counseling & Development, 65*, 308–312.

> Mexican-Americans are reported to underuse counseling services and have counseling needs that are not currently being met. Ponterotto describes the large intracultural diversity of the population and calls for a model inherently flexible in delivery. Multimodal therapy borrows from traditional techniques and therapies to provide the multifaceted and fully comprehensive counseling process necessary when working with Mexican-Americans.

Reynolds, D. K. (1980). *The quiet therapies—Japanese pathways to personal growth*. Honolulu: University of Hawaii Press.

> Five Japanese psychotherapies (Marita, Naikan, Seiza, Shadan, and Zen) are presented along with their common themes and techniques. Collectively, through their own methods of introspection, the therapies address the nature of humans and offer practical advice and techniques for helping people cope with problems. Western practitioners will find this empathic, introspective, and operational approach to human experiences useful.

Singleton, D. K. (1982). *Counseling approaches for enhancing self-esteem of minorities.* Ann Arbor: School of Education/ERIC Counseling and Personnel Services Clearing-house.

> This monograph offers a frame of reference for considering minority group self-esteem and discusses the family, religious, and value orientation as important to the counseling process. Theoretical orientations are presented with implications for counselor behaviors.

Sue, D. W. (1988). *Counseling the culturally different.* New York: Wiley.

> This classic work in the field of crosscultural counseling for all minority groups identifies differences and similarities among ethnic groups in relation to counseling practices, and addresses our social-political system's impact on crosscultural counseling delivery services. "Critical incidents" highlight and illustrate issues and concerns likely to arise in counseling situations.

Sue, S., & Wagner, N. (Eds.). (1973). *Asian Americans: Psychological perspectives.* Palo Alto, CA: Science & Behavior Books.

> Although somewhat outdated, this book provides an overview of the psychological research on Asian Americans. In addition to factual information, it offers insight into the psychohistorical, cultural, and personality factors of Asian Americans.

Vacc, N. A., & Wittmer, J. P. (Eds.). (1980). *Let me be me: Special populations and the helping professional.* Muncie, IN: Accelerated Development.

> This book presents an overview of 10 special populations, with the purpose of exposing counselors to the unique characteristics of these subgroups and to assist professionals as they work with these people. Within each special population group is a wide array of diverse values and individual differences, but the interrelatedness of the groups is the book's emphasis and focus.

16

Group Counseling: Ethics and Professional Issues

Holly Forester-Miller and Robert Lee Rubenstein

Ethics lies at the heart of the counseling process. (Van Hoose, 1980, p. 2)

*E*thics is truly at the heart of the counseling process. This is especially so in group counseling. For many people group counseling is the first opportunity they have had to be open and honest and feel safe in sharing who they are with others. The group leader is responsible for setting the norm of ethical behavior, not only for the counselor but also for the group as a whole, to limit the possibilities of that trust being broken.

> Group counselors, by their very nature in being responsible and responsive to their group members, necessarily embrace a certain potential for ethical vulnerability. It is incumbent upon group counselors to give considerable attention to the intent and context of their actions because the attempts of counselors to influence human behavior through group work always have ethical implications. (Association for Specialists in Group Work, 1989, p. 1)

This quote from the preamble to the Association for Specialists in Group Work (ASGW) *Ethical Guidelines for Group Counselors* stresses the role of group leaders as "ethical agents." As Van Hoose (1980) points out, counseling is effected by much more than the techniques and information in the counseling process, although these are important. It is influenced by "attitudes, beliefs, personal behavior, and views about right and wrong acts" (p. 2), and group members bring many differences, attitudes, beliefs, behaviors, and views to the group. The leader has to assist the group in facilitating each member's growth and development, without imposing any one person's values on any other member. When exploring all the additional aspects of group leaders' responsibilities— some of which may have conflicting demands, such as professional codes, institutional policies, societal expectations, client needs, and state and federal laws—it gets even more confusing. Group leaders must make ethical decisions that satisfy all of the above areas and at the same time satisfy their own sense of ethics and morality. "The awesome responsibility of group leadership is that practitioners must answer ultimately to themselves for their actions" (Kottler, 1982, p. 186).

Each group leader will eventually formulate an individual method of making ethical decisions, based on a personal view of human nature and the process of change. Van Hoose and Paradise (1979) suggest that ethical theory is a systematic way of organizing the "principles or norms that ought to govern one's conduct" (p. 23), and that these norms are based on institutional, societal, and professional policies. By studying ethical principles, guidelines, and decision making, group leaders should be able to form methods of ethical decision making congruent with professional codes and societal expectations. A study by Robinson and Gross (1989) showed that participants who had a university course in ethics were better able to recognize what ethical issues were pertinent in a given situation and to suggest ethical behaviors to correct those situations.

This chapter presents the *Ethical Guidelines for Group Counselors* (Association for Specialists in Group Work, 1989) and the professional and legal issues inherent in group counseling. The overall theme is ethical decision making.

CODE OF ETHICS

Many professional organizations have established codes of ethics for their memberships: the American Association for Counseling and Development (AACD), the Association for Specialists in Group Work (ASGW), the American Psychological Association (APA), the American Mental Health Counselors Association (AMHCA), the National Board for Certified Counselors (NBCC), the American School Counselors Association (ASCA), the National Association for Social Workers (NASW), and the American Association for Marriage and Family Therapy (AAMFT). Each association's guidelines are designed to cover the major areas of concern for its constituency. Each association deals with liability and ethical ramifications according to its own criteria, typically derived from the discipline's code of ethics (Woody, 1988).

Because each set of guidelines has issues in common with the others but also has differences and some areas of disagreement, members of several professional affiliations can get confused. For example, we personally are subject to *Ethical Standards* (American Association for Counseling and Development, 1988), *Code of Ethics for Mental Health Counselors* (American Mental Health Counselors Association, 1987), *Code of Ethics* (National Board for Certified Counselors, 1989), *Ethical Guidelines for Group Counselors* (Association for Specialists in Group Work, 1989), and the ethical guidelines for the state counselor licensing board. As Kibler and Van Hoose (1981) indicate, a counselor can approach "ethical decision making with a whole set of rules and regulations but with few principles to guide his or her behavior" (p. 225).

Knowing the ethical standards that affect practice is not enough. Professionals need to understand the moral principles upon which they are based. Unfortunately, only a few counselor education programs go beyond the introduction of ethical codes and guidelines to examine the moral principles that apply in various situations (Corey, Corey, & Callanan, 1988; Strom & Tennyson, 1989).

Though important, ethical guidelines are limited in their use in professional decision making (Gumaer & Scott, 1985; Mabe & Rollin, 1986; Strom & Tennyson, 1989; Tarvydas, 1987; Van Hoose, 1980; Welfel & Lipsitz, 1984). Ethical guidelines do not provide specific directives for all potential situations; they are not meant to do so. They are meant to provide parameters to "guide" behavior, rather than to give right or wrong answers to difficult questions.

Professionals need to be able to utilize the guidelines as a starting place to explore ethical dilemmas; they also need a set of moral principles and an ethical decision making model to use when the guidelines are in conflict or do not address the issue at hand. As Mabe and Rollin (1986) point out, "There is a limited range of topics covered in the code, and because a code approach is usually reactive to issues already developed elsewhere, the requirement of consensus prevents the code from addressing new issues and problems at the 'cutting edge'" (p. 295). Here, we approach ethics by first examining the guidelines, then exploring moral principles, and last, by presenting an ethical decision-making model.

Purposes of Ethical Guidelines

Codes of ethics serve several purposes (Van Hoose, 1980; Van Hoose & Kottler, 1985).

1. They present standards to aid in ethical decision making.
2. They provide some measure of self-regulation and give some assurance that individual counselor's behaviors will not be detrimental to the profession.
3. They clarify the various areas of counselor's responsibilities—to clients, to society, and to the profession.
4. Codes of ethics offer some protection to clients that professionals will supposedly function in accordance with social mores and expectations.
5. Codes of ethics help counselors safeguard their freedom and integrity by setting acceptable standards of care.

As Gumaer and Scott (1985) stated, "Knowledge of the profession's ethical codes is the key to informed behavior" (p. 199).

As a result of the many and varied sets of ethical codes, we have chosen to present the one set we believe is the most comprehensive and relevant for group leaders—the *Ethical Guidelines for Group Counselors* of the Association for Specialists in Group Work—and some of its implications for practice. Other codes also affect professionals, of course, and group leaders should be familiar with them and spend time thinking about the issues and the morals inherent in them. As Kibler and Van Hoose (1981) point out, "Internalization of morality is the key to effective ethical conduct" (p. 225). "Novices and established professionals alike need to weigh their moral decisions, not in light of legal mandates, but in relation to their personally responsible codes of conduct" (p. 226).

Ethical Guidelines for Group Counselors (ASGW, 1989)

The actual guidelines of the Association for Specialists in Group Work (1989) are contained in their entirety in Appendix B. These are meant to serve as an adjunct to the American Association for Counseling and Development (1988) *Ethical Standards*, found in Appendix C. Here we will spotlight and discuss aspects of each of the 16 ASGW guidelines, to aid in understanding their purposes and implications. Understanding, we hope, will lead to internalization.

Guideline 1: Orientation and Providing Information   To adequately meet the first ethical guideline, we suggest that group leaders develop an "orientation-information checklist" that includes items *a* through *k* from the ASGW guideline. To make a record of having covered these issues with each participant the leader might first explain each item, then have prospective members sign a statement at the bottom of the checklist acknowledging that the group leader has explained each item and that the individual acknowledges an understanding of the content presented.

Guideline 2: Screening of Members   This guideline offers four possible ways to do screening. The preferred screening format is the private, individual session, because this allows both the group leader and the group member the greatest opportunity for interaction and information exchange. The better the understanding of the group and its purpose, and the more information the counselor has about the member's purpose and goals, the better is the potential for matching the group to the person, and vice versa.

Effective pre-group screening can eliminate many potential difficulties that might arise if the person's goals do not correlate with the group's stated purpose—difficulties not only for the leader but for the group members as well. We believe that, regardless of one's theoretical orientation, screening is necessary to establish an effective group. The ideal of one-on-one screening interviews may not always be feasible, but the group leader has to find creative methods of conducting screening in some manageable form. This is vital to protecting the rights of all group members.

Guideline 3: Confidentiality   Confidentiality in any counseling setting is essential, but in a group setting it takes on a few interesting twists. There is no way of guaranteeing that group members will keep confidentiality. Rosenbaum (1982) discusses how Moreno used to have group members take an oath of confidentiality and how this practice was "probably unnecessary since clinical experience indicates that patients learn to trust one another, care for one another, and come to realize that if any patient exposes another outside of the group the same act may in turn be visited upon him" (p. 238). What Rosenbaum seems to be overlooking is the nonmalicious, accidental breaking of confidentiality. A group member rarely would go out and intentionally breech confidentiality, but the potential for accidentally breaking confidentiality is fairly high.

Mary shares with the group that she and her husband are having problems in their sexual relationship. Several group members relate that they have had similar difficulties in their relationships. Sue shares an intimate story about her sexual relationship with her husband and how they dealt with a similar difficulty several years ago. Sue's sharing helps Mary gain some significant insight into her problem, and how her beliefs and attitudes are contributing to the difficulty.

Mary is so excited about her own realization and growth that she can hardly wait to go home and tell her husband about it. In talking to her husband, Mary is careful not to mention any names, but she does share the details of Sue's story in explaining how she has acquired this new insight.

Several weeks later, Mary's husband, John, is telling his best friend how things are so much better sexually between him and Mary. He mentions that it all stems from a story someone told Mary, and John proceeds to tell his friend the story. As he is telling the story in the locker room at the fitness club, a stranger walks in. John continues to tell his friend the story about this other couple without realizing that the stranger is Sue's husband, Mark. Upon arriving home that evening, Mark is quite upset, explaining to his wife that he did not appreciate hearing strangers discuss the intimate details of their sex life.

Obviously, Mary was not maliciously breaking confidentiality. Nonetheless, confidentiality was broken, resulting in some potential difficulties for Sue.

Examples such as the one here should be shared with group members to help them truly understand their part in maintaining confidentiality and to reduce the risk of something similar happening in their group. Participants need to be advised that they can share only their own growth and insights and are obligated to do so in a way that does not mention what anybody else in the group has said or done. Thus, Mary might have said to her husband, "I realized several things about myself tonight that I think may make a difference in our sexual relationship." She could then go on to tell him about her insights without mentioning the group or other members' issues.

Guideline 4: Voluntary/Involuntary Participation   Participation in a group can be challenging. The degree of control over choosing to participate or not can directly influence early interactions between the group leader and members. This is especially important with groups in which membership is involuntary. In the orientation and information phase of a group, informed consent is one method to assist members, whether voluntary or involuntary, to understand group goals. It further ensures that members are aware of the voluntary or involuntary construct of the group.

Informed consent means defining and discussing the participation expectations for group members. It allows for involuntary members to discuss their feeling about being required to participate and to decide at what level they are willing to actively take part in the group.

Gregory and McConnell (1986) stress the importance of using informed consent with children over age 7. They further recommend that the child be questioned briefly after informed consent has been explained, to be sure the child understands this concept.

Guideline 5: Leaving a Group   Members have the right to exit the group at any time, but a member's leaving has ramifications for the individual who leaves prematurely as well as ramifications for the group as a whole, whether it is premature or not. The group leader must advise a departing member of the potential risks involved in early departure and to offer appropriate referrals for the individual. The group leader also has a responsibility to assist the remaining group members in processing the departure of a member.

Whenever an individual leaves the group, for whatever reason, the dynamics of the group change. Ideally, the departing member will come to the group to discuss his or her decision to leave, and this is an expectation that should be shared with members in pre-group screening interviews. If the member indicates to the group that he or she wishes to leave, the leader should make sure that members do not pressure the individual to stay but do have an opportunity to say good-bye and wind up any unfinished business. If the member leaves without mentioning it in the group, the leader should allow the group members time to process their feelings and thoughts about how the individual's departure affects them and the group.

Guideline 6: Coercion and Pressure Group members will probably not truly understand how coercion and pressure directly or indirectly affect group members unless the group leader openly admits that this happens. Kottler (1982) explains that the group leader has a natural tendency to exert pressure and persuasion on people to become and remain group members. The real ethical issue, he says, is to control the degree to which these behaviors surface.

During the course of the group experience, members should be reminded that they have the right to participate or refuse participation in any specific group activity. The group leader should support their decision regarding participation. This fosters the feeling of safety and control within the group. It increases the possibility of growth and exploration of difficult issues and enhances the transference of this knowledge to the extended environment (society).

Guideline 7: Imposing Counselor Values Group leaders have values, and no one can act as if they do not. "The psychotherapist, more than any other student of behavior, presents values to his patients by his very commitment to the affirmation of life" (Rosenbaum, 1982, p. 244). So leaders have to be sure they do not impose their values on the group members, even subtly. Their response in a given situation or the focus they take in questioning a member can be subtle ways of imposing values. For example, if a group member is pregnant and mentions abortion as a possible option, a leader might choose three basic response categories: (a) to present abortion as a plausible option, and possibly the primary option; (b) to mention all options other than abortion (subtle) or clearly indicate that abortion is not a viable option; and (c) to ask the group member what options she sees open to herself and wants to explore, leaving the decision up to the person.

How aware leaders are of their own values will certainly make a difference in how they respond. When they are aware of their values, they can reduce the possibility of unintentionally imposing their values on others, no matter how subtly. Corey, Corey, and Callanan's (1990) article on group leaders' values gives examples of many subtle ways in which leaders might impose their values on group members, and demonstrate "how easy it is to steer clients toward a particular path" (p. 73).

Guideline 8: Equitable Treatment Corey, Corey, and Callanan (1990) state that group leaders must "be able to identify some types of clients with whom they cannot work well, for whatever reason" (p. 69). This identification process is important because group leaders will be working with a variety of lifestyle, cultural, religious, racial, age, and gender issues within their groups. By maintaining a level of awareness of their biases toward individual group members, leaders can attempt to limit any negative effects from these biases.

Using a variety of skills and techniques designed to build group trust and cohesiveness, the group leader can involve all group members, regardless of personal, social or emotional experience. By encouraging active participation and guarding against inappropriate involvement, the group leader can construct an atmosphere of balance for participants.

Guideline 9: Dual Relationships "In a dual role relationship, one person simultaneously or sequentially plays two or more roles with another person" (Kitchener & Harding, 1990, p. 147). Not all dual-role relationships are problematic, but group leaders should understand what causes dual relationships to be difficult and, therefore, how to avoid these potentially harmful or high-risk relationships.

Kitchener (1988) identified three factors to differentiate potentially high-risk dual relationships and ones with little or no risk: (a) incompatibility of expectations between roles, (b) divergence of obligations associated with the roles, and (c) the profesional's power and prestige (Kitchener & Harding, 1990, p. 147). A good example of the difference between high-risk and low-risk relationships is apparent in bartering for goods and services. Typically "goods" and "services" are discussed as though they are one in the same, but the risk levels are significantly different. Exchanging counseling *services* for painting or household repairs represents a high risk. If the repairs are not done properly or prove not to hold up, the group leader has to deal with the member not only with regard to their psychological well-being but also with regard to the leader's dissatisfaction with the work performed.

In bartering *goods* for services with group members, a group member might accept a blanket for "x" number of counseling sessions, as long as both parties agree that this constitutes a reasonable exchange. Many low-income people have a strong sense of pride and will not allow themselves to receive services for which they can not pay (even if they would pay only a nominal amount). Instead, bartering for goods allows these individuals to receive the desired counseling services and keep their pride intact, without all the potential complications involved in exchanging services. In guideline #9(d), the term regarding "goods" is purposely omitted.

Guideline 10: Use of Techniques   No set of techniques exists from which to pick the appropriate one for each situation encountered as group leaders. Therefore, group leaders must continually expand their knowledge and understanding of various techniques and be open to altering them to fit the unique needs of individuals in a group, leaders could create their own techniques when necessary. In doing this, leaders must have a sound rationale and a reasonable idea of what to expect from the techniques utilized. This concept is tied to having a sound theoretical orientation to guide one's practice. According to Corey, Corey, Callanan, and Russell (1982), "We urge group leaders to strike a balance between creativity and irresponsible lack of caution" (p. 140).

In pointing out that even the factors typically considered curative or therapeutic in groups can possibly have counter-therapeutic effects on participants. Lakin (1986) warns:

> Ethical practice is not merely adherence to a professional code, but rather is based on understanding . . . how the modality itself—the group mode in this case—and the techniques that one uses are likely to affect a range of participants. (p. 456)

Guideline 11: Goal Development   Coaches at every level of athletic participation know that the design, implementation, and ongoing evaluation of a game plan are all important determiners of the team's overall success. The same can be said for the group in which the leader actively partakes in this goal-setting process with individual members and also with the group as a whole. Goal setting may help each member gain new skills in identifying and dealing with personal issues. As the group progresses, goals may be reevaluated and redefined.

Guideline 12: Consultation   The group leader has two roles in regard to consultation as addressed in this guideline: (a) consultant to group members, and (b) consultee with other professionals. By virtue of being a counselor, one does not become immune to personal problems, nor does one become versed in healing oneself. Some counselors, for a variety of reasons, either have not acknowledged their own difficulties or would not go to a counselor to deal with their own issues. If group leaders believe that they are above needing help, what is the message this gives to group participants? In a group setting, members already tend to put the leader in a position of higher power, and the leader's attitudes separate him or her even more. The leader's beliefs are basically saying "I'm better than you because I never need help and you do." We question the ethics of group leaders' providing a service that they do not themselves value.

Guideline 13: Termination from the Group   Leaders must not foster dependency in group members. Kottler (1982) reminds us that there comes a point when participating in a group "no longer results in significant products, except further dependency on the leader" (p. 185). As part of group leaders' role, they are to promote the autonomy of members and to help them transfer what they have learned in the group into their everyday lives.

Guideline 14: Evaluation and Follow-up   "Can I drive the car by myself now?" Many people have asked this question as young, aspiring teenage drivers or have been asked this question by their own teenage children. Before an answer is forthcoming, spin-off questions arise: Where are you going? What time will you be home? How late will you be out? How's, what's, when's, where's, why's. So it is with the leader whose group experience is terminating and whose members are being asked to "drive it alone," without support from the group for the first time. During the termination phase of the group, the leader often must face a variety of secondary questions: Should a member be referred for further counseling? When, where, and how will follow-up services be offered? Jacobs, Harvill, and Masson (1988) suggest that group leaders think through these questions before the last session, allowing them to terminate the group with an understanding of where each member is in relation to his or her individual and group goals. At this stage the leader helps members determine where they are, where they want to be, and how they can continue to progress toward their goals.

Guideline 15: Referrals   At any time during the group experience, the group leader may have to refer a group member for individual counseling or other related services. To make these referrals to highly qualified professionals, we suggest that the group leader maintain a referral directory, listing the professional's areas of specialization, qualifications, fee structure, and treatment modalities. Having this type of information enables the group leader to make conscientious referrals according to the unique needs of the group members.

Guideline l6: Professional Development   This guideline recommends clearly that group leaders participate in ongoing professional development activities. Because of rapid growth and changes in technologies and information delivery systems, professionals in all career areas must attempt to stay abreast of new discoveries in their fields so they are able to provide the best services possible. In comparison to other professions, such as law and medicine, the field of counseling and mental health care is still in its infancy. Emerging theories of personality development and understanding of the relationship between physiological and psychological factors and studies of genetic influences on behavior are but a few of the concepts that will directly impact the counseling profession into the next century. Professional involvement at local, regional, and national levels is imperative to keep up to date and, therefore, be competent to provide the best possible assistance to those served.

CASES AND APPLICABLE GUIDELINES

Each of the following three cases represents an actual ethical dilemma of a group leader. For each of the cases, identify which ethical guidelines are pertinent to that situation. Later, we will ask you to apply an ethical decision-making model to each case, but for now, simply review the guidelines in Appendix A and identify which ones are relevant in discussing each case.

Case 1: To support or not to support parents? You are leading a personal growth group for 10th and 12th graders, consisting of 12 members. One of the female members comes to the group with visible bruises. She indicates that she had been in a fight with another student. She had talked to her parents about it, and they had advised her how to handle it. She will ambush the student and then fight, so she can beat her adversary this time. The leader and the group members all seem to feel this was poor advice.

Case 2: The qualified co-leader? You are leading a group for sex offenders in a mental health center. All of the group members have been court-ordered to participate in your treatment group. For some it is part of their parole, and for others it is part of their probation agreement—treatment in place of prison. All of their agreements require that they be "active participants" in the group process, and the group leader has to sign forms each month verifying that the parolee, or probationer, is in fact "actively participating in therapy."

The mental health center often hires part-time people to assist with the groups it offers. A part-time person has been hired as co-leader for your offender's group. This co-leader has a master's degree in counseling with special training in group counseling, and his full-time job is probation officer. He is the probation officer for two of the current group members. Several of the members have approached you about their discomfort with this co-leader. They are afraid that information they share in the group will be used against them in the probation review process or in future court hearings. They also are concerned that if they do not continue to "actively participate," this will be considered a violation of their probation or parole.

Case 3: What to do about a confidentiality breech? You are a school counselor co-leading, with a teacher, an interpersonal problem-solving group. The group consists of 12 eighth graders. This teacher is one of only a few who will allow you to run a group with her class. During the initial stages, each group member, including the teacher, contracted to maintain confidentiality. Around the eighth session, several group members approached the counselor about a suspected breach of confidentiality. They said the teacher/co-leader has been using inside information she heard in the group to entrap and discipline students and has been leaking information to the school principal. You know that this teacher is having stressors on the job as well as at home. The teacher has a history of retaliating against students.

ASGW Guidelines

The ASGW ethical guidelines with revelance to each case are:

Case 1:   3 (a); 6 (a, b, c); 7 (a, e); 10 (d)
Case 2:   3 (g); 4 (a, c, d); 9; 12 (a, b)
Case 3:   1 (c); 3 (b, c, d, f, g); 7 (a, c); 8 (b); 9 (a, g); 12 (c, d, e, f); 14 (c)

ETHICAL DECISION MAKING

As group leaders develop their own method of making ethical decisions, they should explore the applicable ethical guidelines, the moral principles inherent in those guidelines, and the existing ethical decision-making models.

Moral Principles

Kitchener (1984) has identified five moral principles that she sees as critical to evaluating ethical concerns in psychology and counseling. Where ethical codes do not address all situations, the moral principles inherent in these codes can offer direction in ethical dilemmas and provide a consistent framework for ethical decision making (Kitchener, 1984; Stadler, 1986). The five principles are autonomy, justice, beneficence, nonmaleficence, and fidelity.

1. The principle of *autonomy* is basic to the concept of promoting independence. It means allowing individuals both freedom of choice and freedom of action. As Kitchener (1984) points out, autonomy has two limitations. The first limitation to the individual's freedom is based on the concept of not impinging on anyone else's freedom. No one has the right to deprive someone else of autonomy. The second limitation is tied to whether the individual has the ability to make rational decisions. If an individual is not competent to make reasonable choices, such as with small children and people with mental handicaps, that person should not be allowed to act on decisions that could harm themselves or others.

2. *Justice*, when traced to its formal meaning, means "treating equals equally and unequals unequally but in proportion to their relevant differences" (Kitchener, 1984, p. 49). One starts by assuming that everyone is equal. If individuals are not going to be treated as equals, it is necessary to give a rationale for why these individuals warrant different treatment.

3. *Beneficence* means to do good, to provide services beneficial to the other person. Providing beneficial service is what counseling is all about; it is the crux of the profession. As Stadler (1986) indicates, this principle requires us to be proactive, and to actively do good and prevent harm.

4. *Nonmaleficence*, which can be most easily understood as 'above all do no harm' (Kitchener, 1984, p. 47), includes (a) not inflicting intentional harm or (b) engaging in actions that risk harming others. At times these moral principles are in conflict with each other—which is the definition of an ethical dilemma. Obviously, each principle can not be regarded as absolutely binding when they conflict. As indicated by the wording "above all," the principle of not causing harm is often called the most critical of our moral principles (Kitchener, 1984; Rosenbaum, 1982; Stadler, 1986).

5. *Fidelity* addresses the issues of loyalty, faithfulness, and fulfilling obligations. Codes regarding confidentiality stem from this principle. Trust is the foundation on which effective counseling is built, because it is the basic ingredient in a helping relationship. Any actions that threaten this trust or leave obligations unfulfilled have serious implications for the helping relationship and are in conflict with the principle of fidelity.

Decision-Making Model

Applying the ethical decision-making model espoused by Van Hoose and his associates (Van Hoose, 1980; Van Hoose & Kottler, 1985; Van Hoose & Paradise, 1979) to group counseling, Paradise and Siegelwaks (1982) describe the following steps:

1. Identify the problem or dilemma.
2. Do any guidelines or principles exist to help resolve the dilemma?
3. Generate possible and probable courses of action.
4. Consider potential consequences for each course of action.
5. Select the best course of action.

Using this framework, we offer a seven-step decision-making model that also incorporates the work of Kitchener (1984) and Stadler (1986).

1. *Identify the dilemma.* After identifying the source of the conflict, Kitchener (1984) and Stadler (1986) both suggest going back to the moral principles and determining which are involved in this case. If two (or more) moral principles are competing, a "true" ethical dilemma exists. If only one moral principle is involved, no ethical dilemma exists and answers to the question will be found by exploring the applicable moral principle.

2. *Apply existing guidelines or principles.* This next step involves reviewing the applicable codes of ethics to see if they offer any answers. Ethical guidelines seldom can supply answers to a specific situation, especially when it involves competing moral principles. If this does not produce an answer, the competing principles have to be prioritized (Stadler, 1986). This is where a personal sense of ethics comes in. The moral principles have no hierarchy; each is meant to be an absolute, all having equal weight (although, as noted earlier, some ethicists do believe that "to do no harm" is above all else). Each group leader has an ethical sense and should use this personal code to prioritize the moral principles in a given situation. How these are prioritized will determine future decisions. In prioritizing the competing principles, the leader is able to explain the moral reasoning applied in deciding the ranking.

3. *Generate courses of action.* Based on the ranking of the moral principles, the desired outcomes are identified, and then potential alternatives to reaching those outcomes. At this phase, consulting with a colleague is helpful. A colleague can help examine ethical reasoning to this point and see if any issues have been overlooked. Colleagues also can help brainstorm alternative actions.

4. *Consider the consequences.* The implications of each course of action, to the individual, the other group members, the leader, and whomever else each action might affect, should be considered. Examples of people outside the group with whom to explore the implications of the alternatives might be the spouse of a married group member, or the parents of a minor.

5. *Select the best course of action.* "The course of action that is in the best interests of appropriate professional conduct should be chosen" (Paradise & Siegelwaks, 1982, p. 165). Actions should address priorities, as evidenced by the ranked list of desired outcomes that coincides with the ranking of moral principles.

6. *Test your decision.* We would like to add another step to Van Hoose's model—that of testing the chosen course of action. Van Hoose and Paradise (1979) state:

> The counselor or psychotherapist is *probably* acting in an ethically responsible way concerning a client if (1) he or she has maintained personal and professional honesty, coupled with (2) the best interests of the client, (3) without malice or personal gain, and (4) can justify his or her actions as the best judgment of what should be done based upon the current state of the profession. Whenever these four components are present, ethically responsible behavior is likely to be demonstrated. (p. 58)

Before implementing an ethical decision, a group leader should consider these components of ethically responsible behavior and whether they apply to his or her decision. Also, we suggest applying three simple tests suggested by Stadler (1986): universality, publicity, and justice. The test of *universality* is based on whether the group leader could recommend the action to other professionals in similar situations. The test of *publicity* is based on asking: "Would I want my action reported by the press?" The test of *justice* requires that the leader judge the fairness of his or her action by determining if he or she would treat other clients the same in this situation.

7. *Take action.* If the course of action chosen passes all these tests, the leader should take action. As many authors have noted, taking appropriate action in an ethical dilemma is not easy (Kitchener,1984; Paradise & Siegelwaks, 1982; Stadler, 1986; Van Hoose, 1980). Here Stadler offers some especially helpful advice: Identify the concrete steps needed to implement the plan, and strengthen the ego to be able to carry out the decision.

CASES IN RELATION TO THE MODEL

Let's go back to the cases presented earlier. Utilizing the ethical decision-making model, and keeping in mind the guidelines identified as pertinent for each case, answer the following questions. As you answer the questions, explain your ethical rationale and be sure to "test" your decision.

Case 1: How should the leader handle this situation? Would you call the parents or in some way involve them?

Case 2: What would you do if you were the original leader of this group? What would you do if you were the new co-leader and found out that the members were concerned?

Case 3: How would you handle this situation? Typically, in cases of a breach in confidentiality, it is discussed in the group. Would you do so in this case? Why or why not?

PROFESSIONAL ISSUES

Whether working in a school, a mental health center, or other facilities that offer group counseling services, the prudent group leader is aware of professional issues with potential legal or ethical overtones. American society continues to change rapidly. With ever evolving treatments in the field of mental health sciences and ever changing court decisions, relative to societal issues, group leaders have to be well prepared to deal with these issues, both professionally and ethically. Some of the key topics are discussed next.

Privileged Communication

Even though a counselor may have the right of privileged communication in individual counseling, this right does not seem to extend to the area of group counseling. Courts have held that "if more than two people are involved in the conversation the privilege is lost to all, since there is no confidentiality intended" (Fischer & Sorenson, 1991, p. 18). And, "although this now makes little sense in group counseling or therapy, counselors should realize that there is a significant lag between development in their professional technique and law" (p. 18). Many individuals seeking counseling services do not understand the difference between privileged communication and confidentiality. Group leaders have to define the boundaries of privileged communication with prospective group members in the screening process.

Confidentiality

Group leaders should recognize that confidentiality is an ethically based concept with little or no legal basis. Although confidentiality is implied in almost all counseling situations, the legal system traditionally has required that this implied safeguard be relinquished in many legal situations, such as child abuse and potentially life-threatening situations. Most notable is the Tarasoff Case, which deals with the issue of "duty to warn." All group leaders should familiarize themselves with the specifics of this case which defines the boundaries of this concept.

Other situations that have direct implications for counselors are those involving children. Group leaders must help children understand the importance of confidentiality in their groups. Leaders also should assist children in distinguishing between confidentiality and "secret keeping." A leader can do this by using role play to help the child know the difference between sharing appropriate information and not telling information that may potentially harm the child, the child's family, or peers. Group leaders also should be aware of the parents' rights in their states, with regard to information shared within a group experience.

Administrative, Faculty, and Staff Support

For group counseling to be effective in a school setting, administrative, faculty, and staff support are imperative. The group leader should make every effort to provide the following information to all relevant individuals in the school setting:

❑ Topic of the group.
❑ Purpose.
❑ Proposed schedule.
❑ Characteristics of potential members.
❑ Age or grade level.
❑ Length of sessions.
❑ Possible conflicts with academic or other school-sponsored activities.
❑ Any special concerns related to the specific work environment.

To keep disruption to the group process at a minimum, the group leader will establish a mechanism for potential concerns to be addressed and resolved.

Group leaders should further review AACD Ethical Guideline #2, Section A, in regard to professional services and institutional objectives, to ensure that any group experience offered reflects the overall mission of the institution or faculty in which the group is being held.

Permission to Participate

This concept is mostly specific to group leaders working with minors in educational settings. School counselors need to be aware of the policies of their school district related to securing parental permission for children to participate in individual or group counseling. Policies regarding parental permission vary drastically, and could vary from school to school within the same district. Some school administrators believe that counseling is part of the school curriculum, and because no special permission is needed for math, none should be needed for counseling. Others require counselors to get signed permission slips before they even set up an intake interview.

Before applying any specific method, the counselor should review local, regional, and state policies with respect to obtaining parental/guardian permission. Three methods of securing permission to participate are:

1. Send home a form that is specific to the activity offered. This form is to be signed by a parent or guardian and returned to the school before the student can participate.
2. Send home a form that is specific to the activity, requiring parents or guardians to notify the school "only if they do *not* want their child to participate."
3. Develop a policy booklet, newsletter, or information sheet, and give it to all parents or guardians at the beginning of the school year. This should contain information about the variety of counseling services offered to students and specify that it is the students' right to use the services unless the parent or guardian notifies the school in writing of any objections.

These are only a selective sample of the ways a counselor may attempt to notify parents or guardians of the child's participation in group activities. Again, before using any one method, the counselor should review with immediate administrators any policies or mandates that may dictate what method to select

Knowledge of Topic

Group leaders should facilitate groups on topics in which they have had professional training. Group leaders should not lead groups on topics and issues with which they have little or no experience. This recommendation should also bear on selecting co-leaders for the group.

Multi-Cultural Issues

Group leaders should be familiar with potential crosscultural issues that may directly influence the group experience. These should be discussed with prospective group members during the screening process. These issues are not always specific to certain minority populations but may arise in certain geographical regions as well. Chapter 15 presents an in-depth discussion of crosscultural issues

PURPOSE OF THE GROUP

Is it right or wrong? An echo from our childhood or a rule of guidance for adulthood pursuits? One pursuit is developing coping skills to deal with a variety of complex issues in an ever changing world. Group counseling provides an excellent forum to develop coping skills. Various authors (Corey and Corey, 1992; Dyer and Vriend, 1980; Trotzer, 1989) have written extensively about the potential benefits of group counseling. In the context of the forum of group counseling, however, are issues that do not lend themselves to the rigid boundaries set forth by the Rule of Right or Wrong.

Answers that are absolute in being either right or being wrong are difficult to find (Stadler, 1986). Any director of a forum in which ethical or value-related issues are discussed has a moral obligation to assist the audience in not only understanding the purpose of such dialogue but also the process for discussion. The leader of these groups should make every effort to relate the appropriateness of issue discussions to the *purpose* of the group.

Jacobs, Harvill, and Masson (1988) define purpose as knowing the reasons why the group is meeting and what specific goals and objectives are to be met. By defining the purpose of the group to prospective members in the orientation and information-giving phase, the group leader can establish the parameters in which difficult issues can be explored safely and ethically. By keeping the group attuned to the purpose (education, personal growth, issue sharing, or whatever the topic) and by being careful not to change the purpose without the approval of all members, the group leader can assure that issues related to the group's original goals are processed.

Defining the group purpose can also aid its leader in ensuring that other ethical guidelines are being followed. Counseling group leaders in any setting (mental health centers, private practice, public schools, and so on) should clearly define the purpose of the groups they lead. Terress and Larrabee (1985) remind us of the importance of this defining when determining what group topics may be appropriate for certain children. They emphasize the importance of the group leader's knowledge of the topic and the ability to match this content with the potential group participants' needs.

SUMMARY

If "ethics lies at the heart of the counseling process" (Van Hoose, 1980 p. 2), every group leader has a responsibility to be ethically fit so the "heart" beats strong. To be ethically fit means that the group leader will:

— have a working knowledge of the *Ethical Guidelines for Group Counselors* (Association for Specialists in Group Work, 1989).
— be able to apply these guidelines to a variety of situations that may arise in group counseling.
— understand the moral principles inherent in ethical behavior.
— be able to implement an ethical decision-making model.
— be aware of the issues specific to his or her work setting and do what is necessary to deliver group counseling with maximum results and minimum disruptions.
— keep abreast of research, new techniques, and theories, and upgrade counseling skills continually.
— be involved with professional organizations in which all of the issues mentioned in this chapter are routinely addressed.

Taking these guidelines as an ethical foundation, group counseling can be an exciting and rewarding experience for group leaders and participants alike.

REFERENCES

American Association for Counseling and Development. (1988). *Ethical standards*. Alexandria, VA: Author.

American Mental Health Counselors Association. (1987). *Code of ethics for mental health counselors*. Alexandria, VA: Author.

Association for Specialists in Group Work. (1989). *Ethical guidelines for group counselors*. Alexandria, VA: Author.

Corey, M. S., & Corey, G. (1992). *Groups: process and practice* (4th ed.). Pacific Grove, Ca: Brooks/Cole.

Corey, G., Corey, M. S., & Callanan, P. (1988). *Issues and ethics in the helping professions*. Pacific Grove, CA: Brooks/Cole.

Corey, G., Corey, M. S., & Callanan, P. (1990). Role of group leader's values in group counseling. *Journal for Specialists in Group Work, 15*, 68–74.

Corey, G., Corey, M. S., Callanan, P., & Rusell, J. M. (1982). Ethical considerations in using group techniques. *Journal for Specialists in Group Work, 7*, 140–148.

Dyer, W., & Vriend, J. (1980). *Group counseling for personal mastery*. New York: Cornerstone.

Fischer, L., & Sorenson, G. P. (1991). *School law for counselors, psychologists, and social workers*. White Plains, NY: Longman.

Gregory, J. C., & McConnell, S. C., (1986). Ethical issues with psychotherapy in group contexts. *Psychology in Private Practice, 4*(1), 51–62.

Gumaer, J., & Scott, L. (1985). Training group leaders in ethical decision making. *Journal for Specialists in Group Work, 10*, 198–204.

Jacobs, E., Harvill, R., & Masson, R. (1988). *Group counseling strategies and skills*. Pacific Grove, CA: Brooks/Cole.

Kibler, R. D., & Van Hoose, W. H. (1981). Ethics in counseling: Bridging the gap from theory to practice. *Counseling & Values, 25*(4), 219–226.

Kitchener, K. S. (1984). Intuition, critical evaluation and ethical principles: The foundation for ethical decisions in counseling psychology. *Counseling Psychologist, 12*(3), 43–55.

Kitchener, K. S. (1988). Dual role relationships: What makes them so problematic? *Journal of Counseling & Development, 67*, 217–221.

Kitchener, K. S., &Harding, S. S. (1990). Dual role relationships. In B. Herlihy & L. B. Golden, *Ethical standards casebook*. Alexandria, VA: American Association for Counseling and Development.

Kottler, J. A. (1982). Unethical behaviors we all do and pretend we do not. *Journal for Specialists in Group Work*, 7, 182–186.

Lakin, M. (1986). Ethical challenges of group and dyadic psychotherapies: A comparative approach. *Professional Psychology: Research & Practice*, 17, 454–461.

Mabe, A., & Rollin, S. A. (1986). The role of a code of ethics in counseling. *Journal of Counseling & Development*, 64, 294–297.

National Board for Certified Counselors. (1989). *Code of ethics*. Alexandria, VA: Author.

Paradise, L. V., & Siegelwaks, B. J. (1982). Ethical training for group leaders. *Journal for Specialists in Group Work*, 7, 162–166.

Robinson, S. E., & Gross, D. R. (1989). Applied ethics and the mental health counselor. *Journal of Mental Health Counseling*, 11(3), 289–299.

Rosenbaum, M. (1982). Ethical problems of group psychotherapy. In M. Rosenbaum (Ed.), *Ethics and values in psychotherapy: A guidebook* (pp. 237–257). New York: Free Press.

Stadler, H. A. (1986). Making hard choices: Clarifying controversial ethical issues. *Counseling & Human Development*, 19, 1–10.

Strom, S. M.,& Tennyson, W. W. (1989). Developing moral responsibleness through professional education. *Counseling & Values*, 34, 33–44.

Tarvydas, V. M. (1987). Decision-making models in ethics: Models for increased clarity and wisdom. *Journal of Applied Rehabilitation Counseling*, 18(4), 50–52.

Terress, C. K., & Larrabee, M. J. (1985). Ethical issues and group work with children. *Elementary School Guidance and Counseling*, 19, 190–197.

Trotzer, J. (1989). *The counselor and the group*. Muncie, IN: Accelerated Development Inc.

Van Hoose, W. H. (1980). Ethics and counseling. *Counseling & Human Development*, 13(1), 1–12.

Van Hoose, W. H., & Kottler, J. A. (1985). *Ethical and legal issues in counseling and psychotherapy* (2nd ed.). San Francisco: Jossey-Bass.

Van Hoose, W. H., & Paradise, L. V. (1979). *Ethics in counseling and psychotherapy: Perspectives in issues and decision-making*. Cranston, RI: Carroll Press.

Welfel, E. R., & Lipsitz, N. E. (1984). The ethical behavior of professional psychologists: A critical analysis of the research. *The Counseling Psychologist*, 12(3), 31–42.

Woody, R. H. (1988). *Protecting your mental health practice: How to minimize legal and financial risk*. San Francisco: Jossey-Bass.

APPENDIX A

Professional Standards for the
Training of Group Workers

PREAMBLE

All counselors should possess a set of core competencies in general group work. These basic knowledge and skills provide a foundation which specialty training can extend. Mastery of the core competencies does not qualify one to independently practice any group work specialty. Specialists in group work must possess advanced competencies relevant to a particular group work type.

The Association for Specialists in Group Work (ASGW) advocates for the incorporation of core group competencies as part of the Masters level training required in all counselor education programs. The Association also supports preparation of group counseling specialists at the Masters level. ASGW further supports the continued preparation of group work specialists at the post-Masters level (Ed.S. or Certificate, Doctoral, Continuing Education, etc.), recognizing that recommended levels of group work specialty training in many programs will need to be accomplished following completion of the Masters Degree.

This revision of the *Professional Standards for Training of Group Workers* contains two levels of competencies and related training that have been identified by the ASGW Standards Committee: (1) Core Group Competencies: The minimum core of group worker competencies and related training necessary for all counselors, including knowledge, skills, and practice (Minimum: 10 clock hours; Recommended: 20 clock hours); and (2) For Group Work Specialists: Advanced competencies that build on the generalist core in the four identified group work specialties of:

❏ Task/Work groups, including knowledge, skills, and supervised practice beyond core group training (Additional minimum: 30 clock hours; Recommended: 45 clock hours);
❏ Guidance/Psychoeducation groups, including knowledge, skills, and supervised practice beyond core group training (Additional minimum: 30 clock hours; Recommended: 45 clock hours);
❏ Counseling/Interpersonal Problem-Solving groups, including knowledge, skills, and supervised practice beyond core group training (Additional minimum: 45 clock hours; Recommended: 60 clock hours);
❏ Psychotherapy/Personality Reconstruction groups, including knowledge, skills, and supervised practice beyond core group training (Additional minimum: 45 clock hours; Recommended: 60 clock hours).

DEFINITIONS

Group Work

"Group work" is a broad professional practice that refers to the giving of help or the accomplishment of tasks in a group setting. It involves the application of group theory and process by a capa-

---

Source: From the *Professional Standards for Training of Group Workers*, revised 1990. Reprinted by permission of the Association for Specialists in Group Work (ASGW) and the American Association for Counseling and Development (AACD), Alexandria, VA.

ble professional practitioner to assist an interdependent collection of people to reach their mutual goals, which may be personal, interpersonal, or task-related in nature.

Core Training in Group Work for All Counselors

All professional counselors should possess basic fundamental knowledge and skills in group work. Moreover, this set of competencies provides a basic foundation upon which specialization training in group work is built.

Core training group work competencies does not prepare a counseling professional to independently assume responsibility for conducting any of the specialty groups to be defined in these Standards. Additional focused training is required for independent practice in a specialty, as detailed below.

Group Work Specializations

The trainee may proceed beyond core training in group work to specialize in one or more advanced areas of practice. It is to be expected that all Counseling programs would provide core training in group work to all students and most would offer additional training in at least one of the other specializations.

Definitions of each specialization follow.

Task/Work Groups Much work in contemporary Western society is accomplished through group endeavor. The task/work group specialist is able to assist groups such as task forces, committees, planning groups, community organizations, discussion groups, study circles, learning groups, and other similar groups to correct or develop their functioning. The focus is on the application of group dynamics principles and processes to improve practice and the accomplishment of identified work goals.

Guidance/Psychoeducation Groups Education and prevention are critically important goals for the contemporary counselor. The guidance/psychoeducation group specialist seeks to use the group medium to educate group participants who are presently unaffected about a potential threat (such as AIDS), a developmental life event (such as a transition point), or how to cope with an immediate life crisis (such as suicide of a loved one), with the goal of preventing an array of educational and psychological disturbances from occurring.

Counseling/Interpersonal Problem-Solving The group worker who specializes in counseling/interpersonal problem-solving seeks to help group participants to resolve the usual, yet often difficult, problems of living through interpersonal support and problem solving. An additional goal is to help participants to develop their existing interpersonal problem-solving competencies that they may be better able to handle future problems of a similar nature. Non-severe career, educational, personal, social, and developmental concerns are frequently addressed.

Psychotherapy/Personality Reconstruction The group worker who specializes in psychotherapy/personality reconstruction seeks to help individual group members to remediate their in-depth psychological problems. Because the depth and extent of the psychological disturbance is significant, the goal is to aid each individual to reconstruct major personality dimensions.

TRAINING STANDARDS

A. Core Group Work Training for All Counselors: Knowledge Competencies

All counselors can effectively:

1. State for the four major group work specializations identified in this document (task groups, guidance groups, counseling groups, psychotherapy groups) the distinguishing characteristics of each, the commonalities shared by all, and the appropriate instances in which each is to be used.

2. Identify the basic principles of group dynamics.
3. Discuss the basic therapeutic ingredients of groups.
4. Identify the personal characteristics of group workers that have an impact on members; knowledge of personal strengths, weaknesses, biases, values, and their effect on others.
5. Describe the specific ethical issues that are unique to group work.
6. Discuss the body of research on group work and how it relates to one's academic preparation in either school counseling, student personnel education, community counseling, or mental health counseling.
7. Define the process components involved in typical stages of a group's development (i.e., characteristics of group interaction and counselor roles).
8. Describe the major facilitative and debilitative roles that group members may take.
9. State the advantages and disadvantages of group work and the circumstances for which it is indicated or contraindicated.
10. Detail therapeutic factors of group work.
11. Identify principles and strategies for recruiting and screening prospective group members.
12. Detail the importance of group and member evaluation.
13. Deliver a clear, concise, and complete definition of group work.
14. Deliver a clear, concise, and complete definition of each of the four group work specialties.
15. Explain and clarify the purpose of a particular form of group work.

Core Group Work Training for All Counselors: Skill Competencies

All counselors are able to effectively:

1. Encourage participation of group members.
2. Observe and identify group process events.
3. Attend to and acknowledge group member behavior.
4. Clarify and summarize group member statements.
5. Open and close group sessions.
6. Impart information in the group when necessary.
7. Model effective group leader behavior.
8. Engage in appropriate self-disclosure in the group.
9. Give and receive feedback in the group.
10. Ask open-ended questions in the group.
11. Empathize with group members.
12. Confront group members' behavior.
13. Help group members attribute meaning to their experience.
14. Help group members to integrate and apply learnings.
15. Demonstrate ASGW ethical and professional standards in group practice.
16. Keep the group on task in accomplishing its goals.

Core Group Work Training

Knowledge   Core training in group work should include a minimum of one course. Contained in this course should be attention to competencies in the Knowledge and in the Skills domains.

Skills Through Supervised Practice   The Practice domain should include observation and participation in a group experience, which could occur in a classroom group.

> *Minimum* amount of supervised practice: *10 clock hours.*
>
> *Recommended* amount of supervised practice: *20 clock hours.*

B. Group Work Specializations: Knowledge, Skill and Supervised Practice Domains

The counselor trainee, having mastered the core knowledge and skill domains displayed above, can specialize in one or more advanced areas of group work practice. These advanced specialty areas are Task/Work groups, Guidance/Psychoeducation groups, Counseling/Interpersonal Problem-Solving groups, and Psychotherapy/Personality Reconstruction groups. The advanced knowledge and skill competencies associated with each of these specialties are presented below.

TASK/WORK GROUPS

Knowledge Competencies

In addition to Core knowledge, the qualified Task/Work group specialist can effectively:

1. Identify organizational dynamics pertinent to task/work groups.
2. Describe community dynamics pertinent to task/work groups.
3. Identify political dynamics pertinent to task/work groups.
4. Describe standard discussion methodologies appropriate for task/work groups.
5. Identify specific ethical considerations in working with task/work groups.
6. Identify program development and evaluation models appropriate for task/work groups.
7. List consultation principles and approaches appropriate for task/work groups.

Skills Competencies

In addition to Core skills, the qualified Task/Work group specialist is able to effectively:

1. Focus and maintain attention on task and work issues.
2. Obtain goal clarity in a task/work group.
3. Conduct a personally selected task/work group model appropriate to the age and clientele of the group leader's specialty area(s) (e.g., school counseling).
4. Mobilize energies toward a common goal in task/work groups.
5. Implement group decision-making methods in task/work groups.
6. Manage conflict in task/work groups.
7. Blend the predominant task focus with appropriate attention to human relations factors in task/work groups.
8. Sense and use larger organizational and political dynamics in task/work groups.

Specialist Training: Task/Work Groups

Knowledge   Course work should be taken in the broad area of organization development, management, and/or sociology such that the student understands organizational life and how task groups function within it. Course work also should be taken in consultation.

Skills Through Supervised Practice   In addition to Core training acquired through observation and participation in a group (10 clock hours minimum; 20 clock hours recommended), practice should include:

> *Minimum* amount of *30 clock hours* should be obtained in co-leading or leading a task/work group in a field practice setting supervised by qualified faculty or staff personnel.

> *Recommended* amount of *45 clock hours* should be obtained in co-leading or leading a task/work group in a field practice setting supervised by qualified faculty or staff personnel.

GUIDANCE/PSYCHOEDUCATION GROUPS

Knowledge Competencies

In addition to Core knowledge, the qualified Guidance/Psychoeducation group specialist can effectively:

1. Identify the concepts of primary prevention and secondary prevention in guidance/psychoeducation groups.

2. Articulate the concept of "at risk" in guidance/psychoeducation groups.
3. Enumerate principles of instruction relevant to guidance/psychoeducation groups.
4. Develop a knowledge base relevant to the focus of a guidance/psychoeducation group intervention.
5. List principles involved in obtaining healthy and/or at-risk group members for guidance/psychoeducation groups.
6. Describe human development theory pertinent to guidance/psychoeducation groups.
7. Discuss environmental assessment as related to guidance/psychoeducation groups.
8. Discuss principles of structure as related to guidance/psychoeducation groups.
9. Discuss the concept of empowerment in guidance/psychoeducation groups.
10. Identify specific ethical considerations unique to guidance/psychoeducation groups.
11. List advantages of guidance/psychoeducation groups and where indicated or contra-indicated.

Skills Competencies

In addition to Core skills, the qualified Guidance/Psychoeducation group specialist can effectively:

1. Plan a guidance/psychoeducation group in collaboration with "target" population members or representatives.
2. Match a relevant guidance/psychoeducation topic with a relevant (and currently "unaffected") target group.
3. Conduct a personally selected guidance/psychoeducation group model appropriate to the age and clientele of the group leader's specialty area (e.g., student personnel education).
4. Design a guidance/psychoeducation group plan that is developmentally and practically sound.
5. Present information in a guidance/psychoeducation group.
6. Use environmental dynamics to the benefit of the guidance/psychoeducation group.
7. Conduct skill training in guidance/psychoeducation groups.

Specialist Training: Guidance/Psychoeducation Groups

Knowledge Course work should be taken in the broad areas of community psychology, health promotion, marketing, consultation, and curriculum design.

Skills Through Supervised Practice In addition to Core training acquired through observation and participation in a group (10 clock hours minimum; 20 clock hours recommended), practice should include:

Minimum amount of *10 clock hours* should be obtained in co-leading or leading a guidance/psychoeducation group in a field practice setting supervised by qualified faculty or staff personnel.

Recommended amount of *45 clock hours* should be obtained in co-leading or leading a guidance/psychoeducation group in a practice setting supervised by qualified faculty or staff personnel.

COUNSELING/INTERPERSONAL PROBLEM-SOLVING GROUPS

Knowledge Competencies

In addition to Core knowledge, the qualified Counseling/Interpersonal Problem-Solving group specialist can effectively:

1. State for at least three major theoretical approaches to group counseling the distinguishing characteristics of each and the commonalities shared by all.
2. Identify specific ethical problems and considerations unique to group counseling.
3. List advantages and disadvantages of group counseling and the circumstances for which it is indicated or contra-indicated.

4. Describe interpersonal dynamics in group counseling.
5. Describe group problem-solving approaches in relation to group counseling.
6. Discuss interpersonal assessment in group counseling.
7. Identify referral sources and procedures in group counseling.
8. Describe group formation principles in group counseling.

Skills Competencies

In addition to Core skills, the qualified Counseling/Interpersonal Problem-Solving group specialist can effectively:

1. Recruit and screen prospective counseling members.
2. Recognize self-defeating behaviors of counseling group members.
3. Conduct a personally selected group counseling model appropriate to the age and clientele of the group leader's specialty area(s) (e.g., community counseling).
4. Develop reasonable hypotheses about nonverbal behavior among counseling group members.
5. Exhibit appropriate pacing skills involved in stages of a counseling group's development.
6. Intervene effectively at critical incidents in the counseling group process.
7. Work appropriately with disruptive counseling group members.
8. Make use of the major strategies, techniques, and procedures of group counseling.
9. Use procedures to assist transfer and support of changes by group members in the natural environment.
10. Use adjunct group counseling structures such as homework (e.g., goal setting).
11. Work cooperatively and effectively with a counseling group co-leader.
12. Use assessment procedures in evaluating effects and contributions of group counseling.

Specialist Training: Counseling/Interpersonal Problem-Solving Groups

Knowledge   As much course work in group counseling as possible is desirable, but at least one course beyond the generalist is necessary. Other courses in the Counseling program should provide good support for the group counseling specialty.

Skills Through Supervised Practice   In addition to Core training acquired through observation and participation in a group (10 clock hours minimum; 20 clock hours recommended), practice should include:

> *Minimum* amount of *45 clock hours* should be obtained in co-leading or leading a counseling/interpersonal problem-solving group in a field practice setting supervised by qualified faculty or staff personnel.

> *Recommended* amount of *60 clock hours* should be obtained in co-leading or leading a counseling/interpersonal problem-solving group in a field practice setting supervised by qualified faculty or staff personnel.

PSYCHOTHERAPY/PERSONALITY RECONSTRUCTION GROUPS

Knowledge Competencies

In addition to Core knowledge, the Psychotherapy/Personality Reconstruction group specialist can effectively:

1. State for at least three major theoretical approaches to group psychotherapy the distinguishing characteristics of each and the commonalities shared by all.
2. Identify specific ethical problems and considerations unique to group psychotherapy.
3. List advantages and disadvantages of group psychotherapy and the circumstances for which it is indicated or contra-indicated.

4. Specify intrapersonal and interpersonal dynamics in group psychotherapy.
5. Describe group problem-solving approaches in relation to group psychotherapy.
6. Discuss interpersonal assessment and intervention in group psychotherapy.
7. Identify referral sources and procedures in group psychotherapy.
8. Describe group formation principles in group psychotherapy.
9. Identify and describe abnormal behavior in relation to group psychotherapy.
10. Identify psychopathology as related to group psychotherapy.
11. Describe personality theory as related to group psychotherapy.
12. Detail crisis intervention approaches suitable for group psychotherapy.
13. Specify diagnostic and assessment methods appropriate for group psychotherapy.

Skill Competencies

In addition to Core skills, the qualified Psychotherapy/Personality Reconstruction group specialist can effectively:

1. Recruit and screen prospective psychotherapy group members.
2. Recognize self-defeating behaviors of psychotherapy group members.
3. Describe and conduct a personally selected group psychotherapy model appropriate to the age and clientele of the group leader's specialty area (e.g., mental health counseling).
4. Identify and develop reasonable hypotheses about nonverbal behavior among psychotherapy group members.
5. Exhibit appropriate pacing skills involved in stages of a psychotherapy group's development.
6. Identify and intervene effectively at critical incidents in the psychotherapy group process.
7. Work appropriately with disruptive psychotherapy group members.
8. Make use of the major strategies, techniques, and procedures of group psychotherapy.
9. Provide and use procedures to assist transfer and support of changes by group psychotherapy members in the natural environment.
10. Use adjunct group psychotherapy structures such as psychological homework (e.g., self-monitoring, contracting).
11. Work cooperatively and effectively with a psychotherapy group co-leader.
12. Use assessment procedures in evaluating effects and contributions of group psychotherapy.
13. Assist individual change along the full range of development, from "normal" to "abnormal" in the psychotherapy group.
14. Handle psychological emergencies in the psychotherapy group.
15. Institute hospitalization procedures when appropriate and necessary in the psychotherapy group.
16. Assess and diagnose mental and emotional disorders of psychotherapy group members.

Specialist Training: Psychotherapy/Personality Reconstruction Groups

Knowledge   Course work should be taken in the areas of group psychotherapy, abnormal psychology, psychopathology, and diagnostic assessment to assure capabilities in working with more disturbed populations.

Skills Through Supervised Practice   In addition to Core training acquired through observation and participation in a group (10 clock hours minimum; 20 clock hours recommended), practice should include:

Minimum amount of *45 clock hours* should be obtained in co-leading or leading a psychotherapy/personality reconstruction group in a field practice setting supervised by qualified faculty or staff personnel.

Recommended amount of *60 clock hours* should be obtained in co-leading or leading a psychotherapy/personality reconstruction group in a field practice setting supervised by qualified faculty or staff personnel.

IMPLEMENTATION GUIDELINES FOR THE ASGW STANDARDS: INTEGRATION WITH CACREP ACCREDITATION STANDARDS

1. (a) Core group work knowledge for all counseling students can be obtained through a basic course in group theory and practice. Consistent with accreditation standards (CACREP II-J.4), study in the area of *Groups* should provide an understanding of group development, group dynamics, and group leadership styles; group leadership methods and skills; and group types, including group counseling, task groups, guidance groups, and psychotherapy groups. More explicitly, studies would include, but not be limited to the following:

1. Principles of group dynamics including group process components, developmental stage theories, and group members' roles and behaviors.
2. Group leadership styles and approaches including characteristics of various types of group leaders and leadership styles.
3. Knowledge of group work types (counseling, task, guidance, and psychotherapy) including commonalities, distinguishing characteristics, and pertinent research and literature.
4. Group work methods including group leader orientations and behaviors, ethical considerations, appropriate selection criteria and methods, and methods of evaluating effectiveness.
5. Development of skills in explicit and implicit teaching, group process observation, opening and closing sessions, self-disclosing, giving and receiving feedback, modeling, focusing, protecting, managing, recruiting and selecting members, empathizing, confronting, and evaluating.

(b) Core group work training for all counseling students requires a minimum of 10 clock hours of supervised practice, and a recommended amount of 20 clock hours. These skills can be obtained through the basic course in group theory and practice mentioned in 1(a) above (which should provide for direct group participation) and through satisfying the accreditation standard II-F, which provides students with the opportunity to participate in a planned and supervised small group activity. In the latter activity, care must be taken to assure that the AACD and ASGW ethical standard relating to dual relationships is preserved.

2. Specialist group work training can occur beyond the core group work training for programs and students desiring advanced competency development. The specialist training in group work is in Task/Work groups, Guidance/Psychoeducational groups, Counseling/Interpersonal Problem-Solving groups, and/or Psychotherapy/Personality Reconstruction groups.

(a) *Specialized knowledge:* Additional course work is necessary for each of the specialty areas, as follows:

❏ *Task Groups:* As necessary, course work in such areas as organization development, consultation, management, or sociology so students gain a basic understanding of organizations and how task groups function in them.
❏ *Guidance Groups:* As necessary, course work in areas such as community psychology, health promotion, marketing, consultation, and/or curriculum design to provide working knowledge of prevention and structured groups in such areas as stress management, wellness, assertiveness training, problem solving, and smoking cessation.
❏ *Counseling Groups:* At least one course is necessary in group counseling. This additional course should provide opportunities for group membership and leadership, and it should advance conceptual knowledge of group work.
❏ *Psychotherapy Groups:* Course work in such areas as group psychotherapy, abnormal psychology, psychopathology, and diagnostic assessment.

(b) Additional supervised clinical experience is necessary for each of the specialty areas, as follows:

❏ *Task groups:* (30 clock hours minimum, 45 desired)
❏ *Guidance groups:* (30 clock hours minimum, 45 desired)

❑ *Counseling groups:* (45 clock hours minimum, 60 desired)
❑ *Psychotherapy groups:* (45 clock hours minimum, 60 desired)

For *Masters* students, in addition to courses offering content and experience related to the four group work specializations, supervised clinical experience should be obtained in practice and internship, as follows:

Masters Practicum: (CACREP standard III-H). At least 15 hours (of the 40 clock hours stipulated for direct service) should be spent in supervised leadership or co-leadership experience in a group work type designated by ASGW in Counseling, Task, Guidance, or Psychotherapy groups. At the Masters Practicum level, psychotherapy experience ordinarily would be unusual.

Masters Internship: (CACREP standard III-I). At least 90 clock hours (of the 240 clock hours stipulated for direct service) should be spent in supervised leadership or co-leadership. Approximately half of that experience (about 45 clock hours) should be spent leading counseling groups with the remaining time spent leading task, guidance, or psychotherapy groups.

Doctoral Internship: (CACREP standard O). At least 450 clock hours (of the 1200 clock hours stipulated) should be spent in supervised group work leadership or co-leadership. Approximately half of that experience (about 225 clock hours) should be spent leading counseling groups with the remaining time spent leading task, guidance, or psychotherapy groups.

APPENDIX B

Ethical Guidelines for Group Counselors

PREAMBLE

One characteristic of any professional group is the possession of a body of knowledge, skills, and voluntarily, self-professed standards for ethical practice. A Code of Ethics consists of those standards that have been formally and publicly acknowledged by the members of a profession to serve as the guidelines for professional conduct, discharge of duties, and the resolution of moral dilemmas. By this document, the Association for Specialists in Group Work (ASGW) has identified the standards of conduct appropriate for ethical behavior among its members.

The Association for Specialists in Group Work recognizes the basic commitment of its members to the Ethical Standards of its parent organization, the American Association for Counseling and Development (AACD) and nothing in this document shall be construed to supplant that code. These standards are intended to complement the AACD standards in the area of group work by clarifying the nature of ethical responsibility of the counselor in the group setting and by stimulating a greater concern for competent group leadership.

The group counselor is expected to be a professional agent and to take the processes of ethical responsibility seriously. ASGW views "ethical process" as being integral to group work and views group counselors as "ethical agents." Group counselors, by their very nature in being responsible and responsive to their group members, necessarily embrace a certain potential for ethical vulnerability. It is incumbent upon group counselors to give considerable attention to the intent and context of their actions because the attempts of counselors to influence human behavior through group work always have ethical implications.

The following ethical guidelines have been developed to encourage ethical behavior of group counselors. These guidelines are written for students and practitioners, and are meant to stimulate reflection, self-examination, and discussion of issues and practices. They address the group counselor's responsibility for providing information about group work to clients and the group counselor's responsibility for providing group counseling services to clients. A final section discusses the group counselor's responsibility for safeguarding ethical practice and procedures for reporting unethical behavior. Group counselors are expected to make known these standards to group members.

ETHICAL GUIDELINES

1. *Orientation and Providing Information:* Group counselors adequately prepare prospective or new group members by providing as much information about the existing or proposed group as necessary.

   Minimally, information related to each of the following areas should be provided.

   (a) Entrance procedures, time parameters of the group experience, group participation expectations, methods of payment (where appropriate), and termination procedures are explained by the group counselor as appropriate to the level of maturity of group members and the nature and purpose(s) of the group.

Source: Approved by the Association for Specialists in Group Work (ASGW), Executive Board, June 1, 1989. Reprinted by permission of the American Association for Counseling and Development (AACD), Alexandria, VA.

(b) Group counselors have available for distribution a professional disclosure statement that includes information on the group counselor's qualifications and group services that can be provided, particularly as related to the nature and purpose(s) of the specific group.

(c) Group counselors communicate the role expectations, rights, and responsibilities of group members and group counselor(s).

(d) The group goals are stated as concisely as possible by the group counselor including "whose" goal it is (the group counselor's, the institution's, the parent's, the law's, society's, etc.) and the role of group members in influencing or determining the group's goal(s).

(e) Group counselors explore with group members the risks of potential life changes that may occur because of the group experience and help members explore their readiness to face these possibilities.

(f) Group members are informed by the group counselor of unusual or experimental procedures that might be expected in their group experience.

(g) Group counselors explain, as realistically as possible, what services can and cannot be provided within the particular group structure offered.

(h) Group counselors emphasize the need to promote full psychological functioning and presence among group members. They inquire from prospective group members whether they are using any kind of drug or medication that may affect functioning in the group. They do not permit any use of alcohol and/or illegal drugs during group sessions and they discourage the use of alcohol and/or drugs (legal or illegal) prior to group meetings which may affect the physical or emotional presence of the member or other group members.

(i) Group counselors inquire from prospective group members whether they have ever been a client in counseling or psychotherapy. If a prospective group member is already in a counseling relationship with another professional person, the group counselor advises the prospective group member to notify the other professional of their participation in the group.

(j) Group counselors clearly inform group members about the policies pertaining to the group counselor's willingness to consult with them between group sessions.

(k) In establishing fees for group counseling services, group counselors consider the financial status and the locality of prospective group members. Group members are not charged fees for group sessions where the group counselor is not present and the policy of charging for sessions missed by a group member is clearly communicated. Fees for participating as a group member are contracted between group counselor and group member for a specified period of time. Group counselors do not increase fees for group counseling services until the existing contracted fee structure has expired. In the event that the established fee structure is inappropriate for a prospective member, group counselors assist in finding comparable services of acceptable cost.

2. *Screening of Members:* The group counselor screens prospective group members (when appropriate to their theoretical orientation). Insofar as possible, the counselor selects group members whose needs and goals are compatible with the goals of the group, who will not impede the group process, and whose well-being will not be jeopardized by the group experience. An orientation to the group (i.e., ASGW Ethical Guideline number 1), is included during the screening process.

Screening may be accomplished in one or more ways, such as the following:

(a) Individual interview,

(b) Group interview of prospective group members,

(c) Interview as part of a team staffing, and

(d) Completion of a written questionnaire by prospective group members.

3. *Confidentiality:* Group counselors protect members by defining clearly what confidentiality means, why it is important, and the difficulties involved in enforcement.

(a) Group counselors take steps to protect members by defining confidentiality and the limits of confidentiality (i.e., when a group member's condition indicates that there is clear and imminent danger to the member, others, or physical property, the group counselor takes reasonable personal action and/or informs responsible authorities).

    (b) Group counselors stress the importance of confidentiality and set a norm of confidentiality regarding all group participants' disclosures. The importance of maintaining confidentiality is emphasized before the group begins and at various times in the group. The fact that confidentiality cannot be guaranteed is clearly stated.

    (c) Members are made aware of the difficulties involved in enforcing and ensuring confidentiality in a group setting. The counselor provides examples of how confidentiality can non-maliciously be broken to increase members' awareness, and help to lessen the likelihood that this breach of confidence will occur. Group counselors inform group members about the potential consequences of intentionally breaching confidentiality.

    (d) Group counselors can only ensure confidentiality on their part and not on the part of the members.

    (e) Group counselors video or audio tape a group session only with the prior consent, and the members' knowledge of how the tape will be used.

    (f) When working with minors, the group counselor specifies the limits of confidentiality.

    (g) Participants in a mandatory group are made aware of any reporting procedures required of the group counselor.

    (h) Group counselors store or dispose of group member records (written, audio, video, etc.) in ways that maintain confidentiality.

    (i) Instructors of group counseling courses maintain the anonymity of group members whenever discussing group counseling cases.

4. *Voluntary/Involuntary Participation:* Group counselors inform members whether participation is voluntary or involuntary.

    (a) Group counselors take steps to ensure informed consent procedures in both voluntary and involuntary groups.

    (b) When working with minors in a group, counselors are expected to follow the procedures specified by the institution in which they are practicing.

    (c) With involuntary groups, every attempt is made to enlist the cooperation of the members and their continuance in the group on a voluntary basis.

    (d) Group counselors do not certify that group treatment has been received by members who merely attend sessions, but did not meet the defined group expectations. Group members are informed about the consequences for failing to participate in a group.

5. *Leaving a Group:* Provisions are made to assist a group member to terminate in an effective way.

    (a) Procedures to be followed for a group member who chooses to exit a group prematurely are discussed by the counselor with all group members either before the group begins, during a pre-screening interview, or during the initial group session.

    (b) In the case of legally mandated group counseling, group counselors inform members of the possible consequences for premature self-termination.

    (c) Ideally, both the group counselor and the member can work cooperatively to determine the degree to which a group experience is productive or counterproductive for that individual.

    (d) Members ultimately have a right to discontinue membership in the group, at a designated time, if the predetermined trial period proves to be unsatisfactory.

    (e) Members have the right to exit a group, but it is important that they be made aware of the importance of informing the counselor and the group members prior to deciding to leave. The counselor discusses the possible risks of leaving the group prematurely with a member who is considering this option.

    (f) Before leaving a group, the group counselor encourages members (if appropriate) to discuss their reasons for wanting to discontinue membership in the group. Counselors intervene if other members use undue pressure to force a member to remain in the group.

6. *Coercion and Pressure:* Group counselors protect member rights against physical threats, intimidation, coercion, and undue peer pressure insofar as is reasonably possible.

    (a) It is essential to differentiate between "therapeutic pressure" that is part of any group and "undue pressure," which is not therapeutic.

    (b) The purpose of a group is to help participants find their own answer, not to pressure them into doing what the group thinks is appropriate.

(c) Counselors exert care not to coerce participants to change in directions which they clearly state they do not choose.

(d) Counselors have a responsibility to intervene when others use undue pressure or attempt to persuade members against their will.

(e) Counselors intervene when any member attempts to act out aggression in a physical way that might harm another member or themselves.

(f) Counselors intervene when a member is verbally abusive or inappropriately confrontive to another member.

7. *Imposing Counselor Values:* Group counselors develop an awareness of their own values and needs and the potential impact they have on the interventions likely to be made.

(a) Although group counselors take care to avoid imposing their values on members, it is appropriate that they expose their own beliefs, decisions, needs, and values, when concealing them would create problems for the members.

(b) There are values implicit in any group, and these are made clear to potential members before they join the group. (Examples of certain values include: expressing feelings, being direct and honest, sharing personal material with others, learning how to trust, improving interpersonal communication, and deciding for oneself.)

(c) Personal and professional needs of group counselors are not met at the members' expense.

(d) Group counselors avoid using the group for their own therapy.

(e) Group counselors are aware of their own values and assumptions and how these apply in a multicultural context.

(f) Group counselors take steps to increase their awareness of ways that their personal reactions to members might inhibit the group process and they monitor their countertransference. Through an awareness of the impact of stereotyping and discrimination (i.e., biases based on age, disability, ethnicity, gender, race, religion, or sexual preference), group counselors guard the individual rights and personal dignity of all group members.

8. *Equitable Treatment:* Group counselors make every reasonable effort to treat each member individually and equally.

(a) Group counselors recognize and respect differences (e.g., cultural, racial, religious, lifestyle, age, disability, gender) among group members.

(b) Group counselors maintain an awareness of their behavior toward individual group members and are alert to the potential detrimental effects of favoritism or partiality toward any particular group member to the exclusion or detriment of any other member(s). It is likely that group counselors will favor some members over others, yet all group members deserve to be treated equally.

(c) Group counselors ensure equitable use of group time for each member by inviting silent members to become involved, acknowledging nonverbal attempts to communicate, and discouraging rambling and monopolizing of time by members.

(d) If a large group is planned, counselors consider enlisting another qualified professional to serve as a co-leader for the group sessions.

9. *Dual Relationships:* Group counselors avoid dual relationships with group members that might impair their objectivity and professional judgment, as well as those which are likely to compromise a group member's ability to participate fully in the group.

(a) Group counselors do not misuse their professional role and power as group leader to advance personal or social contacts with members throughout the duration of the group.

(b) Group counselors do not use their professional relationship with group members to further their own interest either during the group or after the termination of the group.

(c) Sexual intimacies between group counselors and members are unethical.

(d) Group counselors do not barter (exchange) professional services with group members for services.

(e) Group counselors do not admit their own family members, relatives, employees, or personal friends as members to their groups.

(f) Group counselors discuss with group members the potential detrimental effects of group members engaging in intimate inter-member relationships outside of the group.

(g) Students who participate in a group as a partial course requirement for a group course are not evaluated for an academic grade based upon their degree of participation as a member in a group. Instructors of group counseling courses take steps to minimize the possible negative impact on students when they participate in a group course by separating course grades from participation in the group and by allowing students to decide what issues to explore and when to stop.

(h) It is inappropriate to solicit members from a class (or institutional affiliation) for one's private counseling or therapeutic groups.

10. *Use of Techniques:* Group counselors do not attempt any technique unless trained in its use or under supervision by a counselor familiar with the intervention.

(a) Group counselors are able to articulate a theoretical orientation that guides their practice, and they are able to provide a rationale for their interventions.

(b) Depending upon the type of intervention, group counselors have training commensurate with the potential impact of a technique.

(c) Group counselors are aware of the necessity to modify their techniques to fit the unique needs of various cultural and ethnic groups.

(d) Group counselors assist members in translating in-group learnings to daily life.

11. *Goal Development:* Group counselors make every effort to assist members in developing their personal goals.

(a) Group counselors use their skills to assist members in making their goals specific so that others present in the group will understand the nature of the goals.

(b) Throughout the course of a group, group counselors assist members in assessing the degree to which personal goals are being met, and assist in revising any goals when it is appropriate.

(c) Group counselors help members clarify the degree to which the goals can be met within the context of a particular group.

12. *Consultation:* Group counselors develop and explain policies about between-session consultation to group members.

(a) Group counselors take care to make certain that members do not use between-session consultations to avoid dealing with issues pertaining to the group that would be dealt with best in the group.

(b) Group counselors urge members to bring the issues discussed during between-session consultations into the group if they pertain to the group.

(c) Group counselors seek out consultation and/or supervision regarding ethical concerns or when encountering difficulties which interfere with their effective functioning as group leaders.

(d) Group counselors seek appropriate professional assistance for their own personal problems or conflicts that are likely to impair their professional judgment and work performance.

(e) Group counselors discuss their group cases only for professional consultation and educational purposes.

(f) Group counselors inform members about policies regarding whether consultations will be held confidential.

13. *Termination from the Group:* Depending upon the purpose of participation in the group, counselors promote termination of members from the group in the most efficient period of time.

(a) Group counselors maintain a constant awareness of the progress made by each group member and periodically invite the group members to explore and reevaluate their experiences in the group. It is the responsibility of group counselors to help promote the independence of members from the group in a timely manner.

14. *Evaluation and Follow-up:* Group counselors make every attempt to engage in ongoing assessment and to design follow-up procedures for their groups.

(a) Group counselors recognize the importance of ongoing assessment of a group, and they assist members in evaluating their own progress.

(b) Group counselors conduct evaluation of the total group experience at the final meeting (or before termination), as well as ongoing evaluation.

(c) Group counselors monitor their own behavior and become aware of what they are modeling in the group.

(d) Follow-up procedures might take the form of personal contact, telephone contact, or written contact.

(e) Follow-up meetings might be with individuals, or groups, or both to determine the degree to which: (i) members have reached their goals, (ii) the group had a positive or negative effect on the participants, (iii) members could profit from some type of referral, and (iv) as information for possible modification of future groups. If there is no follow-up meeting, provisions are made available for individual follow-up meetings to any member who needs or requests such a contact.

15. *Referrals:* If the needs of a particular member cannot be met within the type of group being offered, the group counselor suggests other appropriate professional referrals.

(a) Group counselors are knowledgeable of local community resources for assisting group members regarding professional referrals.

(b) Group counselors help members seek further professional assistance, if needed.

16. *Professional Development:* Group counselors recognize that professional growth is a continuous, ongoing, developmental process throughout their career.

(a) Group counselors maintain and upgrade their knowledge and skill competencies through educational activities, clinical experiences, and participation in professional development activities.

(b) Group counselors keep abreast of research findings and new developments as applied to groups.

SAFEGUARDING ETHICAL PRACTICE AND PROCEDURES FOR REPORTING UNETHICAL BEHAVIOR

The preceding remarks have been advanced as guidelines which are generally representative of ethical and professional group practice. They have not been proposed as rigidly defined prescriptions. However, practitioners who are thought to be grossly unresponsive to the ethical concerns addressed in this document may be subject to a review of their practices by the AACD Ethics Committee and ASGW peers.

1. For consultation and/or questions regarding these ASGW Ethical Guidelines or group ethical dilemmas, you may contact the Chairperson of the ASGW Ethics Committee. The name, address, and telephone number of the current ASGW Ethics Committee Chairperson may be acquired by telephoning the AACD office in Alexandria, Virginia at (703) 823-9800.

2. If a group counselor's behavior is suspected as being unethical, the following procedures are to be followed:

(a) Collect more information and investigate further to confirm the unethical practice as determined by the ASGW Ethical Guidelines.

(b) Confront the individual with the apparent violation of ethical guidelines for the purposes of protecting the safety of any clients and to help the group counselor correct any inappropriate behaviors. If satisfactory resolution is not reached through this contact then:

(c) A complaint should be made in writing, including the specific facts and dates of the alleged violation and all relevant supporting data. The complaint should be included in an envelope marked "CONFIDENTIAL" to ensure confidentiality for both the accuser(s) and the alleged violator(s) and forwarded to all of the following sources:

1. The name and address of the Chairperson of the state Counselor Licensure Board for the respective state, if in existence.

2. The Ethics Committee
c/o the President
American Association for Counseling and Development
5999 Stevenson Avenue
Alexandria, Virginia 22304

3. The name and address of all private credentialing agencies that the alleged violator maintains credentials or holds professional membership. Some of these include the following:

National Board for Certified Counselors, Inc.
5999 Stevenson Avenue
Alexandria, Virginia 22304

National Council for Credentialing of Career Counselors
c/o NBCC
5999 Stevenson Avenue
Alexandria, Virginia 22304

National Academy for Certified Clinical Mental Health Counselors
5999 Stevenson Avenue
Alexandria, Virginia 22304

Commission on Rehabilitation Counselor Certification
162 North State Street, Suite 317
Chicago, Illinois 60601

American Association for Marriage and Family Therapy
1717 K Street, N. W., Suite 407
Washington, D. C. 22006

American Psychological Association
1200 Seventeenth Street, N. W.
Washington, D. C. 22036

American Group Psychotherapy Association, Inc.
25 East 21st Street, 6th Floor
New York, New York 10010

APPENDIX C

Ethical Standards of the American Association for Counseling and Development (As Revised by AACD Governing Council, March 1988)

PREAMBLE

The Association is an educational, scientific, and professional organization whose members are dedicated to the enhancement of the worth, dignity, potential, and uniqueness of each individual and thus to the service of society.

The Association recognizes that the role definitions and work settings of its members include a wide variety of academic disciplines, levels of academic preparation, and agency services. This diversity reflects the breadth of the Association's interest and influence. It also poses challenging complexities in efforts to set standards for the performance of members, desired requisite preparation or practice, and supporting social, legal, and ethical controls.

The specification of ethical standards enables the Association to clarify to present and future members and to those served by members the nature of ethical responsibilities held in common by its members.

The existence of such standards serves to stimulate greater concern by members for their own professional functioning and for the conduct of fellow professionals such as counselors, guidance and student personnel workers, and others in the helping professions. As the ethical code of the Association, this document establishes principles that define the ethical behavior of Association members. Additional ethical guidelines developed by the Association's Divisions for their specialty areas may further define a member's ethical behavior.

SECTION A: GENERAL

1. The member influences the development of the profession by continuous efforts to improve professional practices, teaching, services, and research. Professional growth is continuous throughout the member's career and is exemplified by the development of a philosophy that explains why and how a member functions in the helping relationship. Members must gather data on their effectiveness and be guided by the findings. Members recognize the need for continuing education to ensure competent service.
2. The member has a responsibility both to the individual who is served and to the institution within which the service is performed to maintain high standards of professional conduct. The member strives to maintain the highest levels of professional services offered to the individuals to be served. The member also strives to assist the agency, organization, or institution in providing the highest caliber of services. The acceptance of employment in an institution implies that the member is in agreement with the general policies and principles of the institution.

Source: American Association for Counseling and Development, 5999 Stevenson Avenue, Alexandria, VA 22304; 703-823-9800. Reprinted by permission.

Therefore the professional activities of the member are also in accord with the objectives of the institution. If, despite concerted efforts, the member cannot reach agreement with the employer as to acceptable standards of conduct that allow for changes in institutional policy conducive to the positive growth and development of clients, then terminating the affiliation should be seriously considered.

3. Ethical behavior among professional associates, both members and nonmembers, must be expected at all times. When information is possessed that raises doubt as to the ethical behavior of professional colleagues, whether Association members or not, the member must take action to attempt to rectify such a condition. Such action shall use the institution's channels first and then use procedures established by the Association.

4. The member neither claims nor implies professional qualifications exceeding those possessed and is responsible for correcting any misrepresentations of these qualifications by others.

5. In establishing fees for professional counseling services, members must consider the financial status of clients, and locality. In the event that the established fee structure is inappropriate for a client, assistance must be provided in finding comparable services of acceptable cost.

6. When members provide information to the public or to subordinates, peers, or supervisors, they have a responsibility to ensure that the content is general, unidentified client information that is accurate, unbiased, and consists of objective, factual data.

7. Members recognize their boundaries of competence and provide only those services and use only those techniques for which they are qualified by training or experience. Members should only accept those positions for which they are professionally qualified.

8. In the counseling relationship, the counselor is aware of the intimacy of the relationship and maintains respect for the client and avoids engaging in activities that seek to meet the counselor's personal needs at the expense of that client.

9. Members do not condone or engage in sexual harassment which is defined as deliberate or repeated comments, gestures, or physical contacts of a sexual nature.

10. The member avoids bringing personal issues into the counseling relationship, especially if the potential for harm is present. Through awareness of the negative impact of both racial and sexual stereotyping and discrimination, the counselor guards the individual rights and personal dignity of the client in the counseling relationship.

11. Products or services provided by the member by means of classroom instruction, public lectures, demonstrations, written articles, radio or television programs, or other types of media must meet the criteria cited in these standards.

SECTION B: COUNSELING RELATIONSHIP

This section refers to practices and procedures of individual and/or group counseling relationships.
The member must recognize the need for client freedom of choice. Under those circumstances where this is not possible, the member must apprise clients of restrictions that may limit their freedom of choice.

1. The member's primary obligation is to respect the integrity and promote the welfare of the client(s), whether the client(s) is (are) assisted individually or in a group relationship. In a group setting, the member is also responsible for taking reasonable precautions to protect individuals from physical and/or psychological trauma resulting from interaction within the group.

2. Members make provisions for maintaining confidentiality in the storage and disposal of records and follow an established record retention and disposition policy. The counseling relationship and information resulting therefrom must be kept confidential, consistent with the obligations of the member as a professional person. In a group counseling setting, the counselor must set a norm of confidentiality regarding all group participants' disclosures.

3. If an individual is already in a counseling relationship with another professional person, the member does not enter into a counseling relationship without first contacting and receiving the approval of that other professional. If the member discovers that the client is in another counseling relationship after the counseling relationship begins, the member must gain the consent

of the other professional or terminate the relationship, unless the client elects to terminate the other relationship.

4. When the client's condition indicates that there is clear and imminent danger to the client or others, the member must take reasonable personal action or inform responsible authorities. Consultation with other professionals must be used where possible. The assumption of responsibility for the client's(s') behavior must be taken only after careful deliberation. The client must be involved in the resumption of responsibility as quickly as possible.

5. Records of the counseling relationship, including interview notes, test data, correspondence, tape recordings, electronic data storage, and other documents are to be considered professional information for use in counseling, and they should not be considered a part of the records of the institution or agency in which the counselor is employed unless specified by state statute or regulation. Revelation to others of counseling material must occur only upon the expressed consent of the client.

6. In view of the extensive data storage and processing capacities of the computer, the member must ensure that data maintained on a computer is: (a) limited to information that is appropriate and necessary for the services being provided; (b) destroyed after it is determined that the information is no longer of any value in providing services; and (c) restricted in terms of access to appropriate staff members involved in the provision of services by using the best computer security methods available.

7. Use of data derived from a counseling relationship for purposes of counselor training or research shall be confined to content that can be disguised to ensure full protection of the identity of the subject client.

8. The member must inform the client of the purposes, goals, techniques, rules of procedure, and limitations that may affect the relationship at or before the time that the counseling relationship is entered. When working with minors or persons who are unable to give consent, the member protects these clients' best interests.

9. In view of common misconceptions related to the perceived inherent validity of computer-generated data and narrative reports, the member must ensure that the client is provided with information as part of the counseling relationship that adequately explains the limitations of computer technology.

10. The member must screen prospective group participants, especially when the emphasis is on self-understanding and growth through self-disclosure. The member must maintain an awareness of the group participants' compatibility throughout the life of the group.

11. The member may choose to consult with any other professionally competent person about a client. In choosing a consultant, the member must avoid placing the consultant in a conflict of interest situation that would preclude the consultant's being a proper party to the member's efforts to help the client.

12. If the member determines an inability to be of professional assistance to the client, the member must either avoid initiating the counseling relationship or immediately terminate that relationship. In either event, the member must suggest appropriate alternatives. (The member must be knowledgeable about referral resources so that a satisfactory referral can be initiated.) In the event the client declines the suggested referral, the member is not obligated to continue the relationship.

13. When the member has other relationships, particularly of an administrative, supervisory, and/or evaluative nature with an individual seeking counseling services, the member must not serve as the counselor but should refer the individual to another professional. Only in instances where such an alternative is unavailable and where the individual's situation warrants counseling intervention should the member enter into and/or maintain a counseling relationship. Dual relationships with clients that might impair the member's objectivity and professional judgment (e.g., as with close friends or relatives) must be avoided and/or the counseling relationship terminated through referral to another competent professional.

14. The member will avoid any type of sexual intimacies with clients. Sexual relationships with clients are unethical.

15. All experimental methods of treatment must be clearly indicated to prospective recipients, and safety precautions are to be adhered to by the member.

16. When computer applications are used as a component of counseling services, the member must ensure that: (a) the client is intellectually, emotionally, and physically capable of using the computer application; (b) the computer application is appropriate for the needs of the client; (c) the client understands the purpose and operation of the computer application; and (d) a follow-up of client use of a computer application is provided to both correct possible problems (misconceptions or inappropriate use) and assess subsequent needs.

17. When the member is engaged in short-term group treatment/training programs (e.g., marathons and other encounter-type or growth groups), the member ensures that there is professional assistance available during and following the group experience.

18. Should the member be engaged in a work setting that calls for any variation from the above statements, the member is obligated to consult with other professionals whenever possible to consider justifiable alternatives.

19. The member must ensure that members of various ethnic, racial, religious, disability, and socioeconomic groups have equal access to computer applications used to support counseling services and that the content of available computer applications does not discriminate against the groups described above.

20. When computer applications are developed by the member for use by the general public as self-help/stand-alone computer software, the member must ensure that: (a) self-help computer applications are designed from the beginning to function in a stand-alone manner, as opposed to modifying software that was originally designed to require support from a counselor; (b) self-help computer applications will include within the program statements regarding intended user outcomes, suggestions for using the software, a description of the conditions under which self-help computer applications might not be appropriate, and a description of when and how counseling services might be beneficial; and (c) the manual for such applications will include the qualifications of the developer, the development process, validation data, and operating procedures.

SECTION C: MEASUREMENT & EVALUATION

The primary purpose of educational and psychological testing is to provide descriptive measures that are objective and interpretable in either comparative or absolute terms. The member must recognize the need to interpret the statements that follow as applying to the whole range of appraisal techniques including test and nontest data. Test results constitute only one of a variety of pertinent sources of information for personnel, guidance, and counseling decisions.

1. The member must provide specific orientation or information to the examinee(s) prior to and following the test administration so that the results of testing may be placed in proper perspective with other relevant factors. In so doing, the member must recognize the effects of socioeconomic, ethnic, and cultural factors on test scores. It is the member's professional responsibility to use additional unvalidated information carefully in modifying interpretation of the test results.

2. In selecting tests for use in a given situation or with a particular client, the member must consider carefully the specific validity, reliability, and appropriateness of the test(s). General validity, reliability, and related issues may be questioned legally as well as ethically when tests are used for vocational and educational selection, placement, or counseling.

3. When making any statements to the public about tests and testing, the member must give accurate information and avoid false claims or misconceptions. Special efforts are often required to avoid unwarranted connotations of such terms as IQ and grade equivalent scores.

4. Different tests demand different levels of competence for administration, scoring, and interpretation. Members must recognize the limits of their competence and perform only those functions for which they are prepared. In particular, members using computer-based test interpretations must be trained in the construct being measured and the specific instrument being used prior to using this type of computer application.

5. In situations where a computer is used for test administration and scoring, the member is responsible for ensuring that administration and scoring programs function properly to provide clients with accurate test results.

6. Tests must be administered under the same conditions that were established in their standardization. When tests are not administered under standard conditions or when unusual behavior or irregularities occur during the testing session, those conditions must be noted and the results designated as invalid or of questionable validity. Unsupervised or inadequately supervised test-taking, such as the use of tests through the mails, is considered unethical. On the other hand, the use of instruments that are so designed or standardized to be self-administered and self-scored, such as interest inventories, is to be encouraged.

7. The meaningfulness of test results used in personnel, guidance, and counseling functions generally depends on the examinee's unfamiliarity with the specific items on the test. Any prior coaching or dissemination of the test materials can invalidate test results. Therefore, test security is one of the professional obligations of the member. Conditions that produce most favorable test results must be made known to the examinee.

8. The purpose of testing and the explicit use of the results must be made known to the examinee prior to testing. The counselor must ensure that instrument limitations are not exceeded and that periodic review and/or retesting are made to prevent client stereotyping.

9. The examinee's welfare and explicit prior understanding must be the criteria for determining the recipients of the test results. The member must see that specific interpretation accompanies any release of individual or group test data. The interpretation of test data must be related to the examinee's particular concerns.

10. Members responsible for making decisions based on test results have an understanding of educational and psychological measurement, validation criteria, and test research.

11. The member must be cautious when interpreting the results of research instruments possessing insufficient technical data. The specific purposes for the use of such instruments must be stated explicitly to examinees.

12. The member must proceed with caution when attempting to evaluate and interpret the performance of minority group members or other persons who are not represented in the norm group on which the instrument was standardized.

13. When computer-based test interpretations are developed by the member to support the assessment process, the member must ensure that the validity of such interpretations is established prior to the commercial distribution of such a computer application.

14. The member recognizes that test results may become obsolete. The member will avoid and prevent the misuse of obsolete test results.

15. The member must guard against the appropriation, reproduction, or modification of published tests or parts thereof without acknowledgement and permission from the previous publisher.

16. Regarding the preparation, publication, and distribution of tests, reference should be made to:
    a. "Standards for Educational and Psychological Testing," revised edition, 1985, published by the American Psychological Association on behalf of itself, the American Educational Research Association, and the National Council of Measurement in Education.
    b. "The Responsible Use of Tests: A Position Paper of AMEG, APGA, and NCME," *Measurement and Evaluation in Guidance*, 1972, 5, 385-388.
    c. "Responsibilities of Users of Standardized Tests," APGA, *Guidepost*, October 5, 1978, pp. 5-8.

SECTION D: RESEARCH AND PUBLICATION

1. Guidelines on research with human subjects shall be adhered to, such as:
    a. *Ethical Principles in the Conduct of Research with Human Participants*, Washington, D. C.: American Psychological Association, Inc., 1982.
    b. Code of Federal Regulation, Title 45, Subtitle A, Part 46, as currently issued.
    c. *Ethical Principles of Psychologists*, American Psychological Association, Principle #9: Research with Human Participants.
    d. Family Educational Rights and Privacy Act (the Buckley Amendment).
    e. Current federal regulations and various state rights privacy acts.

2. In planning any research activity dealing with human subjects, the member must be aware of and responsive to all pertinent ethical principles and ensure that the research problem, design, and execution are in full compliance with them.

3. Responsibility for ethical research practice lies with the principal researcher, while others involved in the research activities share ethical obligation and full responsibility for their own actions.

4. In research with human subjects, researchers are responsible for the subjects' welfare throughout the experiment, and they must take all reasonable precautions to avoid causing injurious psychological, physical, or social effects on their subjects.

5. All research subjects must be informed of the purpose of the study except when withholding information or providing misinformation to them is essential to the investigation. In such research the member must be responsible for the corrective action as soon as possible following completion of the research.

6. Participation in research must be voluntary. Involuntary participation is appropriate only when it can be demonstrated that participation will have no harmful effects on subjects and is essential to the investigation.

7. When reporting research results, explicit mention must be made of all variables and conditions known to the investigator that might affect the outcome of the investigation or the interpretation of the data.

8. The member must be responsible for conducting and reporting investigations in a manner that minimizes the possibility that results will be misleading.

9. The member has an obligation to make available sufficient original research data to qualified others who may wish to replicate the study.

10. When supplying data, aiding in the research of another person, reporting research results, or making original data available, due care must be taken to disguise the identity of the subjects in the absence of specific authorization from such subjects to do otherwise.

11. When conducting and reporting research, the member must be familiar with and give recognition to previous work on the topic, as well as to observe all copyright laws and to follow the principles of giving full credit to all to whom credit is due.

12. The member must give due credit through joint authorship, acknowledgment, footnote statements, or other appropriate means to those who have contributed significantly to the research and/or publication, in accordance with such contributions.

13. The member must communicate to other members the results of any research judged to be of professional or scientific value. Results reflecting unfavorably on institutions, programs, services, or vested interests must not be withheld for such reasons.

14. If members agree to cooperate with another individual in research and/or publication, they incur an obligation to cooperate as promised in terms of punctuality of performance and with full regard to the completeness and accuracy of the information required.

15. Ethical practice requires that authors not submit the same manuscript or one essentially similar in content for simultaneous publication consideration by two or more journals. In addition, manuscripts published in whole or in substantial part in another journal or published work should not be submitted for publication without acknowledgment and permission from the previous publication.

SECTION E: CONSULTING

Consultation refers to a voluntary relationship between a professional helper and help-needing individual, group, or social unit in which the consultant is providing help to the client(s) in defining and solving a work-related problem or potential problem with a client or client system.

1. The member acting as consultant must have a high degree of self-awareness of his/her own values, knowledge, skills, limitations, and needs in entering a helping relationship that involves human and/or organizational change and that the focus of the relationship be on the issues to be resolved and not on the person(s) presenting the problem.

2. There must be understanding and agreement between member and client for the problem definition, change of goals, and prediction of consequences of interventions selected.
3. The member must be reasonably certain that she/he or the organization represented has the necessary competencies and resources for giving the kind of help that is needed now or may be needed later and that appropriate referral resources are available to the consultant.
4. The consulting relationship must be one in which client adaptability and growth toward self-direction are encouraged and cultivated. The member must maintain this role consistently and not become a decision maker for the client or create a future dependency on the consultant.
5. When announcing consultant availability for services, the member conscientiously adheres to the Association's Ethical Standards.
6. The member must refuse a private fee or other remuneration for consultation with persons who are entitled to these services through the member's employing institution or agency. The policies of a particular agency may make explicit provisions for private practice with agency clients by members of its staff. In such instances, the clients must be apprised of other options open to them should they seek private counseling services.

SECTION F: PRIVATE PRACTICE

1. The member should assist the profession by facilitating the availability of counseling services in private as well as public settings.
2. In advertising services as a private practitioner, the member must advertise the services in a manner that accurately informs the public of professional services, expertise, and techniques of counseling available. A member who assumes an executive leadership role in the organization shall not permit his/her name to be used in professional notices during periods when he/she is not actively engaged in the private practice of counseling.
3. The member may list the following: highest relevant degree, type and level of certification and/or license, address, telephone number, office hours, type and/or description of services, and other relevant information. Such information must not contain false, inaccurate, misleading, partial, out-of-context, or deceptive material or statements.
4. Members do not present their affiliation with any organization in such a way that would imply inaccurate sponsorship or certification by that organization.
5. Members may join in partnership/corporation with other members and/or other professionals provided that each member of the partnership or corporation makes clear the separate specialties by name in compliance with the regulations of the locality.
6. A member has an obligation to withdraw from a counseling relationship if it is believed that employment will result in violation of the Ethical Standards. If the mental or physical condition of the member renders it difficult to carry out an effective professional relationship or if the member is discharged by the client because the counseling relationship is no longer productive for the client, then the member is obligated to terminate the counseling relationship.
7. A member must adhere to the regulations for private practice of the locality where the services are offered.
8. It is unethical to use one's institutional affiliation to recruit clients for one's private practice.

SECTION G: PERSONNEL ADMINISTRATION

It is recognized that most members are employed in public or quasi-public institutions. The functioning of a member within an institution must contribute to the goals of the institution and vice versa if either is to accomplish their respective goals or objectives. It is therefore essential that the member and the institution function in ways to: (a) make the institutional goals specific and public; (b) make the member's contribution to institutional goals specific; and (c) foster mutual accountability for goal achievement.

To accomplish these objectives, it is recognized that the member and the employer must share responsibilities in the formulation and implementation of personnel policies.

1. Members must define and describe the parameters and levels of their professional competency.
2. Members must establish interpersonal relations and working agreements with supervisors and subordinates regarding counseling or clinical relationships, confidentiality, distinction between public and private material, maintenance and dissemination of recorded information, work load, and accountability. Working agreements in each instance must be specified and made known to those concerned.
3. Members must alert their employers to conditions that may be potentially disruptive or damaging.
4. Members must inform employers of conditions that may limit their effectiveness.
5. Members must submit regularly to professional review and evaluation.
6. Members must be responsible for in-service development of self and/or staff.
7. Members must inform their staff of goals and programs.
8. Members must provide personnel practices that guarantee and enhance the rights and welfare of each recipient of their service.
9. Members must select competent persons and assign responsibilities compatible with their skills and experiences.
10. The member, at the onset of a counseling relationship, will inform the client of the member's intended use of supervisors regarding the disclosure of information concerning this case. The member will clearly inform the client of the limits of confidentiality in the relationship.
11. Members, as either employers or employees, do not engage in or condone practices that are inhumane, illegal, or unjustifiable (such as considerations based on sex, handicap, age, race) in hiring, promotion, or training.

SECTION H: PREPARATION STANDARDS

Members who are responsible for training others must be guided by the preparation standards of the Association and relevant Division(s). The member who functions in the capacity of trainer assumes unique ethical responsibilities that frequently go beyond that of the member who does not function in a training capacity. These ethical responsibilities are outlined as follows:

1. Members must orient students to program expectations, basic skills development, and employment prospects prior to admission to the program.
2. Members in charge of learning experiences must establish programs that integrate academic study and supervised practice.
3. Members must establish a program directed toward developing students' skills, knowledge, and self-understanding, stated whenever possible in competency or performance terms.
4. Members must identify the levels of competencies of their students in compliance with relevant Division standards. These competencies must accommodate the paraprofessional as well as the professional.
5. Members, through continual student evaluation and appraisal, must be aware of the personal limitations of the learner that might impede future performance. The instructor must not only assist the learner in securing remedial assistance but also screen from the program those individuals who are unable to provide competent services.
6. Members must provide a program that includes training in research commensurate with levels of role functioning. Paraprofessional and technician-level personnel must be trained as consumers of research. In addition, personnel must learn how to evaluate their own and their program's effectiveness. Graduate training, especially at the doctoral level, would include preparation for original research by the member.
7. Members must make students aware of the ethical responsibilities and standards of the profession.
8. Preparatory programs must encourage students to value the ideals of service to individuals and to society. In this regard, direct financial remuneration or lack thereof must not be allowed to overshadow professional and humanitarian needs.
9. Members responsible for educational programs must be skilled as teachers and practitioners.

10. Members must present thoroughly varied theoretical positions so that students may make comparisons and have the opportunity to select a position.
11. Members must develop clear policies within their educational institutions regarding field placement and the roles of the student and the instructor in such placement.
12. Members must ensure that forms of learning focusing on self-understanding or growth are voluntary, or if required as part of the educational program, are made known to prospective students prior to entering the program. When the educational program offers a growth experience with an emphasis on self-disclosure or other relatively intimate or personal involvement, the member must have no administrative, supervisory, or evaluating authority regarding the participant.
13. The member will at all times provide students with clear and equally acceptable alternatives for self-understanding or growth experiences. The member will assure students that they have a right to accept these alternatives without prejudice or penalty.
14. Members must conduct an educational program in keeping with the current relevant guidelines of the Association.

Author Index

Subject Index

A

A-B-C-D-E paradigm, 68, 69
Abuse victim groups
  context and therapeutic methods in, 172-176
  overview of, 165-166
  selection of individuals for, 166
  stages of work with, 166-172
  transference and concomitant factors in, 176-178
Abused individuals
  adolescent, 179-180
  children, 178-179
  depression in, 168
Acculturation
  definition of, 287
  and group counseling, 295
  and Hispanics, 291
Addicted individuals. *See* Alcoholics; Chemically dependent groups; Chemically dependent individuals
Addiction Severity Index (ASI), 104
Adlerian theory
  concepts and leader dynamics for, 62
  explanation of, 60-61
  techniques for use of, 62-63
Adolescents. *See also* Children
  abused, 179-180
  career counseling for, 223
  "coming out" as gay/lesbian, 193
  depression in, 255-256
  divorce-related groups for, 257-258
  gay/lesbian groups for, 194-195
  with physical disabilities, 158-159
  suicide and, 235, 249-250, 254-258
Adoption, by gays and lesbians, 197
Advice giving, group member, 50
Afro-Americans, 289-290, 297. *See also* Minority groups
AIDS (acquired immunodeficiency syndrome), 186
AIDS groups
  background of, 190, 198-199
  types of, 199-200
Alcoholics. *See also* Chemically dependent groups; Chemically dependent individuals
  gay and lesbian, 198

  hyperactivity in, 109
  impact of learning and education on, 116
  physiological and psychological factors in, 109
  recovery in, 111
Alcoholics Anonymous, 111
Altruism
  in groups, 128, 143
  and self-enhancement, 96-97
American Association for Counseling and Development (AACD)
  background of, 7
  ethical standards of, 308, 343-351
American Association for Marriage and Family Therapy (AAMFT), 308
American Indians, 293-295. *See also* Minority groups
American Mental Health Counselors Association (AMHCA), 308
American Personnel and Guidance Association, 7. *See also* American Association for Counseling and Development
American Psychiatric Association, 183
American Psychological Association (APA), 7, 183, 308
American School Counselors Association (ASCA), 308
Amputees, 155
Anger, 265
Anorexia nervosa
  age and, 135
  cognitive distortions in clients with, 126
  depression and, 256
  etiology of, 123
  explanation of, 121
  problems specific to, 126
Anti-group roles of group members, 44, 47
Antisocial behavior, 86
Anxiety
  in abused individuals, 168
  associated with loss, 266
  produced in heterogeneous groups, 12
Asian Americans, 291-293. *See also*

  Minority groups
Assertiveness, 150
Assertiveness training model, 150
Assessment process
  career group participants and, 227
  for chemically dependent groups, 104-105
Association for Specialists in Group Work (ASGW)
  background of, 6-7
  ethical guidelines of, 41, 307, 308, 335-341
  Professional Standards for Training of Group Work Generalists and of Group Work Specialists, 41, 325-333
Assumptions, culturally biased, 288-289
Athletes, 124
Attention, in chemically dependent groups, 110
Authoritarian group leaders, 39
Authority circle, 27-28
Awareness
  in abuse victims, 173-174
  development of cultural, 287-289
  self-, 16, 167, 226
Awareness raising, 154

B

Band-aiding, 50
Behavioral contracts, 133-134
Behavioral goals, 145
Behavioralism, 84
Black Americans, 289-290, 297. *See also* Minority groups
Blindness, 148-149. *See also* Physically disabled individuals; Visually impaired individuals
Blocking roles of group members, 44, 47
Body image exercises, 132
Borderline process, in abused individuals, 169
Bulimia nervosa
  age and, 135
  cognitive distortions in clients with, 126

of mate, 269-273
mourning process for, 248, 249, 263-264
Decisions, from transactional analysis perspective, 71
Definitive stage
explanation of, 31-32
facilitation of, 44-48
Democratic group leaders, 39
Denial
in chemically dependent individuals, 112-113
in physically disabled individuals, 154
Dependency, 50
Depression
in abused individuals, 168
in adolescents, 255-256
associated with loss, 266
in chemically dependent individuals, 256
in children, 255-256
groups for, 253-254
neurotransmitters present with, 108
overeating and, 135
suicide and, 236, 237, 246, 247, 253-254
Deprivation, and death of mate, 270
Developmental counseling groups, for children and adolescents, 256-257
Diagnostic and Statistical Manual of Mental Disorders (DSM III) (American Psychiatric Association), 121
Diagnostic and Statistical Manual of Mental Disorders Revised Edition (DSM III-R) (American Psychiatric Association), 121, 122
Disabled individuals. *See* Physically disabled individuals
Discrepant behavior, 55
Divorce-related groups, for children and adolescents, 257-258
Dopamine, 108
Drug Abuse Screening Test (DAST), 104
Drug addiction. *See* Chemically dependent groups; Chemically dependent individuals
Dual relationships, 312-313
Dysfunctional behavior
development of, 64
in heterogeneous groups, 11

E

Eating disorders. *See also* Anorexia nervosa; Bulimia nervosa
classification and explanation of, 121-122
etiology of, 122-123
therapeutic considerations for, 123-125

Eating disorders groups
age-specific variations for, 135
curative factors for, 127-129
factors effecting leaders of, 135-136
models of, 125-126
population specific considerations for, 134-135
relational patterns in, 126-127
screening and composition for, 129-130
stages within, 130-131
strategies for, 131-134
Educational background, group functioning and, 111, 116-117
Ego states, 71
Elderly individuals
Afro-American, 289
groups for gay/lesbian, 200
with physical disabilities, 159-160
suicide and, 235, 251-254
Emotionality, in chemically dependent groups, 110
Emotionally abused individuals. *See* Abuse victim groups; Abused individuals
Empathy, as leadership skill, 269
Encounter therapy, 6, 9, 147-148
Endorphin production, 109
Enkelphalins, 109
Esalen Institute, 6
Ethical decision-making model, 317-319
Ethical Guidelines for Group Counselors (Association for Specialists in Group Work)
discussion of, 309-315
preamble to, 307
text of, 335-341
use of, 42, 308
Ethical Standards (American Association for Counseling and Development), 308
Ethics, counseling process and, 307-308
Ethics codes
of American Association for Counseling and Development, 343-351
of Association for Specialists in Group Work, 14, 307, 335-341
background regarding, 308-309
decision making and, 316-319
development of, 7
professional issues and, 319-321
purpose of, 309
sample applications of, 315-316
Ethnic groups, 287. *See also* Minority groups
Ethnicity. *See also* Minority groups
definition of, 287
group composition and, 300
Evaluation, ethics concerning, 314

Exercise
body image, 132
structured, 19
Eye strain, in hearing-impaired individuals, 151

F

Facilitative roles of group members
explanation of, 44
types of, 45
Families
abuse victims and, 170-172, 175
career counseling and, 222
cultural differences in, 297
and eating disorder therapy, 128, 133
resemblance of groups to, 143
Family counseling
as adjunct to group treatment, 124-125
couples group counseling vs., 215-216
Fatigue, in spinal cord injury individuals, 152
Feedback
in career group counseling, 221
myths relating to, 19
Females. *See* Women
Freedom, and death of mate, 270
Frustration, associated with loss, 266

G

Games People Play (Berne), 70
Gay-affirmative counseling, 188-189
Gay Community Services Center (Minneapolis), 200
Gay Forty Plus Club (San Francisco), 200
Gay/lesbian groups
AIDS, 198-200
coming out, 193-194
for couples, 195-197
for elderly, 200
emergence of, 189-192
overview of, 183
for parenting, 197
personal growth, 201
substance abuse, 198
types of, 192
for youth, 194-195
Gay/lesbian individuals
cultural overview of, 184-189
language used to describe, 184
General goals, 8
Generation factor, in cross-cultural counseling, 296
Gentle confrontation, and denial, 154
Geocultural traditions, 297
Gestalt theory
concepts and leader dynamics of, 64-65
explanation of, 63-64